CW00819773

The Therapeutic Alliance

W.W. Meissner, S.J., M.D.

The Therapeutic Alliance

Yale University Press

New Haven & London

Designed by James J. Johnson and set in Ehrhardt Roman type by Keystone Typesetting, Inc., Orwigsburg, Pennsylvania. Printed in the United States of America by BookCrafters, Inc., Chelsea, Michigan.

Library of Congress Cataloging-in-Publication Data

Meissner, W. W. (William W.), 1931–
The therapeutic alliance / W. W. Meissner.
p. cm.
Includes bibliographical references and index.
ISBN 0-300-06684-8
1. Psychoanalysis. 2. Pluralism. 3. Psychoanalytic interpretation. I. Title.
BF173.M3594 1997
616.89′17—dc20 96-13037

A catalogue record for this book is available from the British Library.

The paper in this book meets the guidelines for permanence and durability of the Committee on Production Guidelines for Book Longevity of the Council on Library Resources.

10 9 8 7 6 5 4 3 2 1

Contents

Preface vii

Part I. The Nature of the Therapeutic Alliance

Chapter 1. History and Definition 4
Chapter 2. Alliance and Transference 22
Chapter 3. Alliance and Countertransference 39

Part II. The Real Relationship

Chapter 4. The Analyst as Participant 62
Chapter 5. Reality, Neutrality, and Resistance 74
Chapter 6. Reality and the Analytic Situation: Personal Factors 92
Chapter 7. Reality and the Analytic Situation: Gender-Related and Accidental Factors 107

Part III. Aspects of the Therapeutic Alliance

Chapter 8. Developmental Aspects 128
Chapter 9. The Therapeutic Framework 140
Chapter 10. Empathy and Alliance 154
Chapter 11. Personal Qualities in the Alliance 174
Chapter 12. Personal Factors: Authority, Freedom, and Responsibility 188
Chapter 13. Ethical Dimensions: Confidentiality 200
Chapter 14. Ethical Dimensions: Values 209

Part IV. The Therapeutic Alliance in the Analytic Process

Chapter 15. Establishing the Therapeutic Alliance 226
Chapter 16. Therapeutic Management of Alliance Deviations 245

Chapter 17. Interpretation 257
Chapter 18. Internalization 272
Chapter 19. Termination 288

Appendix: General Guidelines Related to the Maintenance of Boundaries in the Practice of Psychotherapy by Physicians (Adult Patients) 297

Notes 303
References 327
Index 377

Preface

Why, at this juncture in the development of psychoanalysis, would anyone want to study the therapeutic alliance? What does the alliance concept have to do with our understanding of the analytic process, especially in the evolving context of post-Freudian deconstruction and hermeneutic interpretive constructionism, which seem to be racing like a consuming fire across the analytic plain? And what can alliance mean in a theoretical framework in which relational concepts like transference and countertransference assume all-inclusive implications?

To complicate matters even further, the relational perspective in psychoanalysis has become increasingly preoccupied with the real presence of the analyst in the analytic process, so that the prevailing issues at work within the analytic situation have to do with the complex interplay of transference and countertransference, on the one hand, and the real relationship between the analyst and the patient, on the other. These encompassing formulations seem to leave no room for the concept of alliance. Does alliance play a meaningful role in the analytic process? And what difference would it make if it did?

These questions and others have raised a storm of controversy among analytic theorists about how the analytic process is to be understood and particularly about what in the process is therapeutically effective and capable of bringing about meaningful psychic change in our analysands. The problems touch on the nature of the analytic relation and the role of analytic interventions. Is the burden of therapeutic effect carried by interpretation or by aspects of the analytic relation? I am proposing that the therapeutic alliance makes a distinctive contribution to the analytic process, that it is an essential dimension of the therapeutic relation, and particularly that it provides the matrix within which therapeutic effects are wrought.

I should add a word of caution that this is a study of the therapeutic alliance, not of transference or countertransference or the real relation. These aspects of the analytic process have been exhaustively studied and analyzed elsewhere. I shall concern myself with them only to the extent that they pertain to and intersect with the therapeutic alliance. The direction of my effort, therefore, runs counter to the prevailing current of analytic thinking and writing.

Further, the ground to be covered is familiar territory to experienced, perhaps even inexperienced, analysts and therapists. If there is anything revisionist here, it has to do with the theoretical perspective by which I link the therapeutic alliance with the concept of the self as a function of the self, rather than with the ego, as has been the dominant persuasion. This realignment places the alliance in the context of interaction and interconnection between the self and its objects. By implication, the dimensions of the alliance are seen more clearly as involving both self and object in interaction and reciprocal influence.

The effort to define this aspect of the analytic field and account for its implications will carry us unavoidably into controversial areas. Not only does the argument run counter to a variety of contemporary viewpoints, but it takes issue with historical development and therapeutic implementation of the therapeutic alliance. Rethinking the implications of the concept and its role in analysis leads to reconsideration of other aspects of the analytic relation that do not properly belong to transference, countertransference, or the real relation—for example, the therapeutic framework, neutrality and abstinence, empathy, personal factors that enter into the alliance and must be kept separate from the analyst's reality, and, finally, ethical issues and concerns.

In this discussion of the nature of the alliance, my first concern is to distinguish it adequately from transference and countertransference, on the one hand, and the real relation, on the other. At the same time, the alliance itself, as implemented in the analytic process, is a complex phenomenon in complex interaction with both these aspects. I argue that the alliance also involves contributions from the developmental histories of analyst and patient and that these undergo an epigenetic, if somewhat loosely constructed, evolution during the analysis—more in the patient than in the analyst. This is a radical departure from most previous contributions to the study of the alliance.

A second emphasis is on the interactional aspect of the alliance, particularly the manner in which it affects such specific details of the analytic process as setting and maintaining of boundaries, preservation of the analytic frame, development of empathic resonance and understanding, and discovery, formulation, and explication of interpretations. The alliance perspective plays a critical role at every step of the analytic process. Thus alliance cannot be conceived in static or rigid terms, for it is dynamically resonant to the nuances of the analytic process and grows and changes in character and meaning as the analysis progresses.

In the final section, part IV, I focus on the clinical context to demonstrate how the therapeutic alliance plays its essential structuring role in the analytic process. The concept of the alliance I am proposing here is considerably more complex and nuanced than any I have previously encountered.

My debts are so many that it is difficult to name them all. My greatest debt is to my teachers and supervisors who taught me about the alliance, often more by example or discussion of case material than by any explicit verbalization. My special benefactors include Alfred Ludwig, Paul Myerson, Gregory Rochlin, Elvin Semrad, Avery Weisman, and Elizabeth Zetzel. Ludwig, Semrad, and Zetzel have passed on, but their input is reflected implicitly in these pages. I owe a special debt to Zetzel, who was one of the major architects of the alliance concept as most analysts hold it today. I enjoyed the benefit of many hours of discussion during supervision with her before her untimely death. I experienced a tinge of wistful regret when I found myself taking issue with or criticizing her ideas, but I take some consolation from the fantasy that she would have had a good deal to say on the subject, and that she might even concede on a few points I have argued in these pages.

My special thanks are due in the first place to my secretary, Miss Elfriede Banzhaf, for her assiduous and devoted efforts to implement all stages of the preparation of this manuscript. Second, no less appreciation is due to the editorial staff at Yale, especially Gladys Topkis and Noreen O'Connor, for their professional competence and care in preparing these poor efforts for publication—a testament to their skill and dedication. To these contributors I express my thanks and admiration.

For the rest, the reader will have to judge for himself. If he or she finds something clarifying or helpful in this discussion, well and good; if he or she finds something to argue with, even better.

PART I

The Nature of the Therapeutic Alliance

The first part aims at establishing a workable definition of the therapeutic alliance and distinguishing it from other elements of the analytic relation. The triad of elements comprising the analytic relation is, first, components of transference and its correlative, countertransference; second, aspects of the real relation between analyst and analysand; and, finally, the therapeutic alliance. Although I regard these as distinct aspects of the analytic relation, they interact and interpenetrate throughout the course of the analytic process.

In this part I want to draw the distinctions among these components of the analytic process, first, by establishing the basic meaning of the therapeutic alliance (chapter 1), noting particularly how the development of the concept in this study diverges from more classical and familiar formulations, then by exploring their interaction. Second, I shall discuss the relation between the therapeutic alliance and emerging and evolving concepts of transference (chapter 2) and countertransference (chapter 3). In general, transference and countertransference are oppositional to the therapeutic alliance and thus serve as the basis for therapeutic misalliances, but the manner of their interaction and the ways in which they may contribute positively and negatively to the therapeutic relation (rather than to the therapeutic alliance) are explored.

CHAPTER ONE

History and Definition

The "therapeutic alliance" has enjoyed a respectable, if controversial, position among psychoanalytic concepts since it was first articulated.[1] It represents that form of collaboration between analyst and analysand without which the analytic process cannot take place (Olinick 1976). Though its nature and function in the analytic setting continue to be debated, there has been little effort to elaborate the concept itself beyond the level of understanding provided by Zetzel (1956, 1958) and later by Greenson (1965). As Busch (1994) commented: "It is one of those concepts that, while generally accepted as a necessary component of the process, is not fully integrated into our theory. Friedman (personal communication) calls it 'an unscrutinized presupposition of the psychoanalytic procedure'" (p. 373).

The therapeutic relationship in psychoanalysis has several components, including, at a minimum, transference and its correlative, countertransference, the real relationship, and the therapeutic alliance (Meissner 1992). This more or less classical view of the analytic relationship has been challenged by de Jonghe et al. (1991), who add to the basic triad the "primary relationship," reflecting infantile modes of relating and functioning—the kind of pre-oedipal symbiotic tie between mother and child described by Mahler et al. (1975) and reflected in Greenacre's (1954) "primary transference."[2] I regard the primary relationship as a form of pre-oedipal transference.

These components are constantly present and interactive elements of the therapeutic relationship, but for heuristic purposes they require separate description. This line of argument concludes that the therapeutic alliance is distinct from both transference and the real relation and involves a separate line of expression and development in the analytic process. It brings into focus aspects of the analytic interaction other than transference or the real relation. As Modell (1989) commented, "As a precondition of therapeutic change the analysand must be able to experience the analyst as a person in ordinary life, as an analyst functioning within the 'frame' and as an archaic object or an archaic aspect of the self" (p. 81). This line of thinking seems entirely consistent with Anna Freud's (1954) differentiation of transference, the therapeutic relation, and the real relation as intermingled aspects of the analytic relationship and also with Freud's own personal style (Couch 1995).

As a survey from the 1970s suggests, the therapeutic alliance is often intermingled with and poorly distinguished from transference elements (Gutheil and Havens 1979). Olinick (1976) has even suggested a continuum—from alliance as a form of transference to alliance as a form of rational nontransference—rather than a bipolar model. The point is that both elements are usually found in conjunction in the therapeutic interaction and are thus often confounded.

The Therapeutic Alliance

Basic Distinctions

For purposes of discussion, we can start with the "rational alliance" proposed by Gutheil and Havens (1979). Building on the contributions of Sterba (1934), Zetzel (1970), Greenson (1965), and Sandler et al. (1973), they described the therapeutic alliance as "the therapeutic split in the ego which allows the analyst to work with the healthier elements in the patient against resistance and pathology" (p. 479). As such, it is a function of the analyst's "psychoanalytic work ego" (Olinick et al. 1973; Olinick 1976). As Rangell (1992) expresses it, "This analytic relationship, the persistent and ultimately predictable and expectable experience on the part of the patient of the steady, reliable, reasonable, fair, kind, tolerant, non-judgmental, but also non-corruptible attitude of the analyst, is the 'new' relationship that is specifically and uniquely analytic" (p. 420). The therapeutic alliance fits this description specifically.[3]

While a certain consensus regarding definition is possible, difficulties remain in operationalizing therapeutic alliance as it bears on the analytic process. Elements contributing to establishing the therapeutic alliance include contractual arrangements between patient and analyst regarding the logistics of therapy (scheduling, fees, payment, confidentiality, etc.), some agreement as to how the parties will work together and for what purposes, and the understanding and acceptance by both parties of their respective roles and responsibilities. Consequently, the therapeutic alliance embraces many aspects of the relationship between patient and analyst that fall within the scope of neither transference nor the real relationship, even though development and shaping of the therapeutic alliance is intimately related to aspects of both.[4]

Mutual Interaction

The therapeutic alliance involves a process of interaction to which both patient and analyst contribute (Jones 1993; London 1985). The analyst's attitudes, the way in which he* regards and responds to the patient, are important in establishing and maintaining the therapeutic alliance and the shared experience of analysis (Issacharoff 1978). One component relates to the process of participant observation described by Sullivan (1953), by which the analyst's role in the therapeutic transaction is defined. The emphasis shifts from issues of conflict and pathology in the patient to cognitive distortions and faulty communications between patient and analyst. The model of their relationship is less authoritarian and more egalitarian—more of a reciprocal partnership (Chrzanowski 1979).[5]

According to this view, the interacting personalities of analyst and analysand contribute essentially to the alliance. In this sense the therapeutic alliance resembles contemporary intersubjective models, according to which the therapeutic alliance is inseparable from the relational matrix. At the same time, it draws on independent factors from each side of the analytic relation; for example, the analyst's trustworthiness and capacity for autonomy are features of his personality and are not derived from or constituted by his interaction with the analysand. Consequently, the following discussion treads a path between the classical caricature of the impassive objectivity of the analyst and the unqualified relativity of radical intersubjectivity.[6]

Negotiation is a core component of this process (Goldberg 1987b), allowing for meaningful contributions by both participants toward establishing a shared consensual reality. Negotiation stands in contrast to any form of indoctrination, compliance, or submission. Even interpretations become forms of negotiation in which analyst and patient achieve an understanding that is satisfying and meaningful to both. Interaction not only implies a two-way process but also requires engagement and empathy from both participants.[7]

In this process, the analyst's respect, consideration, courtesy, tactfulness, and empathy for the patient are important factors. Further, the analyst must adopt a firm and consistent position vis-à-vis the patient, holding him consistently responsible for participation in the therapeutic process. Gray (1990) comments, "Obviously I am trying to implement and maintain a principle of drawing more and more of the patient's ego into conscious participation in the analytic process" (p. 1087). And again, "the therapeutic results of analytic treatment are lasting in proportion to the extent to which, during the analysis, the patient's unbypassed ego functions have become involved in a consciously and increasingly voluntary co-partnership with the analyst" (Gray, 1982, p. 624). The analyst maintains the expectation that the patient will be meaningfully involved in the therapeutic process and will accept and observe his own responsibilities both within and outside of the therapy. Parallel to this is the analyst's consistent and secure posture, conveying (in behavior as well as words)

*The generic male pronoun is used to avoid awkward constructions; no bias is intended.

that he will meet his responsibilities in the therapy in a mature and constructive manner.

The literature on the outcome of psychotherapy has been preoccupied with whether the effects of psychotherapy can be ascribed to specific therapeutic factors or to spontaneous remission. Strupp (1973) suggested that some nonspecific factors may reflect the influence of the interpersonal relationship of therapist and patient. The relevant nonspecific factors of empathy, understanding, respect, and acceptance would be attributable to the therapeutic alliance as considered here. Freud, of course, realized that a good relationship between the participants was a prerequisite for effective therapy, but for him the relationship remained part of the ground while technique remained in the foreground. However, Luborsky (Luborsky 1984; Luborsky et al. 1980; Luborsky and Crits-Christoph 1990) has shown that the therapeutic alliance is a powerful predictor of the outcome of long-term psychotherapy.[8]

Alliance and the Self

Therapeutic alliance has usually been ascribed to the ego, operating in opposition to id-derived transference manifestations. But as Kanzer (1972) has pointed out, the ego cannot engage in the alliance without involvement of the superego as well. If there is a split in the ego, there must also be a split in the superego. Kanzer envisions four such splits: id-dominated versus more advanced modes of reality testing, continuing inner divisions versus channeling them into transference neurosis, resistances to treatment versus will to recovery, and the split between participant ego and observant ego, as described by Sterba (1934). In these splits the experiencing portion lies closer to childhood affects underlying superego resistance while the observant portion comes closer to critical moral and social ethics allied with conscious rationality. These considerations point our argument for a theoretical basis for the alliance toward a more supraordinate structural concept, in the sense of a hierarchical self allowing for the complex integration of personal functions (Meissner 1986a, 1993), rather than in the ego as an intrapsychically contextualized and delimited entity.

These issues seem to transcend the realm of technique, for they reflect qualities of the analyst's personality and values as they engage with the needs of the patient. The therapeutic alliance has profound implications for the outcome of therapy, providing a matrix within which important interpersonal experiences and crucial identifications, which may modify the patient's pathogenic inner structure, can take place (Meissner 1981).[9]

Definition

There is considerable confusion over use of the term *therapeutic alliance;* in common usage and even in many technical discussions the term seems to indicate little more than that the patient was collaborating and task-oriented (Olinick 1976). Some analysts use it as almost the equivalent of transference (Gutheil and Havens 1979), whereas others reject it as merely an aspect of transference (Brenner 1979; Gill 1979, 1982; Modell 1986). Brenner, for example, rejects any distinction between therapeutic alliance and transference. Alliance concepts are for him neither valid nor useful, but clearly the idea connotes suggestion or corrective emotional experience in his usage (Brenner 1979).

One of the strongest rejections of the idea of alliance came from Lacan (1988), as part of his onslaught against ego psychology: "People tell us about the autonomous ego, about the same part of the ego, about the ego which must be strengthened, about the ego which isn't sufficiently strong to support us in doing an analysis, about the ego which should be the ally of the analyst, the ally of the analyst's ego, etc. You see these two *egos,* arm in arm, the analyst's ego and that of the subject, in fact subordinated to the other in this so-called alliance. Nothing in experience gives us the faintest hint of it, since precisely the contrary takes place—it is at the level of the ego that all the resistances occur" (p. 68). For Lacan, transference and countertransference were forms of turning to the object, so that he regarded the therapeutic alliance as merely part of the analyst's and patient's transferences (Smith 1991). As I hope to show, part of the problem in all these objections lies in difficulties with the original formulations of Zetzel and Greenson.

History

Freud

Freud was not unaware of factors in therapy related to alliance. As early as *Studies on Hysteria* (Breuer and Freud 1893–95), he referred to the need to make the patient a collaborator. The analyst was guided in his work by respect for the patient's individuality and the need to give scope to his developmental potentialities. The insistence on neutrality was motivated by the aim of avoiding therapeutic zeal and protecting the patient from undesirable countertransference intrusions (Kanzer 1981). The principle of abstinence was rooted in the need to minimize acting out of regressive impulses that could threaten both the patient and the analysis (Freud 1914).

Freud's early appeal to a surgical model (1912b), recommending that the analyst put aside all feelings and develop a sort of "emotional coldness," entered into tension with his recognition of the need to draw the patient into the treatment and foster his attachment to the analyst (1913), thus establishing an "analytic atmosphere"—a sense of rapport and sympathy. This required that the analyst have serious interest in and sympathetic understanding of the patient. Freud later (1915a) added truthfulness, lack of pretense, neutrality, and abstinence to the list of recommended responses to transference. Thus, to him analytic neutrality meant neither gratifying the patient's infantile needs and wishes nor maintaining an inhumane emotional distance; rather, it indicated a nonjudgmental, nonmoralizing, impartial, objective, nonintrusive stance. The analyst steers a middle course between overzealousness and therapeutic zeal, between empathic intimacy and unnecessary aloofness (Kanzer 1981). These attitudes and related questions about gratification and deprivation in the analytic situation were in time included in the notion of the therapeutic alliance (Blum 1981).

Freud offered an early approximation of the notion of the alliance in his "unobjectionable aspect of the positive transference" (1912a).[10] He saw this aspect of transference as essential for the success of treatment. But, as Friedman (1969) pointed out, the paradoxical aspect of transference as both resistance and attachment to the analyst called for eliminating interfering factors while putting helpful factors to good use. Ferenczi (1919) added that analysis made contradictory demands on the analyst: to be in touch with his own unconscious as a way of being in contact with the patient's unconscious, but also to scrutinize and process this material continually. The result was an oscillation between uninhibited fantasy and logical scrutiny.

Related to this was Freud's formulation of the "analytic pact." In "Analysis Terminable and Interminable" (1937), he noted, "The analytic situation consists in our allying ourselves with the ego of the person under treatment" (p. 235). The ego in question presumably was the "normal ego . . . which would guarantee unshakable loyalty to the work of analysis" (p. 239)—that is, the aspect of the patient's ego able to engage in the analytic work beyond the constraints of transference and resistance. Resistive defenses could effect an "alteration of the ego" that, if strong enough, would subvert the ego's capacity to do analytic work. Freud (1940) later compared the struggle between the collaborative and resistive parts of the ego to a civil war in which the outcome was determined by an ally outside the conflict: "The analytic physician and the patient's weakened ego, basing themselves on the real external world, have to band themselves together into a party against the enemies, the instinctual demands of the id and the conscientious demands of the super-ego. We form a pact with each other . . . to give his ego back its mastery over lost provinces of his mental life. This pact constitutes the analytic situation" (p. 173).

The tension between the enslavement of the ego to the id and the relative freedom from the id implied in engagement in the analysis, adherence to the fundamental rule, and alliance with the analyst pervades the analytic situation (Friedman 1969). Ultimately, Freud realized that the analyst's humaneness, empathy, and intuition were intertwined with his capacity to establish and maintain basic ground rules, the fundamental rule, and the rule of abstinence, which allowed development of both transference and the analytic pact (Kanzer 1975). The basis of the pact was situated in the real world, reflecting the dichotomous view between transference/resistance and reality. The third alternative, therapeutic alliance, was not formally articulated by Freud, so that his view of the analytic process could not disentangle itself from the paradox involved in these aspects of transference. As Kanzer (1981) notes, Freud's final model of the therapeutic process emphasized a two-person structural framework embracing a continuum of interactive states between the inner and outer realities of both patient and analyst that added a collaborative dimension to the elements of resistance and transference: "The alliance postulated by the pact relates a helpful physician to a sufferer in a carefully regulated operational field and atmosphere suitable for a particular technique and therapeutic goal" (p. 86).

Sterba

The next important step, anticipating Freud's version of the analytic pact, was Sterba's (1934, 1940) distinction of the part of the patient's ego that is attuned to reality, can enter an alliance with the analyst, and opposes the powerful forces of instinct and repression. Sterba's formulation, resting on structural theory, helped resolve the Freudian paradox by putting greater weight on the role of reason and reality—elements that Freud felt did not match the powerful forces involved in neurosis. Freud's "alliance" was a form of libidinal attachment, an aspect of positive transference that was the strongest motivation for the patient to join in the work of analysis (Friedman 1969). If the relatively autonomous ego of Sterba's ally (the "observant ego") were to be separated from drive elements, from where would it derive its motivation? Although Sterba included elements of positive transference, he located the motivational component primarily in the union of purpose between patient and analyst. This made the alliance a function of activity of the ego, a perspective that has pervaded subsequent thinking.[11] His emphasis on the importance of the patient's identification with the analyzing function of the analyst was supported by Bibring (1937). The split in the ego between participant and observant functions leads to identification with the analyst and supports efforts of the ego to reflect on analytic material and gain effective insight.

Yet Friedman (1969) poses the difficult question of whether Sterba's solution escaped the Freudian paradox or only seemed to do so. The Freudian view was that the analyst uses transference to enable the patient to dissolve transference. But what drives the autonomous ego of the alliance if it is divorced from transference? Is it only the patient's infantile, magical expectations that provide the motive power of analysis, so that the illusion that these desires have been analytically fulfilled runs counter to the analytic requirement that they be relinquished?[12]

Sterba's reality-based alliance was dubbed "rational transference" by Fenichel (1941) and "mature transference" by Stone (1961).[13] Fenichel sided with Sterba, relying on the patient's "reasonable ego" and wish for health to motivate him. Dealing with defenses and transferences requires a splitting of the ego into experiencing and judging components with which the patient joins forces through his identification with the analyst. However, transference gratifications can lessen the patient's motivation for analytic work and so may affect the therapeutic alliance. These formulations reflect the mutual contamination of alliance and transference concepts. Stone's view is summarized by Friedman (1969): "The therapeutic alliance thus includes (1) the mature transference derived from this need for guidance, (2) the tender part of the erotic transference, friendly adult feelings and ego identification (Freud's early suggestion), (3) genuine need for help and rational and intuitive appraisal of the analyst, together with adult appropriate confidence in him, and (4) the primordial transference from the wish for the nurturing, body-contact mother as the *driving force*" (p. 147).

Friedman himself seems to have accepted the parental model for alliance, emphasizing the role of rapport and hope. Alliance in his view encompasses both rational and irrational elements, as well as the more infantile primordial maternal transference. Similarly, Novick (1970) objected to the appeal to rational motives in alliance to the neglect of irrational libidinal motives. Adler (1980) suggested that Stone's "primordial transference" and even Gitelson's (1962) "diatrophic function" were synonymous with Kohut's "selfobject transferences" and formed the basis for the patient's collaboration with the analysis.

The so-called therapeutic split lays the basis for the patient's ability to engage in the process, to take an interest in it, to contribute free associations, and to develop the capacity for self-analysis (Stone 1981). This split does not have connotations of a pathological defense, as it does in the work of Klein (Segal 1964) or Kernberg (1975), but reflects relatively autonomous, neutralized, sublimated, and aim-inhibited functions (Olinick 1976). This distinction brought into sharp relief the opposition between therapeutic alliance and transference and the role of autonomous ego functions in facilitating the alliance.

Zetzel

When Zetzel (1956) took up the idea, the interpenetration of aspects of transference with the alliance provided the framework for her thinking, and provided a vehicle for distinguishing between the classical approach and the British object relations school. Transference had taken on a broader meaning that included the whole analytic relationship (Langs 1976). The therapeutic split in the transference resulted in an alliance between the analyst and the patient's adaptive ego (following Bibring) and advanced the distinction between therapeutic alliance and transference neurosis, which Zetzel regarded as the neurotic part of transference. The alliance called on more mature and autonomous ego functions to preserve the real object relationship with the analyst in the face of transference distortions that were the core of the transference neurosis (Zetzel 1966). It involved factors that enabled the patient to continue to work collaboratively and analytically despite conflictual feelings about the analyst and the process.

Further distinction between alliance and unobjectionable or nonneurotic transference was left unclear. In Zetzel's view, alliance was a necessary condition for analysis and interpretation of unconscious derivatives, as well as overcoming resistances and developing and resolving analytic regression. Alliance was based on a pre-oedipal core of secure object relations and called for a "capacity to tolerate anxiety and frustration, to accept certain reality limitations, and to differentiate between mature and infantile aspects of mental life. This relationship acts, on the one hand, as a barrier to significant ego regression, and, on the other, as a fundamental feature of the analytic situation against which the fantasies, memories, and emotions evoked by the transference neurosis can be measured and contrasted" (Zetzel 1958, p. 185). The capacity for alliance required relatively mature ego functions, and the capacity for object relations, an underplaying or disregard of unconscious fantasy and transferential derivatives that might impair or undermine the alliance, an ability to maintain trust in the absence of gratification, ability to maintain self-object differentiation in the absence of a need-satisfying object, and the capacity to accept realistic limitations.

The analyst's part in promoting the alliance was related to his greater activity and presentation of himself as a more real participant in the analytic interaction and as an object for positive identification (Zetzel 1970). The analyst must at times intervene actively in order to establish a working relationship with the patient, fostering the therapeutic split, reality testing, and ego resources to contain transference regressions. Zetzel emphasized not permitting uncontrolled or excessive regression and preventing regressive transference manifestations. Maintenance of the ground rules of therapy and attention to the alliance would buffer these regressive tendencies. She advocated greater participation of the analyst as a partner in the process (Zetzel 1958), bringing into relief the role of the analyst's real personality and individuality. On the part of the patient, the emphasis fell on the capacity for trust as a developmental achievement from very early infantile levels.[14]

Zetzel's (1958) appeal to the model of the mother-child relationship was confusing to many. Tact in managing transference was part of analytic work in the whole process, not just in the opening phase, and need not be based solely on a maternal model. Similarly, for Greenacre (1954), the transference matrix included positive pregenital experiences on which Zetzel's alliance built. In this same vein, Gitelson's (1962) emphasis on care and concern as curative factors independent of interpretation and insight (the so-called diatrophic attitude) raised questions as to whether this was an extension of Freud's notion of neutrality or a deviation in the direction of countertransference.

Greenson

Greenson (1965) defined his version of the "working alliance" as "the relatively nonneurotic, rational rapport which the patient has with his analyst" (p. 157). This alliance between the patient's reasonable ego and the analyst's analyzing ego allowed the patient to maintain an effective working relationship with the analyst. Like Zetzel, Greenson left a piece of positive transference expressed in nonsexual and nonromantic love (Greenson 1967) in the working alliance. Even so, it implied to his mind, "The reliable core of the working alliance is formed by the patient's motivation to overcome his illness, his conscious and rational willingness to cooperate, and his ability to follow the instructions and insights of his analyst" (p. 157). The difference from Zetzel's formulation was not great, even though Greenson stressed the patient's capacity to work in the analysis, but it did seem to elide if not override any distinction between alliance and the real relation between patient and therapist. Analytic success depended on the patient's capacity to develop a transference neurosis and to maintain a reliable working alliance. The effectiveness of the alliance depended on the patient's motivation to overcome his illness, on his willingness to cooperate, and on his capacity to utilize the analyst's interventions (Greenson 1967). He recognized that the patient's identification with the analyst drew upon earlier helpful relationships, but regarding it as part of the real relationship seemed to eliminate it from the usual technical strictures (Gabbard et al. 1988).

Greenson's implementation of working alliance focused on problems in the working relationship since these can give rise to major resistances that may undermine the analysis. But this emphasis also led him to deviations in technique—surface interventions, explanations, directives, discussions of real problems without any effort to search out unconscious determinants, deviations from neutrality—generally leaning toward more direct and manipulative interventions rather than more purely analytic understanding (Langs 1976). Greenson saw the analyst's task as maintaining a balance between appropriate gratification or humaneness and neutrality or abstinence. He (1965) stressed the humanness of the analytic relation, a quality of the analyst "expressed in his compassion, concern, and therapeutic intent toward his patient . . . . [and] in the attitude that the patient is to be respected as an individual. . . . Humanness consists of understanding and insight conveyed in an atmosphere of serious work, straightforwardness, compassion, and restraint" (pp. 178–179).[15]

Criticisms

This aspect of the technical application of alliance by both Zetzel and Greenson gave rise to concerns regarding the clinical utility of the idea (Brenner 1979; Curtis 1979; Stein 1981). Brenner (1979) emphasized interpretation as the effective vehicle rather than human or humane qualities of the analyst. The concern of these criticisms was that an emphasis on alliance might allow aspects of transference to go unanalyzed and uninterpreted, and that behind collaboration, rationality, and identification with the analyst could lurk elements of resistance and transference. These objections, however valid, were focused on a concept of the alliance that did not distinguish it from the real relationship. Others have objected that emphasis on therapeutic alliance gave rise to the risk of overemphasizing one aspect of the therapeutic relation (Evans 1976)—an objection echoed by Novick (1970) in regard to child analyses. The same objection, however, could be leveled against an overemphasis on transference. And Loewenstein (1969) complained, "The terms 'therapeutic alliance' and 'working alliance' may have the disadvantage of failing to cover the fact that some patients are willing to get well but not to work, while others are ready to work but not to get well" (p. 585). Both variants reflect distortions in therapeutic alliance that call for analytic work. Rangell (1969) also observed that the nurturance implied in the diatrophic attitude or in the parent-child model was not consistent with the deprivation and abstinence required to make transference neurosis possible, and he restricted alliance to the connection "between the analyzing function of the analyst and the observing, critical, and judging functions of the ego of the patient; i.e., between the analyst and the *healthy* part of the patient's ego" (p. 72).

Kanzer's (1975) review of these objections questioned Zetzel's analogy between stages of treatment and development, the tendency to rely on genetic derivatives that were difficult to validate rather than on later maturational factors, and the apparent contradictions between the neutrality required for transference neurosis and the diatrophic maternal attitudes aimed at in alliance. He preferred an emphasis on establishing the competence of the analyst over the warm, supportive interventions Zetzel suggested. Kanzer also objected to Greenson's encouragement of real reactions, noting that interpretations help to separate fantasy from reality. While the patient's perceptions and even the analyst's technical errors may prove helpful in certain cases, he asserted that the work of interpretation should not be bypassed.

Langs (1976) added the observation that Zetzel's insistence on the need for an alliance for interpreting unconscious derivatives reflected her neglect of unconscious factors impairing alliance and her underestimation of the role of interpretation of unconscious fantasy in developing alliance. Both Zetzel and

Greenson, he felt, neglected more unconscious and implicit elements of alliance in favor of the conscious and explicit. He further objected to the radical opposition they posed between alliance and transference neurosis, despite the transference elements in their view of alliance. Brenner's (1979) critique, in turn, seemed to downplay actual responses of the participating adults, the modes of perception and expression, attention, interest, and so forth. Stone (1981) observed that a real grievance cannot be simply equated with a transference response, especially when the analyst's error or failure was involved. He commented, "How a patient listens to interpretations, how he utilizes them, indeed the entire complex matter of his will to recover, are influenced by such considerations, as they are by the state of transference with which the adult attitude are in constant, if fluctuating, interaction. But it must not be ignored that it is between the two adults that it all begins and ends" (pp. 112–113).

In all fairness to these objections, the relation between working alliance and real relation was not very clearly maintained in those early presentations. Greenson argued that the real relation was predominant in the opening and closing phases of analysis, while the working alliance emerged toward the end of the introductory phase and receded as the terminal phase approached. Commenting on these developing ideas, Blum (1981) noted: "A wider understanding of the analytic process has evolved, which goes beyond the concepts of transference and resistance and includes studies of the nature and function of the analytic alliance, developmental processes and tendencies in the patient, and noninterpretive ingredients in the analytic process, situation, and relationship. The analytic alliance concept contributes to the understanding of collaborative analytic work and of the prerequisites for effective analytic interpretation" (p. 65).

In his reflection on the role of curiosity in analysis, Nersessian (1995) brings into focus another critical function of therapeutic alliance, but his concept of curiosity would to my reckoning be better cast as "therapeutic interest." He asserts that such "curiosity" is essential in the analytic process on the part of both analyst and analysand, citing precedents for this view in Greenson (1967), Friedman (1988), and Freud himself (1905d, 1910). He draws the important distinction between conflict-free and relatively autonomous curiosity, as in therapeutic interest appropriate to therapeutic alliance and voyeuristic or scoptophilic contaminants reflecting countertransference effects. He further argues that such therapeutic interest is not contrary to therapeutic neutrality, also an inherent quality of therapeutic alliance. The combination of these qualities contributes to an analytic atmosphere of relatively dispassionate inquiry, which is brought to the endeavor by the analyst in his therapeutic role and assimilated and generated by the patient as he acclimates to the analytic modality and participates in the therapeutic alliance.

A more recent contribution impinging on the relative contribution to therapeutic effectiveness of interpretation as opposed to aspects of the analytic relationship focuses on the distinction between mutative interpretation and insight, on the one hand, and mutative support and experience, on the other (de Jonghe et al. 1992). In this two-factor theory of the analytic process, the support provided by the analytic relationship complements technical interpretation-oriented interventions. The supportive dimension of the analytic relationship involves aspects of transference, alliance, and the real relationship. Support can derive from moderate degrees of unobjectionable positive transference, from aspects of the real relation, and especially from the empathic, containing, holding, and ego-reinforcing dimensions of therapeutic alliance—including the sustaining therapeutic interest provided by the analyst. Any deeper understanding of the role and effect of such support in the analytic process would require careful analysis of the supportive aspects of all these dimensions of the analytic relationship. As Stone (1981) commented: "The relative naturalness of the analyst's attitude (within well-defined professional boundaries), and the considered relaxation of superfluous nonrational deprivations, cognitive and affective, become, in my view, even more important than prescribed diatrophic attitudes (other than those implicit in the physicianly role in the context of analytic technique), granted that the absence of the latter to the degree appropriate for a given patient may often be a severe impediment in the initiation and productive continuance of a psychoanalytic process" (p. 116). Despite controversies, recent research efforts have established the relation of the therapeutic alliance to therapeutic outcome (Allen et al. 1984; Bordin 1979; Frieswyk et al. 1986; Hartley and Strupp 1983; Luborsky 1984; Marziali et al. 1981).

There are differences of opinion regarding the use of the terms *therapeutic alliance* and *working alliance*. Curtis (1979) recommended against using them interchangeably, even dropping the term "working alliance." Dickes (1975) interpreted working alliance as the rational relationship between patient and analyst, requiring maturity of ego functions, psychological mindedness, intelligence, and the capacity for reasonable object relationships—reminiscent of Sterba's effort to separate rationality and irrationality—whereas the therapeutic alliance was a more developed and evolved pattern of relationship, including all the elements favoring the patient's participation and the effectiveness of the collaborative therapeutic effort, even unconscious defenses and resistances, as well as transference-based factors related to unconscious transference fantasies and wishes. This would include such elements as the patient's motivation for treatment, aspects of positive transference, and the capacity for rational interaction—similar to the more inclusive sense of rational alliance described by Gutheil and Havens (1979). The working alliance would then be regarded as more limited in scope, involving the basic capacity for patient and therapist to work together and expressing the extent to which the more mature part of the patient's ego can participate in the therapeutic process. The working alliance would then seem to represent the more rational core of the therapeutic alliance (Dickes 1975).[16]

Part of the difficulty in these formulations—one that has contributed to subsequent confusions in conceptualizing the therapeutic alliance—is that a clear line was not drawn between alliance factors and transference, on the one hand, and between alliance and the real relation, on the other. Conceptual clarity often yields ground to the actual concurrence and intermingling of these aspects of the therapeutic relationship. The therapeutic relationship, as I have implied, in fact involves three components that occur simultaneously within the therapeutic relationship but that can be adequately distinguished. These components are therapeutic alliance, transference, and real relationship. The fact that they intersect in complex patterns and are in continual interaction and mutual modification makes it difficult to preserve their distinct intelligibility, but I propose that the effort to keep them at least conceptually separate furthers our understanding better than prevailing approaches that tend to blur the distinction and bring with them a trail of confusion.

Alliance in Child Analysis

The alliance has found a place in the analyses of children and adolescents. When Anna Freud (1965) concluded that in some child analyses transference developed, she noted that the child was also capable of responding to the analyst as a real person. I should add that the capacity to relate to the real person of the analyst and the capacity to engage in therapeutic alliance are different in children than in adults (Schowalter 1976). Account must be taken of the role of the child's parents as auxiliary egos and adjuncts in forming the alliance. The age and developmental abilities of the child and the quality of the relationship between analyst and parents can play a significant part. The place of alliance factors in work with adolescents is better delineated and closer to the adult model (Evans 1976). For many adolescents, involvement of the parents may impede the development of the therapeutic alliance (Schowalter 1976).

In this respect, Novick (1970) pointed out that the child who has a given capacity may or may not be willing to use it, particularly in the work of analysis. The capacity for alliance may be compromised in very young children or in children suffering from pronounced ego deviation, but children naturally resist using such capacities as self-reflection in analysis (Freud 1965; Novick 1970).

Alliance and the Holding Environment

The metaphor of the "holding environment" was used first by Winnicott (1960b, 1965) in reference to patients undergoing regression and the dissolution of a "false self." The model was based on the protective and soothing maternal holding of a needy infant, extended metaphorically to include caretaking functions of older children.[17] The effort to establish the therapeutic context entailed nonverbal aspects of the analyst's activity as diverse as creation and maintenance of ground rules and boundaries of the analytic relationship, concern for the patient, neutrality and anonymity, consistency, regularity of sessions, and timing and quality of silences and interventions (Winnicott 1960b). Langs (1976) added: "The holding qualities are conveyed implicitly and explicitly through the analyst's tolerance, patience, and his ability to respond in nondisruptive and nonretaliatory ways to the patient's initial threats, attacks, or efforts at seduction. The ability to maintain an unswerving attitude of concern, benevolence, anonymity, and neutrality [is] crucial" (II, p. 505). As Winnicott (1963) indicated, "The analyst is *holding* the patient, and this often takes the form of conveying in words at the appropriate moment something that shows that the analyst knows and understands the deepest anxiety that is being experienced, or that is waiting to be experienced" (p. 240). Holding in this sense also conveys the analyst's empathic attunement.

For such false-self patients, the setting assumed increased importance, in contrast with neurotic patients for whom interpretive work was more salient, a view endorsed by Khan (1960a, 1969) as well. For the former type of patient, the analyst's good-enough adaptation to the patient's needs was crucial, allowing the patient to risk dependence on the analyst and raising the hope for emergence of the true self (Winnicott 1956). The patient will test the analyst before daring to overcome the dread that the analyst will not believe his primitive fears of annihilation or disintegration (Winnicott 1963). Khan (1972) distinguished two ways of relating to the patient, the first involving decoding the meaning of the patient's conflicts and transference involvements, the second a more affective environmental holding to facilitate the patient's engagement in the analytic situation and his capacity to manage the regression accompanying the unfolding of his self-experience. Unveiling this self-experience called for different responses from the analyst than are demanded in more neurotically structured transferences. Modell (1976) expanded analytic characteristics mimicking such idealized maternal functions: "The analyst is constant and reliable; he responds to the patient's affects; he accepts the patient, and his judgment is less critical and more benign; he is there primarily for the patient's needs and not for his own; he does not retaliate; and he does at times have a better grasp of the patient's inner psychic reality than does the patient himself and therefore may clarify what is bewildering and confusing" (p. 291).

The concept of the holding environment entered the literature as a contribution to understanding therapeutic action with primitive personalities suffering from disorders of ego development, particularly narcissistic character disorders (Modell 1976). By implication, emphasis on the holding environment shifted the focus from Strachey's model of mutative interpretation to the affective relatedness between analyst and patient, providing a safe context for the analytic process. Some patients developed neither a transference neurosis nor a therapeutic alliance (Modell 1976); where, then, was the "point of urgency" to provide the motive force behind therapeutic action? This model has become increasingly influential in understanding the initial aspects of establishing analytic rapport, expressed largely though the analyst's understanding of and empathy for the patient's anxieties (Stone 1981). Modell (1976, 1988a, 1988b) enlarged the concept to include a largely silent component of standard interpretive analytic work in the "cocoon" phase of therapy with patients with narcissistic personality disorders and as a necessary backdrop for standard interpretive work. Holding thus provides an illusion of safety and protection from dangers both within and without. The patient will not be slow to test these factors as the analysis progresses.

But holding is possible only when the patient allows it. The patient's response either facilitates or distorts the holding environment. For more disturbed patients, such holding assumes a crucial curative role; for narcissistic and schizoid patients, whose tolerance for the analytic relationship is limited, such a noninterpretive stance may help make further treatment possible, at least in the beginning stages (Modell 1975, 1976; Stone 1981). In Modell's reconstruction, the early "cocoon" transference is marked by isolation, self-sufficiency, and a dearth of affective communication; the analyst's response is empathic holding, and his interpretations convey his empathy and are nonmutative. In the middle phase, narcissistic rage fueled by envy emerges along with the beginnings of a therapeutic alliance, and the analyst adopts a more interpretive stance. The final phase is marked by consolidation of the alliance and potentially mutative interpretations.

One aspect of the holding environment concept that can enunciate a partial truth and at the same time lead to a potential misunderstanding is its implicit appeal to a parental, even maternal, model of the analyst-patient relation (Arlow and Brenner 1966; Mayer and Spence 1994). Could the analytic situation be thought of as mobilizing developmental potentialities, even without interpretation of unconscious conflict? Did the permission to regress in the presence of a nonthreatening, empathic, and reliable analyst open the way to completing developmental processes that had become stalled (Blum 1981)? There are limits and risks to this line of thinking: the analyst is not the patient's parent, and the patient is not a child relating to a parental figure.[18] Spruiell (1983) pointed up this issue nicely:

> While we experience ourselves—temporarily within the frame—as taken to be, for example, parents, and our responses are authentic within the frame,

> we know that the analyst is an adult involved in a game which is sometimes quite playful but hardly ever trivial. Even within the frame we do not act like parents; we do not succor, ignore, reward, spank, cajole, argue with, instruct, bathe, forbid, etc. Nor do we act like lovers, enemies, friends, siblings, or the patient himself or some part of him. We act like analysts—a fact sometimes forgotten in the literature where one finds assertions that within the "alliance" the analyst is "really" being a better parent than the patient ever had. It is as disastrous for analysts to actually treat their patients like children as it is for analysts to treat their own children as patients. (p. 12)

Mitchell (1988) similarly noted that the maternal-deprivation model makes the analyst into a good or bad maternal object and the patient into the passive recipient of good or bad mothering; that is, the role of aggression and object-relations conflicts is minimized, and the patient's role as victim is reinforced. As Pine (1993) emphasizes, what counts is the context of safety, but this merely echoes the holding environment of childhood and may be as different from the childhood model as similar to it.[19] "In providing a holding environment," Sandbank (1993) observes, "analysts are not holding patients in the same way that mothers hold babies. . . . What makes for similarity . . . is connected to the idea that both analysts and parents aim to facilitate psychological growth. In order to achieve this they are constantly moving back and forth between two poles. At one pole is the unconditional acceptance of the child/patient, identification with his distress, making it possible for him to feel very close, affirmed, mirrored and often serving as an auxiliary ego for him. At the other pole is the parent's/analyst's vision of the child/patient's potential development as an individual, the facilitation of feelings of separateness, individuation and autonomy" (p. 717).

A related conception is the Kleinian metaphor of containment (Bion 1962, 1963, 1965, 1970; Klein 1974). This model also appeals to imagery in which the mother-analyst contains elements of the patient's rudimentary identity (Grinberg and Grinberg 1974). Such containment allows the analysand to accept the regression necessary for successful analysis, to tolerate inevitable anxieties, and to lay a foundation for effective interpretation. Containment of the patient's rage and violent projections helps both patient and analyst survive these assaults and makes the analyst a good and protective container guaranteeing a safe context for emotional discharge (Green 1975) or an "envelope" whose limits help preserve transference disruptions (Gehrie 1993). Thus the patient's basic anxieties and fears of annihilation of both self and object can be alleviated (Klein 1974). The analyst's capacity to tolerate and contain the patient's projections and to metabolize them appropriately, helping both the patient and himself to gain clearer understanding of their meaning through interpretation, is integral to the containing function.[20]

A related perspective on the function of the therapeutic alliance is that one of its purposes is to establish and maintain the analytic space—that is, the metaphorical space between analyst and analysand within which crucial illusions are allowed to emerge that fuel the analytic process and provide the essential ground for therapeutic effects (Gehrie 1993). The alliance facilitates the use of the analyst as a transitional object and the analytic space as a field of illusion (Eickhoff 1993; Green 1975; Loewald 1975; Person 1993) in which distinctions among transference, therapeutic alliance, and reality can be maintained (Gehrie 1993). The therapeutic alliance can be viewed as embracing those components of the analytic situation where the central analytic illusions—transference and countertransference, with all their implications and vicissitudes, take root and flourish.

The metaphoric usages of holding and containment aim to create the optimal therapeutic milieu for the analyst and analysand. Renik (1992), for instance, reminds us not only of the importance of this function to the analytic process but also of the difficulties that it can create. This illusory middle ground of analysis can itself become fetishized and replaced by a gratifying transference fantasy that escapes further investigation and leads to therapeutic impasse. Fantasy and reality become confused and magical expectations continue to flourish. The illusion of fulfilling a cherished fantasy, not uncommon in borderline and some narcissistic patients (Abend et al. 1983; Meissner 1988), replaces analytic collaboration and consensual goals of treatment.

CHAPTER TWO

Alliance and Transference

The distinction between therapeutic alliance and transference has always been a subject of intense controversy. Analytic opinions cover a broad spectrum from denial of any distinction or the effort to do away with the alliance concept altogether through an array of viewpoints introducing transference components into alliance in various degrees and forms and extending to insistence on the separateness of alliance and transference. The seeds of controversy were sown by Freud's view of an unobjectionable transference, which made way for the emergence of alliance concepts. Many analysts have since been concerned with the danger that unobjectionable transference, along with its alliance congeners, might go unanalyzed or open the way to unattended transference/countertransference enactments that leave analytic work distorted or incomplete (Wallerstein 1993).

Alliance versus Transference

By far the greatest portion of analytic theoretical endeavor has gone into delineating the complexities of transference in the analytic relation and process. The forms of transference are protean; in a previous effort (Meissner 1988), I found room for variants of transferences based on displacement or projection, classical forms of positive libidinally based transferences, negative aggressively determined transferences, narcissistic transferences, selfobject transferences, transitional transference relatedness, and transference psychosis. Another classification was advanced by the Hampstead group (Sandler et al. 1969, 1973): (1) transference representing in manifest or latent content revivals of past experience, impulse, fantasy, and conflict in relation to the analyst (these are the classic transferences based on displacement);[1] (2) transference neurosis, involving the concentration of past repressed derivatives onto the analyst with diminished expression elsewhere; (3) externalization (projection) of characteristics from the patient's inner world and psychic structure onto the analyst;[2] (4) displacements of other current relationships into the analytic relation; (5) character transferences based on habitual and characteristic patterns of interaction (I would question whether these reactions belong in the category of transference); (6) transferences contributing to the therapeutic alliance (I would prefer "contaminating" rather than "contributing"); and (7) transference readinesses, in which previously operative wishes, fantasies, and expectations are brought to the analytic interaction.[3] To this list we should add the distinction between transference of impulse and transference of defense (Freud 1936), in which the defense against the impulse rather than the impulse finds its way into the transference. Gray (1987, 1991) envisions the latter as forms of superego externalization, casting the analyst either as an authoritarian inhibitor, controlling and critical, or as a permissive, approving, even affectionate protector. Gill (1982) sees these as defenses against both transference and transference wish. These portrayals of the analyst can also be recognized as manifesting forms of transference/countertransference interaction and associated therapeutic misalliances.

There is a general trend in contemporary analysis to regard the classic view of transference, based on displacements from past objects, as inadequate and to include components reflecting the need of each participant to draw the other into a stance corresponding to his or her own intrapsychic configuration (Sandler 1976; Jacobs 1991). Transference has undergone further diffusion of meaning, at its height arriving at a notion of transference as "just the psyche's characteristic activity of creating a meaningful world in which to live" (Lear 1993, p. 741), or "simply the idiosyncratic, unconscious side of the psyche's fundamental activity: to inform the world with meaning" (p. 748). Thus, transference is extended so that we lose any distinction between the meanings we give to reality and the meanings inherent in transference. Transference becomes all-encompassing, and the meaning of reality (or alliance, for that matter) fades into obscurity.

Transference and therapeutic alliance have essentially different roots and express themselves in different ways in the analytic process. The all-encompassing connotation given to transference—embracing the total relation between patient and analyst—overrides critical distinctions, allows a number of technical confusions to persist, tends to emphasize the patient's neurotic contributions to the analytic process while de-emphasizing the analyst's contributions, and does not give adequate play to the patient's more positive and therapeutic contributions (Langs 1976).

Freud's (1915) basic insight that transference love is an effort to destroy the analyst's authority and thus undermine analytic work led him to the conclusion that the therapeutic response lay in neither acceptance nor rejection but in maintaining a stance of truthfulness and neutrality, keeping countertransference in line, and the rule of abstinence. Without these countermeasures, as he put it, "The patient would achieve *her* aim, but he [the analyst] would never achieve *his*" (p. 165). He recognized that factors allowing the patient to persist in the analytic effort in the face of powerful resistances were found in the relation to the analyst, but he had no place for these motives except in transference. In his view it was basically positive transference that saw the analyst as an authority to be trusted and believed (Freud 1916–17); alliance as a separate concept was not at that point part of the analytic lexicon. There is some argument as to whether Freud ever abandoned his reliance on some modification of positive transference to maintain the patient's involvement—Kanzer (1980) seems to think that he did, Gill (1982, 1993) that he did not. In any case, Freud also recognized that transference was basically antithetical to the pact made in the beginning to share in their common effort (Freud 1940).[4]

Sources of Motivation

In the context of ego psychology, most advocates of the alliance concept, following Hartmann's (1950) lead, attributed alliance to the ego and stipulated antagonism between alliance as an ego-derivative and transference as an id-derivative (Loewenstein 1969; Zavitzianos 1974).[5] Hartmann developed the idea of ego-interests originating in id-strivings, but becoming neutralized and deinstinctualized, thus relatively autonomous and drawn to the service of the ego. Thus, ego-interests can become antagonistic to id-strivings. Insofar as these motivations enter the therapeutic alliance, they must be kept distinct from other motives closer to instinctual desires. Although the alliance had its roots in Freud's view of the unobjectionable positive transference, Loewenstein (1969) maintained that willingness to cooperate could not be attributed to transference alone, but was also based on trust and confidence in the analyst founded on autonomy and the capacity for reliable object relations and for aim-inhibited libidinal object-ties. This view was echoed by Blum (1971b), for whom the alliance was based on conflict-free ego-capacities, as opposed to the conflictual origin of transference, and might include elements of positive transference, basic trust, and relatively permissive superego derivatives.[6]

Zetzel (1965), in turn, noted that regression required to reopen earlier conflicts and modify defenses, but this was not a regression undermining basic ego capacities. Therapeutic regression was made possible by maintenance and integration of therapeutic alliance, facilitating the patient's continuing positive identification with the analyst (1970). Such therapeutic regression opened the way to transference and its infantile wishes and fantasies, but the ability to maintain ego structure and capacity in the face of regression was indispensable for the analytic process. The alliance and the real relationship offered the basis for a stable analytic situation, allowing the infinite mutability of the transference to find expression (1970). For Zetzel, the intactness of the alliance rested on these ego capacities; in the present study, alliance is conceived in more object relational terms and as such is properly attributable to the self-system rather than solely to the ego.

Rangell (1969) made a further discrimination between alliance and transference. In addition to his neutral attitude, which is also empathic and compassionate, the analyst brings to the analytic encounter a giving and nurturing stance, like Gitelson's diatrophic attitude or Zetzel's appeal to the mother-child bond. Both Zetzel and Greenson emphasized the role of alliance in nurturing the patient's infantile needs so that the patient's more mature self could tolerate the stress of neutrality and transference regression. However, Rangell makes the point that alliance is not based on such nurturance but takes place between the analyst's analyzing function and the healthy critical and judging capacities of the patient's ego. Fixated infantile needs were to be analyzed; relying on them for the therapeutic relation led only to a corrective emotional experience and gratifications. Alliance was based instead on the stance of neutrality, deprivation, and limitation, characteristics that elicit a more classical transference neurosis. Swartz (1969) added that in patients in whom the alliance was weak or nonexistent, emergence of the transference neurosis was correspondingly impeded.[7]

From one point of view, then, there is a kind of negative proportionality: if alliance becomes dominant in the clinical interaction, transference tends to recede, and vice versa (Binstock 1973). Such was the case for Novick's (1970) Erika, for whom positive transference played a major role in her cooperation with treatment. Novick summarized the situation: "When it [positive transference] was too intense or too highly resisted it destroyed the alliance. Equally, the alliance was lost when the libidinal wishes were displaced and enacted outside the transference. The ego attitude by itself was not sufficient and she could not speak to me because she no longer loved me. The alliance was re-established when I became, once more, an object of libidinal interest" (p. 243). It seems that alliance is understood here as a form of modulated libidinal attachment that can be disrupted by excess or resistance—thus making it a form of transference. But for Binstock (1973) the distinction was based on a qualitative difference. Transference was neither actual nor directed at a whole object, while alliance in contrast was actual; the analyst relates to the patient as a whole actual object and the goal of analysis is to enable the patient to relate to the analyst as an object that is both whole and actual. While transference is subject to regression, alliance is not—it can diminish or be suspended, but it cannot regress.[8]

Differentiating Alliance

Failure to distinguish between real relationship and alliance, as Kernberg (1993) notes, "may unwittingly foster a distortion of the psychoanalytic situation into a direction of conventionality, in which unacknowledged, culturally and socially determined joint biases of patient and analyst contribute to restrict the full investigation of the transference" (p. 666). This may obtain with respect to the reality of the analytic relation, but not in the alliance; rather, the alliance should provide the basis for acknowledging and exploring such differences and their impact on transference and therapeutic work.

Nevertheless, in certain respects the distinction seems uncertain. If we consider Erikson's (1963) basic trust as a component of the patient's capacity for alliance, it is often difficult to keep aspects of early infantile positive transferential determinants distinct from basic trust itself (Stein 1981). For the most part, they go together and are mutually influential and supportive. But primitive positive transference carries other connotations that are not part of basic trust—wishes for dependency, merger, symbiotic reunion, even idealization, for example—and that are in many ways antithetical to it. Resistance to giving up the illness and losing the analyst, associated with symbiotic dependence on the analyst, can undermine any effective alliance (Schevin 1963). The distinction is clearer in relation to issues of autonomy. The patient's capacity for an autonomous relationship with the therapist may be influenced by a variety of transference dispositions, whether positive or negative, including wishes to separate, but autonomy itself is a present and concurrent quality of the object relation and cannot be regarded as synonymous with any of the related transference dynamics.

Freud's idea of an unobjectionable transference and later versions of mature transference (Stone 1961, 1981) fall short of the more central concept of transference in the context of the transference neurosis. Stone's (1961, 1967, 1981) primordial transference seeking symbiotic reunion expresses archaic preoedipal needs, but the mature transference seeking to bridge the gap from the mother of separation is seen as an irrational energizing component of therapeutic alliance. The mature transference,[9] in these terms, is at once distinct from alliance and an integral part of it. It aims toward achieving separation, individuation, and mastery over internal and external environments. This view of mature transference rests on the assumption that the wish to be understood, to understand, to learn and mature is essentially transferential—a view that the present analysis challenges, whether the dynamic falls to the aegis of ego or to a more evolved conception of self (Meissner 1981, 1986a). This watered-down transference would have to be relatively neutralized and autonomous. Even so, it is not equivalent to alliance, although it may also contribute to a positive relationship.[10] Rather than complicating the understanding of alliance by mixing it with transferential *formes frustres*, I would prefer to maintain the conceptual distinction and see such transferential derivatives as contaminants of alliance. Even the "matrix transference" (Langs 1976), arising from the earliest mother-child interaction but including later developmental components and contributing to the patient's positive relation with the analyst, remains open to all the vicissitudes of transference and stands in opposition to nontransference. Such transferential contaminants require analysis and resolution to complete the analytic process. In addition, there is always the tendency to be more accepting of these "rational" or "mature" aspects of transference and to expend our interpretive capital on more irrational expressions lying closer to the heart of transference neurosis.

Along the same line, Loewenstein (1954) took the view that any alliance regarded as conflict-free would be precarious without the added force of transference, implying that transference would reinforce the alliance. The same ambiguity was built into Zetzel's (1956) and Greenson's (1965) contributions. As Greenson (1965) expressed it:

> This differentiation between transference neurosis and working alliance, however, is not absolute since the working alliance may contain elements of the infantile neurosis which eventually will require analysis. For example, the patient may work well temporarily in order to gain the analyst's love, and this ultimately will lead to strong resistances; or the overvaluation of the analyst's character and ability may also serve the working alliance well in the beginning of the analysis, only to become a source of strong resistance later. Not only can the transference neurosis invade the working alliance but the working alliance itself can be misused defensively to ward off the more regressive transference phenomena. Despite these intermixtures, the separation of the patient's reactions to the analyst into these two groupings, transference neurosis and working alliance, seems to have clinical and technical value. (p. 158)

Along similar lines, Jacobs (1991) provided an account of a case in which the initial course of therapy had been marked by a strong positive transference and therapeutic alliance, but subsequent analysis began under an onslaught of negative transference in which the patient saw his analyst as unreliable, incompetent, and untrustworthy. This lasted for more than a year before it began to dissipate and some semblance of an alliance could be established. The reactivation of these powerful negative elements was due to the previous termination of the therapy which the patient had experienced as rejection and abandonment derived from devastating childhood traumata. Alliance was out of the question until the force of these negative transference elements could be dispelled. Others have noted that when the patient's transference experience of the analyst lies too close to internal representations of highly conflictual, ambivalent, or negative primary objects, development of the therapeutic alliance can be significantly impeded (Roland 1967; Viederman 1976). Serious resistances can also arise from failures of the analyst to lend credence, under some circumstances, to the patient's accurate perception of problematic character traits or errors of the analyst (Greenson and Wexler 1969). Another source of potentially serious difficulties arises when the patient's transference image lies too close to real characteristics of the analyst that mimic characteristics of primary objects—tone of voice, physical appearance, choice of words, and so on.

In the light of these formulations, transference and alliance must be kept separate, but they interact in complex ways. To the extent that they interact positively, they remain distinct, so that if the analyst is inclined to accept positive transference as a support to the analytic work, he cannot forget that it is transference and ultimately antithetical to the alliance. Transference always involves a resistance—a point that was not ignored by Freud (1917). As Zavitzianos (1974) commented:

> True transference arouses resistances and is always a resistance itself. As long as it exists and is not analyzed, therapeutic progress is hindered. . . . The goal of the transference is not recovery. During positive transference the patient does not make any more constructive use of the analyst's interpretations than he does during negative transference. The greater receptivity of the patient during positive transference is deceptive. It indicates only a hunger for libidinal gratification. Accepting treatment for the sake of such gratification is entirely different from accepting it for the purpose of recovery. The latter requires a readiness to accept the frustration of transference wishes. (p. 305)

Alliance Motivation

But the patient's wish for help is not necessarily a transference wish: it may be rational, reasonable, and realistic and may motivate him. The wish to cooperate with the analyst and realize the goals of the analysis may not be the same as the wish to get better, for the latter may embrace unreal and magical fantasies and expectations contrary to alliance (Sandler et al. 1973). As Stone (1981) has observed, there are gratifications implicit in the psychoanalytic situation, such as freedom of expression, tolerance, unconditional acceptance, reliability, including initial positive transference elements such as expectations for parental protectiveness, care, interest, and relief from suffering, that help sustain the treatment process. While these expectations may carry an infantile cast in some degree, they may not be limited to that constraint but may reflect more developed, reasonable, and realistic motives consistent with alliance and involving the patient's intellectual interest and curiosity (Fields 1985). That such complex levels of motivation are simultaneously operative in the analytic process does not force us to conclude that they are synonymous or reducible in any fashion.[11]

For example, Greenacre's (1954, 1968) use of the term *transference* to embrace the total relationship between analyst and patient overrides any distinction between alliance and transference. To the extent that it plays any role, alliance is regarded (à la Zetzel) as a secondary component, along with transference neurosis, of the analytic relationship (Greenacre 1959; Panel 1958). Her tendency to use the term *transference* to indicate the total relationship between analyst and patient meant that attitudes leading to positive collaboration and rapport were part of transference along with transference neurosis. As they enter the alliance they are reinforced by identification with the analyst. Alliance becomes synonymous with positive transference rooted in the early mother-infant bond (Greenacre 1968). This tends to shift the emphasis toward basic trust as the essential element in alliance and toward maternal and need-fulfilling functions of the analyst—reminiscent of Zetzel's emphasis on trust. Alliance, then, becomes just another form of transference based on early, primitive, and infantile contributions from early developmental strata. Many analysts maintain that distinction of alliance from transference is simply not possible or, if done, is meaningless (Brenner 1979; Curtis 1979; Novick 1970). A similar emphasis can be found in Stone's (1961) appeal to transference to the mother of separation. Heimann (1970) came to the same conclusion from a more Kleinian perspective, that there had to be an element of positive transference in the basic trust that enabled the patient to accept the doctor's advice, and whether behavior toward the analyst seemed realistic or not, there was transference in every response to the analyst. Similarly, in Stein's (1981) discussion of so-called unobjectionable transference and its connection with transference neurosis, he questions whether transference elements can ever be unobjectionable or immune from analysis; they may also mask negative transference (Gill 1993) or screen out other undesirable elements (Jacobs 1991).

From another direction, Langs' (1976) objections bring into sharp relief the issue of whether there are unconscious transference or fantasy elements embedded in alliance or whether the alliance and transference sectors of the patient's experience of the relationship with the analyst are continually and mutually interacting. Olinick (1976) observed this same blurring of the lines of distinction:

> Alliances are based upon a continuing dynamic ebb and flow of reality factors and transference. They disconcertingly vanish into the transference at times of resistance; regression claims them, and only careful attention to the analysis of transference and resistance may release them again. Yet even during times of obdurate resistance, there is some part of the psychoanalytic patient that attends and listens to what is happening. Analysands will often tell us, for instance, that months earlier we had offered an inter-

> pretation that they had rejected, but which now they recognize as having always been valid. Not always does this represent effects of a premature interpretation. Rather, a considerable period of working through has been necessary before the patient can rediscover the issues besetting him. The fact is that, even while the alliance seems to be in abeyance, some agency within the patient is preconsciously active—monitoring, viewing, testing, and evaluating. (pp. 3–4)

Adler (1980) takes the similar position that alliance derives from transference and reflects certain childhood experiences and early developmental achievements. In contrast, I prefer to understand alliance as distinct from both reality factors and transference, even though there is presumptively no therapeutic alliance without transference contaminants of one kind or degree or other. The alliance may at times be overridden by transference and/or resistance, but it runs its own course.

Transference and Alliance Interplay

Other more pragmatic connotations come into play in the analytic relationship and may have implications for therapeutic processing and response. Alliance comes into play from the first moment of contact between patient and therapist, even if the initial exchange takes place over the telephone. The alliance is generated and shaped at every moment of the therapeutic interaction by both patient and therapist. Transference factors may or may not come into play from the beginning. For some patients, pieces of transference material become active quite early in the process; for others, transference emerges more gradually and is often delayed, coming to the fore only as the analytic process deepens and regression increasingly takes hold. In other cases, elements of preformed transference can be at work even before any contact between patient and analyst, but alliance issues cannot come into play until contact is made. These differences may have diagnostic implications (Meissner 1984a).

One implication of this distinction with immediate relevance to analytic praxis is that alliance factors arise immediately within the ongoing analytic relationship itself, while transference aspects derive from nonanalytic frameworks and enter into the analytic relationship from the outside. Transference elements may facilitate or inhibit the therapeutic relationship, but they always undermine the therapeutic alliance, whether they are positive or negative in content. As Novick (1970) put it, "The alliance can be swept aside by resistance to the negative transference, by the emergence of the negative transference, by the enactment of the positive transference in the sessions, by the displacement of positive libidinal wishes and their enactment outside the transference. In addition, we have seen that the intensification of internalized conflicts can lead to the use of externalizations, a defensive process which can overwhelm all the motives for maintaining an alliance" (p. 245). Negative transference elements undermine the essential collaborative nature of the alliance, and for the most part this distortion of alliance is easily recognized. Positive transference elements may provide a more subtle and often confusing picture insofar as their motivational elements may reinforce or sustain the therapeutic relationship. They do so, however, at the cost of the therapeutic alliance. Elements of positive libidinal regard or attachment, dependency, aspects of idealization, and other aspects of a positive transferential attitude—even Freud's unobjectionable positive transference—may under certain conditions contribute to the therapeutic process, but they ultimately undermine the alliance. If there is a therapeutic gain to be extracted from the influence of such factors, it is more often short term and is purchased at the longer-term cost of distorting or undermining therapeutic alliance. These contribute to the forms of distortion of therapeutic alliance that Langs (1975a, 1975b, 1976) described as "misalliances." Transference in these situations is not synonymous with therapeutic misalliance: transference distortions may give rise to such misalliances, but they are conceptually different.[12] Here a firm distinction between alliance and real relation is helpful insofar as transference tends to react to real characteristics of the analyst; as Fox (1984) puts it, "It is not merely a displacement of past figures on to the blank screen of the analyst but a finding of these fantasied figures in the person of the other" (p. 233). In contrast, impingement of transference on the alliance transforms alliance into misalliance.

An example may help to clarify the point. Early in a series of evaluative sessions in which a patient and therapist were working toward a decision to undertake a course of therapy, the patient, a woman in her late twenties who had had difficulties in the past with an eating disorder and had recently experienced the abrupt and unexplained termination of a therapeutic relationship that had lasted more than six years, described her mother as an alcoholic and her father as an overeater. She tearfully complained that her mother would drink and become unavailable to her and that her father would eat and become similarly unavailable. With some hesitation, a few minutes later in the discussion she commented that the therapist seemed to be overweight and that made her afraid that he would not listen to her and would not be able to hear her pain.

This material could and should easily be heard in transference terms, namely, a negative father transference triggered by the similarity between the father's corpulence and the therapist's. I would suggest, however, that what was also being expressed was the patient's concern that the therapist would be unable to hear her internal distress, that he would be unavailable to her and be unable to stay with her during painful experiences. The patient was clearly suffering from an unresolved mourning of the former therapist and was struggling with issues of trust on the brink of entering another such relationship. I would regard these as alliance issues, arising as an aspect of the immediate situation to which both patient and therapist are contributing.. The result took the form of denying any meaning to the analytic relation and of trying to reproduce the pre-loss relation with the analyst. The continuing object need affected not only adult object relations, but was also expressed in the relation to the analyst during the initial phase of analysis. In both cases, the alliance suffered, emergence of an analyzable transference neurosis was thwarted, and analytic effectiveness diminished. Hani (1973) described a similar outcome in patients suffering from traumatic maternal separation, a point consistent with Zetzel's view that traumatic shortcomings of the mother could impair the development of object relations and thus affect the patient's ability to establish a therapeutic alliance. In addition, patients who successfully achieve and resolve oedipal conflict tend to have a better capacity for alliance. Fleming's (1972) view was that the analyst's diatrophic and empathic responses to the patient's object need to find an auxiliary helper to facilitate separation and individuation of a relatively autonomous self contribute to alliance. Establishing a foundation for this need in the alliance opens the way for release of other childhood hopes and expectations and development of the transference neurosis. She concluded, "The analyst's knowledge of the effect of separation experiences, with their potential for trauma but also for normal development, will enable him to recognize the problem of interrupted mourning work and facilitate its continuance to completion. On the basis of such an empathic symbiotic working alliance and a break-through of resistances against mourning work, the psychoanalytic process can proceed and patients suffering from childhood object deprivation can be helped" (p. 45). Such formulations are reminiscent of Nacht's (1957, 1962; Nacht and Viderman 1960) earlier view of the need for absolute union and lack of separation—not a form of transference but representing a wished-for and never-attained state. Efforts to interpret the infantile wish only renewed the vulnerability to separation; the authors recommended a noninterpretive intervention of modified neutrality that would create a sense of "presence" rooted in the analyst's reality, not unlike Winnicott's "holding."

Many negative reactions to the work of Zetzel and Greenson were based on this view. If the analyst paid too much attention to alliance, he would interfere with the transference and its development in the analytic process (Brenner 1980; Curtis 1979). Heimann (1970) criticized the attitude that alliance was to be encouraged and not subjected to analysis. Efforts to support the therapeutic alliance would, it was feared, reinforce the analyst's countertransference, in particular his denial of unconscious fantasies and transference material; analyst and patient would collusively avoid unconscious conflicts and fantasies. Similar difficulties arise with respect to reconstruction: an effective reconstruction can reduce the intensity of transference by resolving it, yet concentration on the transference can lead to resistance to remembering (Reed 1993). *A pari,* attention to alliance issues may at times diminish transference intensity, but an exclusive focus on transference may also run the risk of avoiding alliance difficulties.

The reciprocal connection between the therapeutic alliance and transference is not the only pattern of activation that can prevail. Establishment and consolidation of a secure and firm alliance may also become a necessary condition for the more regressive emergence of powerful, meaningful, and even dangerous transference dimensions (Hani 1973; Zavitzianos 1974). In such cases, the alliance offers a safe context within which intense and frightening transference derivatives can be allowed access to consciousness and analytic processing (Sandler 1960). Stone (1961) emphasized that alliance is necessary when the patient's transference is exceptionally intense and his vulnerability to regression makes interpretation difficult. And Greenson (1965) argued that stalemate is most common when the analyst becomes exclusively preoccupied with the analysis of transference and resistance, neglecting the alliance. These views, generally based in some version of ego psychology, tend to see alliance as necessary for transference interpretation rather than the other way around (Panel 1971). The opposite tack is followed by Kleinian analysts, who emphasize transference interpretation as leading to alliance, although this tendency opens the way to neglect of nontransferential aspects of the analytic relation (Langs 1976). For the most part, Kleinian analysts not only do not find the alliance concept helpful, many regarding it as manipulative, even antitherapeutic (Hamilton 1993), but also regard transference interpretations as effective without any need for alliance (Modell 1976).

More often than not, distortions in alliance reflect underlying transference issues, so that interpretation of these transference distortions becomes necessary to establish or salvage the alliance. Gabbard et al. (1988) documented how transference interpretations resulted in increased collaboration with a difficult borderline patient. They speculated that the patient's fears of angry retaliation or humiliating ridicule from the therapist were clarified, allowing the patient to explore these fears and realize that they were the product of irrational internal sources and not real external threats. Likewise, Khan (1960b) reported a case in which interpretation of the patient's intense object need based on childhood object deprivation diminished transference resistance and established a meaningful therapeutic alliance.

There are cases, however, in which any attempt to interpret transference will place the alliance in jeopardy. Such patients tend to have fragile self-organizations marked by either paranoid or severely narcissistic features. They experience any attempt to interpret their transferences as controlling, intrusive, hurtful, humiliating, or repeating an infantile trauma (Stern 1992).[14] Where interpretation of transference is either not possible or stimulates such negative responses, the ground of the alliance has to shift toward a holding model, allowing background factors of safety and security greater room to develop. Modell (1976) described the process of undoing a "cocoon" transference—from the initial holding phase, in which any effort to interpret is frustrated and ineffective, through a stormy period in which the release of pent-up rage gives way to rudiments of an alliance in which interpretation can begin to effect dissolution of the cocoon, and a final stage of relatively firm therapeutic alliance and more effective interpretation. In contrast to classic neurotic transference, dissolution of the cocoon transference opens the way for establishing an alliance. Interpretations in the first phase express only the analyst's empathy and acceptance as part of the holding function.

Alliance and "Selfobject" Transferences

The line of demarcation between alliance factors and transference is somewhat obscured in so-called selfobject transferences. In my view, it is not clear to what extent selfobject relations differ from Balint's (1965, 1968) "primary love" relation or from the holding environment, this ambiguity arising from the question of whether selfobject transferences are truly transferences or *formes frustres* of alliance. As London (1985) noted, selfobject transferences are quite different from transferences as understood in drive-conflict terms and have similarities to the holding concept with additional emphasis on the role of empathy. They are based on needs rather than wishes, reflecting certain developmental vicissitudes and forms of environmental input: "The patient has no wish to be mirrored but he doesn't function very well unless he is mirrored" (p. 98). The Ornsteins' (1994) description is clarifying:

> Selfobject transference (Kohut 1971) has to be distinguished from the traditional view of transference, in that it becomes established in relation to structural deficits, rather than in relation to intrapsychic conflicts. Neither displacement nor projection is considered to operate in the selfobject transference. The underlying structural deficit reactivates the patient's thwarted need to grow—hence, the various selfobject transferences (mirror, idealising and twinship) manifest themselves ubiquitously and may be especially intensely and insistently focused on the analyst during the analytic process. Rather than displacing or projecting, patients in their selfobject transferences express currently-felt needs; needs that have remained unresponded to, or unreliably responded to, ever since infancy and childhood and left them with structural deficits in the self. We might say that a selfobject transference reflects the re-opening of the patient's deficiently structuralised psyche for belated maturation and development. (p. 977)

Others have pointed out that selfobject transferences refer back to the real relation with the mother or with the analyst in his reparative role (Rothstein 1980) or that there is no displacement of an object (Treurniet 1983).[15]

In Kohut's (1971, 1977) view, emergence and stabilization of narcissistic or self-object transferences through the analyst's empathic understanding provide the basis for a stable clinical analyzable situation. These selfobject experiences (mirroring, idealizing, and twinship or alter ego) are necessary for emergence and maintenance of a cohesive self (Wolf 1993). There are technical implications in Kohut's approach to narcissistic transferences: these patients' inability to form a realistic bond with the analyst should not be met with active interventions attempting to establish the alliance but by attention to disturbances in the self (1971). If this seems to gainsay or replace the idea of alliance with empathic acceptance, Adler (1980) calls attention to Kohut's description in the same work of a form of alliance reminiscent of Sterba: "The observing segment of the personality of the analysand which, in cooperation with the analyst, has actively shouldered the task of analyzing, is not, in essence, different in analyzable narcissistic disorders from that found in analyzable transference neuroses. In both types of cases an adequate area of realistic cooperation derived from positive experiences in childhood (in the object-cathected and narcissistic realm) is the precondition for the analysand's maintenance of the therapeutic split of the ego and for that fondness for the analyst which assures the maintenance of a sufficient trust in the processes and goals of analysis during stressful periods" (Kohut 1971, p. 207). The extent to which this formulation mingles rather than confuses (Gutheil and Havens 1979) alliance and transference is open to question. It can be argued, in reference to the widening scope of analysis, that the selfobject stance is another form of analytic neutrality that encourages archaic responses in the selfobject transference that will yield to further analytic exploration if the foundation is laid for such an effort in a trusting and secure relation to the analyst (London 1985; Jacobs 1991). In my view, this latter component *is* the therapeutic alliance.

The problem is compounded by the extent to which alliance factors and transferential factors are confused in the literature. Zetzel (1956) and Fleming (1972) tend to derive alliance from primitive pregenital transferences, even suggesting a symbiotic quality akin to the selfobject model. Even Langs (1976), who otherwise makes a strong case for the importance of alliance, argues that "the therapeutic alliance is a sector of the analytic relationship with contributions from every aspect of the patient's intrapsychic structures and self, and from both the transference and nontransference realms. The rational and non-neurotic aspects of the alliance are, in this view, its surface manifestations, while both rational and irrational components may lie beneath them" (II, p. 200). I would argue, contrary to all these trends, that the concurrent and interactive nature of these components of the analytic relation does not argue for their conceptual conflation, nor does their distinction eliminate their intimate interconnection and involvement. Langs (1976) goes on to say, "Derivatives of erotic and hostile transference fantasies and wishes may at times contribute positively to the alliance sector, although their distorted and distorting elements will generally prove interfering at some juncture and will require analytic resolution—the fate of all of the transference-based contributions to the therapeutic alliance" (II, p. 212). The task of analysis and resolution would be better served by a clear discrimination between what belongs to the alliance and what enters from the transference.

The underlying needs of the self, as expressed in "selfobject" transferences, are at least partially responded to in the therapeutic alliance (Treurniet 1980; Levine 1983). This aspect is at least suggested by Stolorow's (1993) distinction between repetitive and selfobject dimensions of transference. The former leads to conflict and resistance and is closer to traditional notions of transference, whereas the latter seeks selfobject experiences from the analyst that were lacking during development. These dimensions are described as oscillating: when the analyst is malattuned and unempathic the repetitive dimension comes to the fore, and when the analyst is empathic and understanding the selfobject dimension is reinforced. But the analyst's attuned understanding may intensify conflict and resistance if it activates walled-off longings and hopes along with fears of repeating the trauma. The selfobject language here lends itself to formulation in alliance terms. The dependence and need expressed by selfobject language is familiar for patients of all descriptions, not simply narcissistic, so that such transferences can emerge in the course of any analysis (Jacobs 1991).

But there is another side to this coin. To the extent that neurotic or self-related needs expressed in selfobject transferences are responded to by the object, there would seem to be a high risk for developing transference/countertransference interactions and/or misalliances. For example, if an ideal-hungry self finds an object that responds to its need and becomes an idealized object, the transference on the part of the subject would seem to correspond to a countertransference on the part of the object. This would be analogous to the case of a negative transference, in which, for example, the victimized and vulnerable self of the patient would be matched by a sadistic, hostile, or destructive image of the therapist. While a good therapeutic alliance would not respond to the sense of victimization in this sort of negative transference, a good therapeutic alliance would respond to the basic need being expressed in the selfobject transference, but not in transferential terms. While an alliance for the idealizing subject would not immediately satisfy his need to idealize, it would offer him a context of understanding, security, acceptance, and confidence that would allow his idealizing need to be accepted and empathically understood, so that whatever factors might underlie the need to idealize would be satisfied by an object responsive to other fundamental nonnarcissistic needs. If the underlying narcissistic inferiority contributes to the patient's need to idealize, then participation in a meaningful therapeutic alliance would provide some restitutive balm. The view from the selfobject is akin to Balint's (1968) assessment of the basic fault: transference in these patients is basically different from that in the classic neurotic and requires a different mode of listening and responding, and relational factors take precedence over interpretation. This view of therapeutic interaction comes close to the notion of a corrective emotional experience, but it is far from being simply that; rather, it involves significant dynamic issues and processes, activated within the interpersonal relationship, that involve patterning of projections and introjections central to the process of cure (Meissner 1981).

Relation of Transference to Therapeutic Misalliance

Transferences lie at the root of most therapeutic misalliances. Whenever the therapist recognizes a misalliance he has good reason to search behind it for transference components that may be giving rise to or contributing to it. As Freud (1912a, 1915) observed, a certain degree of benign and positive attachment to the therapist may be a necessary component in setting the therapeutic process on the right footing and allowing the patient to feel sufficiently comfortable to proceed with analytic work. This degree of positive transference, which usually is admissible to consciousness, can thus make an important contribution to establishing a therapeutic alliance. It is only when transference, usually in a negative form, becomes a resistance to forming the therapeutic relationship that it serves as a focus for concern and interpretation. Negative transferences, whether in merely negative or paranoid form, always contribute to formation of a therapeutic misalliance.[16] In distortions, based on negative transferences, the therapist may be seen as judgmental, critical, unsympathetic, rigid, harsh, sadistic, hostile, powerful, controlling, threatening, abandoning, and so on. If these aggressive dynamics are extended to the psychotic level, transference becomes paranoid, and the alliance is correspondingly disrupted.

Narcissistic transferences are somewhat similar to positive transferences in the manner in which they may or may not contribute to a therapeutic misalliance. If the narcissistic transference is relatively muted and mild—as is often the case, for example, in higher-order borderlines (particularly primitive hysterics) and narcissistic personalities—it may not distort the potential therapeutic alliance to any significant degree. But even in higher-order patients (Meissner 1984a, 1988), the degree of idealization or mirroring must be carefully assessed in connection with its impact on the therapeutic alliance. Distortion may not be severe, but it may contribute to a subtle narcissistic alliance, requiring specific attention in the hope that it can evolve toward a more meaningful therapeutic alliance.[17] As narcissistic distortion becomes more severe, however, risk of narcissistic alliance increases, as well as the tendency to form a narcissistically determined therapeutic misalliance. In such cases, risk of a transference/countertransference interaction in response to the patient's narcissistic need is high (Meissner 1988).

The situation with selfobject transferences is similar in regard to transference/countertransference risk. To the extent that selfobject interaction takes place on this level, it always involves some degree of therapeutic misalliance. Insofar as it is possible, approaching and responding to the needs expressed in selfobject transference in terms of therapeutic alliance, as I have indicated already, is preferable by far to the transference/countertransference option. By the same token, transitional object transferences and the demand placed on the object to respond in terms of transitional relatedness always involves some degree of therapeutic misalliance and introduces a degree of distortion. The analyst can be valued too much and become overly responsible for the patient, thus diminishing the patient's autonomy (Treurniet 1983). This situation tends to be found more characteristically in lower-order borderline patients (Meissner 1984a, 1988). Finally, transference psychosis not only represents acute and regressive disruption and breakdown of therapeutic alliance but can also reflect an underlying therapeutic misalliance, usually of a severe, profound, and long-lasting variety.

CHAPTER THREE

Alliance and Countertransference

Definition

Countertransference, along with therapeutic alliance and transference, is a primary locus of therapeutic action in the analytic process. The term has been used with various connotations, some referring to all the therapist's responses to the patient (Kernberg 1984; Gunderson 1984), others to specific unconscious transference-like reactions. Early usage implied that countertransference always introduced some distortion or interference into the therapeutic interaction, reflecting unconscious reactions deriving from infantile residues in the therapist's own personality. Countertransference reactions are generally regarded as forms of transference in the therapist, at times in response to and/or in conjunction with eliciting stimulation of the patient's transference (transference/countertransference interactions) or motivated solely by factors within the therapist (Jacobs 1991).

Chediak (1979) distinguished between counterreactions and countertransference:

> When the analyst's state of mind pertains to the dyadic interaction, it would be necessary to differentiate among (1) *intellectual understanding* based on information given by the patient and intellectual knowledge possessed by the analyst; (2) *the general response to the patient as a person,* the counterpart of what Strupp (1960) stresses when talking about the patient's reaction to the analyst's personality; (3) *the analyst's transference* to the patient, i.e., reliving of early part object relationships as elicited by certain features in the patient; (4) *the analyst's countertransference,* i.e., the reaction in the analyst to the role he is assigned by the patient's transference; (5) *empathic identification* with the patient (p. 117).

The last four categories are forms of counterreaction, while countertransference is given a more restrictive and specific meaning.[1]

In contrast I regard both the third and fourth categories, rather than simply the fourth, as forms of countertransference. The third corresponds to what has been called "subjective countertransference" and the fourth to "objective countertransference" (Kirman 1980; Spotnitz 1969).[2] This does not exclude the therapist's other emotional and cognitive reactions to the patient. Although primarily unconscious in origin, countertransference reactions in varying degrees can give rise to conscious derivatives.[3] Empathic understanding, as understood in this study, falls outside the realm of countertransference.[4]

Current trends in psychoanalytic clinical thinking tend to shift the emphasis from transference to countertransference, with an emerging paradigm that visualizes all forms of transaction or relation between analyst and analysand in relational and interactional terms. Gabbard (1995), for example, focuses his analysis of this "common ground" on the processes of "projective identification" and countertransference enactment as constituting components, both envisioned as joint creations by analyst and patient. The participating functions are better described in terms of interlocking projections and introjections (Meissner 1974a, 1978c, 1981, 1984a, 1988); countertransference responses do not arise unless corresponding introjective potential is elicited in the analyst. And if there is no countertransference response, there is no transference/countertransference interaction and no countertransference enactment. The continuum of possible responses runs from countertransference to counterresponse. Such responses often, but not always or exclusively, reflect the stimulatory input from the patient.

Some reactions of the therapist to the patient may involve aspects of the real relationship or the therapeutic alliance, both distinct from countertransference (Jacobs 1991; Winnicott 1949).[5] The therapist experiences a wide range of responses to the patient, many of which may reflect his current interaction with the patient's personality.[6] The tendency to feel assaulted after a patient's angry attack may simply be a normal and immediate defense, but it may also stimulate a countertransference reaction.

A useful example has come to my attention. In an article on countertransference in treatment of eating disorders, Zerbe (1995) describes an unpremeditated and spontaneous reaction to critical assault from a difficult, multiply hospitalized, and chronically unresponsive-to-treatment patient suffering from anorexia with bulimia. In a group setting, the patient accused Zerbe of being rigid and unhelpful and thus defeating rather than fostering therapeutic benefit. Zerbe responded, "I'm tired of how you are trying to devalue and destroy your treatment and that of the other patients who are also here. You bludgeon the staff with your criticisms, but you don't do anything about yourself. When is it going to stop?" (p. 161). I would regard this response as reasonable and effective, and by her own acknowledgment abetted the therapeutic alliance. But why should this be regarded as countertransference? I would think of it as a form of confrontation quite appropriate to the context regardless of its unpremeditated spontaneity. It was an appropriate reaction to a provocative attack from the patient and was cast in therapeutically meaningful terms. To make a further point, Zerbe accounts this as attributable to the "real relation," but once more I would differ. The feelings and the actions are real enough, but they should be viewed as cast in the framework of the therapeutic alliance. This therapeutically formed response has a quite different implication than any response in real terms and is so experienced and interpreted by the patient. The result was to establish Zerbe as a meaningful and effective therapeutic agent.

In such cases, the therapist's subjective self-awareness and reflective self-knowledge may help to discriminate. These noncountertransference aspects may be conscious or unconscious or both, but they tend to provide a more realistic and valid basis for the therapist's interaction with the patient. Non-countertransference aspects encompass both factors contributing to therapeutic alliance and the real relationship and may involve reactions to the patient's transference that do not involve countertransference (Greenson and Wexler 1969).[7] By the same token, feelings of liking or disliking the patient are over-determined by transferential and realistic factors but, properly speaking, have nothing to do with therapeutic alliance.

Moreover, one person's therapeutic alliance may turn out to be another's countertransference. The gradation between possible approaches to the patient's transference or therapeutic misalliance may vary among therapists and may to differing degrees reflect countertransference vicissitudes. Some self psychologists have labeled Kernberg's approach to narcissistic transferences as a form of countertransference acting out, reflecting the therapist's own conflicts about grandiosity and envy and turning interpretation into a narcissistic assault. *E contra,* Kohut's approach has been criticized as an exercise in futility, collusion, and overidentification with the patient's narcissistic needs and illusions (Mitchell 1986). Consequently the degree to which countertransference, as opposed to other operative factors, is involved at any point in the interaction between therapist and patient remains a continuing and unremitting problem. Difficulties created by countertransference in effective analytic listening are well recognized (Schwaber 1992), but another view is more consistent with the therapeutic alliance perspective. Renik (1993) notes: "Instead of saying that it is *difficult* for an analyst to *maintain* a position in which his or her analytic activity objectively focuses on a patient's inner reality, I would say that it is *impossible* for an analyst to be in that position *even for an instant:* since we are constantly acting in the analytic situation on the basic of personal motivations of which we cannot be aware until after the fact, our technique, listening included, is *inescapably* subjective" (p. 560). At the same time, I would insist that our listening rather than an exercise in exclusive subjectivity, involves a complex intermeshing of subjective and objective. And, at times, as Renik also acknowledges, the analyst's capacity for independent objectivity can play a decisive role in the analytic process.

Countertransference Model

Introjective / Projective Basis

The model of transference/countertransference interactions I shall use is based on the paranoid process and on the interaction between introjective and projective processes (Meissner 1970, 1971, 1972, 1978, 1981). The patient's pathological sense of self is structured around a core set of pathogenic introjects, internalizations of significant ambivalent and defensively elaborated object relationships experienced during development (Meissner 1979). The potential for countertransference is based on the therapist's similar introjective organization—one hopes less defensive, less pathogenic, and better integrated and differentiated (Finell 1985; Grinberg 1962; Langs 1978–79; Loewald 1986; Racker 1968; Searles 1978–79). Dimensions of the introjective configurations in the therapist or analyst are the same as those underlying expressions of transference in patients and give rise to corresponding forms of countertransference, based on erotic, aggressive, and narcissistic dynamics or other aspects of the self-system (Meissner 1978, 1984a, 1986b). As Loewald (1986) emphasized, analyst and analysand become enmeshed in a complex therapeutic interaction, a kind of psychic force field compounded out of intermingled transference and countertransference processes.[8]

Analysis of the introjective organization provides a basis for understanding transference/countertransference interactions. The introjective organization gives rise to projections coloring the experience of objects and modifying the quality of object relations—the so-called projective or "externalizing" transferences (Berg 1977). The corresponding process in the therapist forms the basis for countertransference (Money-Kyrle 1956). Projections are usually based on repressed aspects of the patient's introjective configuration. The patient who is functioning in terms of the victim-introject, for example, will tend to project elements derived from the polar opposite aggressor-introject so that the patient casts the therapist in the role of victimizer and aggressive persecutor. Similarly, the patient who is functioning in terms of the narcissistically inferior configuration will tend to project the narcissistic opposite in a form of idealization of the therapist.

The projective device is not simply an intrapsychic or subjective phenomenon; it may, in fact, correspond in some degree to actual qualities or traits of the therapist that become exaggerated to meet the patient's pathological needs (Langs 1978–79; Searles 1978). The projection also creates pressure in the interpersonal interaction to draw the other member of that interaction to fulfill the expectations and inherent demands of the projection. The therapist in such a situation not only is seen by the patient as, for example, an aggressive persecutor, but the projection has an inherent gradient eliciting an aggressive response from the therapist in his interaction with the patient. The process is further sustained by the extent to which the patient's projection meshes with aspects of the therapist's unresolved aggressive conflicts and introjective components. Transference/countertransference interactions reinforce the patient's pathological needs (Appel 1974; Giovacchini 1972; Langs 1975a, 1975b), and, more specifically, the patient's pathogenic introjective configuration (Meissner 1984a). In this sense, the patient unconsciously seeks countertransference reactions in the therapist (Clifton 1974; Searles 1978).

Coercive pressures generated by transference seek to draw the therapist into the position of answering to the inherent pathological needs of the patient (Searles 1984). Where mirroring needs enter the picture, transference needs will seek out an object that resembles the subject in some fashion, in some cases facilitating creation of a symbiotic dyad (McGlashan 1983). Some schizoid patients tend to induce in the therapist feelings that resemble their own, including boredom, isolation, disengagement, and even rage (Appel 1974; Modell 1975).

Transference/Countertransference Interaction

The patient's projections can create a counterresponse in the therapist, who may introject the content of the patient's projection and begin to function in terms of the inherent demands of those introjections. This may set the stage for and mobilize a counterprojective response on the part of the therapist derived from the combined influence of the introjected content, based on the patient's projections and the therapist's own introjective configurations. The resulting introjective organization and the derivative counterprojections from therapist to patient form the core of countertransference (Feinsilver 1983). In addition, within transference/countertransference interactions, aspects of the therapist's introjective configuration are reciprocally projected onto the patient and become internalized by the patient as "identifications" with the therapist's often unconscious and poorly integrated introjects (Searles 1985).[9] These complex transference/countertransference interactions have also been described as aspects of an intersubjective process (Stolorow et al. 1981, 1983).

These mechanisms were described in some detail by Racker (1953, 1957), who (1957) distinguished concordant identifications (recognition of the other's experience as similar to one's own) from complementary identifications resulting from the patient's projection and the corresponding internalization by the therapist.[10] In concordant identifications (introjections), the therapist may identify aspects of his own psychic structure with those of the patient (ego, superego, or other aspects of the patient's psychic organization and functioning: introjective configurations, self-representations or images, affective states, and so on). Such introjections may serve as the basis for empathy but may be drawn into countertransference by way of overidentification.[11] Complementary introjections always involve countertransference and elicit corresponding emotional responses in the therapist (Boyer 1983). Racker also underscored the potential threat of mutually reinforcing transference/countertransference interactions forming a vicious neurotic circle.

These patterns of transference/countertransference interaction have also been described in representational terms by Stolorow et al. (1981, 1983). They conceptualize the transference/countertransference interaction as an intersubjective process marked either by "representational conjunction" or by "representational disjunction." The former describes a situation in which the therapist assimilates representational configurations and affective significances structuring the patient's experience into similar configurations in his own psychic life. In disjunction, by contrast, the therapist assimilates misreadings of the patient's experience into his own configurations and affective connotations, thus distorting its subjective meaning. While this formulation is cast in representational (cognitive) terms, in contrast to my emphasis on introjective (structural) aspects, I argue that countertransference cannot be adequately understood on the basis of the differential organization of subjective worlds. Some forms of countertransference are, in fact, based on the similarities between the subjective worlds of therapist and patient. In any case, the intersubjective view has the advantage of focusing on the interactional and intersubjective nature of transference/countertransference interactions.

Interactive Process

A useful schema for understanding the progressive emergence of transference/countertransference interactions has been provided by Burke and Tansey (1985; Tansey and Burke 1989). The process is divided into two phases: reception and internal processing.

> *Phase I. Reception.* The first phase deals with the therapist's reception and experience of a set of self-representations or experiences stimulated by the patient's projections.
>
> *Subphase 1. Mental Set.* The therapist's mental set enables him to attend and listen optimally to the patient's communications. This optimal set can be disrupted by characterological difficulties or conflicts in his own mind (blind spots, sensitivities, insensitivities, prejudices, narcissism, unresolved conflicts, usually aggressive or libidinal, arrogance, authoritarian attitudes,

etc.) or situational problems (lack of sleep, personal crises, pregnancy, overwork, illness, etc.).

Subphase 2. Pressure of the Interaction. The therapist begins to experience the pull of the patient's emotional interaction. Disruptions come from unconscious needs in the therapist to shut off or limit the patient's communications and projections, to avoid the emotional interaction and limit any introjective response.

Subphase 3. Identification—Signal Affect. The interaction progresses to a stage of internalization of the patient's projective elements. The introjection is unconscious, but can result in alterations of the therapist's self-experience in the form of signal affects. Disruptions occur in the therapist's reaction to or handling of these affects, either in the form of discomfort, anxiety or depression, or in the form of excessive gratification or self-enhancement (e.g., in response to the patient's idealization). Defenses may be set in motion to block the affect and interfere with its signal function.

Phase II. Internal Processing. This phase leads to utilization of the therapist's subjective experience as a tool for understanding the patient.

Subphase 4. Containment-Separateness. The therapeutic task is twofold: to contain and integrate consciously the internal alterations and inner affective experiences stimulated by interaction with the patient and particularly in response to the patient's projections; and secondly, to separate sufficiently from the immediate experience and involvement with the patient to observe, analyze, and understand what is being experienced in the interaction.

Subphase 5. Working Model. The therapist constructs a "working model" or representation of the patient and of the interaction between himself and the patient, as a basis for empathic attunement for both affective and cognitive understanding of the patient's inner experience and of meanings inherent in the transference / countertransference interaction. Disruptions at this subphase arise from the therapist's inability to achieve an adequate working model, or from his ability to utilize only one aspect of the model successfully, i.e., he may be able to assess his own experience and interaction with the patient ("therapist-interaction working model") but may have difficulty achieving an understanding of the patient's internal experience and his experience of the therapist and the therapeutic interaction.

Subphase 6: Empathic Connection. The working models serve as a basis for the therapist to understand his own affective experience, the extent to which his experience is determined by the patient's projection as opposed to being internally determined, to assess the degree of correspondence between his own internal states and the patient's (the degree of concordant versus complementary identification), and to understand the patterns of projection and introjection reciprocally involved in transference / counter-

> transference interactions. Each of these tasks has its corresponding forms of disruption. The therapist's failures may enter into the process at any point. He may not be able to grasp or understand certain aspects of the process or his own experience. Even if his understanding at all points is adequate, he may lack the capacity or skill to communicate what he has learned to the patient in ways that can be assimilated by the patient and are useful to the patient in dealing with his problems.

Although the basic dynamics of transference/countertransference interactions are primarily unconscious, they may have conscious reverberations and concomitants that can alert the therapist to their operation. Unconscious countertransference reactions usually disrupt or distort the therapeutic interaction and interfere with an effective therapeutic alliance (Langs 1975a, 1975b). However, when such dynamics can be identified and consciously processed, aspects of the patient's pathology and the therapeutic interaction may be recognized and resolved (Joseph 1985). McDougall (1978) refers to these forms of unconscious communication as "primitive communications," flowing from the patient's need to reconstruct in the analytic relationship traumatic contexts from childhood. In this sense countertransference can become a useful instrument attuned to a level of otherwise unavailable unconscious communication between patient and therapist (Boyer 1978).

However, exclusive attention to countertransference enactments can run definite risks. Sonnenberg (1995), for example, emphasizes the role of self-analytic processing of countertransference reactions as the basis for empathic "trial identifications" allowing access to the patient's inner world. But he also notes: "I believe that when analysts allow themselves to regress in the service of their analysands, allow themselves to be drawn in various role responsive ways into the worlds of their analysands so as to understand their analysands' experiences more vividly, inevitable errors will occur and blind spots will effect their work. That is because when we analysts work in that way we often rely heavily on our own experiences to understand those of our patients, and it is then inevitable that our own conflicts about our experiences will stand in the way of our understanding that we are trying to tell ourselves about ourselves and our patients" (p. 341). The risk is twofold—first, interpreting the patient's experience on the basis of one's own (a form of projection) and, second, distorting the therapeutic alliance, thus perpetuating a therapeutic misalliance.

Countertransference and Misalliance

In many patients, more so in narcissistic and character-disordered patients than in neurotic personalities, transference/countertransference difficulties frequently serve as a basis for subtle distortions of therapeutic alliance, which tend to be pervasive and persistent. The therapist does not become aware of countertransference reactions and their derivatives directly, but may find himself experiencing stalemate or some faltering in therapeutic work. His own aggressive or narcissistic conflicts may lead him to collude with the patient's subtle neurotic stance. Appropriate interpretations may be withheld because the patient's inherently victimized stance elicits aggressive elements in the therapist that obtrude on his ability to be appropriately assertive or confronting. Narcissistic aspects of the interaction may provoke the therapist's narcissistic vulnerability or, conversely, draw him into a position of therapeutic omnipotence on the basis of a presumed but unexamined inadequacy in the patient. These deviations or therapeutic misalliances (Langs 1975a) are often slow to develop to the point at which the therapist can recognize them. Early detection and therapeutic response to initial alliance deviations can help in maintaining an effective therapeutic relationship. The difficulties may take the form of persistent resistance that does not seem to yield or modify under the influence of continuing and extensive interpretation and working through. Such patients can comply with the amenities of analytic work yet effectively avoid any authentic or meaningful involvement with the analyst.

Aggressive Aspects

Aggressive aspects of transference/countertransference interactions express themselves in the interplay between aggressor- and victim-introjects in both therapist and patient (Meissner 1978c, 1981). Aggressive projections onto the therapist may be expressed as intensified distrust or fear of the therapist, who is seen as hurtful and attacking, and may result in sadistic or destructive defensive efforts on the part of the patient. The patient's rejection and demeaning of the therapist and the correlative projection can arouse feelings of worthlessness and impotence in the therapist and correspondingly evoke his own restitutive aggression (Maltsberger and Buie 1974).

Under such countertransference pressures, the therapist may find himself resorting to deviations in technique or failing to maintain an adequate therapeutic framework (Langs 1975b), both of which may profoundly affect the patient and the therapeutic process. He may decide to terminate the therapy prematurely, thus relieving himself of a relationship in which he feels trapped, defeated, helpless—obviously an acting out of the therapist's wishes to be rid of a patient who provokes such uncomfortable feelings (Wile 1972; Nadelson 1976). Or the analyst's feelings of impotence and ineffectiveness may cause him to regard the patient as untreatable (Boyer and Giovacchini 1980). The therapist's aggressive impulse may also take the form of becoming more interactive with the patient, either to overcome the sense of frustration and helplessness or to exert control over an otherwise anxiety-producing situation. This process may even influence decisions regarding the prescribing of drugs as a way of escaping from transference and the need to understand it or as a magical potion (Chessick 1978).

The therapist, whose own sadomasochistic conflicts remain to some degree unresolved, must be cautious of sadomasochistic acting out, which often masks underlying narcissistic transferences (Oremland and Windholz 1971). The therapist who believes himself to be invulnerable to such feelings or conflicts may miss an essential part of the therapy and fall into countertransference difficulties (Nadelson 1976). The awareness of countertransference hate can signal to the therapist that he is masochistically absorbing too much of the patient's abuse. An aggressive countertransference stance may also express itself in the therapist's need to reassert his authority, defensively insisting to the patient on the therapist's own professional competence and value. The patient may then respond, also defensively, with increased anger or anxiety, or may resort to a more compliant stance in which anger is withheld. The need for the patient to protect and buffer such a therapist becomes part of the therapeutic interaction and further undermines the therapeutic alliance.

Projection of derivatives of the victim-introject onto the therapist can stimulate the therapist's own conflicts over aggression and defensively reactivate his masochism (Racker 1958). The therapist's guilt over counteraggressive impulses may result in a reactive masochistic submission to the patient's aggression by which he begins to doubt his own competence and to assimilate masochistically tinged victim-introjective elements. The patient's aggressive posture, acting out the aggressor-introject, is accompanied by projection of the elements of vulnerability and victimization onto the therapist. The masochistic introjection of these elements can gradually erode the therapist's self-esteem and sense of professional identity. There is a strong temptation for a masochistic submission to the patient's efforts at control, expressed in guilt, depression, and shame that the therapist is unable to gratify the patient's magical expectations.

The patient's failure to respond, accompanied by a continual effort to frustrate the aims of the therapy, creates a sense of helplessness and hopelessness in the therapist. The patient may respond not so much with rage as with a sense of sadness and disillusionment reflecting original disappointments in an incompetent or unresponsive mother. These aspects of the patient's self-image may be projected onto the therapist and produce a therapeutic stalemate in which the therapist feels impotent and frustrated and feels he has to do something, anything to relieve the sense of helpless frustration, even though it may be ultimately unproductive or countertherapeutic. At such points the therapist may resort to transferring the patient or terminating the therapy. Countertransference, then, becomes a vehicle for redeeming the therapist's own injured narcissism and for preserving a sense of competency and self-esteem, but at the cost of devaluing the patient.

Narcissistic Aspects

Transference/countertransference interactions can also take place on the basis of narcissistic projections. When the inferior side of the narcissistic introjective organization is projected, this frequently takes the form of devaluing or demeaning the therapist (Adler 1970). In virtue of projection, the therapist may be seen as angry and rejecting. The therapist may introject this implicit projection in a way that reinforces and plays into his own narcissistic vulnerability, may resort to self-defense in a variety of aggressive manifestations (Thomson 1993), or may try to redeem his tottering narcissism by proving to the patient that he can be the good, loving, and giving parent that the patient demands (Greenacre 1956). Circumstances in which the analyst's ignorance or impotent frustration contribute to his narcissistic vulnerability may induce a counterprojective defense by which the patient is seen as ignorant or defective and the analyst can entertain fantasies of superiority, even falling back on his presumed theoretical competence to bolster his shaken self-image (Mitrani 1993).

Idealizing Interaction. Idealization involves projection of superior aspects of the narcissistic organization. These patients may approach therapy with an attitude of submissive compliance to a powerful and all-wise therapist whom they invest with the capacity to fulfill their needs and transform their lives magically. The therapist's own unresolved narcissistic needs to assume an omnipotent role and provide for all the patient's needs, or deal effectively with all of the patient's pathological difficulties, can make him vulnerable (Finell 1985). In the face of an idealizing transference, the therapist's own narcissistic need to be admired or to counter defensively his own feelings of inadequacy can easily draw him into an implicit magical contract with the patient or acceptance of the patient's idealization (Greenacre 1956; Finell 1985). However, such idealizations set up transference/countertransference distortions that undermine any possibility of an effective therapeutic alliance.

At the same time, the therapist's reaction can be subtle and often quite well disguised, giving rise to significant countertransference vicissitudes. Such patients may engage the therapist by an attitude of hopefulness and compliance, attributing special power and wisdom to the therapist. This often has the quality of an attempt to re-experience a kind of symbiotic relationship with a powerful object who will bring about some form of magical rebirth—something that the inadequate and vulnerable mother was unable to accomplish. The patient's helpless impotence is matched by the projective magical power of the therapist, which can run the risk of ignoring or minimizing the patient's pathology or of raising the level of therapeutic expectation beyond the patient's inherent limitations. This may lead to inevitable disappointment and disillusionment in the patient and a sense of frustration and impotence in the therapist.[12] Similar reactions can be experienced in connection with so-called selfobject transferences: the therapist may feel despair and anger at the patient's neediness and at his own failure to meet the patient's needs. The result is often a repetition of infantile traumata rather than their amelioration (Adler 1985). Or, in the face of devaluation by a grandiose and superior patient, the therapist finds himself reacting defensively with impulses to mock, criticize, laugh at, and otherwise devalue the patient's offensive self-inflation and entitlement.

Erotic Aspects

The original libidinal sense of Freud's observations on erotized transferences and their correlative countertransference reactions has been broadened to include a diversity of related phenomena, including demands for physical contact, the more disguised desire for sexual relations manifested as wishes for adult love or as assaultive antagonism, demands for approval and admiration, wishes to gain acceptance by compliance, dependent clinging, fears of object loss, and so on (Blum 1973; Gabbard 1994e). Erotized transferences are characterized frequently by intensity, tenacity, resistance to interpretation, and tendencies to act out erotic feelings. The patient tries to seduce the analyst into mutual acting out, or frequently acts out transference with substitute objects. The patient is thus caught up in an infantile reaction in which the distinction between transference and alliance, on one hand, and reality, on the other, is obscured if not overridden. As Blum (1973) noted: "Patients developing such erotized transference delusions have been predisposed by early ego impairment. The analyst may be 'loved' as the single most precious object tie and reality representative" (pp. 63–64). Such patients may freely express and indulge themselves with highly erotic and even perverse fantasies about the analyst that have a highly seductive quality, but at the same time they may experience a sense of frustration and disappointment that the real relationship with the analyst offers something quite different. To this must be added the underlying hostility of negative transference undermining the analyst's authority and his alliance function (Schafer 1993). The analyst may feel drawn into an incestuous negative transference enactment and react with defensive countertransference (Cesio 1993). Continual self-monitoring and attention to alliance factors in such circumstances becomes mandatory (Panel 1974). Particular care is required for anything in the analyst's manner that might elicit or contribute to the patient's erotic transference response.

Therapeutic Response to Countertransference Difficulties

The spectrum of possible countertransference reactions covers a wide range of forms and degrees of difficulty. Divergent features of countertransference experience and the quality of transference/countertransference interactions account for variations in the therapist's capacity to listen effectively (Jackson

1992), in the nature and quality of his therapeutic response, and in priorities for therapeutic intervention. For the most part, well-trained and experienced analysts, bolstered by a strong professional identity and confidence in the analytic paradigm, can absorb the patient's projective and other transferential inputs. But often enough the threshold of the analyst's defenses is broached and can result in guilt, shame, and self-reproach that escape effective self-monitoring and therapeutic processing and contribute to departures from sound therapeutic technique. Often these take the form of collusive distortions of the alliance and the analytic frame (Moraitis 1993; Robertson and Yack 1993), as when transferential feelings are experienced and regarded as "real" (Gabbard 1994d, 1994e). Such deviations can arise from the analyst's failure to recognize countertransference responses (Spruiell 1984) or even his unconscious use of countertransference reactions to screen out other resistances that might distort the alliance (Jacobs 1991).

Countertransference enactments. At a minimum, the influence of the therapist expresses itself on the level not only of verbal exchange, but also of behavior and action. What therapists say to patients must be placed alongside how they treat their patients, how they behave with them, what the affective quality of their interaction is, and how they react in the various contexts arising in a course of therapy. These "countertransference enactments" (Jacobs 1986, 1991) all communicate significant messages to the patient about the therapist's thoughts and feelings about him. Ideally, the therapist's thoughts, verbalizations, and actions should be consistent and directed to therapeutic goals. The potential for countertransference difficulties to influence the therapist's thoughts, feelings, attitudes, and words is great enough; the potential for these unconscious processes to find expression in the therapist's manner, behavior, and action is even greater. Even when they can be turned to therapeutic advantage, they remain deviations in technique and are best dealt with when countertransference awareness takes precedence over countertransference enactment (Renik 1993)—a transition that would move the interaction from the transferential to the alliance sector.

A supervisory experience with an advanced resident provides an example. The resident, who prided herself on her ability to be empathic and sensitive to the needs of her patients, was working with a woman whose pathology was at a high borderline level, probably in the primitive hysteric range (Meissner 1984a). The patient used therapy as a vehicle to express, seemingly indefatigably, her tale of misery and woe, presenting herself repeatedly as taken advantage of, particularly at the hands of important others in her environment. The therapist's reaction was to feel sorry for the patient, to sympathize with her victimization, and to ally herself with the patient against uncaring and exploitative individuals in her life. She would become the concerned and caring object the patient sought, rather than finding some effective footing that would allow the patient to explore her victimized feelings and begin to process and understand them. Comments such as "Oh! You poor thing!" or "What a terrible thing to have happen!" were not infrequent. The therapist's intention was to be empathic and understanding, but the tone of her interventions was pitying, condescending, and to a degree infantilizing. Real understanding and empathy, which would have allowed the therapist to deal with the patient's victimized posture rather than colluding with it and reinforcing it, was lacking.

Interaction versus interpretation. The pressure generated by some patients for real interaction can result in transference/countertransference interactions in which the priorities fall not on the more usual technique of interpretation, but on aspects of action and reaction that have a much more immediate quality. Only when these aspects have been adjusted and the regressive strain eased is further associative exploration and interpretation feasible (Little 1966). For other more primitive character disorders, some sense of the reality and presence of the therapist is essential to maintain the therapeutic relationship. In these cases, qualities of the relationship take precedence over interpretation in the therapeutic process.

One patient presented superficially as a classical obsessional personality. Analytic hours were filled with superficial and largely irrelevant material. As the analytic regression began to take effect, hints of the patient's underlying narcissistic vulnerability and intense rage began to appear. Moments of affective turmoil were quickly covered over and denied. Gradually, the hours were increasingly silent. Occasional gentle attempts to ease the patient's aloof retreat were futile. Whole hours would pass without a word. The analyst became impatient, frustrated, and bored. His mind would wander and get lost in distracting reflections, none of which had anything to do with his patient. He found himself frequently dozing and falling asleep.[13] Even worse, he began to think that the patient was unanalyzable, that he should have had better sense than to have accepted him for analysis, wishing that the patient would quit the analysis, and so on. The analyst's narcissism was on the line and was suffering considerable duress.

The patient finally expressed a wish to stop the analysis. Thus, they were able to find out that the patient's magical conviction was that the analyst could alleviate his difficulties if he wanted to. All the patient had to do was come to the hours, be there for the required time, and that was enough. The rest was up to the analyst. The patient would exert no effort, undergo no pain, and take no responsibility for the progress of his analysis. He was simply waiting the analyst out. If the analyst refused to perform the magic, the patient would quit. This reflected powerful transference issues having to do with his infantile expectations of his parents, which had been severely disappointed. He was an only child with no history of real friendships or other meaningful human involvements beyond his parents. As an only child, he cherished bitter resentments that his parents would not make him the center of their lives and that they had not given him more or done more for him. He felt that his mother had not wanted him and that she was more involved and committed to her artistic career than to him. He saw his father as inadequate and impotent, a failure in life who had failed to provide him a model of real manhood. He saw the analyst as more concerned with scientific study of his "case" than with him as a human being. The analyst was also inadequate and impotent as an analyst, in his view, because he could not deal effectively with the patient's difficulties. Quitting the analysis would confirm both these transferential convictions.

The patient clung to his posture of blaming his parents for his problems. They had made him the way he was, and he would make no effort to change himself. It was up to them to do for him what they had not done. It was up to the analyst to do for him what they had not done. Any notion that he had to take responsibility for his own life and happiness was rejected out of hand. When it became clear to him that the analyst could not or would not meet his demands, he stopped coming. Despite the analyst's conscious efforts to the contrary, the hostile countertransference wish was fulfilled. The patient was able to fulfill and live out his fantasy of becoming the analyst's victim, and the analyst's countertransference played out the role of victimizer.[14]

Emotional reactivity. It is important to the therapeutic work for the therapist not only to be in touch with his emotional responsiveness to the patient, but also to be able to acknowledge freely such reactions to himself and, where appropriate, to the patient. The capacity for the therapist to become conscious of, identify, and acknowledge his initially unconscious countertransference reactions is primary and essential to effective therapeutic management. This internal acknowledgment may alert the therapist to hidden therapeutic issues or to failures in therapeutic alliance. Self-analysis and monitoring of his own responses may be adequate and appropriate. Where therapeutic alliance is severely threatened, the therapist's capacity to be open and frank about such reactions can confirm the patient's perceptions of the reality of the therapist and help to consolidate the discrimination between fantasy and reality—and, in terms of technical implications, between transference and therapeutic alliance. Failure to acknowledge such reactions, however, can be extremely disruptive and may even contribute to malignant regression. As Langs (1976a, 1976b) noted, such regressions may reflect failure of the therapeutic alliance. In addition, such therapeutic misalliances and the push toward regression are often caused by unresolved countertransference difficulties.

A clinical example may help clarify these issues. The patient, a primitive borderline woman with many pseudoschizophrenic characteristics, would, at points of severe regressive crisis, look psychotic and have a strong propensity for acting out aggressive impulses in suicidal and self-destructive ways, including repeated overdosing and episodes of self-laceration. After I had been seeing this woman for about a year in twice-weekly psychotherapy, it happened that a holiday came along and I neglected to remind her that we would not be meeting on that particular day. As it turned out, the patient came to my office door and found it locked.

She went away in a rage, but much to her credit was able to call me the following day, still angry, and tearfully reproach me for my oversight. I replied with some concern that she had been inconvenienced, apologized, and told her that we would talk about it when I next saw her. When she subsequently came to my office, she still harbored a simmering resentment about the episode. I asked about her feelings, and she told me about the fantasies she had had on coming to the locked door. At first, she said, she felt bitterly disappointed and hurt, and then was overwhelmed by a wave of anger in which she imagined herself screaming at me and finally throwing things at me. She was afraid that her anger would destroy me somehow, and was able to acknowledge that she was angry enough at that point to want to kill me. Moreover, quite consistently with her paranoid disposition, she felt that this oversight had been deliberate and derived from my anger at her and my wish to retaliate because of the angry wishes and feelings she had about me. She felt that my behavior had resulted from my own wish to lock her out in the hope that she would leave treatment.

In the course of the discussion, I told her that I was really not aware of the sorts of feelings she ascribed to me, but that, in looking at the behavior, both she and I had reason to be suspicious. When she had called me to tell me that she had come to my office on the holiday, I had been truly surprised and somewhat chagrined that I had forgotten to tell her about the holiday. But the fact remained that her perception might in some way be accurate.

The effect of this admission was quite striking. She seemed to be relieved, almost immediately relaxed her tense and worried demeanor, and seemed considerably mollified. In fact, my admission had legitimated and justified her anger, which began to look more realistic and in some degree reasonable, rather than the product of her distorted thinking and her craziness. The discussion led to consideration of her fear of my anger and of the possibility of my retaliation, and moved from there to an extremely useful exploration of her fear of her father's explosive and somewhat paranoid anger. She recounted several episodes in which she had been terrified of his seemingly capricious, rejecting rages. She was able to talk about her difficulty in dealing with such feelings in appropriate and constructive ways.

It became clear to her that, even though such angry feelings might arise in the context of the therapeutic relationship, they could still be put in perspective and did not necessarily destroy the relationship. Nor did they mean that such feelings operating in me would eliminate the warm feelings I might have toward her or my wishes to be therapeutically helpful to her. My admission decisively undermined any supposition that I was always right and sane and that she was always wrong and crazy. This understanding between us made it considerably easier for her to express her angry feelings without fear of retaliation from me and, consequently, to explore and understand them.

Countertransference monitoring. In dealing with projective-introjective interactions, the therapist must carefully discriminate between the patient's projection as such and potential countertransference responses. It can be countertherapeutic to ascribe such countertransferences simply to the patient's projections, since this would fail to acknowledge the validity of the patient's perception. Patients who have a propensity for acting out may have a unique ability to read unconscious id impulses of the analyst and exploit them to get the analyst to act out in collusion with them (Bird 1957). This can both undermine the patient's hold on reality and jeopardize the therapeutic alliance, contributing to further regression in the patient (Giovacchini 1973; Krohn 1974). Such discounting of the patient's perception and reduction to projection can be both hostile and demeaning, and may represent a form of countertransference counteraggression (Nadelson 1976). This would certainly have been the case for this patient. On the other hand, an open and honest focus on countertransference reactions, whether actual or potential, and their further exploration in terms of meaning for the therapeutic interaction can be extremely helpful (Giovacchini 1972).

This does not mean that the therapist will necessarily communicate all thoughts and feelings, even those reflecting countertransference difficulties, to the patient (Greenson 1967; Little 1957; Reich 1966). It is extremely important, however, that the therapist be in touch with such feelings and attitudes and be ready and able to explore them with the patient when it becomes therapeutically useful for working through a transference/countertransference interaction or in the interest of re-establishing or maintaining the therapeutic alliance.

Negative transference. In the interest of maintaining the therapeutic alliance, the therapist must pay careful attention to negative transference elements. A consistent element is the patient's efforts to defeat the therapist, to make the therapy into a meaningless and ineffectual game. Behind this lies the inner necessity on the part of the patient to maintain the introjective configuration at the core of his often fragile and unstable self-organization. As I have already suggested, preservation of the pathogenic introjective organization motivates the projective elaboration underlying transference/countertransference interactions. Thus, constant attention to focusing, clarifying, and interpreting negative transference elements is of particular importance in establishing and maintaining the therapeutic alliance (Friedman 1975; Kernberg 1970).

Therapeutic confrontation is particularly useful when the patient adopts the victimized position, reflecting an underlying victim-introject. A clear statement of the patient's victimized position, or of the potential victimizing effects of a projected course of acting out, can focus on related underlying dynamics and motivations and their effects on therapeutic work, particularly on the alliance. Such clarifications and confrontations with the patient's potential self-destructiveness and need to assume the victimized position may reassure the patient that he is not on this account abandoned or rejected and undercut the pull in the countertransference reaction to play into the patient's victimization and thus reinforce it.

Idealization. When the patient views the therapist as an omnipotent and magically powerful rescuer, the task of undoing such idealizations requires that the therapist clarify the transference distortion while accepting the patient's positive feelings. This task is particularly difficult since such idealizations are often accompanied by feelings of worthlessness and shame in the patient, who looks to the therapist to overcome these painful and self-demeaning feelings. The therapist's failure to respond to these needs may be translated into his withholding and rejection—the therapist becomes the idealized figure who refuses to give the patient the good things that the patient so desperately desires and needs (a situation that repeats original traumatic experiences in relationship to parental figures). Insofar as possible, the therapist's interventions should be approached from the perspective of the therapeutic alliance.

Acting out. The therapist's task in dealing with tendencies to act out is to maintain a firm, consistent, and assertive stance in setting limits without entering into transference/countertransference interactions that would recapitulate the patient's victimization and put the analyst in a threatening, prohibiting, accusatory, and chastizing position. The therapist's introduction of limit setting and controlling parameters can be easily translated by projective distortion into hostile and sadistic images. An attempt to explore the meaning of any acting out is always indicated: unresolved aggressive conflicts or unconscious hostile or destructive wishes toward the patient can inhibit appropriate and effective action. When possible, interpretation and exploration of meaning in terms of the therapeutic relationship are more effective. Emphasis on alliance factors in this connection is particularly important, since acting out is almost always a reflection of underlying transference/countertransference difficulties (Langs 1975a, 1975b, 1976). The therapist needs to maintain his autonomy and accept responsibility for his interventions and their consequences.

Internalization. A significant component of the therapeutic process is the role of internalizations within the patient-therapist interaction. The patient's projection of aggressive, erotic, or narcissistic components onto the transitional object created within the context of the relationship with the therapist is the basis for transference. The therapist's corresponding introjection of that projective content and his internal processing of it provides the basis for countertransference. The interaction sets up a process of mutually interacting projections and introjections on the part of both patient and therapist. For example, the patient might project idealized elements onto the therapist. If the therapist can accept this projection, assimilate it, and integrate it with the ongoing flow of his responsiveness to the patient, he remains unconflicted and comfortable with the idealization and with his own inherent limitations. To the extent that he avoids the countertransference trap, he can respond to the patient not as an idealized superior or omnipotent object, but as an ordinary human being who remains interested, respectful, and appropriately committed to the patient and his welfare. He reflects back to the patient from this idealization a sense of the patient's value in the therapist's eyes and a projective content calling forth a qualitatively different affective response from the patient, of greater equality, balance, mutual involvement, and collaboration from the patient, rather than a sense of devaluation, contempt, or trivializing disregard. The latter response would play out the countertransference paradigm and reinforce corresponding feelings in the patient of narcissistic inferiority, unimportance, inadequacy, and even shame.

This process takes place in contexts of immediate transference/countertransference interaction but may also develop over much longer periods of time. The patient's need to idealize the therapist is constantly eroded by the flow of realistic impressions of the failings and human limitations of the therapist gathered over long periods of therapeutic interaction. The patient must ultimately integrate this flow of awarenesses into his ongoing assessment of the stature and narcissistically invested superiority of his therapist. But in a good therapeutic relationship, the idealized object is not at all discomforted or conflicted by his own obvious weakness and shortcomings. He is comfortably and easily able to assimilate and integrate these into his overall functioning and suffers no deficit of self-esteem when these inadequacies come to light.

The patient learns that it is possible to be competent, to be effective, and to have a meaningful place in the world without having to scale the heights of grandiosity and perfection. He learns that there is such a thing as being good enough, that to be imperfect and limited does not necessarily imply worthlessness and shamefulness. In the ongoing interplay of projections and introjections, owing to these gradual modifications of what is internalized from the therapeutic relationship, the narcissistic titer is modified and the pressure of narcissistic demands is shifted from the extreme basis underlying the patient's psychopathology to a more moderate middle ground allowing for emergence and development of meaningful ideals, values, and ambitions. A similar process of projective/introjective interchange and internalized transformation can take place for aggressively derived introjections as well.

PART II

The Real Relationship

This section takes up the question of the relation between therapeutic alliance and reality. The presence and influence of reality factors in the analytic situation and process are ubiquitous and cannot be avoided. They are of two kinds—those intrinsic to the situation and process, and those impinging on them from outside. The former group of realistic factors have to do with the real personalities of the participants as they enter the analytic situation and engage in the analytic process. This brings into focus the inherent distinction between therapeutic alliance and real relation, and the manner in which they interact in contributing to the analytic relation (chapter 4). The distinction is primary to my argument and has important technical implications. In addition, the role of reality in the analytic process demands reformulation, especially with regard to neutrality, abstinence, and, by implication, the ways in which reality can serve the interests of resistance (chapter 5). Here the central tensions created by pulls toward reality and away from the therapeutic alliance call for technical reflection.

Some factors impinging on the analytic situation from the outside are directly related to the real existence and person of analyst and patient and immediately affect the persons and their participation in the process and over which they have little or no control (chapter 6). These include death, illness, aging, and race (the categories are somewhat arbitrary and are not meant to be all-inclusive). Another set of factors that come to bear on the analytic situation in a more accidental or personally peripheral way include gender, pregnancy, and other reality-based factors (money, malpractice concerns, interruptions, and so on) (chapter 7). In all these instances, my concern is limited to their implications for, and especially what problems they may create in managing the therapeutic alliance. I shall confine myself to indicating the dimensions of the related problems and referring to the available literature where further explorations of the issues can be found.

CHAPTER FOUR

The Analyst as Participant

The operative distinctions in part I were between transference and countertransference, as expressions of intrapsychic dynamic forces entering into and modifying the therapeutic relation, and the therapeutic alliance. In this chapter I shall focus on the place of the real relation in this interaction. Controversy prevails between those who emphasize real or nontransferential factors and others who regard real factors as incidental or irrelevant. A useful cautionary note comes from Hoffman (1994) in response to the question: if spontaneous personal engagement with the patient has potential benefit, why bother with technical directives and ground rules? He answers, "We would then simply be entering personal relationships with our patients with the arrogant claim, masked as egalitarianism, that to spend time with us will somehow be therapeutic. Also, we would be promoting allegedly 'authentic' personal involvement as an encompassing technique, an approach that would be just as suspect in terms of its genuineness as any fanatically ascetic stance. No, clearly there is much wisdom in the requirement that the analyst abstain from the kind of personal involvement with the patients that might develop in an ordinary social situation" (p. 193). But then another division arises between those who take the real context as a condition for interpretation and those who regard the real relation as itself curative (Levine 1993). The question is not one of involvement versus noninvolvement, but rather what kind of involvement, as the analyst is necessarily involved in personal interaction.

The analytic space can be divided into three component psychic spaces—intersubjective, intrasubjective, and transsubjective (Gampel 1992). Reality is imbricated in intersubjective and transsubjective spheres. In this chapter I shall consider real aspects of the analyst's person and personality as they engage in the relationship with the patient—the intersubjective space. This will encompass aspects of the analyst's personality, character, and style. In chapter 5 I shall take up issues related to neutrality, abstinence, and resistance in its various guises. In chapters 6 and 7 I shall discuss impingement of reality factors on the analytic process—the transsubjective space. I shall examine issues of age, sex, illness, death, pregnancy, relocation, and so on. The overlap between those aspects personal to the analyst and reality factors impinging on the analysis can be significant—there is nothing more personal, for example, than sex or pregnancy—but these are not inherently part of the analyst's personality.

The Problem

The literature on the therapeutic relation has been plagued by the overriding dominance of the distinction between transference on one hand and real relation on the other. A further distinction, central to my argument but little acknowledged and less utilized, is between therapeutic alliance and real relation. As a result of the preoccupation with the distinction between transference and real relation, insofar as the therapeutic alliance is also distinguished from transference, it has been lumped together with the real relation as though they were synonymous or any differences between them were of no consequence.[1] This failure to distinguish between alliance and real relation persists; in his introductory text, Gabbard (1994a) writes: "The patient's relationship to the therapist is a mixture of a transference relationship and a real relationship. The real relationship has been termed the *therapeutic alliance* (Zetzel 1956) or the *working alliance* (Greenson 1965/1978)" (p. 104). This sort of misunderstanding allows Thomä and Kächele (1987), in their comprehensive discussion, to write: "It is said that if the negative transferences gain the upper hand, they can completely paralyze the analytic situation. The basic prerequisite for cure, namely the realistic relationship, is then undermined. Here Freud introduced an apparently objective or external truth—patient and analyst are based in the real external world (1940, p. 173)—which, examined more closely, is in fact no less subjective than the truth which comes from transference. The introduction of the real person, the subject, into the working alliance does not prevent verification of the truth; on the contrary, it makes the subjectivity of our theories manifest" (p. 63).

Kernberg (1993) focuses on the distinction between transference and real relation and contrasts the approach of ego psychology, de-emphasizing the importance of the analyst's personality, with the interpersonal approach, in which the analyst's personality inevitably influences transference. "My own view is that the reality of the analyst's personality becomes important only in so far as it serves as an anchoring point for the transference, where it requires on-going self-scrutiny by the analyst of his own behaviour and countertransference reactions. . . . In contrast, the analyst's regression to his own defensive character patterns, as a consequence of severely pathological transference-countertransference developments with chronically regressed patients, requires the protection of the treatment frame, and analytic working through of the transference simultaneously with the analyst's work on and attempts to utilise the understanding derived from his own countertransference" (p. 667). The frame and structural conditions required for working through of transference and countertransference are, of course, the therapeutic alliance.

If there is ambiguity regarding the distinction of alliance and real relationship, we cannot think that ambiguity does not invade what we would have thought to be a relatively secure distinction—that between transference and reality. Spruiell (1983) highlighted this problem when he wrote: "Despite its own theoretical thrust and however eroded older concepts of reality may be, psychoanalysis continues to utilize them. References to what is psychologically real, what is rational, irrational, delusionary, realistic, the nature of reality testing, the supposed 'real' relationship as opposed to the 'transference' relationship, the sense of reality, what is or is not psychotic, distorted, appropriate, inappropriate, adaptive, maladaptive—all of these judgmental references are to matters lying at the heart of our profession. Yet most of these references, while they remain for the most part operationally satisfactory, are no longer conceptually tenable; the philosophical position of 'naive realism' is obsolete" (p. 5). And he later adds: "There is nothing imaginary about the affective erotic and destructive swirls of currents in the consulting room. They are real in their own sense, and it is a mistake to interpret them 'away' as 'really' concerning past figures. Nor is there anything more 'factual' about the patient and analyst working together cognitively as an adult 'team'; there are transferences there too. Following this view, questions like *the* real relationship and *the* transference relationship simply evaporate" (pp. 16–17).

The statement is troublesome—one that I hesitate to endorse without qualification.[2] The deconstructionist twist in Spruiell's position captures a truth about the analytic relation, but, in my view, at the cost of relinquishing other salient truths. There is no argument that, from the point of view of the patient, transference can seem real, even that it *is* real. But it is real qua experience, not qua reality. The analyst does not become, and for the most part is not, what the patient's transference dictates. The distinction here is between psychic reality (of the patient's transference experience) and the actual reality (of the analyst's person). The distinction is not all that clean, however, since we know well that the analyst can be drawn into transference/countertransference interactions that can result in the analyst playing a role corresponding to the terms of the patient's transferential demand. And, conversely, a real reaction on the part of the patient that is interpreted as transference can undermine the alliance (Langs 1973a, 1973b).[3] But is there not some point in keeping such transferential and countertransferential processes at least conceptually distinct from another level of interaction in terms of the real relationship? I prefer the line of thinking that infers that the psychic reality, whether of patient or therapist, does not undermine or abolish the real relationship and its vicissitudes.[4]

Part of the problem is the multiple meanings of *real* in analytic discourse.[5] We speak of the reality of transference, feelings, fantasies, psychic reality, and now even virtual reality (Cesio 1993). Is the patient's love "real" (Hoffer 1993)? Freud's (1915a) question "opens up the question of the nature of reality, the question of what is illusory and what real, and of what constitutes the difference" (Person 1993, p. 4). In this discussion, I shall maintain that a firm distinction exists between psychic reality and the actual reality of the real persons involved in the analytic transaction, and, further, that the basic prerequisite for cure in analysis lies in alliance rather than in realistic relationship. Correspondingly, it is not the real person who engages in the alliance, but the analyst in his role as therapeutic agent.[6] The real relationship is itself worthy of more extensive investigation, but my discussion will attempt to draw a clear distinction between these intertwined aspects of the analytic process, review some of the history of this problem, and consider application of this distinction in the therapeutic setting.

Alliance versus Real Relationship

Previous discussions of therapeutic alliance have suffered from the necessity to distinguish it from transference. The therapeutic relationship includes both transference and nontransference components, but little effort has been expended in drawing a line between alliance and the real relation, both of which are nontransferential. In Viederman's (1991) excellent clinical discussion of the reality of the analyst in the analytic process, for example, he does not distinguish between real relation and therapeutic alliance, which can lead to some misunderstandings. The same problem arises in Kantrowitz's (1993) explication of the interaction between real characteristics of the patient with those of the analyst; some of these interactions can influence transference, some, therapeutic alliance, and some remain in the realm of real interaction. The relative failure to draw these distinctions is perhaps understandable, insofar as these factors intermingle and interact in the actuality of the therapeutic relation—a fact that tends to obscure distinctions between them and different ways in which they contribute to the overall relation.

Intermingling of fantasy and reality in the analytic process complicates the effort to keep them distinct. There is always tension between transference dynamics and real involvement with the analyst for all patients (Zavitzianos 1974), becoming more intense and troublesome for patients in the borderline spectrum and severe narcissistic disorders (Adler 1980; Blum 1971b, 1973; Kernberg 1968; Levin 1969; Meissner 1988; Rappaport 1956; Zetzel 1956).[7] If a part of every patient finds gratification and relief in the analyst's even-handed tolerance and acceptance of transference derivatives, a part also finds his adherence to the analytic process and the analytic framework dissatisfying and artificial. As Caper (1992) notes, "This part of the patient seems to regard transference figures that act out their roles as external phantasy objects as absolutely real, and the real figure of the analyst as artificial. Such patients will often refer to their relationship with external phantasy objects as 'real relationships,' in contrast to the supposed 'artificiality' of the relationship with the real analyst" (p. 288). This reversal of fantasy and reality is due to the analyst's adherence to the terms of the alliance—the "careful avoidance of the manifold collusions with the patient's unconscious fantasies" (p. 288).[8] An appeal to the humanness of the analytic relation (Greenson 1967, 1972) as part of alliance is misguided—humanness does not belong to alliance, but to the real relationship. Emphasis on the human or humane aspects of the analytic relation have often enough led to collusion with the patient's neurotic needs and contributed to distortions of the alliance (Langs 1976).

De Jonghe et al. (1991) offer a further clarification. They argue that the classic psychoanalytic view divided the analytic relation into three components—transference, working relationship (alliance), and real relation. A post-classical view, however, adds the primary relationship to the list as a fourth dimension. They define the primary relationship as "the reliving or re-experiencing of early infantile modes of functioning: affects, needs and wishes dating from the pre-oedipal, even the earliest pre-verbal period. It is essentially a recapitulation of the very early relationship between mother and infant, the experience of the undifferentiated self-object representation of the mother-child symbiotic phase and the separation-individuation phase (Mahler et al. 1975). It is a tie or bond of a pre-oedipal nature, not a relationship between separate individuals" (p. 699). Thus, in their view, real relationship and alliance derive from more mature object relations based predominantly on object cathexis. Transference derivatives are also object related, but the objects are more infantile. The primary relationship in contrast is derived from involvement with an infantile object, but the relation is rooted in narcissism rather than object cathexis. These distinctions are helpful in locating concepts like primary love (Balint 1965) and selfobject transferences (Kohut 1984), or even Stone's (1961) "primary maternal transference" in the transference paradigm.

The "realistic relationship" in this approach refers "to mature, realistic and healthy aspects of the relationship other than the working relationship. These aspects relate to the other person in his own right, not as a parent substitute nor as a working partner. It is the relationship between the patient and the analyst as real persons, not in their functions of analyst and analysand" (de Jonghe et al. 1991, p. 696). This formulation clearly distinguishes real relation from transference on the one hand and alliance on the other. The distinction from transference is valid, even though transference and reality can fall into conjunction (Greenacre 1959). For example, an overweight analyst may stimulate associations to an overweight parent and thus offer support to transference displacements.

This point is brought into focus in Thomä and Kächele's (1987) emphasis on the dependence of the patient's transference and transference resistance on shaping of the analytic situation by the analyst, and by Langs' (1992) advocacy of an interactional perspective: transference is not simply determined by unconscious drive-derivative displacements on the part of the patient but may also involve responses of the patient to stimuli coming from the experience of the encounter with the real analyst.[9] Rangell (1985) observed, "The 'real' as well as the distorted exist in life and in analysis. Both, not one, are also reflected in the transference" (p. 328). Baudry (1991) reinforces this understanding when he comments: "I believe that the analyst's real character traits serve as hooks on which patients can hang their transference reactions and give them a measure of plausibility. It is important for the analyst to be in touch with his characteristic responses so as to be able to monitor his own contributions and see how the patient uses them" (p. 928).[10] The same phenomenon can involve any real attribute of the analyst or, conversely, the patient (Bernal y del Rio 1984). A somewhat more operational description is offered by Baudry (1991): "By real relationship I mean one in which the analyst interacts with the patient outside the boundaries of what is commonly defined as the therapeutic role—for example, gives advice, acts as a friend, socializes with the patient, tells him about himself and his own life, freely responds directly to questions" (p. 921).[11]

The "mature, realistic and healthy" (de Jonghe et al. 1991, p. 696) part of the real relation may be open to question. The reality of the patient, as well as the analyst, may be somewhat less than mature, realistic, or healthy. If so, these qualities enter the analytic relation as characteristics of the actual personality of the analyst or patient. For Viederman (1991), the "real person" of the analyst refers "not only to his outward traits, but to his unique characteristics as a person and to his behavior in the analytic situation which goes beyond interpretation and clarification. The analyst's presence is rooted in the revelation of his personality and at times certain aspects of his experience, and in the idiosyncratic ways that two people develop a relationship and establish a dialogue with characteristics unique to that dyad" (pp. 452–453).

The qualities entering into the alliance, however, as opposed to the real relation, are dictated not immediately by the personality of either participant, but by the analytic situation and work and by the engagement capacity of each.[12] Winnicott (1949), for example, wrote about "objective and justified hatred" toward a patient that was merely the analyst's natural reaction to disagreeable aspects of the patient's personality rather than any form of transference. Such a reaction may stem from the real relation and not pertain to therapeutic alliance; in fact, it may contradict it.

Personalities in Interaction

The most important and central reality for the patient is the person of the analyst, and any split of that person into transference object and working analyst requires further integration. Patients develop feelings, positive and negative, about their analysts based not merely on transference but on qualities related to his actual personality and character traits (Dewald 1976; Dickes 1967; Goz 1975; Greenson 1967, 1971; Jacobs 1991; Langs 1973a; Menaker 1942). Negative personality characteristics of the analyst can interfere with the analytic process (Ticho 1972; Heimann in Ticho 1972). Every analyst has his or her own constellation of personal characteristics, mannerisms, style of behavior and speech, habits of dress, sex/gender (Appelbaum and Diamond 1993; Lester 1990), way of managing the therapeutic situation, attitudes toward the patient as a human being, prejudices, moral and political views, sense of humor (Bader 1993), and personal beliefs and values (Greenson and Wexler 1969; Klauber 1968).[13] Even the therapist's style of dressing makes a statement about his personality, reflecting his formality or casualness. The patient's choice of apparel also makes a similar statement, or can serve as an enactment of transference or other dynamic issues in relation to the therapist; the woman who dresses revealingly or seductively, for example, or a man who dresses sloppily. To a certain extent, analysts can vary or adapt their style to the characteristics of individual patients (Jacobs 1991). A degree of adapting on the part of both patient and analyst takes place on an unconscious level—probably reflecting successful empathy on both parts.[14]

These are all relevant aspects of the analyst's real existence and personality and belong to the real relationship (Adler 1980). The analyst's adherence to an exclusive transference model can serve a defensive need to avoid the reality of the analyst or to circumvent alliance issues (Moraitis 1993). By the same token, excessive focus on reality may collude with the patient's defenses and avoid areas of conflict (Levine 1993). Certainly Freud was not adverse to asserting his personality into his analytic work and having his personal identity accessible to his patients, as Lipton's (1977, 1979) re-evaluation of the Rat Man's treatment suggests (Stone 1981). Freud missed aspects of Dora's transference (Freud 1905a), but was also oblivious to the influence of his own reality (Cesio 1993). These aspects of the real relation seem to have been excluded in his mind from issues of technique (Shapiro 1984).

But these aspects of the analyst's real personality—humor, for example—

may become a vehicle for countertransference dynamics and undermine the alliance (Kubie 1971) or may strengthen the alliance and promote analytic work (Christie 1994; Poland 1971, 1990). Schafer (1970) included the comic among the visions of reality inherent in the psychoanalytic outlook. Again, humor within the context of alliance can serve therapeutic purposes, not outside of it. As Jacobson (1993) observes, "Our real task is to maintain the optimal tension for analytic experiencing, learning, and change, to provide enough human connection to facilitate the process, but not on occasions or in ways where it will interfere with the development of the internal experiences the patient must come to know and understand" (p. 537).

The real personality of the analyst may play as important a role as his verbal communications, and this interpenetration of the reality of the therapist's personality is consistent with maintenance of neutrality (Ottenheimer 1979; Skolnikoff 1993). The interpretive and the relational are inextricably linked—to the extent that interpretation is effective, the relation is having its maximal effect (Pine 1993). Such real personal characteristics condition the therapeutic relationship, influencing the form of transference, or, the form of enactments, contributing to resistances or transference/countertransference involvements (Kantrowitz 1993; Simon 1993; Skolnikoff 1993; Smith 1993; Strupp 1973). Negative personality characteristics of the analyst can interfere with the analytic process (Ticho 1972; Heimann in Ticho 1972). The analyst not only serves as a transference object, but also offers the patient a real and new relationship (Blum 1971a, 1981; Loewald 1960). As Torras de Beà (1992) stated: "Besides, our way of listening, of tolerating frustration and anxiety, the associations we choose in interpretation, the way we articulate them and the new meanings we convey, tell the patient quite a lot about us, about what we are, and both about our fears, anxieties and defence mechanisms as well as about our courage, solidity and constancy. Any patient . . . gets to know his analyst more and more, and I think it is a favourable sign when he ventures to do so and to become progressively more realistic about him" (p. 162). Among the things the patient gets to know are the real limitations and fallibility of his analyst (Sterba 1941). These real aspects are entirely distinct from transference and countertransference (Langs 1976). None of this is lost on the patient who is exquisitely observant and sensitive to the least details of the analyst's real person (Hann-Kende 1933), although he may also have to overcome his fears of consequences and develop greater trust in the relation before he can address them (Heimann in Ticho 1972). The real precipitants of transference reactions can be grouped into those coming from appropriate or necessary interventions of the analyst; from aspects of the analytic situation or the analyst's therapeutic stance; from other behaviors of the analyst such as separations, termination, illness, moving an office, and so on; or from outside information about the analyst (Langs 1976).

While it is true and fundamental to the analytic process that, as Blum (1981) notes, "Patients . . . react to the analyst's personality and possible problems in terms of their own personality and transference dispositions" (p. 60), the transference channel is not the only vehicle for patient-analyst interaction.[15]

A similar set of realities operates with regard to the therapist's view of the patient. As he enters the consulting room, the patient carries with him certain determinate real qualities and characteristics stamping him as this human individual. Central components are aspects of the patient's personality and behavioral style. Certain mannerisms or forms of behavior may elicit a reaction from the analyst. A female patient may be beautiful and behave in a sexually seductive manner—aspects of her usual style of behavior and mode of interaction with men. These are real aspects of her person that cannot be reduced to transferential components. They may elicit responses from the therapist, especially if male, that may even be affective in tone but have nothing to do with countertransference. He is simply responding to the reality of an attractive woman. By the same token, a handsome, appealing, subtly seductive and attractive male patient can exercise an influence on a female analyst that might be erotic in implication. These transactions occur within the real relation and need not have any countertransference implications.

Similarly, objective qualities of both participants come into play continually to shape the quality and course of their interaction, which undoubtedly plays a part in shaping the analyst's experience of the engagement, how he relates to the patient, and how he implements his analytic role (Smith 1993). This may even affect the choice of analyst (Alexander et al. 1993; Thompson 1938b); a female patient with a history of poor relations with inadequate male figures (especially her father) chose a male analyst in an effort to experience a desexualized, trusting, and mutually respectful relation with a strong and reliable male figure (Ottenheimer 1979). The analyst may be authoritarian and directive in his style of intervention and interpretation. His approach to the analytic situation and interaction may simply express his habitual manner of interacting, or it may in some degree be dictated by defensive needs and even derived from underlying unresolved conflicts, and still not necessarily express countertransference. Analysts, like patients, are often poorly attuned to their own personality traits, how they appear to their patients, and especially how these traits can influence the analytic process. Attunement to countertransference issues, by and large, tends to be much better (Ticho 1972).

The analyst's personal characteristics may be a facet of his personal style and his habitual mannerisms in approaching and dealing with a particular patient (Kantrowitz 1992, 1993). From one perspective, no active measures are required to open the analyst's real personality to the patient, which is unavoidably expressed even in standard classical technique (Modell 1976; Pine 1993).

Similarly, another version of countertransference cloaked in the garb of strict adherence to norms of abstinence and neutrality may in certain cases create a situation of deprivation for the patient and result in an angry counterattack or submissive avoidance (Viederman 1991). Masochistic patients may experience emotional distance or studied indifference as sadistic. Acknowledgment of the reality of the other carries with it the realization of separation and the attendant risks and threats of loss and abandonment that may lead to attempts to actualize the relationship in the interest of gaining assurance (Feldman 1993b). Yet the most therapeutic reassurance is to be found within alliance. These aspects of the therapeutic interaction can occasionally influence the patient's dreams, sometimes signaling some faltering in the alliance (Rosenbaum 1965) or wishes for the analyst to be a real figure (Bradlow and Coen 1975; Rappaport 1959).[16]

The influence of the analyst's personality on the analytic process is seen frequently in cases of a second analysis. Often the patient's complaints about the previous analyst reflect antipathy to that analyst's personality traits (Ticho 1972), although such reactions may also reflect transference difficulties that were unresolved or poorly handled. At times, patients in a second analysis will idealize the previous analyst and hold him up as a model for comparison with the present analyst. The second analyst in these circumstances comes off poorly in the patient's splitting. However, differences may be compounded by the personalities and styles of the respective analysts. Aspects of negative transference potential that were either circumvented or simply not elicited with one analyst are drawn into full flower with another.[17] Impasse or stalemate may not be attributable to unconscious guilt or to the errors or ignorance of the analyst, but may reflect matters of style and manner of which neither patient nor analyst are aware (Jacobs 1991). Careful attention to this issue may pay dividends when characteristics of the analyst seem to parallel or overlap with those of the patient or when they share a common blind spot regarding problems that can underlie transference/countertransference interactions or can act as reality-based factors impeding analytic progress (Kantrowitz 1993).

While the distinction between these real aspects of the therapeutic interaction and elements of transference is more familiar and accepted in the analytic purview, the related distinction between such real factors and the therapeutic alliance is more difficult. Alliance requires specific negotiations and forms of interaction between therapist and patient for effective and meaningful therapeutic interaction. Trust, for example, is not part of the real relation, even though it arises between real people and reflects aspects of their real functioning and interacting. It entails a quality of the interaction within the object relationship that must be engendered by specific behaviors aiming at establishing and sustaining such trust. The capacity for trust may be a part of the reality of the patient's personality structure and functioning, but this capacity must be realized in the ongoing interaction between analyst and patient in the specifically therapeutic context, and in this sense contributes an essential element to the therapeutic alliance. Trust, then, as it enters the therapeutic alliance is quite different than a trusting disposition that the patient may have toward any significant figure in his environment. Trust in the alliance is specifically focused in the analytic setting as a contributing element of the analytic process and directed to mutual involvement and collaboration with the analyst specifically in the work of the process. Authentic trust in the alliance allows a patient in analysis to reveal his deepest and most shameful secrets and perverted fantasies, but it would not call for him to give the analyst the key to his safe-deposit box. Trust in the alliance is specifically invested in the analytic object for purposes of the analytic process.

Similarly, a patient may have a real capacity for autonomous functioning, but that capacity must be allowed to emerge as an aspect of the analytic relationship and interaction in order to be regarded as a factor in therapeutic alliance. Yet the reality of the patient's personality structure pervades his whole life experience and relationships. Insofar as these qualities contribute to the mutually reinforcing collaboration of analyst and patient, they are part of therapeutic alliance. Outside the analysis they belong to the patient's real personality.

The Character of the Analyst and the Patient

The character, as distinguished from personality, of the analyst impinges on the analytic process in a variety of ways. It contributes significantly to the real relation and to the alliance. It may also influence transference by providing characteristics congruent with transference determinants.[18] The character of the analyst is one of the real factors framing the analytic process. Fenichel (1945) defined character as "the ego's habitual modes of adjustment to the external world, the id, and the superego and the characteristic types of combining these modes with one another" (p. 467); personality adds to this "the analyst's professional competence and commitment, the range of his education, human values, ideals, language, sensitivity, interests, customs, and other residues of his life experiences" (Ticho 1972, p. 138). Baudry (1991) provides a useful inquiry into the role of the analyst's character in the analytic process; I shall comment on and broaden his reflection to include the question of the character of the patient and its influence on the analytic process as another salient component of the real relation.

The personality of the analyst is an unavoidable dimension of the analytic interaction that tends to be numbered among "those subtle, unfathomable, intuitive aspects of the professional behavior of an analyst that provide much of the frame and background of the analytic relationship" (Baudry 1991, p. 917). It may be expressed in aspects of the analyst's individual style, although links between style and character may be somewhat loose. Personality attributes impinging on the analytic process may include the analyst's competence as an analyst, his commitment to the process, his values; ideals; training and education; use of language;[19] habits; interests; physique; life experience; and tendencies to be active or passive, action-oriented or reflective, enthusiastic and alive or dull; tendencies to see events in positive or negative light; sense of humor; tendencies to be stiff or flexible, gruff or tender, cautious or risk-taking, even-tempered or moody, patient or impatient, authoritarian or not (Cooper 1986; Ticho 1972). The same list of characteristics applies mutatis mutandis to the patient. Both parties may react to the personality characteristics of the other in ways that are outside alliance and transference (Stone 1961).

Baudry (1991) raises the question of whether and how the analyst's character influences his technique. He offers three possibilities: "(1) general self-syntonic beliefs and attitudes which permeate all aspects of the analyst's functioning both personal and professional: pessimism / optimism, degree of permissiveness, activity vs. passivity, degree of warmth vs. distance, rigidity / flexibility, authoritarian tendencies, and so forth; (2) aspects of the style of the given analyst—tone, manner, verbosity, use of humor, degree of irony; (3) the analyst's characteristic reactions to various affects of the patient or to problems in the treatment, such as stalemated situations" (p. 922).

While all of these possibilities can influence the interaction between analyst and patient, these are not necessarily aspects of countertransference. Countertransference dynamics may enter the picture, but the qualities discussed here belong to the analyst's personality exclusive of transference. Distance, for example, is a matter of the degree of affective relation between patient and analyst. There is an optimal distance that facilitates meaningful communication consistent with demands of the alliance,—excessive closeness or intimacy can lead to potential seductiveness and the risk of transgression of therapeutic boundaries, and excessive distance can lead to heightened defensiveness, resistance, and feelings of rejection. Both alternatives open the way for transference distortions and misalliances.

For purposes of clarity, I favor a definition of countertransference based on the analyst's neurotic transference to the patient, whether that reaction is conscious or unconscious, affective or cognitive, or whether the reaction facilitates or impedes the analytic process.[20] Thus, the analyst's tendency to assume a relatively authoritarian position may be a personality characteristic and may not reflect countertransference at all. At the same time, the patient's response—whether rebellious or compliant—may or may not reflect transference, but may represent no more than a characteristic of his adaptive style. Attribution of such forms of behavior and / or interaction to transference or countertransference are more reliably made when there is specific evidence to support that claim.

CHAPTER FIVE

Reality, Neutrality, and Resistance

Neutrality and Abstinence

Neutrality has long been honored as an essential component of the analytic situation and process. As Freud (1915a) used the term, it implied avoidance of countertransference (Shapiro 1984), but quickly became linked to the notion of abstinence, meaning withholding of gratifications and preservation of anonymity (Pine 1993). It also came to imply respect for the patient's individuality (Freud 1912b, 1923b; Schachter 1994). These notions can and should be distinguished (Poland 1984). Neutrality is "one of the defining characteristics of the attitude of the analyst during the treatment. The analyst must be neutral in respect of religion, ethical and social values—that is to say, he must not direct the treatment according to some ideal, and should abstain from counseling the patient; and he must be neutral too as regards manifestations of transference . . . ; finally, he must be neutral towards the discourse of the patient: in other words, he must not, *a priori,* lend a special ear to particular parts of this discourse, or read particular meanings into it, according to his theoretical preconceptions" (Laplanche and Pontalis 1973, p. 271). The same source describes abstinence as the "rule according to which the analytic treatment should be so organized as to ensure that the patient finds as few substitutive satisfactions for his symptoms as possible. The implication for the analyst is that he should refuse on principle to satisfy the patient's demands and to fulfill the roles which the patient tends to impose upon him" (p. 2).

Opinions regarding neutrality range from regarding it as the touchstone of psychoanalytic method to regarding it as meaningless or irrelevant (Hamilton 1993). Franklin (1990) surveyed the forms of neutrality—behavioral, attitudinal, interpersonal, interactional, and essential. This last seems to refer to the basic ambiguity and open-endedness of analytic hypotheses and interpretations, such that any conclusions remain tentative and open to further modification. This emphasizes the quest for meaning so central to the analytic process rather than arrival at answers or conclusions and increasingly characterizes participation of both analyst and analysand. Hoffer (1985), like Poland (1984), spoke of neutrality of appearance, referring to what the analyst reveals of himself, especially feelings, and neutrality of power or influence, referring to the analyst's aims and goals, or to the influence of one person over another. To this Poland (1984) added the analyst's neutralization and mastery of his own inner processes. Kris (1990) advocated a form of "functional neutrality" rooted in the patient's experience of the analyst that facilitates free association and advances the psychoanalytic process. Such functional neutrality implies that the analyst can respond empathically and flexibly to needs of the patient at times when shame and guilt interfere with free self-expression, in contrast to classical neutrality, which might reinforce the patient's punitive self-criticism (Treurniet 1993). Forms of essential or functional neutrality and their congeners are consistent with the view of neutrality in the context of therapeutic alliance.[1]

Aspects of the analyst's personality and style addressed previously may be less relevant to the issue of neutrality; the issue in all such matters concerns more the extent to which they remain part of the acceptable analytic background or whether they intrude on and distort the analytic process and material (Levy and Inderbitzin 1992). The point of both neutrality and abstinence is to facilitate uncovering of the unconscious (Shapiro 1984), but this crucial aim of analysis must allow for acceptance and processing by the patient. The realization of the importance of the real person of the analyst as a participant in the analytic situation has led some analysts to advocate sharing his feelings with the patient (Berman 1949; Gitelson 1952; Little 1951; Renik 1995a; Schachter 1995). Alger (1966) advocated the analyst's role as a model for expressing feelings and joining the patient in the mutual endeavor of exploring their relation, an approach similar to that recommended by Ferenczi.[2] My own view is that such self-exposure has a place if it is consistent with and sustains the alliance, not otherwise.[3] Reich (1960) cautioned that some self-revelation may be at times advisable, especially of obvious errors or countertransference expressions, but not to the point of burdening the patient with the analyst's concerns. Errors can be acknowledged and discussed not only without detriment to the alliance, but can have a positive effect in undermining any detrimental imbalance in the analytic relation.[4] Greenson (1967, 1971, 1972; Greenson and Wexler 1969) suggested principles for processing such errors, an approach taken up and expanded by Langs (1976). Langs, however, tended to take a somewhat univocal view of such modifications of neutrality as forms of countertransference acting out with consistent unconsciously negative effects. He expressed concern that the flexibility and modifications of neutrality, recommended by Stone (1954, 1961) and supported by the views of Zetzel (1956) and Greenson (1965), would justify discarding basic analytic principles and creating misalliances.

Stone (1961) argued for an appropriate degree of gratification in the patient's relation with the analyst, which seems unobjectionably consistent with demands of the alliance. The question is always how much and with which patients. In these terms, he urges that a variety of ancillary techniques—advice, encouragement, reassurance, and so on—have a place in analysis. I would argue that the standard of judgment as to when these interventions are helpful or appropriate should be the therapeutic alliance. The analyst who says nothing when his patient is on a path of harmful acting out or self-injury from poor judgment or unresolved conflict is not doing his job. The alliance does not allow the analyst to sit quietly and allow the patient to harm himself.

The question of self-revelation cannot be conclusively resolved and remains largely a matter of personal style. The point of Freud's (1912b) appeal to the surgeon or mirror models was for protection of the analyst's emotional life and the futility of trying to overcome resistance by self-revelation (Stone 1961). He regarded self-revelation as a form of suggestion that did not contribute to uncovering the unconscious. Stone (1961), however, questioned indiscriminate withholding of information in response to simple questions. There would seem to be a middle ground between impersonal rigidity and intrusion of too much of the analyst's reality into the analytic space.[5] Total anonymity is impossible, and there is much about the analyst's real person that is open and accessible to the patient.[6] Deviation from a comfortable and appropriate middle ground opens the process to deviations from the alliance whether or not these are generated by countertransference. The analyst can best negotiate these waters if he observes the requirements and boundaries of the alliance. All questions have explorable meaning and implication, but straightforward questions—"Are we meeting on Washington's birthday?" or "When is your vacation?"—could readily be answered. The question of when a question is better explored than answered is a matter of clinical judgment. Idle curiosity about the analyst's person or life or prurient interest are different matters. The intersection of fantasy and reality, always part of the fascinating complexity of analytic experience and related to the generative matrix of transference, is a constant factor in all these considerations. It is not always clear the extent to which real information about the analyst facilitates emergence of transference and serves consolidation of the alliance and, conversely, the extent to which it impedes transference and distorts alliance.[7] Stone's (1961) view that knowledge of the analyst's hobbies and interests or where he goes on vacation would not disturb transference must be assessed critically in light of their impact on the individual patient and analytic process. Determination of the extent to which the patient's efforts to gain greater access to the reality of the analyst are deviations from the alliance is always germane.

Neutrality and abstinence, however, are entirely consistent with the alliance as described here. Poland (1984) proposes certain characteristics of neutrality that echo aspects of the alliance—emphasis on the two-person system of mutual interaction and influence, issues of power (one does not dominate the other), the avoidance of regressive pulls in the analyst, respect for the individuality of the patient, circumscription of eccentric intrusions of the analyst's unconscious, increasing freedom of the patient as a goal of analysis, the importance of empathy, care of imposition of values, and so on. I would enlist these characteristics in support of my argument that neutrality is essential for the alliance and that its implementation within the alliance sector is its proper context within the analytic relationship.[8]

The same argument suggests that neutrality and abstinence are also compatible with empathy and other qualities of therapeutic alliance (Hoffer 1993).[9] Kohut (1980) was careful to distinguish psychoanalytic empathy, which he regarded as neutral and objective, from "the cluster of ill-defined meanings, calling forth associations of friendliness and emotional warmth, that the term 'empathy' tends to evoke" (p. 484). The view of neutrality and empathy as antithetical has been challenged (Levy 1985; Levy and Inderbitzin 1992). Empathy should serve as the guide to maintaining neutrality, which, in the specific interaction with the patient, depends on the analyst's sense of the patient's subjective experience. This is not possible without the blend of detachment and involvement called for by Greenson (1978). Neutrality and abstinence are not the same as, and should be kept distinct from, anonymity. Neutrality can be violated either by excessive self-detachment or by excessive self-revelation. As Jacobson (1993) notes, "We should be aware also that such withholding of responses, if applied excessively—relentlessly, mechanically, or insensitively—may introduce needlessly painful and unproductive turbulence into the psychoanalytic situation, constituting a distortion rather than a facilitation of the process" (p. 534). I contend that neutrality is preserved within the alliance sector and, correspondingly, that neutrality suffers when the analyst is drawn into interacting with the patient either in terms of transference or the real relation. The long-held view that the ideal of technical neutrality was somehow separate from the personality of the analyst has been laid to rest. The impact of the analyst's personality on the process is a given and cannot be eliminated, for the analyst's technical interventions are permeated with his presence[10] and personality (Peters 1991).

Analysts have more or less abandoned Freud's early metaphors of the mirror or the surgeon to express this aspect of analytic interaction (Rioch 1943). These stark images lean too much in the direction of unempathic remoteness, another countertransference pitfall (Stone 1981). Even for Freud, neutrality did not connote emotional distance or coldness or a dehumanizing lack of human warmth and sympathy, but rather an approach that was nonjudgmental, nonmoralizing, not imposing one's own personal attitudes or values, not intruding on the patient's personal life, staying impartial and objective (Blum 1981). It is the position of equidistance from id, ego, and superego recommended by Anna Freud (1936), as well as a stance that an intelligent and attuned patient could respond to as reasonable and appropriate (Stone 1981). As Stone observed, "To the extent that 'neutrality' with an affirmative affective tone is genuinely achieved, it is an excellent contribution both to the legitimate principle of abstinence and to the high tolerance and acceptance which characterize the analytic work in its best sense" (p. 101).[11] As Bader (1993) notes, the humorless analyst is a caricature of analytic abstinence and neutrality; even humor has a place. He writes: "The unique feature of depression and affective rigidity among analysts is that we have a theory of technique that can be misread as justifying our neuroses, and we can enact them under the guise of abstinence and neutrality. . . . Misalliances or impasses can be the end result of what, to us, looks like a treatment based on good technique" (p. 49).[12]

Real Relation as Resistance

We usually think of resistance in terms of specific defensive maneuvers of the patient to divert or frustrate the analytic process and the analytic effort. However, if we accept the broader notion of resistance as anything impeding the analytic process, then reality and the real relationship between analyst and patient can under certain circumstances serve that function (G. Bibring 1936; Chused 1992). Not only can the real serve as resistance for the patient, but it can be used for the same purpose by the analyst, however repugnant the idea that the analyst might introduce resistances into the analytic process. My major point here is that reality and the real relation are not always positive or promotional factors in performance of the analytic task.

In analytic material there is always tension between factual data and the patient's recounting (Trad 1992), between fact and fantasy, between historical and narrative truth (Spence 1982). Patients' adherence to their version of their own life history as factual can become a resistance to the extent that it obscures exploration of psychodynamic factors determining the form the history takes (Modell 1991). Along the same vein, if the analyst accepts the account of the patient as veridical, he short-circuits exploration of the dynamic determinants that enter into the telling and the story—a form of analyst resistance.

The communicative structure of the analytic relation is further complicated by idiosyncratic theories of pathogenesis (Goldberg 1991) and narrative incommensurability. As Hunter (1991) described in some detail, the account of his illness and his experience that the patient brings to the treatment setting is fundamentally divergent from the account the physician develops in the course of his examination and diagnosis. Even though the essence of the difference is why the patient seeks help, the disparity in narrative comprehension can provide the basis for misunderstandings and adversely affect the relationship between patient and physician. The same disparity affects the respective accounts of the patient in analysis and his analyst.[13]

As the patient tells his story, dimensions of the recounting of his past can assume different colorations and levels of meaning in his own ear as opposed to his analyst's ears. The view of the patient's reality, as it evolves in the analysis, may find congruence between analyst and patient, or it may not (Feldman 1993a). We cannot forget Kris' (1956) cautions regarding the personal myth and the unreliability of memory. Variants of the story—as narrative truth versus historical truth (Spence 1982), or narrative representation versus narrative enactment (Morris 1993)—become polarities in terms of which the discourse assumes intelligibility. The emphasis, focusing, and implication in the minds of the participants in the narrative process can distill these elements in different proportions and mixes.

The challenge to the analyst is to reconstruct the patient's account in terms that make it relevant to the structure of scientific thought generated by his culture and theory and that lend understanding to both the story and its teller. Yet, however well the treater's reconstruction explains the patient's account, it does not replace it; both accounts persist side by side, neither one adequately translating the other. They are simply incommensurable—neither fully comprehended nor reduced by the other. The core difficulty is the radical impossibility of explaining the consciousness and experience of another human being. While the professional account may render an intelligible version of the patient's experience, it risks losing touch with the meaning of the original narrative and so mistranslating it. The analytic rendition focuses on selected aspects of the patient's story and weaves them into a coherent account, abandoning or allowing to recede into the background those elements that are irrelevant or noncontributory. Yet this same information may seem salient and more persuasive to the patient. The analyst develops his own plot to embrace the relevant data, a plot that may and often does differ considerably from the patient's.

In this complex process, as Hunter (1991) makes clear, the relative incommensurability does not imply the inadmissibility of either account. The patient's narrative remains the basis of the analyst's narrative, which recasts the story in more objective and scientifically relevant terms. These tensions impinge on the analytic relation since the validity of the respective accounts must be preserved and understood. To what extent does the analytic narrative reflect the patient's subjective experience? To what extent does the analytic construction enable the patient to both feel understood and gain deeper understanding of that experience? Where is reality to be located in these accounts? Is the real story being told by the patient or by the analyst, and how do we decide? Or are both accounts relevant to reality, each capturing a different perspective? In terms of the alliance, the analytic task is to bring the analytic account into meaningful dialogue with the patient's account in ways that allow their integration and result in healing effects for the patient. The dialogue takes place not on the level of the data involved in the telling, but on the level of the meaning, implication, and consequences of the story and its telling. These differences can easily become the vehicle for some of the difficulties in metacommunication that can erode the alliance or contribute to misalliances (Jacobs 1991). Some of these factors can be engaged and relatively resolved in the therapeutic alliance: as Goldberg (1994) commented, "Any life history or theory of pathogenesis serves defensive functions and constrains access to other interpretive and reconstructive possibilities. Each participant in the process is loath to give up his or her preferred explanatory possibilities, and yet, to some extent, this must occur on both sides if optimal analytic work is to take place" (p. 70).

To take this a step further, the real relationship can also become a vehicle of resistance. For some patients, adherence to the real relationship provides a way of avoiding transference with its associated affects (Grossman 1993).[14] For others, some real characteristics of the analyst may stimulate transference reactions—a circumstance that not only abets the analytic process but can lead to further exploration and clarification of transference dynamics. But for some patients, the resemblance of the transference object to real objects, whether erotically stimulating or traumatically damaging, can serve as the basis for resistance to transference that takes the form of failure to acknowledge transference and any differences that may occur in the transference object along with the similarities. Chused (1992) points out the usefulness of listening carefully to the patient's perceptions of the analyst and his technique, particularly when the patient's view accords with the analyst's own self-perceptions—such perceptions may be masking transferences but may also contain them. A similar obliteration can be used to preserve and keep from analysis transference fantasies, leading to extension of the analytic process and use of the analyst as a fetish (Renik 1992). For other patients the differentiation between transference and reality is obliterated so that transference is experienced as an intolerable repetition of previous trauma. If the analyst's real characteristics are more congruent with the fantasy, transference illusion overrides the distinction of fantasy and reality and the alliance is bypassed. In such cases, if an adequate footing cannot be gained in the alliance to explore both the reality and the transference aspects, therapeutic progress may be frustrated and prospects for resolution doomed.

By the same token, were the analyst to accept the patient's transference as real, he would introduce a distortion into the analytic process. Just as taking the patient's account of himself as reflecting a veridical reality can become a resistance to analytic exploration, so acceptance of transference manifestations as real undermines analytic investigation and understanding. Analogously, if the analyst introduces a real factor into the analytic interaction with his patient, it can distort the analytic process and serve as a focus of resistance.

To take a benign example, an analyst had been seeing his patient for a reduced fee that, on further reflection, seemed inappropriate. He informed his patient that he wanted to raise the fee and opened a negotiation to determine what a reasonable fee would be. The reality of payment of a fee for services rendered was thus brought into the analytic process. The analyst's approach to the question was cast in terms of the alliance with due respect for the patient's autonomy and freedom to decide. This led to a further exploration with the patient of the meaning of the fee, the issues of entitlement and expectation that it brought to the surface, and a consolidation and deepening of the alliance. The same proposal could have been imposed on the patient in a way that demanded his submissive acceptance. The expectable resentment and anger of a patient to such authoritarian treatment could easily lead to discontent and rebellion to the detriment of treatment. The troublesome question as to when introduction of real factors into the analysis facilitates or impedes the analytic process pervades the rest of this discussion.

By the same token, for some patients, transference fantasies are experienced as real insofar as they have real effects in the analytic interaction. But, operating in terms of the alliance, the analyst's job is to analyze both transference and countertransference fantasies and understand their meaning. Anything else, as Caper (1992) observes, "such as love, advice, guidance, or support for his self-esteem is the analyst's acting in his countertransference, and represents *his* resistance to analysis" (p. 288).

Freud brought this issue into clear focus in his paper on transference love (1915a).[15] Development of an erotic transference involved erosion of the boundaries between fantasy and reality and between the analytic relation and a real relation (Schafer 1993). The analyst's sense of the transference as unreal did not match the patient's perception of it as real. This is a classical example of the drive in the patient to draw the analytic relation in the direction of the real, therefore away from the constraints of the alliance, and thus bring about an erosion of the analytic space (Blum 1971b, 1973; Hernández 1993; Joseph 1993). But as Freud (1915a) observed, "It is, therefore, just as disastrous for the analysis if the patient's craving for love is gratified as if it is suppressed. The course the analyst must pursue is neither of these; it is one for which there *is no model* in real life" (p. 166). This middle ground is defined by the alliance.

Therapeutic Mismatch

It seems likely that many factors having to do with reality, in addition to unanalyzed transference/countertransference issues, play a significant role in the problem of matching. No analyst is equipped to deal as effectively and competently with all sorts and variations of patients. We all do better with some sorts of cases than with others. By the same token, most patients will do better with some analysts than with others. The mesh of personal characteristics and styles that make for successful analysis are not well understood, but in practice we need to keep the possibility of mismatch between analyst and patient in perspective whenever there is question of stalemate or impasse (Olinick 1976). Available data point toward the conclusion that the match between patient and analyst plays a significant role in determining therapeutic outcome (Kantrowitz et al. 1989, 1995), particularly transference resolution (Kantrowitz et al. 1990). As Heimann (in Ticho 1972) put it, "If personal idiosyncrasies are unfavorable for forming sensitive and imaginative perceptions of the patient, neither a real therapeutic or working alliance nor a fertile transference neurosis will come into existence" (p. 156). A female patient, for example, with severe difficulties with object relations may find the distance and reserve of her analyst at first reassuring to her basic anxieties, but over time the collusive match between the analyst's personality and her pathology can become more threatening and lead to stalemate. As Ticho (1972) noted, "A closer and stronger therapeutic alliance would have carried the patient over such critical periods when the regression endangered the therapeutic alliance" (p. 140).

Prediction in this area is pitifully weak. Usually we can detect a mismatch only after the fact. If an analyst senses his own dislike, irritation, impatience, or perhaps even lack of sympathy with a given patient, it may be better to refer the patient rather than venture into an analysis. But these are highly subjective criteria bearing little weight. More often one finds out only in the course of analytic effort. And, from the side of the patient, criteria of judgment are no better. Perhaps a feeling of comfort, a sense that this analyst can understand and be helpful, a feeling of security, are as much as can be hoped for. Entering analysis, like marriage, always involves an element of risk. Jacobson (1993) may be correct in saying that "the notion of therapeutic fit may boil down to knowing when to explore or confront and when to accept; when to participate responsively to facilitate the deepening of the transference, and when silence will provide optimal facilitation for an unconscious transference fantasy to come to full flower; when a period of conflict between patient and analyst is a sign of failure of empathy, and when it is a necessary part of the analytic process for a given individual, vital to his or her individuation" (p. 537).

Complicating the picture are the inevitable dimensions introduced by interaction between two individuals who bring to the process distinctive orientations, backgrounds, attitudes, and commitments. The analyst, in his role as therapist and inheritor of a medical tradition, is the healer, the one who diagnoses and treats. The patient seeks treatment because he has been unable to resolve his difficulties on his own, and so must submit to the expertise and skill of the therapist. The disparity of roles and approaches to the problem may take on aspects of resistance when these modes of engagement come into conflict. The treater carries a set of convictions, theories and values distinctively his own that may or may not be shared by the patient, and vice versa[16]—including not only theories of cure, but basic philosophical premises regarding the nature of man and mental disorder (Chessick 1977; Goldberg 1991, 1994). Analytic pursuit of the subjective involves philosophical commitments on the nature of truth (whether based on correspondence or coherence [Hanly 1990]), reality, and meaning. Patient and analyst may even approach the analytic encounter with differing theories of mind, whether other minds are similar or different (Abend 1979; Raphling 1994; Spence 1993). Tensions exist between the view of the mind in the frame of post-Cartesian irresolvable dichotomies and a postmodern, post-Wittgenstein revolt against the myth of the subjective and the primacy of internal, wordless thought (Cavell 1988a, 1988b, 1993). The internalist assumption of priority of the subjective, more familiar to traditional analysts, stands in tension with an externalist view of mental states constituted though object relations and environmental relatedness (Cavell 1991, 1993).[17] Religious perspectives and attitudes may also diverge and influence the therapeutic matrix (McDargh 1992). Differences in use of language and metaphor may promote shared meanings and alliance or lead to misunderstandings and misalliance (Levenson 1979; Rhodes 1984; Skolnikoff 1993; Warner 1976–77). Lear (1993) refers to "idiolects," personalized versions of shared natural language with their own special meanings and resonances that the analyst must learn if he is to understand unconscious connections and reverberations of the patient's conscious language. Lear writes: "The dynamics of intrapsychic transference reveal that even when a person participates in shared cultural activities, they will tend to have an idiosyncratic, unconscious meaning for that person. This, I believe, is one of Freud's greatest discoveries. We have seen that a person's thoughts, words, and activities are embedded in a web of unconscious associations that are both archaic and idiosyncratic. Just as each person, when speaking a natural language, also unconsciously speaks an idiolect, does he not also, as he participates in the culture's activities, unconsciously inhabit an idiosyncratic world?" (pp. 747–748).

The patient, for his part, may assume a position of dependence on the therapist, who may be cast in the role of powerful and magical healer, who will reward the patient's submission by resolving his difficulties. This rescue theory is a form of misalliance (Wile 1977). Others may approach therapy with their own personal theory of cure, through problem solving or willpower or resolutions of self-improvement. Such individuals commonly look for self-help devices, behavioral routines, reading recommendations, and so on. The analyst is cast in the role of advice-giver, problem-solver, or technical expert. These efforts to control the therapeutic situation are inconsistent with meaningful alliance. Others may seek self-justification and resort to various blaming devices, often with a paranoid tinge (Meissner 1978c). Wile (1977) offers additional misalliance approaches—the bromide theory characterized by rationalizations for the patient's difficulties, attributing his misfortune to bad luck, the fates, denial of seriousness of the problem, or even appeal to biological theories of causation. Some individuals look to faith healing, astrology, conversion experiences, or prayer for a way out of their difficulties. All of these approaches to the analytic situation can elicit collusion on the part of the therapist, who may respond to the patient's need for rescue or to the need for vindication, forming a misalliance on the basis of collusive opposition against the victimizing agencies lined up against the patient. My point is that these parameters of individual orientation to the treatment situation for both patient and therapist lay the ground for distortions in the therapeutic alliance and are part of their individuality as personal agents.

When there is an unresolvable impasse, considerations of transferring the patient to another analyst require careful evaluation of the potential personality match. Some patients develop similar transference reactions, regardless of the analyst's personality, but many patients manifest sensitivity to this aspect of the relationship. Coming to such a conclusion is always difficult and painful. The analyst may realize only slowly that his personality or way of thinking, even of theorizing, is part of the problem, and estimates of the potential match with another analyst are tenuous at best (Ticho 1972).

The Freud-Ferenczi Debate

From the perspective of this discussion, we can argue that the place of the real relation and its association with alliance was at issue in the differences between Freud and Ferenczi found in their correspondence (Brabant et al. 1994; Ferenczi 1949; Grubrich-Simitis 1986) and in Ferenczi's (1932) clinical diary. Many of Ferenczi's ideas have found increasing acceptance—the interactive quality of the analytic relation, the role of the analyst's feelings in understanding the analytic process, and influence of the mother in transference—but his understanding of mutuality and the revival of childhood traumata have not (Haynal and Falzeder 1993). As the diary (1932) reveals, Ferenczi was sensitive to the role of trauma in the patient's history and to its effects in the analytic relation, particularly the extent to which classical technique might replicate early traumata (Simon 1992).

He was apparently not uncomfortable with physical contact with his patients, for he took blood pressures and conducted neurological examinations. He likewise encouraged open discussion of his own mistakes and errors with the patient, a point Freud found reprehensible (Gay 1988). Ferenczi regarded such experiences as open to exploration as to their meaning and was quite cognizant of the risk that the patient might interpret such contacts as seductive or sexual advances (Simon 1992). At issue were Ferenczi's experiments with his active technique that included displays of affection—even hugging and kissing—and other realistic intrusions into the patient's life, and, in the 1920s, his relaxation technique. This approach was a reaction to the earlier active technique and emphasized empathic acceptance and security in the analytic relation, similar to subsequent advocates of the holding environment, containment, and empathy. Hoffer (1990) puts Ferenczi's approach in these terms: "In keeping with the consistent portrayal of the patient as child and victim of the insensitive parent and analyst, overwhelming trauma to the ego serves as the paradigm for Ferenczi's understanding of his disturbed patients. Psychological surrender in the service of psychological survival is vividly described as the basis for a group of defence mechanisms. The analyst's task, repeatedly articulated by Ferenczi, is to provide a safe, accepting, loving, empathic, relaxed setting where the trauma necessitating these disruptive defences can be re-experienced, remembered and thereby ultimately resolved" (p. 725).

Freud disapproved of such developments as deviations from the work of analysis. For Freud (1912a), the analytic field was defined by transference: "This struggle between the doctor and the patient, between intellect and instinctual life, between understanding and seeking to act, is played out almost exclusively in the phenomena of transference. It is on that field that the victory must be won—the victory whose expression is the permanent cure of the neurosis" (p. 108). And as far as the analytic relationship was concerned, Freud (1915a) wrote succinctly: "It is, therefore, just as disastrous for the analysis if the patient's craving for love is gratified as if it is suppressed. The course the analyst must pursue is neither of these; it is one for which there is no model in real life" (p. 166).[18]

The active technique was a direct challenge and refutation of Freud's principle of abstinence. But, as Hoffer (1991) points out, criticisms of his approach made Ferenczi more aware that the active technique could be harsh and abusive of patients and excessively authoritarian. At times patients became compliant out of fear, thus reproducing earlier infantile traumata. In retreat from this tendency and from Freud's advice, he advocated a more positive approach. As Hoffer (1991) comments, "By this time, Ferenczi had come to view Freud's technical recommendations as essentially negative ones. He took it upon himself to enrich psychoanalytic technique by including the 'positives' which he felt Freud omitted, including 'tact,' 'empathy' (*Einfühlung*), elasticity, indulgence, warmth, candour and responsiveness, in an egalitarian rather than in an authoritarian atmosphere" (p. 467).

The difference between the two men lay in their conceptions of the analytic relation. For Freud, the analysis was encapsulated, removed from the patient's real life, and focused in the confines of the analytic hours. This allowed him to analyze his own daughter, as well as Ferenczi, a close and valued colleague. For Ferenczi, analysis could not be corralled within designated hours, but instead embraced his entire relationship with Freud. For him there was no distinction between the analytic and the real relation, nor could he conceive of the analytic situation as divorced from the personality of the analyst and the unconscious communication between them (Blum 1994a). The analytic relation was the only relation, so that the reality of the patient, his life and personality, and the reality of the analyst were included on the same terms. Their viewpoints became polarized: Freud's emphasis on frustration, abstinence, and understanding versus Ferenczi's appeal to gratification, indulgence, and feeling, and Freud's insistence on insight gained through remembering and reconstruction versus Ferenczi's focus on revitalized experience leading to recovery of traumatic memories.[19] This persuasion reached an extreme in Ferenczi's practice of mutual analysis, in which patient and analyst took turns analyzing each other. Ferenczi had to abandon the experiment because of his fear of violating the confidentiality of his other patients in the course of free associating (Hoffer 1991).

From a historical perspective, I conclude that in Ferenczi's technique the analytic relation was absorbed into the real relationship in such a way that the effects of transference were obscured. Many recommendations of his positive technique would fall within the perspective of therapeutic alliance. From Freud's side, without a concept of therapeutic alliance, there was no basis for accepting any of Ferenczi's modifications of analytic technique without casting them as intrusions of reality violating the essential transference experience. A distinction between the alliance and the real relation might have offered a middle ground on which both Freud and Ferenczi could have reached agreement. Without a concept of alliance, Freud had no way to come to terms with Ferenczi's insistence on the demands of reality, and Ferenczi had no basis for dealing with nontransferential aspects of the patient that would respect Freud's principle of neutrality and abstinence.

In any case, the issues embedded in their controversy have not disappeared. Debate continues on the relative therapeutic merits of interpretation versus interpersonal and interactional aspects of the relationship between analyst and patient. Where does the curative power of analysis lie? In mutative interpretations? In the quality of personal relation between participants in the process? Both? To what degree? The balance may differ from patient to patient. We presume that Ferenczi was dealing with patients that were somewhat lower on the scale of character pathology. His emphasis on relational aspects may come closer to the view of many contemporary theorists concerning the broadening scope of psychoanalysis. It has reverberations in the self psychology of Kohut, who seeks to provide the empathy that might have been lacking in the self-objects of infancy (Stone 1981).

Clinical Relevance

To the extent that reality factors enter into the analytic process, they raise the question as to how much and in what manner they contribute to or interfere with the therapeutic effort. Does impingement of reality erode the analytic abstinence and neutrality Freud thought so important to analytic work? Must they always be taken as a form of resistance to the analytic process? Baudry takes an unequivocal position on this question: "I do not believe I am overstating the case in seeing the purpose of technique and its structure as an effort to tame the personality of the analyst so as to allow psychoanalytic work to be done. That is, the rule of abstinence limits the development of a real relationship between the patient and the analyst" (p. 920).

Effects of the real relation cannot be excluded from the process. Commenting on changes in the patient's relation to the analyst, Balint (1965) observed that "all these changes appear to point into one direction, which is accepting the analyst as a 'real' person. That means that the patient tries to find out his analyst's wishes and desires, interests, needs and sensitivities and then is at pains to adapt his behaviour and associations, even his use of phrases and forms of speech, to the image formed of his analyst, in order to find pleasure in the analyst's eyes" (p. 132). Even the analyst's proper role, consistent with the alliance, includes certain gratifications that fulfill transference fantasies of certain patients. The patient may also employ available clues to the reality of the analyst's attitudes, reactions, and values to satisfy transferential wishes, or seek to induce reactions in the analyst that would gratify transference wishes, a process termed "actualization" (Chused 1991; Roughton 1993).[20]

But this need also evolves; presumably reacting to Ferenczi's stress on mutuality, Balint (1965) continues: "The patient gradually realizes, understands and accepts his analyst's shortcomings, especially in relation to himself (the patient). Parallel with this process he renounces bit by bit his wish to change the analyst into a co-operative partner, i.e., to establish a harmonious relation in which the two partners—patient and analyst—will desire the same satisfaction in the same *mutual* act, and turning towards the world of reality tries to find someone else there, better suited for such a purpose" (p. 133). In other words, the patient in this view would seek to draw the reality of the analyst into the transference. The analyst's abstinence and resistance to the transference pull sets the stage for transference analysis and surrender of transference desire. I would argue that an essential part of this process falls in the alliance sector, as the patient will only surrender his wishes to the extent that he can join the analyst in the therapeutic effort and intent. The gradual shift in accepting characteristics and limitations of the analyst reflects greater focus of the analytic effort in the alliance. The point of abstinence, it seems to me, is to maintain the alliance in the face of both transferential pressures and the patient's desire to erode the alliance by putting the relation on a realistic basis. This is a salient component of every analytic process and forms one of its most significant resistances. The distinction between the reality of the analyst in the analytic process and the intrusion of personal influence outside the accepted channels of the analytic interaction is central. The former is unavoidable and a natural component of the interaction; the latter is a violation of abstinence in the analyst and a form of resistance in the patient.

The Demand for Reality

The role of reality becomes most problematic in the analytic process in those instances in which the patient demands some intrusion of reality into the analytic process. This was the bone of contention in the debate between Freud and Ferenczi; Ferenczi did not hesitate to introduce such reality factors, probably responding to the demand, explicit or implicit, of more primitive character-disordered patients (Hoffer 1991). One striking example of such an explicit demand was recorded by Casement (1982). The episode has been commented on by several authors, and I will add my own observations since the material lends itself so well to this discussion. The point is not to pass judgment on Casement's solution of the dilemma but to focus the issues pertaining to the role of alliance versus reality in the analytic process.

Casement's patient was a young woman who had suffered a severe scalding at the age of ten months. At the age of seventeen months, the scar tissue was operated on under local anesthesia. Her mother, who was holding her hand, fainted and could no longer hold the child's hand to comfort her. The surgeon continued the procedure nevertheless. The experience of facing the surgeon alone without the support of her mother was traumatic. In recalling and re-experiencing the terror of this trauma, the patient begged Casement to hold her hand so that she could tolerate the anxiety. She further threatened that if he did not comply, she would leave the analysis. Casement judiciously explained that many analysts would not permit such a thing, but that he also appreciated that her need was so great that holding his hand might be the only way to tolerate the reliving experience. He said he would think about it and let her know after the intervening weekend.

The rationalization for holding the patient's hand would look to a corrective experience—the reliving of the trauma, this time with the support of the protecting mother-figure. Realizing that he was excessively influenced by fear of losing the patient, Casement decided not to hold the patient's hand, feeling that it would not have helped her that much; no doubt Ferenczi would have acceded to the request with little hesitation. Hoffer (1991) summarizes the dilemma: "Does the analyst, by acceding to the demand, provide a corrective emotional experience which then *precludes* a genuine resolution of the affects originating in the traumatic event? Or, by not acceding to the expressed need, does the analyst anti-therapeutically *re-traumatize* the patient?" (pp. 469–470). Fox (1984) comments: "The principle of abstinence must be viewed in terms of the management of the clinical situation in order to create the conditions for the development of an interpretable transference. In this case, too great a frustration (or absence) seemed to precipitate a delusional transference. Optimal frustration-distance, however, enabled the transference illusion of the mother who failed to emerge and to be worked through" (pp. 231–232). And further: "In his [Casement's] carefully articulated description, he shows the critical need for an optimal presence-absence in a patient who was struggling to maintain an analysable relationship with him. He demonstrated how he was able to substitute an ongoing empathic attitude for her request for physical contact so that she was able to work through a critical separation in her early development. As is perhaps most clear in this case, a degree of gratification is necessary to maintain an analytic presence. Some of the recent work of Kohut and his followers may be viewed in the light of this reformulation of the principle of abstinence" (p. 234).

Hoffer (1991) supports Fox's (1984) view that abstinence guides management of dimensions of frustration-gratification and isolation-involvement in the analytic situation. He adds a further consideration: "In my view, the crucial point is that the analyst be free to 'consider such a possibility,' and be willing to do the active work of re-thinking the technical 'principles' in each clinical situation. The analyst must tolerate the tension and the 'essential ambiguity' (Adler 1989) of the analytic situation in order to maintain the genuineness of the analytic relationship. Rigid adherence to any 'absolute rule' of treatment can remove the immediacy required for a genuine analytic relationship. Analysands will deal with questions and the associated feelings and fantasies in an 'as-if' way if they know the analyst's thinking is foreclosed by strict adherence to any preformed doctrine" (p. 470). We need to remind ourselves that the options cover a considerable ground. As for handholding, Margaret Little (1990) reported that in her analysis with Winnicott, he had apparently held her hands for a good many hours while she struggled on the couch with her near-psychotic anxieties.

At this point I should like to review Casement's experience in terms of the tension between alliance and real relation. There are a number of indications in the case material that Casement was dealing with a patient whose personality structure was pitched at a more or less borderline level. The intense vulnerability to regression, the tendency to act out tensions, the relative intolerance of anxiety or other dysphoric affects, the relatively poor capacity for delay of gratification, the tendency to relate to significant objects on a need-satisfying basis, and the poor capacity to maintain discrimination between fantasy and reality indicate relatively poor structure and are consistent with a diagnosis of primitive character disorder (Meissner 1984a). This is part of the context for the dilemma posed by the patient's acute need.

In terms of the tension between reality and alliance, the patient is seeking relief of intolerable anxiety by appealing for a disruption of the alliance. Casement had to make a judgment—what need was primary in the patient in terms of the facilitation of the analysis: the infantile need for physical contact and support experienced in the intensity of reliving uppermost, or the kind of support that would help her tolerate affects and work them through? Was the first a necessary prologue to the second—in other terms, was the introduction of a real element necessary to preserve or re-establish the alliance? Casement's decision not to participate collusively in the enactment brought the maternal transference into full bloom, while his concern and forbearance enabled his patient to bear the terror and feel understood and supported (Roughton 1993).

Casement's resolution of the difficulty was admirable, but why? Was it because he at least offered the possibility of real gratification? Would the real gratification have served this purpose better—as Ferenczi might argue? Would the experience have been corrective? I would argue that the essential element was his restitution of the alliance in the face of the patient's transference demand. The elements contributing to this resolution were his empathy with the patient's need and terror, his understanding of their traumatic roots, his avoidance of a rigid or authoritarian stance, his willingness to leave the question open to consideration (whether to gratify the patient's wish or not), and his openness to discuss the dilemma with her. These are all stances that I would regard as aspects of therapeutic alliance. One might view the dynamics of the situation in terms of the patient's feeling victimized and vulnerable in the analytic situation and her attempt to turn the analytic tables, victimizing the analyst by virtue of her demand that he abandon his analytic stance and accede to her wishes. Casement found a way to avoid the Scylla of gratification and violation of analytic boundaries and the Charybdis of unempathic distance. These tensions can only be resolved, I would contend, within the therapeutic alliance, which supports the patient's more mature capacities to tolerate anxiety and work through the traumatic experience in an analytically useful way. The analytic situation offers ample gratification and support to the patient without violation of physical boundaries. But these supportive elements, in some degree required for all patients, are dependent on the therapeutic alliance. The analyst's willingness to consider options and discuss them openly and nondefensively with the patient are also integral parts of the alliance-based interaction.

In this sense, intrusion of reality factors in the analytic process are substantially a form of resistance that challenges and erodes the alliance, and their correction lies in the reconstitution and confirmation of the alliance. Even so, at times analysts appeal to the introduction of reality as a means of confirming or re-establishing the alliance. Fields (1985), for example, cites the case of a man who resisted his transference interpretations and demanded that Fields advise him about what to do about his wife's suspected infidelity. Fields' effort to explain his reasons for not gratifying the patient's wish went nowhere. In the face of this impasse, Fields decided to offer advice in order to regain the alliance. Rather than seeing this approach as building the alliance, I would see it as undermining it. Over and above the patient's potentially paranoid outlook, a cautious analyst would have to consider the possibility of a transferential trap in which he could be held accountable for any unfortunate consequences of his advice. Giving advice crosses the boundary between alliance and reality and undermines the alliance. In contrast, an approach through the alliance would have some empathy for the patient's anxiety and find a way to explore the patient's wish for advice and the potential consequences of gratifying or denying the wish.

But from another perspective, this conclusion may not be quite so compelling. Here the distinction between reality and alliance plays a significant role. The analyst's intervention lies not in the path of absolute abstinence and interpretation in such cases, and by approaching the patient in terms of the alliance, the involvement and presence of the analyst is cast in nontransferential terms. The analyst's presence in the interaction is not in these terms reality-based, but alliance-based. The alliance demands some degree of personal involvement in the analytic relation, but the give-and-take is cast within the framework of the consistent and firm boundaries of the therapeutic alliance. Any principle of genuine abstinence and analytic neutrality must consider the essential role of the alliance in all analytic work. When the foundation of the analytic process in the alliance is not possible or becomes so distorted that it is beyond redemption, analytic work is no longer possible. I would endorse Blum's (1981) comment that "analytic change does not depend on either a transference cure or a cure through the 'real' relationship, though noninterpretive elements may be therapeutically beneficial and also promote development. Many different ingredients in the analytic situation operate synergistically in reducing resistance, undoing fixation, promoting insight. Neither a diatrophic attitude nor a positive countertransference are regarded as technically advantageous to Freud's recommendations of neutrality and 'sympathetic understanding' " (p. 66).

CHAPTER SIX

Reality and the Analytic Situation: Personal Factors

In previous chapters, my focus was on exploration of the role of reality in the analytic relationship, specifically factors intrinsic to the relation and personalities of the participants. The interplay of such factors with transference, countertransference, and therapeutic alliance is impressive, but these personal and interpersonal elements of the analytic relation do not exhaust reality-based influences on the course and intricacies of the analytic process.[1] A multiplicity of real events and influences come to bear on the analytic process, often with decisive impact, affecting both transference and therapeutic alliance and operating quite independently of personal factors stemming from either participant.

Some reality-based issues, although closely involved in the personal lives of either patient or analyst—for example, payment of fee, illness, or pregnancy—are separate from the personal qualities or personality of individuals affected. Other aspects, including maintaining the analytic schedule and setting (where therapy is done), might also have relevance to the analytic framework and therapeutic boundaries. My selection, therefore, in this chapter will be relatively arbitrary and certainly not complete; I shall refer to relevant literature for more detailed exposition. My purpose is to develop a sense of the degree to which such extrinsic reality factors intersect with transference dynamics and play a vital role in the development and course of therapeutic alliance in any analytic process.

Realities of time, place, and circumstance pervade the analytic situation: the location of the analyst's office, physical surroundings, furniture and decorations in the room, and even how the analyst dresses. Surrounding circumstances modify the framework for the analytic effort: the patient's financial situation, job demands, arrangements for payment of fee, whether the patient has insurance and what kind, what pressures are pushing the patient into treatment. All these reality factors are extrinsic to the analysis, but they significantly influence the analytic relation and how it is established and maintained.

Reality also exercises influences through external circumstances and events impinging on the experience of both patient and analyst, separately or in tandem. I want to consider first factors affecting the person of the participants, and then accidental factors impinging on the situation. External factors coming to bear directly on analyst or patient include death (obviously actual death of either party terminates the therapeutic process, but also the threatened death of either participant has an impact), illness, pregnancy, and the aging process. I would classify as accidental external factors time, space, use of medications, monetary considerations, insurance negotiations, economic or political conditions, and cultural differences. I do not regard these factors as countertransference issues, although they may trigger transference or countertransference reactions. Pregnancy, for example, in either analyst or patient, may stimulate important transference or countertransference expressions, but pregnancy is not part of either—it is a real fact influencing the analytic process. I would hold to this distinction in line with my overall effort to discriminate between factors related to transference and those related to reality.[2]

Reality Factors Directly Affecting the Participants

The following categories represent ways in which reality can provoke a variety of transference and countertransference reactions and interactions. The analyst must be alert to these influences and deal with them in therapeutically appropriate ways. The guiding norm remains the therapeutic alliance—the closer the therapist remains to the terms of the alliance, the more he can be sure of moving in the right direction. I am not concerned here with developing transference and countertransference implications connected with these phenomena, since that has been done quite effectively by others. My focus is on explicating some implications of these occurrences for the alliance and on clarifying the division of such realistic factors from the therapeutic alliance.

Death

Death is a stark reality faced by every human being. Although, as Freud (1915b) pointed out, "Our unconscious, then, does not believe in its own death, it behaves as if it were immortal" (p. 296), it is a reality faced by analysts and patients alike. It is somewhat paradoxical, as Mayer (1994) notes, that "the idea that an ongoing *psychoanalytic* process is possible and productive as patients face death is treated skeptically by most authors—though often with the explicit disclaimer that it may be the analyst rather than the patient who finds such work too difficult to undertake" (p. 3). My concern in this section is the effect of the occurrence of death or the imminence of certain death of either analyst or patient on the analytic process and in particular on therapeutic alliance. The effects of serious or even life-threatening illness will be considered in the following section.

First, death of the analyst. Termination of the analyst automatically terminates the relation, and the patient is left to mourn the loss. Data collected by Lord et al. (1978) indicate that the expected mourning response to such loss is normal for some patients, pathological for others. Early life experiences of loss and deprivation increase the likelihood of pathological mourning. Also, the mourning reaction seemed more severe in older patients.

I have had several experiences of dealing with the death of a colleague, one the unexpected demise of a supervisor. Shortly after the obsequies, I was called by two of the abandoned patients—both psychotherapy patients who had been in treatment for years. The problem was the same for both—a depressive reaction and a frustrated mourning process. They both did some relatively effective crisis therapy which mobilized their capacity to mourn, largely by way of unveiling their negative feelings toward the dead analyst for dying and leaving them in the lurch. A second experience came in the wake of the anticipated death of another senior colleague from cancer, a situation he had discussed with his patients. After the therapy was appropriately terminated, the patient was referred to me. Our therapy began with the consequences of his therapist's death and the issues of unresolved mourning associated with it, a dynamic that revitalized aspects of the death of the patient's father. As the work progressed and deepened, we reached a decision to pursue analysis.

Experiences of this sort bring home the impact of the therapist's death—realized or imminent—on the analytic process.[3] When the analyst is facing certain death, does he have an obligation to inform his patients? Some would answer yes (Cohen 1983), but from the perspective of alliance the issue may be more complex. Others have argued that discussion of the analyst's impending death may be harmful (Abend 1982). On one hand, the patient has every right to be forewarned of a potential separation and loss that may be painful if not devastating. This right has to be balanced against difficulties involved in the degree of self-revelation inherent in communicating the fact.

The pain of facing, accepting, planning, and preparing for one's own death can be overwhelming[4] and can deter a therapist from dealing with this difficult reality. The difficulties in dealing with death are universal in the healing professions and medicine. No one is comfortable in dealing with the termination of one's own existence. Denial plays its part. Residues of narcissistic invulnerability and illusions of immortality are shattered, particularly when the threat of death is imminent and inevitable. Loss of the capacity to function and fears of isolation and abandonment play their part in therapists as in all human beings. With all these factors operating, it may require courage for a therapist to inform his patient that he is going to die. The technical problem has to do with how much to tell the patient, how, and when. These are matters of individual judgment that have to be based on the capacity of the patient to deal with them and the overall therapeutic situation.

The alliance plays a central role, in that the more secure the alliance, the better both therapist and patient will be able to work it through. The imminence of the analyst's death can provoke significant and effective work in therapy. Not only is there time pressure, but the therapist and patient are working on an issue that confronts or will confront them both—the inevitability of death and its meaning. In this context, issues of self-revelation fade into the background but not completely. The important information for the patient is the fact of death, the arrangements to be made around it, and the need to deal with issues of loss, separation, abandonment, and the limitations of existence. The therapist must still persevere in the work of the therapy and attend to problems of the therapeutic alliance, transference, and his own countertransference. A collusion of patient and therapist to avoid or circumvent the issue would constitute a misalliance based on transference/countertransference influences.[5]

The issues would be somewhat similar in the case of therapy with patients facing imminent death,[6] which brings to bear specific and powerful issues. The dying patient tends to experience anger and depression as part of anticipatory grief or mourning (Kübler-Ross 1969), along with fear of the unknown, of loneliness and abandonment (Rochlin 1965), of loss of bodily functions and control, of loss of identity and self-cohesion (Pattison 1967; Tasman 1982). The therapeutic task is to help the patient deal with issues of loss and fears of abandonment (Schwartz and Karasu 1977) and to work through whatever narcissistic traumata are involved in the prospect of death. Mourning work with dying patients requires not only mourning loss of the world and attachments to it, but mourning loss of one's own body and self. This latter loss is a narcissistic trauma that the dying person struggles to accept as reality, a trauma diametrically opposed to the unconscious conviction of immortality (Hägglund 1981). Weakening of the body and increasing pain intensify the fear of death expressed as fear of separation and annihilation.

In terms of the alliance, the patient needs the therapist's empathic understanding and acceptance, especially with reference to the infantile rage and regressive vicissitudes they have to face and endure together; he needs the therapist's assurance that he will continue to be there for him as a sustaining object for his dependency needs. Unlike ordinary therapy, where the objective is to resolve such needs in the interest of greater autonomy and maturity, the dying patient will often need continuing support. The effort to maintain a therapeutic focus can be readily sidelined by painful and threatening aspects of death for therapist and patient. Both are mortal, and for both the patient's struggle with his imminent demise stirs difficult and troublesome feelings and conflicts. They may resort to various forms of collusion to avoid dealing with these painful issues, but these forms of misalliance serve neither the therapeutic process nor the best interests of the patient. If the patient senses the analyst's discomfort or anxiety, his conscious fears of death are likely to recede into the background (Schwartz and Karasu 1977).

Elements of alliance come into play with particular poignancy. Empathic acceptance holds primary place, along with the capacity to share the dying person's experience, fears, and doubts. The sense of connection and shared empathy counters primitive fears of abandonment and aloneness. The problem for the therapist is that confrontation with death stirs his own sense of helplessness and vulnerability (Dahlberg 1980). Again, I would not regard these fears as forms of countertransference, as they do not derive from the therapist's relation with earlier objects, nor are they specifically reactions to transference dynamics of the patient. They are fears experienced by all human beings, based on a fundamental and universally feared reality (Zilboorg 1943). However, at times the underlying fear of death may give rise to countertransference enactments that foster collusive avoidances and mutually reinforcing defenses in both patient and analyst (Lacocque and Loeb 1988). The pressures to abandon neutrality and assume the role of benign, helpful, and protective parent can erode the therapeutic alliance and produce a counterproductive misalliance (Inderbitzin and Levy 1994). The analyst owes it to the patient to exercise his capacities and skills to preserve the alliance intact and correct misalliances when they occur. This requires that the analyst achieve some degree of mastery of his own anxieties and conflicts with regard to death. In the face of these fundamental fears and anxieties, the therapeutic task and contract remain in effect, now with somewhat different purposes and meaning. Strengthening of the alliance facilitates this process, and confirming and stabilizing it are essential to helping the patient come to his end with resignation and integration of the fact of death as an inherent part in his life trajectory.

Although the impact is of a quite different order and quality than in the death of the analyst or patient, death of a loved one can create reverberations for the analytic process. A depressive reaction to such a loss is frequently the precipitating event bringing the patient to therapy. The loss and consequent mourning, whether successful or unsuccessful, tends to set the agenda for the analytic work.[7] Deaths of significant political or popular figures may also have an influence; Fairbairn (1936) recorded the effect of the death of King George V on some of his patients, and many will readily recall the effects of the Kennedy or King assassinations.

This is familiar analytic ground, overshadowed by dynamics described so effectively by Freud in "Mourning and Melancholia" (1917). Matters become a bit more complex when the loss is suffered by the analyst. Death can deprive him of the sources of love and support that are essential for his adaptation to life and its demands. Loss of a spouse, a child, or a dear friend can wreak havoc with the analyst's emotional life. The first problem is what and how much to tell the patient. Usually, death of a loved one means interruption of the analysis.[8] How much information will rationalize the interruption and avoid excessive self-revelation? The decision must be made in light of the nature of the relation with the patient, the status of the alliance, the quality of the patient's transference, with awareness of potential countertransference implications, and with the intent to do as little harm to the analytic process as possible. Moreover, the interruption is rarely one that can be anticipated. Death comes quickly and disruptively. The patient is informed on short notice—making the interruption potentially more traumatic than otherwise. When faced with this situation, I have informed the patient immediately and left the message that I have had to interrupt our work because of an unexpected death in the family, that I plan to be back within a few days, and that I shall call when I return.

When analytic work resumes, several issues come to the fore. The alliance requires a degree of emotional availability and attunement difficult to maintain in the face of one's own loss and bereavement. If the work of mourning brings with it an excessive degree of self-absorption, distraction, inability to tolerate the affective currents swirling around the analytic couch, or a significantly impaired capacity to concentrate and listen attentively to the patient's productions, the analyst is falling short of the agreement inherent in the alliance. He may have to face a choice between continuing analytic work, or interrupting the analysis until he is better able to bring to it the proper mind-set and emotional balance. The former brings with it distortion of the alliance and impediments to effective analytic work; the latter imposes the burden of further separation and postponement of the analytic process. Both operate to the detriment of the patient and depart from the ground of alliance.

In addition, the fact of the analyst's loss and the interruption have implications for the analytic process. The patient may be resentful of the interruption, angry at the abandonment, sadistically gratified at the analyst's misfortune, or commiserate and empathize with the analyst's loss and mourning. The former reactions and feelings are usually masked, requiring the analyst to be attuned to their harmonics and to focus them effectively. Countertransference needs, as well as unconscious conflictual aspects of the analyst's own mourning process, can impede dealing with such issues. The latter responses may channel sincere feelings of the patient but may also mask more hostile feelings or deter the patient from dealing with painful issues out of excess concern for the analyst's vulnerability. Transference/countertransference combinations can easily arise out of these patterns and undermine the alliance.

Illness

Short of the extreme situation of terminal illness for either party, illness and injury are recurrent afflictions that no one can escape. Few analysts have not had to deal with the issue of illness, either their own or the patient's. The reverberations of an illness for the analytic process are a function of the severity and duration of the illness and whether or not the illness is recurrent (Panel 1993b).[9] Such episodes can become the vehicle for enactment of variations on sadomasochistic themes. Illness in either participant can intensify the sense of vulnerability and victimization and play into underlying pathogenic introjective configurations. This reaction in the therapist can precipitate countertransference reactions of guilt, inadequacy, helplessness, shame, or other regressive patterns interacting with the patient's pathological needs (Abend 1982; Clark 1995; Dewald 1982; Kriechman 1984; Schwartz 1987; van Dam 1987). The literature is illustrative of transference and countertransference issues attending illness, but my focus here, given motivational and transferential variants, falls on what are the implications and consequences of illness for the therapeutic alliance?

The first issue is whether interruption of the analysis because of illness constitutes a breach of the alliance. There is the illusion of immunity from untoward interference: "The nature of the therapeutic liaison—with its emphasis on constancy, commitment and expectations for the future—generates in both therapist and patient alike a fantasy of a therapist invulnerable to unexpected catastrophes. Both sides assume that the therapeutic dyad will continue unabated for the good and improvement of the patient until the controlled completion of the treatment" (Durban et al. 1993, p. 705). These authors then observe that "the therapist's illness is experienced by both him and his patient as a breach of contract" (p. 705). Despite the experience of interruption, I would argue that it is not a breach of contract and, therefore, not a violation of the terms of the alliance. For the analyst to be available to continue his work with the patient even if ill or incapacitated would be completely unreasonable and therefore no alliance at all. Rather, the alliance offers a guarantee of the analyst's constancy and presence within reasonable limits; not only will he not be available when he is sick or has suffered an injury, but he might not be available when he goes to a convention or takes a vacation. Legitimate absences and interruptions are part of the understanding of alliance for both parties.[10] As Durban et al. (1993) assert, threat of illness disturbs the therapeutic relation and process: "A number of components are regarded as necessary, even essential, for therapeutic observation and change. Among these are regularity of time, place and presence, and the activity of the therapist as an observing partner. The therapist serves as a kind of background, envelope and container for everything that the patient deems fit to raise during his sessions. A threat to these basic functions from illness may impinge upon the essence of the therapeutic process. The bodily menace makes the background salient and the therapist's possible absence a real and disturbing presence" (p. 707). In my view, alliance provides the essentials of constancy, regularity, and containment, but not with some fantasied absolute guarantee. An effective and well-founded alliance enables both analyst and patient to contain anxieties connected with illness and therapeutic work to continue within limits determined by the analyst's or the patient's illness. The threat of the illness and the menace of the analyst's potential absence, then, would be matters for analytic exploration and understanding. In a sense in all therapeutic situations, the container is always "cracked."

The literature on illness or injury of the analyst is sparse, probably for reasons related to transgression of some analytic ideal or from shame connected with regressive aspects of the illness (Abend 1982; Schwartz 1987). Among the few early accounts there was the Wolf Man's reaction to Freud's advancing cancer (Brunswick 1928), but little else.[11] The ice was broken by Dewald's (1982) courageous recounting of his experience of severe illness and the effects it had on his analytic work, particularly the role of denial and the regressive dimensions of his experience and how they affected his dealings with his patients. Abend's (1982) account of his illness endorsed many of Dewald's findings. A question preoccupying both accounts, as in most attempts to deal with this problem (Lasky 1992), is what and how to tell the patient.[12] As Dewald observes, the more real information given the patient, the more contaminated subsequent transference distortions will be. For the analyst, illness introduces uncertainty about boundaries between personal and professional roles, and for patients blurring of the line between fantasy and reality (Schwartz 1987). Abend makes a central point that any aspect of reality in the analytic relation is intertwined with and contaminated by transference, even affecting the analyst's ability to make reasonable judgments in the matter.[13] He takes a firm position that "optimal analytic technique is more likely to suffer from an analyst's explicit focus, in conjunction with the analysand, on the reality relationship than it will by the analyst's insistence on attending to its unconscious meanings instead" (p. 367). But the vacuum of information together with lack of opportunity to explore transference implications may overly burden vulnerable patients. However, as Dewald (1982) notes, "To give extensive factual information may unnecessarily allay anxiety and the occurrence of transference fantasies if the illness turns out to be relatively benign. But to provide detailed factual information may further activate and intensify frightening fantasies if . . . the illness becomes increasingly life-threatening" (pp. 349–350).

I agree with Abend that reality is overlaid, sometimes heavily, with transference derivatives and that analysts should pay attention to these unconscious derivatives. But analysts ought not overlook the impact of the reality itself and its meaning, independent of transferential responses. Abend acknowledges the reality but urges that it should never be considered without its unconscious connections. I would flip the coin: psychic reality of both analyst and patient should not be the exclusive object of analytic reflection without attending to the reality giving rise to it. The bottom line is that countertransference pitfalls lie underfoot on both sides of this path (Schwartz 1987). For this reason, consultation with an experienced and uninvolved colleague should be encouraged (Clark 1995).

The question of what to tell patients can be resolved only individually, taking into account the nature of the patient's pathology, the available resources that would provide support for the patient and enable him to deal with the crisis of loss and separation—and, in the case of a severe life-threatening illness, of the fear of death—as well as the status of transference and alliance. Alliance provides some operative guidelines as to how the analyst deals with the onset of serious illness and what he decides to communicate to his patients. The patient has a right to pertinent information since the analyst's illness forces him to transgress the terms of the alliance: the therapy time and scheduling he is responsible for providing is being violated. But too much information bridges interpersonal barriers safeguarding the unique psychic space the therapist is committed to preserving. Countertransference traps loom in saying too much or too little. The analyst makes his decision with respect to whatever he judges to be in the interest of supporting the alliance and minimally disturbing the therapeutic frame.[14] Moreover, the illness may well present a personal crisis in the therapist's life, and he has every right to protect the integrity and privacy of his personal life, regardless of the patient's personal desires or needs.

Additional problems may arise after the crisis is over and the analyst returns to work. He may resume his usual pattern of work, but in the course of his illness his sense of narcissistic invulnerability, personal integrity, and even competence may have been eroded; also, the struggle with reactivated regressive needs may have not been fully resolved (Schwartz 1987). Guilt over interrupting the treatment and uncertainty about effects of the illness on analytic competence may cause him to resume work prematurely or may affect his narcissistic and superego equilibrium after returning (Clark 1995; Lasky 1990a, 1990b, 1992; Schwartz 1987; Schwartz and Schlessing-Silver 1990). As Lasky (1992) notes, these regressive countertransference features are seen most clearly in therapists who may be dying or have permanent impairments but continue to practice.[15] This can provide a way of dealing with depressive aspects of their condition by maintaining self-esteem and denying implications of the reality. The idealized exemplar of Freud continuing to work courageously in the face of the pain and torment of his advancing cancer (Schur 1972) is less than corrective of this dynamic.[16] There is also an ego-ideal model of carrying on regardless of pain or personal cost.[17] As Durban et al. (1993) put it, "A therapist whose body is 'wounded' will be seen, both consciously and unconsciously, as deficient in his healing capacities. Winnicott (1962) describes how the patient needs the healer as a kind of 'ideal version' of himself and projects all health on to the therapist in order to become healthy. An unwritten and unconscious pact between them establishes this idealisation, in the service of effective therapy, and the ethical code of the profession even protects the patient against this pact being abused in any way" (pp. 706–707). I question the latter aspect of this statement, since clearly the unconscious idealizing "pact" has nothing to do with therapeutic alliance.

An additional factor is loss of income suffered by the analyst as a result of his illness (Dewald 1982; Lasky 1990a) and conversely how to address the issue of payment with patients who might be in arrears. Financial need and the push to defend against neurotic fears of being displaced, losing patients, and assuring oneself that one's skills and personal capacity (related to castrative components of the illness) are intact and may pressure the analyst into resuming work before he is really ready for it. Guilt for abandoning patients may also take its toll.

Upon return to practice, the encounter with patients and their transferences and feelings brings further problems (Little 1967). Fantasies, factual distortions, misconceptions, and exaggerations abound. Much may be determined by the patient's previous experience with his own illness or that of important figures in his life (Schwartz 1987). And reality has a way of intruding, as residual disability or other signs of weakness after illness. Dewald was forced to wear an eye patch for some residual effects of his disease, a fact that stimulated a variety of transference fantasies. Feelings of resentment, anger, depression, and disillusionment are usually connected with separation and the sense of abandonment. The analyst may experience exhibitionistic or masochistic fantasies related to his pain and suffering, or a sense of narcissistic entitlement and wishes for compensation for his ordeal. The patient's resistance to discussing feelings about the illness and interruption can trigger countertransference responses having to do with the analyst's wish to have been missed, to feel important to the patient, or to seek other subtle gratifications, or, in contrast, to experience guilt for abandoning the patient, doubts about his capacity to function effectively, or difficulties tolerating the patient's anger and resentment (Lasky 1992; Silver 1982). Almost any information given to the patient may serve as a vehicle for subtle countertransference elements. Such covert and hidden messages may avert the patient's anticipated anger and elicit concern and sympathy, invite patients to worry or offer reassurance, all functions that would be far from our conscious intentions (Abend 1982).

Working through these reactions and feelings on both sides may take a long time. Fantasies of recurrence of the illness and anniversary reactions may occur. As Dewald (1982) commented: "The major technical issue is the question of how extensively can and should the patient be encouraged or helped to describe and deal with the multiple conscious and unconscious reactions to the analyst's illness, both during the time of the separation and when the analysis is being resumed. The meanings which the analyst's illness has vary widely from patient to patient. They depend simultaneously on transferences from earlier life experiences and fantasies, the duration and progress of the analysis prior to the illness, the nature of the patient's neurotic disturbances, previous transference fantasies which may be confirmed or contradicted by the occurrence of illness in the analyst, as well as the nontransference components of the patient-analyst relationship, and how much factual information the patient had about the illness" (p. 355). The analyst in this difficult situation is caught between too little information and too much, between demands of reality and distortions of transference, between the perils of self-revelation and impersonal distancing from the patient. Wherein lies the course of true neutrality? How to find one's way among these multiple countertransference traps? The analyst cannot allow himself to be deterred from exploring the patient's feelings and fantasies about his illness, regardless of his own inner fears, conflicts, and anxieties.

The fact of physical illness can stir unconscious residues and fantasies in the patient regarding the meaning of sickness and the patient role, usually centering around themes of castration and narcissistic vulnerability (Brodsky 1959; Halpert 1989). But regressive fantasies can be stimulated in the analyst as well (Frayn 1987), reflecting interplay between the patient's latent transference fantasies and the analyst's corresponding countertransference fantasies.

From the point of view of the alliance, the patient's illness should not except him or the analyst from the therapeutic frame. Decisions as to how to manage scheduling around the illness should be regarded within the context of the alliance. This has to do with the question of charging for missed appointments—a subject I shall consider in greater depth in chapter 9. I do charge for missed appointments, even those occasioned by illness. For minor illnesses or interruptions of a day or two for colds or flu, this does not present much of a problem. If the patient informs me of his absence, I have the option of filling the hour and, if I do, the patient is not charged. Sudden illnesses requiring longer absence or hospitalization, e.g., acute appendicitis, I charge for missed appointments, but when the patient notifies me that his recuperation will involve missing further appointments I again can take the opportunity of filling the time. In the case of serious, long-term illnesses that involve lengthy interruption of the analysis, I agree with the patient not to charge for missed time, but also not to hold the time open for the patient. When he has recovered and is ready to resume analysis, we renegotiate a new schedule. However one comes to such arrangements, whatever is consistent with the alliance and supportive of it will be therapeutically reasonable. The pattern I have chosen has the advantages of preserving the patient's autonomy and freedom as well as continuing his responsibility for the therapeutic process insofar as decisions regarding when to return to treatment are left in his hands. The added advantage, often more important than anything else, is that it tends to avoid a variety of countertransference traps.

Aging

The effects of aging are another of those inexorable realities that play upon the analytic situation and process. The basic contribution to this topic was made by Eissler (1975),[18] who focused on effects of aging on the analyst and effects of aging of the analyst on the patient. The elderly analyst creates quite a different aura in the office than a younger person. The reverberations affect many aspects of the situation, including posture, level of activity, vigor, appearance, decor, handshake, sound of the voice, and so on. These factors can affect the patient's unconscious in ways that may facilitate or impede the analytic process. There are also internal changes associated with the aging process—changes in superego and ego-ideal (usually softened and less rigorous), or even tendencies to rigidity, authoritarian attitudes, compulsivity, or depression. Tolerance for the unceasing demands of the therapeutic situation may suffer. Modifications in narcissistic equilibrium and vulnerability may have their effect. The analyst may feel less bound by ordinary norms of practice and technique, or more willing to explore technical innovations. These can reflect advances in maturity and self-confidence, or may become the playground for narcissistic needs to feel special, different, or even omnipotent. Anxieties about competition with younger colleagues and fears of eroding capacities (memory, for example) or fear of failure may increase and create difficulties.

The analyst may be less able to empathize with younger patients in the face of changing values, societal expectations and mores, patterns of behavior and dress, and other aspects of the generation gap (Rangell 1981). This may be compounded by underlying envy of youth and the promise and potential belonging to the young and not the old. Yet aging has its advantages as well as disadvantages. Eissler noted that increased tolerance for the patient's pathology and less compulsion to cure, may develop and paradoxically offer a degree of relief to the pressured patient. Exposure of the patient's deeper vulnerability may result in defensive counterattacks against the analyst—paranoid acting out meant to protect the open wound—and the older analyst may be in a better position than in his younger days to respond positively to this reaction, owing to the increase in tolerance and decrease in therapeutic ambition.

Walking hand in hand with advancing age is fear of death (Roth 1978). If the analyst has not resolved his conflicts about death, aging will not relieve him of these burdens. To that extent, his ability to help his patients deal with death will be compromised. This may become a pressing problem and stir transference anxieties and painful countertransference reactions around the issues of death and illness described above. The patient is more likely to develop anxieties around the issue of the therapist's death with an older analyst, a preoccupation that the vulnerable analyst will find difficult to tolerate. If the aging analyst has worked through and resolved these fears, he is better able to engage the patient's fears therapeutically. Eissler warned against a danger, even in this arena, of a nondefensive and stoical attitude to death that the patient may come to regard as idealized and heroic, to the detriment of his own sense of worth and possibly contributing to guilt. The stoic façade may mask hidden unresolved conflicts in the analyst's unconscious that may contain residues of counterphobic defense. The patient's transference reaction can provide a useful signal for the analyst.

Therapeutic alliance with elderly or aging patients is no different than with any other patient. The same configuration of constituents that attend any alliance—therapeutic frame, contractual components, responsibilities, honesty and integrity—are relevant. However, adherence to the alliance on the part of the aging analyst may require an honest confrontation with issues of physical impairment that may accompany the aging process, diminishing capacity to carry on analytic or therapeutic work effectively, and related issues concerning possible retirement and the increasing proximity of death.

Views of psychological treatment for elderly patients have changed radically since Freud's (1933) pessimistic opinion that the psychical rigidity associated with aging limited the therapeutic effectiveness of psychoanalysis. In subsequent years, the view has gradually found expression that therapy with patients in advanced age groups was not only possible but potentially quite successful. Beginning in the 1970s, a number of authors (King 1974, 1980; Sandler 1978; Shainess 1979) reported successful psychoanalyses with patients in older age brackets. Even when organic deterioration is found in the clinical picture, there are indications that ego functions may be diminished but not lost permanently (Grunes 1981).

Clinical experience suggests that elderly patients bring certain elements to the therapeutic situation that may promote therapeutic work. Along with a fear of illness that may limit or terminate their lives, they also bring hope that therapy will be able to help. Frequently in contexts of loneliness and isolation, they bring an intense desire for meaningful human contact and attention, which are often translated into regressive transference fantasies (Coltart 1991). Elderly patients often come to treatment because of increasing awareness of changes in their lives and the way in which the aging process affects their physical, psychological, and social well-being. Aging is a threatening prospect, bringing with it fears of fragmentation or disintegration and death. But these fears also bring a sense of dynamic and urgent necessity to their involvement in analytic treatment, a motivation that facilitates establishment and consolidation of an effective therapeutic alliance, thus promoting and abetting the therapeutic work.

Race

The last of these real factors impinging on the person of both analyst and patient is race. Everyone has racial characteristics, readily open to observation and often immediately evident, that identify the individual as a member of a particular racial group. Racial differences inevitably stir racial stereotypes as well as transference and countertransference reactions in both parties, and these differences are often compounded by cultural and subcultural differences (Lambley and Cooper 1975; Schachter and Butts 1968; Zaphiropoulos 1982). One possible impediment to interracial therapy stems from prejudices each party brings to the therapeutic encounter. Black patients, for example, tend to enter therapy with greater fear and distrust (Wohlberg 1975) and characteristically present their life experiences as expressions of racial oppression and only secondarily as personal—the opposite of trends among white patients (Kennedy 1952). While these prejudices may be inherent in patients' respective psychological makeups, they tend to be reinforced by socially derived attitudes reflecting aspects of their respective subcultures (Wohlberg 1975).

It would be easy to rationalize these attitudes as forms of transference and countertransference, but it is not clear to me that they are such, at least not simply so. Transferential responses are products of therapeutic interaction that reflect developmental experiences and are appropriately dealt with in the analytic setting. While racial prejudices of whatever degree may provoke transferential effects (Fischer 1971), these effects would be secondary to primary prejudicial attitudes and feelings, by-products of social conditions and influences pre-dating the therapy. A white therapist might take a devaluing and pejorative view of his black patient without this having countertransference implications. Or he might respond to the patient's paranoid feelings by attributing them to racial oppression. These may be defective or prejudicial attitudes of the therapist, but not in themselves transferential (Griffith 1977). Nonetheless, if a therapist is not able to put himself in a truly empathic position vis-à-vis his patient, he should not try to treat him.

Social prejudices bring with them cynical and distrusting attitudes toward any efforts to engage the patient in a therapeutic alliance (Griffith 1977; Wohlberg 1975). One of the striking aspects of my training experience in a psychiatric facility serving patients of different races was the infrequency and reluctance of black patients to utilize a neighborhood facility staffed with white doctors and mental health professionals. There were black psychiatrists and other professionals on the staff, but the facility had been labeled as "white" and that was enough to deter black patients from turning to it for help. In the therapy framework, different sets of expectations can operate in terms of what treatment and help mean. It was not always clear that what the treaters envisioned as purposeful care and treatment was what the patients had in mind. The resentment and envy of underprivileged black patients found expression in resistance to treatment and attempts to induce guilt in the treaters and to engage them in debates over black-white differences and social injustices rather than more immediate therapeutic issues (Lambley and Cooper 1975). Common features of such interracial analyses were rapid onset of erotic and masochistic transferences, and countertransference-determined tendencies to undercharge, impulses to be overly supportive and sympathetic, denial of differences, and (among Jewish analysts) reacting to anti-Jewish sentiments (Goldberg et al. 1974; Wohlberg 1975).

While these difficulties are introduced into the therapeutic setting by racial differences, racial homogeneity is neither a guarantee of good treatment nor necessary for it. Black therapists can harbor prejudicial attitudes toward black patients, and, black or white, a good therapist needs an awareness of his own racial, social, and socioeconomic prejudices and how they can affect his work with patients of other racial backgrounds. While these differences are more striking in black-white combinations, problems of interracial differences and tensions affect relations between individuals of any national or ethnic origin. Each group carries its own cultural and historical animosities that can find expression in the prejudices of individuals. Because of the paranoid tinge of often embedded prejudicial attitudes, the success of therapy rests on the success with which patient and therapist can find a basis for trust that will allow a meaningful alliance to develop (Meissner 1978, 1986b).

CHAPTER SEVEN

Reality and the Analytic Situation: Gender-Related and Accidental Factors

Gender

The sex of both analyst and patient is part of the reality attending the analytic situation and plays a decisive role in the dynamics of the process (Bibring 1936; Greenacre 1959; Ticho 1972). The sex of both participants is immediately evident—"an actuality that punctures the illusion of anonymity from the first moment" (Appelbaum and Diamond 1993, p. 146)—and may influence the choice of analyst (Goz 1973; Person 1983; Thompson 1938b). Transference, as we have seen, tends to amalgamate with aspects of the reality of the analyst, and age and sex (also race) are among the few real components of the analyst's person the patient knows from the beginning, giving rise to sexual stereotypes and stimulating transference reactions in all patients.[1]

While transference often crosses gender lines—in every analytic process the analyst, whether male or female, becomes the focus of transference derivatives from both parents—the reality of the analyst's sex plays a particular role in determining how these derivatives will align themselves and the role they play in the analysis (Brickman 1993; Kulish and Mayman 1993; Raphling and Chused 1988).[2] As Diamond (1993) puts it, "The consensus is that gender is an organizing force that elicits particular conscious and unconscious fantasies, aids or impedes resistances, and affects the sequences through which psychosexual conflicts emerge and are played out in the overall transference arena" (p. 208).

In their research on this matter, Kulish and Mayman (1993) offered several hypotheses:

1. The patients' transferences as perceived by the judges are more likely to be congruent with the therapists' gender: paternal transferences with male therapists; maternal transferences with female therapists.

2. Male therapists are more likely to see themselves as paternal figures in the transference and female therapists as maternal figures, regardless of the gender of the patient. Discrepancies between the independent raters' and the therapists' perceptions will provide a measure of the distortion introduced by the therapists in their perceptions of the transference themes.
3. However, male therapists also occasionally see themselves as maternal figures, whereas female therapists will rarely see themselves as paternal figures.
4. Different psychosexual themes will characterize the interactions between patient and therapist as a function of the genders of different therapist-patient pairings.
5. The more talented or experienced therapists will be less prone to gender-related misperceptions. (pp. 293–294)

The data supported the hypotheses and led to the conclusions that patients tend to develop initial transferences according to the gender of the therapist, that therapists have a strong bias against seeing themselves in opposite gender roles (more so in females than males), and that therapists may collusively encourage development of gender-consistent transferences. More talented or experienced therapists reported more opposite-gender transferences.

Sexual stereotypes of both forms can play a role—women as sensual, dependent, maternal, nurturant, hysterical, and accommodating, and men as virile, strong, macho, aggressive, predatory, competitive, and phallic—and influence both transference and countertransference (Guttman 1984). Stereotypes are embedded in a cultural matrix reflecting images of the respective sexes reinforced by social forces.[3] These stereotypes have often found reinforcement from theoretical stances—the classical Freudian analysis of feminine psychology may well be prejudicial to women, and is yielding to more balanced and solidly based revision (Guttman 1984; Wittkower and Robertson 1977). The effect of such determinants is reflected in the tendency for a female analyst to elicit from patients and see herself in terms of qualities of maternal caring consistent with feminine gender role, a tendency that might allow for relative loosening of boundaries for both participants, in contrast to the tendency of male analysts to see themselves as more independent of patients' needs and demands, making them seem less involved and emotionally responsive (Mendell 1993).

More recent research has revised some of our thinking about patterning of transference reactions in cross-sex analyses. The stereotype of the hysterical female patient's erotic transference to her male analyst is familiar enough.[4] But the ability of male analysts to work effectively with female patients entails a capacity to empathize with feminine concerns and dynamics and to master the castration anxieties associated with such alignments, especially in dealing with pre-oedipal and prephallic material (Lasky 1989). It has also been thought that male patients did not develop strong erotic feelings toward female analysts, so that paternal transferences are overridden by images of the phallic mother (Kulish 1984, 1986; Lester 1985, 1985–86). Contrary evidence made it clear that the potential for strong erotized transferences toward female analysts was available in some male patients (Goldberger and Evans 1985; Goldberger and Holmes 1993).

Particular difficulties seem to arise for some male analysts in dealing with strong regressive attachment and dependency wishes in some female patients. Regressive maternal transferences tend to be less intense and sustained in male-female dyads than in female-female dyads, possibly reflecting differentiations in gender-related psychology and patterns of development (Lester 1993). This disparity can lead to conflicts over the patient's regressive demands, weakening and even transgressing of boundaries, and a variety of countertransference reactions. Therapeutic relations involving opposite-sex participants have at times given rise to difficulties that constitute clear violations and disruptions of the alliance (Voth 1972).[5] Particular difficulties can arise in situations in which untoward pressure for sexual acting out comes from the patient and the therapist is forced toward violating sexual boundaries. This is often the case in the treatment of borderline patients who are more disturbed and who act out more, in whom the need for sexual gratification and real emotional involvement is peremptory. The patient's rage in response to the therapist's efforts to maintain boundaries, together with his intense neediness and dependency, entitlement, and manipulativeness, coerces the therapist into relaxing boundaries and makes holding to limits difficult. Fear of the patient's rage and rescue fantasies can set the stage for bending rules and becoming overinvolved and overinvested in the patient. Collusion in boundary confusion can lead to intensified and distorted affects, behavioral improprieties, and even affectionate or sexual expression, leaving the therapist vulnerable to litigation and charges of malpractice (Gutheil 1989).

Effects are also detectable in the realm of countertransference (Lester 1985). Differences in gender-role-related countertransference patterns may reflect developmental or cultural influences, but female analysts tend to be more sensitive and empathically nurturant, may collude in fostering dependency needs in male patients, and experience differences in affective countertransference dreams. Such dreams contain more explicit erotic and hostile material with males, while pre-oedipal themes and self-other boundary issues are more common with females (Diamond 1993; Lester et al. 1989). As Mendell (1993) notes, "In dealing with female patients, the female therapist tends to experience a pull toward an early, archaic mother-child interaction, in which fluid boundaries and conflicts revolving around competition, compliance, dependency and separation abound" (p. 284), probably reflecting predominance of maternal identifications. By the same token, a corresponding weakness of paternal identification may have something to do with the paucity of paternal transferences of male patients in relation to female analysts. Fear and avoidance of aggressively sexual or hostile transference expressions from male patients can complicate the therapeutic relation and lead to countertransference difficulties or disruptions of therapeutic alliance.

In contrast to the rich complexity and diversity of transference and countertransference vicissitudes focused around issues of gender in both patient and therapist, the alliance sector operates relatively independently of these factors. In this respect, contrast between the reality of gender and the transference derivatives it evokes and the consistency of the alliance provides a striking justification for the distinction between alliance and reality. Whether the analyst is male or female, and whether the patient is male or female, makes no difference in the nature and characteristics of alliance. The same conditions, requirements, and responsibilities apply. In these terms, then, alliance acts as a stabilizing and containing component of the analytic relation that opens the illusory transitional space, within which transference and countertransference variants can find expression, and provides the framework within which these elements can be explored and understood.

Pregnancy

Analysts occasionally become pregnant, and another unavoidable reality enters the analytic arena. As Appelbaum and Diamond (1993) say so well: "An analyst's pregnancy is a breach of anonymity that cannot be circumvented. Even the most polite and well-trained patient can preserve for only so long the fictive ignorance of the pregnancy or of how it happened. The actuality of what is usually the most private and personal of all realities of the analyst's life—the sexual act—is now forced upon the patient and is there to be contended with in the conversation" (p. 146). Pregnancy raises the familiar questions—does the analyst inform the patient? If so, how? When? And with what consequences for the progress of the analysis and analytic work?

The analyst's pregnancy can become a focus for intensification of transference/countertransference dynamics that may have been soft-pedaled during the course of analysis (Fenster et al. 1986; Lax 1969; Uyehara et al. 1995; Van Niel 1993). Patterns of aggressive and victimizing interaction can be precipitated, stirring powerful currents of envy and destructive hatred in both male and female patients against the therapist for her good fortune and fulfillment and against the fetus, which they may view as depriving the patient of the therapist's care and investment. In such cases, severely pathological, primitive, and destructive feelings and wishes can be mobilized to create a situation of considerable stress and threat for the therapist, even in otherwise well-functioning and even presumably analyzable patients.

Pregnancy can elicit a variety of reactions in patients, including dependency conflicts, fears of loss and abandonment, separation anxiety, envy, jealousy, sexual competitiveness, resentment at exclusion, wishes and fears of pregnancy, anxiety and guilt over death wishes or vengeful feelings toward the fetus and / or analyst, and sibling rivalry (Deben-Mager 1993, and so on ; Bassen 1988; Uyehara et al. 1995). Pregnancy can involve a developmental crisis resulting in a variety of regressive pulls, not the least of which is the "maternal preoccupation" involving feelings of passivity, dependency, and involution (Bibring 1959; Bibring et al. 1961; Notman and Lester 1988; Van Niel 1993). These can become the source of affective reactions impinging on the alliance, even though they might not qualify as countertransference reactions.

The power of these forces is unforgettable for anyone who has been exposed to them. I shall not forget one case in which a female analysand—fortyish, unmarried, unable to establish a meaningful and satisfying relationship with a man, and desperately yearning to be pregnant—harbored envious and narcissistically vulnerable feelings toward her analyst, a slightly younger woman. The analyst's pregnancy unleashed painful, rageful feelings of profound hatred and envy, wishes that the baby would abort or be a monster—an onslaught of such affective intensity that the analyst had great difficulty in tolerating and maintaining perspective on the countertransference feelings it stirred. Toward the end of the pregnancy she miscarried. How much the emotional turmoil connected with the analysis had to do with it remains an open question.

When the analysis resumed, the patient was thrown into an emotional maelstrom of guilt for her envious and destructive wishes, sadistic satisfaction that her revenge against the analyst for daring to replace her with another child had been accomplished (an echo of earlier oedipal disappointments and sibling rivalry), rage at the analyst for interrupting the analysis and frustrating her wishes to have a relationship and family, for emotionally displacing her with the unborn baby and treating her like another patient rather than as her favored (indeed, only) child. Struggling with her own grief and the inevitably difficult countertransference feelings, the analyst struggled heroically to maintain some semblance of an analytic process.

Some of the dust seemed to have settled over the course of several months, when a second round was precipitated by the analyst's second pregnancy. The results were much the same: the patient expressed outrage, intense hatred, and powerful negative transference elements largely based on narcissistic rage at a mother who was unable to respond empathically to her narcissistically wounded daughter in the wake of subsequent pregnancies. Not only was the analyst depriving her of the affective attunement that she felt entitled to, but interruption of the analytic work was frustrating her wishes to get what she wanted out of the analysis—to become pregnant like the analyst. To the patient, the analyst was, in a sense, flaunting her sexuality in the patient's face and rubbing her nose in the hateful fact of her pregnancy. Under these unrelenting pressures, the analysis could not continue, and the patient broke off the process in a rage, declaring that she would make the analyst pay for what she had done to her. She subsequently brought suit against the analyst for malpractice, based largely on the fact of the analyst's pregnancy. Fortunately the suit was finally dropped, but not without a good many anxious moments for the analyst, who did, however, deliver a healthy baby.

The story is not that unusual; Lazar (Panel 1993b) reported on her experiences with seven pregnancies, five ending in miscarriages. While transference/countertransference dynamics were intensified in all cases, resulting in anger, anxiety, and withdrawal, the effect of the miscarriages on patients seemed related to their personal histories of loss and sadness, and proved helpful to some and unbearable to others. Uyehara et al. (1995) also report several cases of premature termination. A common element in premature ruptures of treatment was intensified guilt regarding the miscarriages. Male patients seemed to experience fantasies related to early maternal identifications including womb and pregnancy envy. For both male and female patients, the degree of denial was striking.

But the impact of pregnancy on analysis is not altogether negative. By far the majority of therapists who have been through the experience report that it proved positive for the therapeutic work and facilitated development of transference issues (Bassen 1988; Fenster et al. 1986). Both transference and resistance tend to become intensified, the pregnancy serving as a catalyst to precipitate deeply unconscious and conflictual wishes and needs (Bassen 1988).

Practical details also arise in dealing with pregnancy. The first issue is what to tell patients and when. A second concerns the amount of pregnancy leave to take and when to resume the analysis. In Bassen's (1988) study, those who informed their patients early (before the pregnancy was evident) may have done so on the basis of countertransference feelings and experienced the pregnancy as having a negative effect on the analysis. This approach may have provided patients a convenient defense against unconscious transference reactions and collusion to avoid other meanings of the pregnancy. Countertransference dilemmas are not unlike those in informing patients of illness, but in this instance issues of preserving anonymity are somewhat different and the likelihood of the patient becoming aware of the analyst's condition greater. More analysts than not chose to wait for patients to make their own observations and then work with associations and fantasy material as it developed. At a certain point, the patient's failure to mention the subject may require investigation; denial or avoidance can have important dynamic roots. In general, analysts seemed uncertain in dealing with these issues (Bassen 1988).[6]

From the perspective of the alliance, the analyst has a better chance of responding effectively and avoiding potential countertransference traps by keeping the alliance in view as a guide for decision making and responding to the patient. My experience in supervising analysts dealing with this situation underlines the degree to which the relevant variables are highly individual to both analyst and patient. As far as telling the patient goes, my tendency is to preserve the autonomy and neutrality of the analyst so far as possible. Waiting for the patient to bring the matter up, either directly or indirectly in dream or other displaced material, honors this dimension of the analytic process more than premature revelation. But with certain patients, the analyst may choose to inform the patient of the change in the analytic situation. Such patients may be excessively sensitive to issues of separation, abandonment, or rejection, and extension of this confidence may have beneficial effects. The analyst would have to be relatively certain that this tack did not reflect underlying countertransference determinants—guilt at depriving the patient, imposing a separation, and so on. The timing and manner of informing are best attuned to the status of the transference and the degree to which alliance can be utilized as a firm basis of communication. Different analysts will have different degrees of comfort and stylistic preferences in making these decisions.

Arranging pregnancy leave can be a delicate matter. Because of uncertainties in bringing pregnancy to term, possible postpartum reactions, unforeseeable demands for mothering and care of the newborn, and other indeterminable variables, leaving the duration of the leave open seems preferable. The analyst can arrange to contact the patient when she is ready to resume analytic work. Some analysts will determine a point at which they decide to return to work, others may work back into a regular schedule gradually. The range of time taken for maternity leave is quite variable; Bassen (1988) found the time ranged from eight days to three months, the majority being between one and two months.

These decisions should be made according to the requirements of the mothering situation and the needs of the child rather than any pressures or demands from patients. The analyst has a right to set her own priorities, and the needs of the baby take precedence over needs of patients. I regard this as an objective principle, however, one that can be contaminated by countertransference issues. But this arena reflects issues related to the autonomy and separateness of the analyst, who accepts certain basic responsibilities in her personal life, and these, for a time, outweigh her duty to her patients. The transference and nontransference consequences for whatever decisions the analyst takes in the interest of herself and her baby can and must be dealt with in their proper time and place. The perspective of the alliance, then, offers the ground on which demands of reality can productively be integrated with requirements of the analytic situation.

Regardless of the timing and specific decisions made in this process, engagement of the patient in a mutual exchange and decision-making process is consistent with the alliance and can confirm it, despite regressive needs and transferential contaminants introduced by the pregnancy. In this manner, the patient can feel that he or she is being treated respectfully as a participant in the decision-making process. This more egalitarian approach is more consistent with the alliance than unilateral decisions made without patient participation and imposed in an authoritarian manner. Even setting a date for interrupting, a matter largely up to the analyst in terms of how far along in her pregnancy she is able or willing to work, is better negotiated with respect for the patient's needs and wishes; it will serve the alliance if the patient feels that his needs and wishes have been considered, even if the analyst's preference takes precedence at this juncture. The same principles apply in making arrangements with the pregnant patient. Her priorities may dictate that she interrupt analysis for a significant period in order to go through delivery, postpartum adjustments, and early stages of mothering. The decision as to when to resume analysis should remain entirely in the patient's hands, but negotiating these details takes place in the context of the alliance and contributes to the consolidation of the analytic process.

Accidental Factors

Money

Money is a reality that affects everyone: how we live, what we can buy, where we send our children to school, what kind of house we live in, what kind of car we drive, and so on. It also plays a role in what kind of therapy we can have and on what terms. The subject of money paid for psychoanalysis or psychotherapy is rather complex, but I will postpone a more detailed discussion of problems involved in dealing with it to the consideration of the therapeutic frame (see chapter 9).

For most patients, the money they expend for psychological treatment is not a small matter. Fees for private and/or long-term psychotherapy or psychoanalysis are high and for most patients represent a significant portion of their income. This can stimulate transference and other reactions and provide the basis for significant countertransference responses in therapists. But, as Gutheil (1977) noted, the subject is frequently omitted or neglected in negotiations setting up the therapeutic frame prior to therapy.

With respect to the therapeutic alliance, I regard arrangements for paying the fee as essential to the therapeutic framework and part of the alliance. This requires not only that these financial matters be discussed, but also that agreement regarding the fee and manner of payment should be reached by a process of exploration and decision making in which patient and therapist have an equal say and in which the final fee should be one that the patient can comfortably pay and that the therapist feels is adequately rewarding for his efforts. The process of negotiation is not simply a decision about the fee, but makes a vital contribution to the alliance itself, more by concrete enactment than by any verbal communication, and thus becomes an integral part of the therapeutic frame.

Malpractice

Malpractice litigation or the threat of it can disrupt the therapeutic situation and destroy any hope for continuing alliance. The threat of suit by a patient against a therapist usually comes about as a result of disruption in the alliance and can be symptomatic of a poorly established therapeutic alliance to begin with (Gutheil et al. 1991; Menninger 1989).[7] But we do not know exactly what circumstances lead to threats of litigation, although risk of litigation increases among patients at higher risk for hospitalization, suicide, or physically invasive treatments, e.g., drugs, ECT, psychosurgery (Charles 1993). If the patient implements a suit or even suggests that he is about to do so—e.g., by consulting a lawyer—the alliance no longer exists and therapy is at an end. At that point, the therapist appropriately stops seeing the patient and consults his own lawyer. By the same token, in the face of legal action all the therapist's ordinary responsibilities to the patient in the alliance are abrogated. A basic principle of the alliance is involved: the therapist's right to protect himself and his interest as part of his commitment to his profession and therapeutic work, while maintaining his responsibility to the patient to provide appropriate care and service. If the patient distorts or disrupts the basic agreement on which the alliance is based, the therapist's investments and responsibilities shift accordingly.

The experience of the legal process and the scrutiny it subjects the therapist to (apart from any judgment or settlement) can be devastating and stressful. Studies of this matter have revealed the degree to which depression, premature retirement, divorce, alcoholism, and even suicide can be precipitated by the malpractice ordeal, whether or not the therapist is found to be at fault (Charles et al. 1984, 1985, 1987, 1993; Ferrell and Price 1993).[8] Requirements of informed consent and patient participation are best served by the deliberative model in which the patient is engaged in a dialogue leading to the desirable course of action. This is consistent with a more balanced conception of therapeutic alliance and involves the patient in a greater degree of responsible participation in the therapeutic process.

However, in the current context of predatory litigation, the therapist must also be circumspect about opening himself to malpractice risk. Recommendations that the therapist openly admit his errors and mistakes needs some qualification. Judgment is required as to what errors are admissible and how. When the patient correctly identifies some mistake the therapist made, and it is clearly recognizable as a mistake, then there is little harm and at times significant gain in recognizing it for what it is. The therapist may be wrong about an interpretation or not understand something correctly, and acknowledgment of the error can serve the alliance well. But such matters are not the stuff of malpractice litigation. Other matters may well prove actionable—especially when some harm is suffered by the patient. The usual problems accounting for litigation involve violence by patients, suicide, injuries from negligent treatment, faulty initiation or termination of treatment, and problems arising from employer, supervisory, or consultative relations (Menninger 1989). This may turn out to be the case when therapy ends unsuccessfully, for whatever reason. In such circumstances, the therapist—whatever his concern and care for the well-being of the patient—must tread cautiously and must protect his own interests.

Culture and Politics

The sociocultural and political ambiance in which analysis is practiced can have a significant impact on the analytic process. Not infrequently, for example, patients from a particular ethnic or cultural background may find it necessary to deal with attitudes and feelings about cultural stereotypes and family values and attitudes that may have been devalued and scorned as part of their effort to dissociate themselves from conflictual attachments to immigrant parents (Davidson 1980a, 1980b). Not only is the culture derivative from generational networks a part of the patient's personality that he must integrate with his sense of self as it is discovered and created in the analytic process, but also certain cultural dictates may influence how he undertakes and experiences the analytic process itself.

By the same token, every patient brings his own cultural acquisitions that influence his approach to and expectations of analysis. All patients were raised in a culture from birth and have assimilated its norms, values, and beliefs. And all social groupings are composed of subcultural groupings with their own individuating characteristics and contribute to the sense of identity of their members. Cultural variations in which pre-oedipal issues and oedipal conflicts are shaped and resolved can find expression in transference/countertransference involvements in the analysis.

The same assertions apply to analysts. Analysts who work in or across cultural boundaries are immediately confronted with cultural stereotypes—not unlike those in interracial analyses—which interact with development of transference and can precipitate countertransference reactions (Ticho 1971). When these two bearers of cultural significance come into analytic conjunction, they may prove in some degree congruent but also will predictably encounter subcultural disjunctions. As Kernberg (1993) noted, "In support of the concern over ideological distortions, the avoidance of covert—and overt—political issues, including psychoanalytic politics, may reflect an unconscious collusion between patient and analyst" (pp. 669–670). The transcultural perspective has taught us much about the variety and implications of individual cultural diversity (Devereux 1953).[9]

Analysis and therapy are embedded in a sociocultural matrix within which political and ideological forces often come into violent collision and create a context of social violence (Gampel 1992). Such social violence becomes present in the analysis in powerfully determinative ways in the awareness of both analyst and patient. Should it be ignored or not? Gampel (1992), writing against the backdrop of the Nazi Holocaust, the tensions of the Arab-Israeli conflict in Israel, and the Gulf War, describes the dilemma succinctly: "When terror and social violence exist in the patient's and analyst's environment, should the analyst introduce this external reality into the session if the patient does not make any associations that connect with what is going on outside? Is it an ethical misdemeanor for the analyst to hear what is happening outside more than what is going on within the patient's inner world? Conversely, if the analyst refrains from bringing in the social violence that is taking place in the present, is that an act of participation in the patient's denial?" (p. 534)[10] Not doing so would seem to endorse a view of analysis as concerned only with the inner world and its vicissitudes. Doing so acknowledges that analysis is open to forces of reality stemming from the patient's personal life and from the world he lives in. The analytic task is to encompass and understand both the real impact of external events and their symbolic meaning for the patient, for implications of both may be significant for the patient's understanding of himself and his world.

Training

A rather selective but nonetheless significant reality-based context of analysis is training, either as a candidate in a psychoanalytic institute or in a training program in psychoanalytic psychotherapy. The training situation introduces a wealth of factors impinging on the analytic situation and can readily induce transference/countertransference interactions. The situation, in which analysis is conducted by a training analyst with a candidate or analyst-in-training as analysand, sets the stage for conflicts with authority or some sense that the institute—through its students committee, education committee, or committee of training analysts—is checking up on the candidate's performance and progress; this can lead to transferential distortions of the therapeutic relation and particularly of the therapeutic alliance. The realization that any such authoritative or oversight structure could impair the analytic situation and contaminate the analytic relation has led most American institutes to adopt a nonreporting system whereby minimal information passes from the training analyst to bodies responsible for regulating the training process. An education committee, for example, may be told nothing beyond dates of the beginning and end of the analysis.[11]

Every training analyst has had experiences in which the issue of his role as representative of a body exercising jurisdiction over the progress and final approval of the candidate has come into question. This issue has been little studied, but a particularly useful area for exploring implications of this circumstance seems to be the experience of candidates who may have had multiple analyses, a first analysis not in the training context and a second as a training analysis. The differences in transference reactions and alliance difficulties between these settings could be illuminating. In one such experience, the initial analysis with a candidate in training was benign, helpful, and regarded positively, and the second training analysis, which was fraught with negative transference from the beginning, suffered from pervasive misalliances and ended poorly.

Part of the problem may arise from the candidate's idealization of analytic training and even of the analyst. When the inevitable disillusionment and disappointment set in, the reaction may be angry criticism or devaluation of psychoanalysis, the institute, the training program, the courses, the teachers, and the analyst. But, as Torras de Beà (1992) noted: "When the patient is a candidate, the Institute and training can also come in for such criticism. Interpreting this indiscriminately as aggression or negative transference would be to lose important elements of contact with reality in the relationship. As I see it, the only way to overcome idealization (and also, of course, the competitive and devaluing relationship) is to confront and work through the successive disappointments and loses which must be dealt with in any analysis. Only the constant analysis of all these reactions will direct the patient to healthy identifications" (p. 162). Idealization also involves a form of misalliance, and for some candidates, the implicit fantasy is that by submission to the power of the wizard-analyst the candidate will acquire the power and status to perform marvelous feats of analytic magic as required by a narcissistically inflated ego ideal. The fantasy and idealizing transference also involve a faulty alliance riding on this narcissistic substructure. By implication, then, part of what needs to be explored and adjusted is the alliance itself, and this can help to resolve some of the distortions and draw the candidate's psyche in the direction of constructive identifications. After all, realization of a meaningful and authentic alliance as a lived experience is one of the essential goals of any training analysis.

Interruptions

Interruptions are a common occurrence in analytic work. They may occur for a variety of reasons—illness, vacations, holidays, family deaths, bad weather, personal or professional commitments, and so on. Interruptions may arise from the side of the patient or the analyst. They frequently give rise to transference reactions, usually having to do with feelings of loss, abandonment, or rejection or fears of separation and loss. Depressive affects and feelings of loss and abandonment can be triggered even by the ordinary scheduled weekend break. One patient, whose characterological defense against feelings consisted in a wall of studied indifference, found himself becoming depressed and suddenly feeling suicidal during a long holiday weekend, thinking anxiously that I was not in my office and was not available to him. Such transference reactions must be listened for in the course of any interruption of the regular analytic schedule. In this patient, the disconcerting experience revived memories of being unable to mourn his father's death associated with childhood memories of his father's absences and emotional remoteness. His depressively averted rage at me for abandoning him put him into touch with the deeper rage and disappointment at his unavailable father.[12]

In terms of the alliance, such breaks are experienced by the patient in transference terms, but they are not deviations from alliance on the part of either party. If the patient schedules an interruption, he remains responsible for the time. Insofar as he has a claim on any given hour, he can choose to use it as he sees fit—a basic stipulation of the alliance with respect to the patient's freedom and responsibility.[13] If his exercise of that freedom of choice begins to look like resistance, it becomes a matter for exploration—but the right and power to decide remain his. However, if the analyst is responsible for the interruption, the situation is somewhat different. Breaks that are foreseen—holidays, vacations, attendance at meetings, presentation of papers, elective surgery, dental appointments, and so on—require that the patient be informed. In this circumstance, a further question arises whether the analyst should make any effort to make up the lost time or arrange a substitute appointment. I do not, because I regard such interruptions as inherent in the therapeutic frame. If the patient enjoys that degree of freedom, so does the analyst. I include this stipulation in the "ground rules" affecting our respective participations in the analytic situation and process, which are spelled out and discussed at the outset, so that when occasion arises for interruptions, scheduled or not, they are accepted as part of the working situation. Mutual respect for the needs, individuality, autonomy, and freedom of both participants is thus incorporated into the therapeutic alliance.

Moving

Most analysts will move their offices several times in the course of their careers. I have moved my office four times in my years of active practice, all within a geographically limited area. Moving an office to another part of the country is a bit different than moving across the street. In the former case, the result is forced terminations, with all the inherent difficulties (Aarons 1975; Schwarz 1974; Weiss 1972). But even moderate shifts of location can trigger meaningful reactions in patients. In my experience, patients show curiosity regarding reasons for the move and its meaning: is the analyst cutting back? Does it mean that he might want to terminate any of his patients? If the office is smaller, does it mean he is less successful in his work? If larger, does it mean he is more prosperous? In addition, the change elicits a certain nostalgia for the old office, particularly in patients who had been coming there over a long period of time. Comparisons of new and old location and decor can reveal emotional responses to the move. Complaints about difficulties finding the new place, problems with bus service or parking, and so on, are potentially displaced complaints about the change and its meaning.

In terms of the alliance, any plans for moving the office are shared with patients as soon as there is something definite to tell. Reactions are explored insofar as possible in anticipation of the move, and transference and nontransference implications developed. What and how much to convey to the patient is again a matter of self-revelation and anonymity, taking into consideration what the patient needs to know and what will be therapeutically useful. The alliance would dictate care regarding preservation of anonymity, maintaining appropriate boundaries, and striking a therapeutic balance between the patient's needs and maintenance of the therapeutic structure and frame.

Gifts

Giving and receiving gifts between analyst and patient are beyond the pale of therapeutic alliance. The alliance encompasses a set of transactions including provision of certain services by the treater and payment of a fee by the patient—nothing else in terms of the exchange of goods and services. But even this norm is not without flexibility. In the course of several years of relatively intensive therapy, a patient came one day with a shopping bag and at the top of the hour began to reach into the bag saying that she had brought something for me. I stopped her at that point. I expressed my appreciation for her good wishes and intentions, but observed that I did not understand how her bringing of a gift fit with our work together and whether it contributed to that effort or not—an alliance-based inquiry. The discussion and fleshing out of the pros and cons of the situation resulted in her leaving the purchased gift in the shopping bag—to the benefit of her alliance with me and ultimately the outcome of her therapeutic work. Many months later, her therapy was drawing to a close. She had organized a charity marathon for the benefit of a local hospital, and in the flush of her accomplishment brought one of the T-shirts promoting the race and presented it to me—a gift that I received comfortably and with mutual good feeling.

What does this suggest about gifts and their place in the therapeutic alliance? I judged the former gift as counterproductive, expressive of certain unresolved transference issues, and deviant from a proper alliance. Among the unconscious meanings of a gift from an adult patient to an analyst is the narcissistic promise that binds the receiver symbolically to the giver (Silber 1969). In this case, I detected a need in her to assure herself that I would continue to work with her in her best interest—all inherent in the alliance. Accepting the gift would have colluded with her anxiety and undermined the alliance. The latter gift was more in the spirit of sharing a feeling of comradeship and mutual good feeling in recognition of something we had accomplished together, for the race was symbolic of something gained in the therapy that she valued and wanted to share with me. The T-shirt cost her little or nothing, but what it expressed was much more meaningful.

My point is that gifts are not part of the alliance, but their acceptance is best determined in the context of whether the acceptance contributes to the therapeutic work or not.[14] If it does not, or if the question is in doubt, I would say the gift is not to be accepted—but again, in the spirit of the alliance, the nonacceptance is matter for discussion and exploration in terms of the function it plays in regard to the therapeutic alliance. Discrimination depends on the quality of the relation with the patient, the state of transference, the stage of the therapeutic process, and the terms of the alliance. Accepted or not, the patient's motivation for giving the gift and its meaning for the alliance and the therapeutic process should be explored. Langs (1976) took a "No never" view of this matter, but later modified his position somewhat.

Any decision is made with reference to the meaning to the patient and the place of accepting or not for the process. One analytic patient brings me a small jar of fruit preserves at Christmastime—a small token at a time of festive giving, and something he makes himself. I accept it with good grace and friendly feelings. I feel sensitive to this patient's need to establish some less formal bond than is inherent in the therapeutic frame, and my feeling is that a refusal would be rejecting and traumatizing. At some later point in our work together, this gesture can more profitably be scrutinized and evaluated. If the implication is that the alliance is narcissistic, as Langs (1976) would suggest, I am willing to accept this misalliance condition until we reach a point at which it can be examined analytically. In this case, I would argue that flexibility at this stage promises better dividends for the alliance and the therapeutic outcome at a later stage.

Recording

Another reality intrusion on the analytic process arises from the recording analytic sessions for research purposes, to study details of the analytic process and its mechanisms. I have not participated in such an effort, but the results of those who have persuade me that this is an important area of research that is making and will continue to make significant contributions to our understanding of the analytic process. But there is no getting away from the fact that it modifies the analytic situation: someone is listening. One cannot have it both ways, despite disclaimers of advocates of the method. If you want detailed and recorded data—and there are good reasons for it—you will have to sacrifice the purity of the context (Gill et al. 1968).

But this does not necessarily erode or distort the alliance. The terms of the research and recording have to be worked out in advance with the patient so that nothing transpires that he or she does not understand and has not agreed to. At the same time, all conditions of confidentiality and the limits of utilization of research data must be specified and mutually agreed upon in advance. Problems arise during the course of any analysis conducted under these conditions, even with recording of single sessions or parts of sessions (Robbins 1988; Stern 1970). They may become the focus for transference/countertransference interactions, including intrusions on the analyst's privacy affecting empathic and introspective functions (Simon et al. 1970) If so, they should become the focus of analytic work like any other behavioral data reflecting underlying unconscious and motivational influences, whether in analyst or patient. Whatever research methods are employed, the contemporary medicolegal climate requires informed consent of the patient. In my book, this is a requirement that is supportive of therapeutic alliance, in which nothing is done without full knowledge, understanding, and cooperation of the patient. Without the patient's agreement and cooperation, there is no alliance and, therefore, no therapy.

Extra-analytic Contact

One of the ground rules of the therapeutic frame is that contact between therapist and patient is restricted to the therapist's office and nowhere else (Langs 1973b). However, extra-analytic contacts between patient and therapist occur willy-nilly. In the community in which I practice, academic and cultural circles are small and the likelihood of encountering a patient is high. If I go to the theater, a movie, a museum, a concert, a basketball game, or a restaurant, the likelihood is high that I will run into one of my patients. The encounter always has reverberations within the analysis: these may be wishes to be close, to join in some activity, to have a cup of coffee together in the Square, to share some activity in a spirit of friendship, or they may be anxieties of being known, observed, perhaps criticized, judged, rejected, and so on. Such encounters invariably arouse the patient's curiosity, stimulate exhibitionist, scopophilic, and even primary scene fantasies (Ganzarain 1991; Inderbitzin and Levy 1994).

Such spontaneous and unrehearsed encounters are usually not a problem and can be explored and their meanings and implications brought to the surface.

They are best handled circumspectly, with respect for the patient's wish and need to maintain anonymity and distance, responding in a friendly, hopefully warm, yet limited way to any initiatives on the part of the patient to extend contact. Whatever the quality of the interchange, it is fresh material for exploration in subsequent analytic hours, particularly in reference to its meaning and implications for the analytic relation. The problem for the analytic process is that the patient's frequent effort to avoid talking about such experiences in the analysis can be joined collusively by the analyst's discomfort and the anxiety aroused in both parties. Part of the problem is the intrusion of a piece of reality on the analytic space. The analyst, I would suggest, is well advised in such circumstances to measure his response in terms of what seems to be in the interest of the therapeutic relationship and alliance. A clear conception of the reality, the transference and countertransference phenomena attached to it, and the differentiation between these and the alliance are basic components of dealing with such contacts therapeutically (Tarnower 1966).

Medication

Use of medications for patients in analysis has been a controversial subject. In the years following introduction of effective psychotropic medications, especially anti-anxiety and antidepressive agents, the prevailing wisdom was that use of such agents during the course of an analysis would diminish symptom intensity and thus possibly undermine motivation for continuing analytic work, or at least serve as a complicating parameter that would contaminate transference and possibly become a vehicle for enactment of countertransference (Sarwer-Foner 1960; Ostow 1962). This early view has undergone considerable revision since more effective medications have found their way into the pharmacological armamentarium and analysts have gained increasing experience in combining analysis or analytically oriented psychotherapy with these drugs (Esman 1989; Roose 1990; Wylie and Wylie 1987). In certain cases, addition of some psychopharmacological agent seemed not only advantageous, but necessary for effective therapeutic management (Kantor 1989, 1993).

Along with greater openness to use of these agents, the analytic sophistication regarding implications of the use of medication on transference and the analytic process grew apace. The role of pills as vehicles for transference and countertransference expression and their function as transitional objects (Adelman 1985; Gutheil 1982; Hausner 1985–86) became better understood. The prevailing view at this juncture is that use of medications is not at all incompatible with an ongoing analytic process, especially in the treatment of mood or anxiety disorders. Not only do a fair percentage of analysts use such combined therapy, but the incidence is significant even in training cases (Roose and Stern 1995).

I regard medication as another reality-based factor that impinges on the analytic process and has important reverberations for the analytic relation and transference. If the analyst is persuaded that medication may serve his patient well, he needs to keep in mind implicit messages he may convey in introducing the subject. Will the patient experience it as an expression of the analyst's disappointment in him for not being able to manage his feelings without artificial help? Will he take it as affirming his inferiority and weakness? Will he accept it compliantly as a magical talisman from the powerful analyst? The possibilities are multiple and can insert themselves subtly and by implication. As with other similar accidental factors impinging on the therapeutic alliance, the issue of taking medication is a matter for mutual exploration and decision between analyst and analysand. Implications for the analytic work should be discussed, possible transference issues explored in detail, and reverberations for therapeutic alliance sorted out. Lurking in the background inevitably is the medical model, according to which the magician-doctor, who has the power and knowledge to heal, applies his wisdom to the ignorant, suffering, helpless, and accommodating patient. To the extent that it goes unaddressed, this model will contaminate the analytic process and lead to a potentially problematic misalliance.

Even when the decision-making process is adequately conducted, the ongoing technology of drug management may continue to create problems. The elaborate ritual of drug taking and drug monitoring—the necessity for explaining side effects, obtaining informed consent, checking on side effects (orthostatic pressure), checking on compliance, taking plasma-level measurements—can create myriad complications in the analytic process on the level of transference, countertransference, and transference/countertransference. The potential for distortion of therapeutic alliance and problematic misalliances is not insignificant. In my own practice, for these reasons and for more personal ones—I am not interested in drug management—I prefer to have a colleague who is more practiced and up-to-date on psychopharmacology do the job. This by no means eliminates the issues of drugs from analytic consideration, but it allows for a freer and less encumbered exploration of its meaning and effectiveness (or lack thereof) in the analytic setting. This is somewhat analogous to the therapist/administrator split more familiar in hospital and clinic settings, with similar advantages and disadvantages. However this issue is addressed and managed, therapeutic alliance is a point of reference that requires continual consideration and in most cases should be explicitly addressed.

PART III

Aspects of the Therapeutic Alliance

On the assumption that the distinction between therapeutic alliance and transference, countertransference, and transference/countertransference interactions on the one hand (part I) and the distinction between therapeutic alliance and aspects of the real relation (part II) on the other have been established, we can turn our attention to a closer examination of some of the inherent qualities of the therapeutic alliance itself. The following seven chapters are given over to exposition of what I regard as the essential components of the therapeutic alliance in order to approach a more complete and clinically relevant understanding of its nature and practical implications.

The first aspect to be considered is the fact that the therapeutic alliance has a developmental perspective. Not only are there certain specific developmental attainments that contribute to the therapeutic alliance as it takes shape in analysis, but in the course of the analysis itself the therapeutic alliance undergoes an epigenetic evolution analogous to the developmental process (chapter 8). The therapeutic alliance at the beginning of analysis is not the same as that found in the middle phase and is again different from that found in the termination phase. To emphasize a point—more is involved developmentally in the therapeutic alliance than trust, much more!

Other essential components include the therapeutic framework, embracing the therapeutic contract and boundary issues (chapter 9), the central roles of empathic attunement and listening (chapter 10), personal qualities of the analyst and the analysand, including those that reflect each participant's own personal development and capacities for alliance (chapter 11), and those that accrue to them by virtue of their participation in the analysis and play a critical role in the manner and effectiveness of their involvement—specifically, authority, freedom, and responsibility (chapter 12). Finally, ethical considerations, which play an essential part in the development and sustaining of the therapeutic alliance, are considered. I shall pay particular attention to confidentiality and issues related to preserving it (chapter 13) and the values, both personal and technical, and their function within the analytic relation and process (chapter 14).

CHAPTER EIGHT

Developmental Aspects

Early attempts to articulate the therapeutic alliance tended to view it restrictively as reflecting accomplishments from quite early developmental strata. The emphasis in Zetzel's (1956, 1965, 1966) rendition, for example, fell on residues of caretaker vicissitudes from earliest child-mother interactions centering around issues of trust—much along the lines of Erikson's (1963) discussion of trust. In this view, the basic capacity for alliance was laid down at a pregenital level at the point at which the capacity for object relationship and object constancy began (Zetzel 1958; Fleming 1975). Greenacre (1956) also located the primitive basis of alliance in characteristics of the early mother-child relationship. Thus, patients who had been able to establish sufficient trust and object constancy in their relations with their mothers were thought to be able to establish and maintain a therapeutic alliance, whereas patients who had experienced early traumatic separation from their mothers had difficulties in the alliance. With the latter patients, development of a capacity for object relationships by way of positive identification with the analyst became essential for analysis to progress (Hani 1973).

The conception of therapeutic alliance I have been advocating does not allow such a univocal or reductive understanding. I shall argue in this chapter that therapeutic alliance involves assimilation and integration of contributions from all developmental levels. If trust is an important building block of alliance, autonomy is no less significant, along with the other components I shall address. Moreover, each of these components has undergone a process of ontogenetic evolution in the course of the patient's life history and will develop progressively in the course of successful analysis. My purpose in this chapter is to focus on aspects of the patient's developmental experience that might contribute to these qualities as he enters the analytic process. Later I shall take up the vicissitudes of these personal factors as they may evolve during the analytic process (see chapters 11 and 12).

In her attempt to analyze the therapeutic alliance, Zetzel (1970) focused on the one-to-one relationship in the child's early environment, particularly the mother-child relationship, where she envisioned the capacity for alliance to be rooted. To see therapeutic alliance simply in these terms, however, makes it a unitary capacity, limited to the patient's ability to trust the analyst. Such a view of therapeutic alliance is reductive, while the alliance itself is considerably more complex. A variety of developmental attainments may qualify the patient's capacity to relate to the nontransferential and therapeutic person of the therapist. These factors stem not only from early one-to-one maternal involvement, but may also derive from more complex involvements in later triadic situations, as well as other later involvements with significant figures. My point is that the characteristics of therapeutic alliance derive from the full range of the child's developmental vicissitudes and reflect different qualities of this developmental experience at various stages of the analytic process. Therapeutic alliance and the capacity for it reflect certain developmental processes which must be distinguished from regressive introjective components that contribute to elaboration of transference distortions and transference neurosis.

Developmental Parameters

Development is a complicated process with many facets, the exploration and deepening understanding of which provides the background for this discussion. I shall not review that rich literature, but shall focus on selected developmental issues that seem immediately relevant to therapeutic alliance. Enlarging the developmental matrix has important reverberations for how we conceptualize the alliance and its role in the analytic process. As Novick and Novick (1994) commented: "The effect of the search for ever earlier causes combined with the view that postoedipal development is a recapitulation of infantile experiences relegates adult memories of latency and adolescence to serving mainly a defensive screen function. This conceptualization has a profound effect on technique. If, alternatively, we retain Freud's earlier view that important transformations occur in latency and adolescence, how would this affect our understanding and handling of the adult patient's material?" (p. 145).

Consequently, the therapeutic alliance within the analysis has a course of development. In large measure, articulation of this aspect of the analytic process remains virgin territory. The development of the alliance in the analytic process can be envisioned, in broad terms, as following a progressive epigenetic course. Erikson's (1959, 1963) schedule of developmental crises provides us with an epigenetic schema and a set of categories and vocabulary in terms of which we can discuss these issues. One can, for example, define the therapeutic alliance's relevant parameters around issues of trust, autonomy, initiative, industry, identity, intimacy, and so on. Erikson (1964) has also provided us with a schema of strengths or virtues, including hope, will, purpose, competence, fidelity, love, care, and wisdom. Their development is linked to the schema of developmental crises, and their function vis-à-vis the alliance and its evolution during the course of an analysis are goals the analytic process seeks to approximate. Whether Erikson's categories will be the most useful in understanding the therapeutic alliance remains to be seen.

I shall follow Erikson's (1959, 1963) epigenetic schema as a convenient framework for discussing these aspects of alliance and their role in the course of the analytic process. A subsidiary point deserving emphasis is that these qualities are specifically self-qualities rather than ego-qualities. I regard Erikson's formulations of these developmental attainments as relevant to the self rather than the ego, a perspective left indeterminate in Erikson's own writing because of his ambiguous views on the relationship between ego and self, an unresolved phase of psychoanalytic theoretical development (Meissner 1986a, 1993).

Trust

There is little question that the capacity for trust and hope has its roots in early maternal involvement (Evans 1976; Meissner 1973, 1987a). Trust itself is a more complex phenomenon than can be accounted for by appeal to an infantile model. There are layers in the development and expression of trust that require later developmental acquisitions for satisfactory understanding. In addition, activation of other qualities and dispositions in the analytic relation draws on multiple levels of development and object ties (Arlow and Brenner 1966). As Novick (1970) pointed out, the capacity for trust may have its roots in the oral period, but other factors from other developmental periods also contribute to the alliance—autonomy from the anal period, pride and pleasure in achievement from the phallic period, and so on.

In keeping with the overall epigenetic frame of reference, the individual elements of the schema may also have their own ontogeny. Mehlman (1976), for instance, has described a form of secondary trust, which differs from basic trust in that, given the establishment of basic trust, it maintains a certain state of openness vis-à-vis the parents. According to Mehlman: "Secondary trust has to do with the willingness to cede over to the parental object some of those adaptive and defensive ego functions that would otherwise represent a closed system of previously internalized archaic parental images irrespective of their quality" (pp. 23–24). Thus the element of trust can be seen to have its own relatively independent ontogeny reflecting specific vicissitudes in the child's developmental experience.

If we shift the discussion to the problem of internalization, secondary trust implies a continual openness to and acceptance of direction and influence from parental objects. It implies a relative lack of ambivalence, the persistence of basic trust, and a receptiveness to positive, supportive, and constructive relationships with parental objects. Premature closure, implicit in the failure of secondary trust, however, suggests not only defensive fixation and separation from the influence of the parental object, but also a premature and defensively motivated internalization, namely, forming a pathogenic introject tinged with paranoid elements. Both elaboration of secondary trust and its failure are accompanied by significant internalizations—in the one case, constructive imitations and identifications, and, in the other, relatively pathogenic and defensively motivated introjections (Meissner 1974a, 1981).

Autonomy

Erikson's developmental schema locates the rudiments of autonomy roughly during the anal period, connected with the emergence of sphincter competence and the struggle over autonomous control of bodily functions and the submission to parental control. The anal zone becomes a source of erotic stimulation related to functions of retaining and releasing—"holding on" and "letting go" in Erikson's terms. In psychosocial terms, the child becomes increasingly aware of himself as separate and independent. Greater muscular control leads to an increasing capacity for autonomous expression and self-regulation. The child begins to interact assertively with others, especially the parents.

Successful resolution of the autonomy crisis lays the foundation for a more mature capacity for self-assertion and self-expression, for respect for the autonomy of others, and for self-control without loss of self-esteem. The maturely autonomous adult can engage in rewarding and effective cooperation with others without falling into the trap set by a deficient autonomy (masochistic subjection or submissiveness) or into the opposite trap of hyperautonomous domination or authoritarian control. A failure to resolve the crisis of autonomy effectively contributes to a false autonomy that feeds on the autonomy of others by domination or excessive demands or in the fragile autonomy of the compulsive (anal) personality.

Thus rudiments of autonomy laid down in these early developmental experiences play a vital role in the subsequent emergence of the personality, particularly in reference to the capacity for independent action and agency that plays such a central role in later self-integration and adaptive functioning (Meissner 1993; Modell 1993). Moreover, the autonomy in question here is specifically a capacity of the self-system as an emergent quality of self-organization embracing and building on the substructural contributions of ego and superego autonomy. It is this autonomy of the self that comes into play in the self-determining deliberations and actions that maintain the relative independence of the individual in the face of external pressures and in contexts of interaction and interdependence with others. Insofar, then, as therapeutic alliance is a form of object relation, the autonomy involved in it belongs to the self rather than to isolated ego functions.

In these terms, early infantile autonomy of the anal phase represents only the initial stage of a developmental process continuing into adulthood in which the significance of autonomy as a personal capacity assumes a meaningful place in the structure of the personality. Development of the capacity for autonomous functioning and relating through the vicissitudes of oedipal and post-oedipal (latency and adolescent) phases moves in the direction of increasing independence along with relative dependence, of a capacity for self-determination in the service of self-oriented goals and objectives—in the face of inner drive-derivative conflicts and external opposition and disapproval. Philosophers have called this mature capacity "will" (analysts do not know what to call it), but it clearly involves a certain independence of drive and reality and allows for a degree of self-choice and decision.

Autonomy in this key strikes a somewhat different chord than that sounded by Rapaport (1958) or Hartmann (1939) in that it requires an idea of how superego and ego structures can be integrated in relation to critical narcissistic transformations. Here Erikson's psychosocial crises can be envisioned in terms of the critical resolution of narcissistic issues at various stages of the life cycle and their integration with progressive structural modifications and integrations of superego and ego. Another critical theoretical issue concerns internalization, especially internalizations having to do with higher order, culturally derived components, particularly value systems. This interface among cultural influences, learning phenomena, and organization and integration of inner psychic structure becomes crucial. Historically, no one was more sensitive to the difficulty of integration of inner structure and inputs provided from learning than Rapaport. The problem of integrating learning parameters with structural formation and modification was a central focus of his life's work, and one which he himself had to declare unsatisfactory. The problem remains alive in our theoretical approach to such issues.

Rapaport's (1958) model of autonomy concerns independence from drives and reality determinants. Thus the guarantee of relative autonomy from drives comes from the side of reality or the environment, while the guarantee of independence from reality determinants comes through the operation of drives and drive derivatives. In this sense, Rapaport's notion of ego autonomy is negative, connoting independence of specific determinants, and ends up trapped between instinctual forces and environment. Autonomy is an autonomy *from* instincts and *from* environment.

The problem with such a negative model of autonomy can be seen clearly in the obsessional patient, who preserves his autonomy by immersion in details of reality, thus presumably defending himself against drive derivatives. However, it seems ludicrous to think of the obsessive-compulsive syndrome as autonomous with respect to drive influences. Indeed, such patients are plagued by drive-derivatives. In such a case, the model seems to break down. Rather than considering autonomy as caught between these dichotomous polarities, it may be more useful to think of it as an internalized attribute, simultaneously independent of both drives and environment. Alternatively, we may be able to think of it as involving simultaneous congruence with both drives and reality. In this sense, the ego can be strengthened by drive components, rather than weakened.

These complications lead us in the direction of a somewhat different notion of autonomy than that articulated by Hartmann and Rapaport. To begin with, in the Hartmann-Rapaport model autonomy is strictly speaking a functional autonomy, that is, an autonomy of specific ego functions. This functional view, related to the ego-psychological notion of ego as an organization of functional systems, is relatively impersonal and concerns itself with maintenance of structural integrity in the functions of the ego. Such autonomy is then a matter of conflict-free functioning within an average expectable environment (Hartmann 1939). Consequently, ego autonomy must be reduced to the autonomy of separate functions, an argument articulated by Beres (1971).

This limitation of the functional view of autonomy sets it apart from the notion of autonomy that has to do with the cohesiveness, integration, and independence of the self, that is, as an inherent quality or possession of the self. Erikson tried to describe this form of autonomy in his epigenetic schema as a critical developmental achievement for the growing child. The Rapaport model, stressing the role of stimulus nutriment and social learning, tends to ignore or underplay the role of narcissistic factors involved in integration of self-autonomy and the maintenance of self-coherence. Rather, such an approach tends to settle for a form of "social compliance" along lines described by Hartmann (1944). Hartmann understood such compliance as referring to the relation of congruence between the person's mental structure and his social environment: "This gives us the right to speak of *social compliance,* by which we understand the fact that social factors must also be described psychologically in such a way as to demonstrate their selective effects; they operate in the direction of the selection and effectuation of certain tendencies and their expression, and of certain developmental trends, among those which, at any given moment, are potentially demonstrable in the structure of the individual" (p. 27).

Reliance exclusively on extrinsic factors, however, creates a risk of substituting a form of "false self" conformity for real autonomy. The false self-organization, as Winnicott (1960a) pointed out, is based on conformity to social and extrinsic expectations and norms, resulting in splitting of the inner organization of the personality with potentially serious pathological results.

Initiative

The last Eriksonian developmental phases I shall consider here are initiative, associated with the play age, and industry, a facet of latency development and school age. As with trust and autonomy, these developmental crises carry a history and an ontogeny reaching beyond the phase with which they are associated. The crisis of autonomy, with its links to the anal period and practicing and rapprochement stages (Mahler et al. 1975), allows emergence of precursory expressions of initiative that gain increasing scope with consolidation of autonomy and find increasing expression in the child's exploration of the world of play. By the same token, resolution of the crisis of initiative undergoes further evolution in ensuing stages of development leading toward identity formation and adulthood.

Entrance into the play age is accompanied by maturation of capacities for locomotion and language allowing the child to reach beyond the limits of his childhood experience and to explore his immediate environment. Motor equipment has developed enough to permit not merely performance of motions, but wide-ranging experimentation in locomotion. The child begins to test the limits of his newfound capability. His activity becomes vigorous and intrusive. A similar crystallization occurs in the use of language, which becomes an exciting new toy calling for experimentation and the satisfaction of curiosity. Intrusion characterizes the child's activity: physically into other bodies, into other people's attention by activity and aggressive talking, into space by vigorous locomotion, and into the unknown by lively curiosity. All this is accompanied by growing sexual curiosity and specifically masculine or feminine initiative, conditioned by development of phallic eroticism.

In the psychosocial sphere, the child's experience is directed by an expanding imagination that begins to mesh with the world's real structure, physical and social. The child's fancy meets the nonfanciful demands of reality, and, in the area of phallic activity and sexual curiosity, the conflict takes on serious proportions. Excessively severe rebuke or prohibitions can bring about unnecessary repressions and restrict the play of the child's imagination and initiative. If the crisis of initiative is successfully resolved, positive residues are provided for development of conscience, a sense of responsibility and dependability, self-discipline, and a certain independence in the mature personality. This is therefore a crucial stage for formation of superego, based on introjection of authoritative (especially parental) prohibitions. Unsuccessful resolution of the crisis provides a basis for the harsh, rigid, moralistic, and self-punishing superego that is the dynamic source of a sense of guilt.

Interplay of parental prohibitions and identifications can inhibit that sense of initiative which lends spontaneity and freedom to the child's inquiring intrusions. The child assimilates an internalized system of parental norms and prohibitions that guide the course of behavior and serve as seeds for development of a mature value-system. If the assimilated elements are fundamentally realistic in foundation and orientation, they can be synthesized into the evolving structure of the mature ego. In this instance, the pattern of identifications is well defined and supported by mature parental identities, and parental prohibitions are balanced and reasonable. Much of the development of superego at this level reflects patterns of parental superego adjustment and maturity. Disturbed parental role functions, however, may threaten the child's successful resolution of this psychosocial crisis.

The child's emerging phallic interests need the support and formative influence of secure, stable identifications in order to establish foundations of a mature sense of sexual identity and gender role function. Inability of parents to provide models of sexual functioning impairs the child's identification in this essential area of self-awareness. This dimension of superego formation is important for achieving a guilt-free sexual adjustment.

Moreover, if parental demands are reasonable and realistic, conjoint functioning of ego and superego are made possible. But if demands and prohibitions become the vehicle of parental immaturities, superego formation is impaired and the ground is laid for future conflict and guilt feelings. Guilt, then, arises from the disparity between activity of the ego and value-dependent prescriptions of the superego. Where internalized norms of the superego are based on unresolved infantile conflicts (oedipal conflicts, in Freud's terms), this primitive unreasonableness of the superego underlies unrealistic and therefore neurotic guilt feelings. But even if the value system is realistically oriented, guilt is still possible, not because of the inherent punitiveness of the superego but because of the defection of the ego.

Industry

The periods of infantile (phallic) sexuality and adolescent sexuality (puberty) are separated by the latency period, in which the child's interest is generally diverted to other matters. The child steps up from the level of imaginative exploration and play to a level in which his participation in the adult world is foreshadowed. In our culture, the child is sent to school, where he begins to learn skills that will equip him one day to take his place in adult society. His interest turns to doing and making things—in general, he becomes involved in developing the necessary technology for adult living. He is drawn away from home and its close association and learns the reward systems of the school society and assimilates its values of application and diligence. He also achieves a sense of the pleasure of work and productivity, of satisfaction of a task accomplished, and of the merit of perseverance in difficult enterprises. In other words, the normally developing child adds to his evolving personality a sense of industry.

There is danger at this stage that a child's lack of success in the school society will produce a sense of inadequacy and inferiority. Failure to achieve a sense of industry may also indicate defects in the resolution of previous crises. Excessive emotional dependency on the family can impair the child's ability to compete and cooperate with peers at school

Maturational Multidimensionality

If we examine earlier understandings of therapeutic alliance in the context of development, it seems clear that Zetzel's approach fell into a too-facile dichotomy between pre-oedipal and oedipal levels, in which transference dynamics tended to be viewed in oedipal terms and alliance factors in pre-oedipal terms. We would now tend to view transference as reflecting conflictual issues at all levels: pre-oedipal, oedipal, and post-oedipal. The same is true of the therapeutic alliance, which also reflects achievements drawn from all levels of developmental experience. Anna Freud (1962) made the point nicely when she commented: "I think you will not misunderstand me if I say that the therapeutic alliance between analyst and patient is *not* carried by any of these earlier stages of object-relationship, although all these earlier stages are 'material.' The therapeutic alliance is based, I believe, on ego attitudes that go with later stages, namely, on self-observation, insight, give-and-take in object relationship, the willingness to make sacrifices" (p. 192). My only demur from this cogent observation is my preference to see the capacity for alliance and alliance itself in object relational terms and as a function of the self-organization, and not restrictively of the ego.

At the same time, a developmental aspect of the interchange between therapist and patient involves mutual cuing and relatedness reaching back to early strata of mother-infant interaction. To the extent that positive dimensions of earlier developmental experiences can be recaptured, the potential for constructive alliance building can be reinforced. To the extent that such factors are lacking or that negative aspects of the mother-child interaction are tapped into, the basis for disruption of alliance or for therapeutic misalliance is reinforced. More is involved on this level than merely specifiable aspects of the contemporary interchange.

Alliance and Epigenesis

During the regressive phase of the analytic process, then, the therapeutic alliance serves sustaining and buffering functions, allowing this process to take place. However, as the analysis moves into a more progressive phase in which elements of transference neurosis begin to be analyzed, interpreted, and worked through, the therapeutic alliance itself undergoes reworkings of developmental crises forming an epigenetic progression. The working through and progressive resolution of associated and underlying instinctual conflicts provides the frame of reference within which these epigenetic crises can be successively resolved. Thus, as the analysis moves forward, the quality and organization of the therapeutic alliance also shift and undergo progressive change.

These qualities and capacities for adaptive personality functioning, consequently, have their own inherent history in the course of the analytic process. They evolve in somewhat epigenetic fashion during the course of the analytic work. Trust may thus play a more telling role than autonomy in the opening phase of the analysis. The patient must be able to tolerate a degree of dependence in order for the analytic process to take hold. Evolution of trust within the analysis may involve increasing dependence, even of a fairly primitive kind, but that dependence will have to be worked through and gradually resolved to make way for a trusting relationship that allows for the emergence and facilitation of basic autonomy within the therapeutic relationship. As autonomy begins to grow, the patient can begin to take responsibility for progression of the analytic work and assume more initiative and industry in directing the course of analytic inquiry, including the interpretive process. I would argue, then, that the therapeutic alliance rides on multiple levels of developmental determination, that these determinants follow their own pattern of epigenetic articulation within the analytic process, and that the study and therapeutic enhancement of these issues and the putative resolution of the developmental crises as they arise in the analysis are crucial matters of technique and the theory of therapy.

In postulating an epigenetic progression, I am not suggesting some apodictic organic sequence. Rather, the process varies considerably from patient to patient in terms of the underlying developmental issues, the patterning of the analytic process, the empathic and responsive capacities of the analyst, and a host of other variables. Moreover, as with any epigenetic sequence, the process does not involve an exclusive shift from one critical focus to another; rather, all aspects of the developmental sequence are involved at every phase. In the sequence suggested here, for example, issues of autonomy simultaneously implicate related components of trust and initiative. Nonetheless, the inherent sequencing and internal logic to phases observed in the analytic process are not in an ironclad order.

A specific issue related to working through of the alliance may predominate at one point, then the focus may shift to a different issue, returning to the first issue at yet another point. Nor are these issues cast in all-or-nothing terms. Rather, they arise in varying degrees and are worked through in varying proportions at different phases of a given analysis. Thus, while secondary trust may be essential for inaugurating a genuine therapeutic alliance, even basic trust may play an important part in the terminal phases of a given analysis.

In other words, the critical focus in the present consideration is that therapeutic alliance is composed of a variety of operative qualities which undergo developmental progression both as a result of and as an active component of the analytic process. Moreover, developmental aspects of this progression are inherent in the analytic process and, therefore, require analytic attention. These are real issues within the analytic process, operating in parallel to and often interacting critically with aspects of the transference neurosis. This reciprocal interaction takes place throughout the analytic process and provides a critical working area of therapeutic effects. I shall discuss this area later in terms of critical internalizations involved (see chapter 18). At this point, however, I am concerned only with descriptive aspects of the progression in the therapeutic alliance itself.

I have not been able to improve on the epigenetic schema suggested by Erikson (1963, 1968) for articulating these developmental contributions. His categories do not exhaust dimensions of the therapeutic alliance, but they do offer a preliminary set of concepts articulated within a developmental framework. Identificatory elements that provide the substructure for the therapeutic alliance derive from all levels of the patient's developmental experience. The therapeutic alliance is consequently neither a simple nor a univocal aspect of the psychoanalytic situation. Rather, its quality and basis differ for every patient, depending on the phase of analysis and on the level of regressive reactivation experienced by the patient. The patient's experience of a trusting relationship and the quality of identifications associated with it are considerably different in early developmental strata, when the first rudiments of trust are being elaborated, than in much later developmental strata, when more complex derivative issues of trust are being elaborated and worked through. Similarly, development of autonomy in the alliance progresses through earlier phases, in which regressive forms of dependence may become more dominant, through stages in which autonomy is gradually formed and consolidated, and on to a final stage in which autonomy is established along with a capacity for mature dependence and appropriate independence. A parallel progression takes place in other dimensions of the alliance, each in its own fashion and time, as the analytic process moves forward (see chapters 11 and 12).

At each level of developmental attainment, from the rudimentary level of basic trust, through development of autonomy, initiative, the achievement of identity, industry, and even generativity, we have a resolution of developmental crises that constructs a basic capacity and source of strength within the evolving structure of the self. These constructive resolutions draw the developmental course of the individual away from unresolved conflicts and pathological compromises toward a greater capacity for more mature, adaptive and effective ego-functioning and self-integration. These are capacities in the analytic relation that the therapeutic alliance builds on and toward which its therapeutic efforts are directed. Therapeutic alliance both builds on basic trust and builds it. It both builds on the patient's capacity for autonomy and reinforces it.

CHAPTER NINE

The Therapeutic Framework

The concept of the therapeutic frame or framework has many connotations. Spruiell (1983) observed: "The situation that develops between an ordinary analyst and an ordinary patient is indeed a social situation, but a most peculiar one. In this social situation a number of usual rules governing two-party relationships are specifically abrogated—in particular, the to-and-fro dance of organized, eye-to-eye dialogue, the ubiquitous censorship of thoughts which might disrupt rational communication and interaction, and amenities of a (usually amiable) hypocritical nature. The analytic situation has a frame, if one thinks of a frame as referring to *unchanging basic elements or principles of organization defining a specific social event and distinguishing it from other events*" (p. 9). As with many other dimensions of the analytic process, opinions vary on the question of the therapeutic framework. Some therapists even claim therapeutic benefit from interventions outside the analytic framework. As Hanly (1994) observes:

> There are also analysts who are experimenting with interventions outside the analytic hour. I refer here to events such as encounters with patients *en route* to the office; a session conducted while walking in a park; visits to a female patient in the maternity ward; attendance at a patient's concert; and telephone calls to the analyst's home. Analysts have long been familiar with the use of parameters. One may accept calls from a patient struggling with a suicidal depression while preparing the way for them to become unnecessary. The interventions to which I refer here are different because they are claimed to be therapeutic precisely because they occur outside the usual analytic situation and no effort is made to bring them into it, to interpret them or to facilitate their wearing away. The claim is that they are therapeutic precisely because they are non-interpretive. And they remain uninterpreted because they are part of and contribute to the real relation with the patient by demonstrating the analyst's humanity in its realistic proportions and his care and concern for the patient. (p. 457)

I shall treat the analytic frame here as an essential component of therapeutic alliance that refers to the terms and conditions required in order to provide a context within which analytic interaction and the analytic process can take place (Langs 1976). The therapeutic framework includes the negotiated terms on which analyst and patient agree to work together (Bleger 1967; Green 1975; Langs 1973b). If they cannot find a common ground on which to engage in the analytic process, therapy is not possible.

Purpose

Why is a framework necessary and what does it have to do with alliance? The framework provides a structure within which the appropriate conditions can be maintained, allowing the psychoanalytic process to emerge and develop.[1] For the patient the framework guarantees consistency and stability in the therapeutic milieu—a context within which more regressed, conflicted, shameful, anxiety-ridden, and guilty parts of the self can find expression. The frame contributes to the security essential for any analytic work to be done (Sandler 1960). Only when the framework is adequately established can both patient and analyst have the freedom to venture, make mistakes, or reveal vulnerabilities. As Levenson (1992) comments, "Frame prevents Freud's 'playground' from becoming a battlefield" (p. 559).

The frame also contributes important elements to the role of the analyst. Anxiety pervades the analytic situation for both participants, analyst no less than patient. The analytic frame can serve as container for anxiety generated on both sides of the analytic divide. Levenson (1992) put the matter succinctly: "Analysts require a carefully contrived and maintained psychoanalytic frame which defines, in advance and somewhat arbitrarily, all those conditions of therapy which may be considered as superordinate to content: i.e., time, money, place (is one's office in the home?), limited extent of social and personal contact with the patient, gifts, cancellation agreements, the requirements of scrupulous self-report from the patient, the analyst's care about self-revelation" (p. 558).

The frame, therefore, establishes the terrain on which the analytic encounter takes place. That terrain is fraught with peril for the analyst, as his participation in the process entails becoming the object and repository of painful and destructive wishes and affects stemming from the patient, which he is called on to suffer without recrimination or retribution. The analytic situation is one of unrelieved strain inevitably taking its toll on the analyst. The frame sets the limits of this space, preserving the analyst's privacy and appropriate anonymity. In addition, the frame provides a buffer against any inappropriate gratifications and wishes aroused in the course of interaction with the patient (Langs 1976).

The frame, then, creates the analytic space and makes meaningful participation in the analytic process possible for both parties. The frame is another safeguard against countertransference deviations, such that any modification of it can open the door to countertransference problems.

Components of the Analytic Frame

All of the elements contributing to the therapeutic frame have been the subject of a considerable literature and provide a focus for extensive clinical investigation in their own right. My effort here has a more limited focus, namely, that each of these components represent an aspect of the alliance, so that how they are dealt with and on what terms becomes salient to establishing and maintaining the alliance, and therefore has significance for the rest of the therapeutic effort.

The Therapeutic Contract

One aspect of the therapeutic alliance includes those elements described in terms of "therapeutic contract." Roland Barthes (1982) cited Brecht on this matter: "Most of the time, the relations between humans suffer, often to the point of destruction, from the fact that the contract established in those relations is not respected. As soon as two human beings enter into reciprocal relationship, their contract, generally tacit, comes into force, regulating the form of their relations, etc." (p. 384). This saying is especially pertinent to psychoanalysis and psychotherapy. *Contract* may not be the best term for this aspect of the alliance in view of its legalistic connotations—some have suggested *covenant* as a better term. Veatch (1981) objected to the former term because it does not focus ethical connections and fidelity. The covenant model stipulates mutual commitments, fidelities, expectations, and principles that shape the attitudes and behaviors of the participants. In any case, this idea refers to the collaborative nature of the enterprise and the fact that therapist and patient enter into a mutual relationship based on reciprocally satisfactory terms that are negotiated and agreed on as the ground rules by which they will work together—including the ground rule of free association (Kanzer 1957). The contract is roughly synonymous with Freud's analytic pact.

As a foundation for medical ethics, Veatch (1981) proposed a triple contractual approach involving a social contract affecting social principles or conventions for social interaction, a second contract or covenant between healing professions and society, and the contract between individual healer and patient. The second and third contracts derive from the first and specify its principles. Essential to the idea of a contract is free participation of the involved parties. Conditions for a collaborative enterprise cannot be unilaterally stipulated. The patient cannot specify the conditions for successful therapy—that is the domain and responsibility of the therapist—but the patient does not engage in the process without informed consent. Attaining that degree of mutual understanding and agreement without coercion or compromise is essential to establishing the therapeutic alliance (Kultgen 1985).

Shapiro (1989) objects to the idea of the contract on the grounds that the patient's ego is not sufficiently disengaged from neurotic needs to undertake the required self-observation. He writes: "This assumption is also contained in the attractive-sounding but problematical concept of 'therapeutic alliance,' at least in one of its meanings. The supposed 'contemplative ego' or 'observing ego' of the patient that is critical to such an 'alliance' is just such an introspective agency. But the fact that the patient's articulation of his subjective experience serves and is not detached from the dynamics of the neurotic personality precludes reliance on such a 'contemplative ego' or any 'alliance' that, in turn, depends on it" (pp. 72–73). The framework, however, is more a statement of the necessary conditions for therapeutic engagement than a demand imposed on the patient.

Certainly, therapeutic alliance includes more than is suggested by a merely contractual model. The framework refers to those conditions required on the part of both therapist and patient in order that good and effective therapeutic work can be conducted. Included among other things are scheduling (the place and time for analytic appointments), fees and the method of their payment (including management of any insurance payments), arrangements for missed appointments or vacations, delay in making important decisions, and questions regarding confidentiality (A. Freud 1954a; Gabbard 1994b; Gutheil and Gabbard 1993; Langs 1976; Meissner 1979, 1986b; Stone 1961; Uchill, 1978).

Boundaries

While the therapeutic frame can be regarded as defining the therapeutic space as distinct from nontherapeutic space (in analysis, the analytic situation), the internal structure of the frame also consists of certain boundaries essential for the analytic process. The primary responsibility for management of these boundaries falls to the analyst, but the responsibility is shared by the patient as a partner in the therapeutic process.

All patients, to some degree, try to bend or erode the boundaries inherent in the therapeutic frame, in both psychotherapy and psychoanalysis (Bleger 1967). This may become a problem especially in narcissistic patients whose entitlement and/or grandiosity does not allow them to tolerate limits of the frame well (Kron 1971). In most cases, such efforts to undermine the frame can be readily managed, but in extreme cases it can become a source of disruption. These difficulties are a major focus in the treatment of patients in the borderline spectrum who experience limitations and frustrations with the therapeutic alliance (Meissner 1988). In lower-order cases, even experienced clinicians may be intimidated by borderline rage, neediness or dependency, entitlement, manipulativeness, and boundary erosion, among other factors. Resulting pressures often force therapists to yield to the patient's demands and to feel that any effort to set limits or keep firm boundaries will precipitate unmanageable outbursts and irreparably disrupt therapy. Appeal to the therapist's nurturance may foster overinvolvement or overinvestment and generate rescue fantasies corresponding to the patient's neediness. These can be recognized readily as countertransference reactions, but they often lead to boundary relaxations and infringements that may not only undermine the therapeutic process but also lead to dire ethical and medicolegal complications (Gutheil 1989).

While firmness in maintenance of therapeutic ground rules is mandatory, flexible maintenance of rules is quite different from violating or disregarding them (Nacht 1958; Weigert 1954b). As Freud remarked in a letter to Ferenczi: "I thought it most important to stress what one should not do, to point out the temptations that run counter to analysis. Almost everything one should do in a positive sense, I left to the 'tact' that you have introduced. What I achieved thereby was that the Obedient submitted to these admonitions as if they were taboos and did not notice their elasticity. This would have had to be reversed some day, but without setting aside the obligations" (Grubrich-Simitis 1986, p. 271).

Any of the analytic ground rules can be employed flexibly even as the rule is insisted on and reinforced (Langs 1976). Part of the analytic frame, for example, is lying on the couch, but exceptional circumstances may call for modifying this practice—for physical or psychological reasons—even as both analyst and patient accept the reasons for using the couch and recognize return to the couch as preferable.[2] On occasions when I have thought it advisable for an analytic patient to sit up as a temporary expedient, in the face of excessive anxiety, for example, the decision was reached by my suggestion and discussion of the pros and cons and reasons in some detail before the patient decides to sit up or not. In addition, the therapist must be alert to possible countertransference dimensions of any wish to bend or modify the ground rules. Hidden rebellious, antinomian, or narcissistic components of the therapist's personality may find expression in wishes to modify or bend the frame (Allen 1956).

The notion of boundaries has an important role to play in professional medicolegal contexts, such that transgression of boundaries becomes a matter of violation of the contractual terms of the relationship. Here again, risk of legal action is more prominent among lower-order forms of character pathology, often motivated by primitive rage and entitlement that allows the patient to bring charges regardless of truth or falsity, motivated by vengeful feelings and intensely self-justifying affects. But in addressing these issues in relation to the therapeutic alliance, the emphasis falls more on the structuring impact of these conditions on therapeutic work and the manner in which they facilitate the therapeutic process.

The relaxation of boundaries can become a slippery slope often leading to ethical or medicolegal transgressions. Any transaction between therapist and patient not prescribed by the alliance—no matter how benign or trivial—must be scrutinized for its deviations from the therapeutic frame: a patient gives a gift, invites the therapist to lunch, party, or other social gathering, offers privileged information that would profit the therapist in some way (stock tips, special deals), gives advice in an area of the patient's expertise, or the therapist reduces the fee for referring another patient or as a favor, solicits support for research or other interests, indulges in any physical touching beyond a casual handshake, reveals personal information to the patient, accepts an invitation to speak from a patient, agrees to write an introduction for a book the patient is publishing, or has any social relationship with members of the patient's family. Also we would have to include any favors a patient may do for the therapist (even favors of minor moment like bringing in the therapist's morning paper) as well as the therapist's holding therapy sessions in places other than the usual without good reason, attending social functions also attended by the patient, giving a patient a lift to the bus stop, and so on. However innocent and plausible such boundary erosions may seem, they send conscious and unconscious messages readily contradicting the alliance and have immanent potential for leading to further abuse of and deviations from the alliance.

Roles

Respective roles of both analyst and patient are part of the framework. What specific functions does the therapist perform in the course of the therapeutic process? And what specific functions does the patient perform in the course of that process? How each contributes to the process and what they can expect from each other in the course of their work together should be matters of explicit discussion and consensus. These are matters for clarification and discussion at the very beginning of treatment and may require re-examination in the light of subsequent difficulties arising in the course of therapy.

There are no set rules governing roles of analyst and patient. My own persuasion is that the analyst should think through his understanding of the nature of the analytic relationship and process to reach an evolving sense of what these respective roles require. Sorting out these roles necessarily involves a clear notion of what responsibilities each participant undertakes and how these responsibilities are to be fulfilled. The functional conditions lay the ground for asymmetrical roles for both analyst and analysand (Baranger 1993; Stone 1961).

For the patient this involves coming to the hours on time, paying the fee regularly, and engaging in the work of the analysis (bringing up meaningful material, associating according to the fundamental rule [Freud 1905c], collaborating with the analyst in the effort to find meaning and understanding, and so on). For the analyst it means being present for appointed hours, being on time, preserving the integrity of time and place of the analysis (keeping to the agreed time and not allowing interruptions such as telephone calls), listening carefully and doing his best to understand the patient's material, engaging with the patient in a mutual effort to find meaning and purpose in the patient's experience through collaborative exploration, and preserving confidentiality. The roles carry implicit boundaries and responsibilities, the observance and maintenance of which is part of the therapeutic contract. Both analyst and patient are participant observers in this process.[3]

Time and Place

Other elements of the framework have to do with maintenance of the conditions for the analytic setting. All these are matters for discussion, negotiation, and agreement. Part of the framework, therefore, is the consistency of the place of meeting, adherence to specifics of scheduling, maintaining integrity of the therapeutic hour (meaning no interruptions, no telephone calls) as far as is reasonably possible. Specifically, therapy takes place in the agreed-upon appointment times, and at no other time.[4] With regard to space, therapy occurs in the therapist's consulting room, and in no other place. A meeting between analyst and patient in any other setting constitutes a violation of the frame and is simply not therapy. If the patient is sick, hospital or home visits may be generous and charitable, but they are not therapeutic nor should they be regarded as part of the therapy. Even casual or accidental meeting of the patient—even momentary contact on the street—does not go without its reverberations in the analytic process. Any less casual or more structured extra-analytic meeting can be expected to carry an even heavier burden of connotations, transferential and otherwise. Because of such potential complications, such contacts should not be arranged (Greenacre 1959), but when they happen by chance they can readily be managed in an easy and friendly manner, without anxiety or phobic avoidance (Tarnower 1966). But because of the same implications, they should be explored in the analytic process.

Extra Sessions

Holding extra therapy sessions that are not part of the regular schedule is a deviation from the frame, but one that may or may not be indicated. In analytic treatment, extra sessions are unusual and rare—probably due to frequent scheduling of sessions. But in the psychotherapeutic setting, the need for extra sessions may arise, particularly with patients in the borderline spectrum (Meissner 1988) who may be in a regressive crisis. An inability to tolerate emotional turmoil and anxiety prompts them to pressure the therapist for extra therapeutic sessions. While there may be certain advantages to extra sessions in the initial stage of therapy as a way of dealing with the patient's immediate anxiety and consolidating the therapeutic alliance, there is also considerable benefit for many patients in *not* having this urgent need responded to immediately by a therapist. A balance is called for between the therapist's extra availability and support when indicated and the possibility of reinforcing the patient's regressive need. The therapist must judge what is in the best interest of the patient and the therapeutic process. My personal preference is to test the patient's capacity to tolerate the anxiety until the next scheduled appointment, but if a patient does not respond to this effort, I would rather offer an extra session than have the patient resort to desperate telephone calls.

Granting such an extra session to an anxious patient at the same time opens an opportunity to explore potential implications of such a course of action, for example, reinforcing the patient's sense of weakness and defectiveness and its implications for the therapy. Generally, this process of confrontation and clarification diminishes this kind of acting out. My objective is to bring the therapy into a regular pattern consistent with the therapeutic frame, limiting therapeutic contacts to the agreed-upon schedule of hours and focusing attention of the therapeutic work on long-standing, chronic issues in the patient's life rather than on crisis situations that disrupt rather than contribute to the therapeutic process. The purpose of therapy is to facilitate the patient's psychological growth rather than to alleviate anxiety. If the latter objective must be attended to, it should not be at the expense of the former.[5]

Telephone Contact

Some telephone contacts are unavoidable—arranging and canceling appointments and other factual matters. They always carry potential for deviation from the frame, especially when patients try to engage the therapist in more extensive discussions. I follow a similar pattern in dealing with telephone calls as extra sessions. When, in the beginning of therapy, the patient's inability to tolerate anxiety or depression or suicidal impulses leads to urgent telephone calls seeking help and reassurance, I respond initially but gradually impose increasingly stringent limitations. During the first few telephone calls I try to understand the patient's turmoil and offer reassuring comments. Often, little more is required than a few minutes of sympathetic listening and a reassurance that we will talk about the problem at the next scheduled session. I do not let such calls drag on, however, and progressively decrease the time for such conversation, so that the patient gradually gets the idea that the telephone is not an open channel for communication. If this behavior continues, I indicate to the patient that the call is inappropriate and that we will have to discuss the matter at our next meeting and then hang up. The question of telephone calls and the patient's anxiety and the unwillingness or inability to tolerate anxiety then becomes a focus of concern within the therapeutic work.

I believe that beneficial therapy does not take place over the telephone and that the patient's use of the telephone is a vehicle for acting out that diverts the work of the therapeutic process from its proper context.[6] A therapist may encounter rare exceptions to this view, but if a therapist uses the telephone as part of therapy, I would regard it as something other than therapy, or at best a diluted and partial form.[7] Often it is enough that the patient be able to communicate the anxiety or upset to the therapist, realize that the issues are not necessarily urgent, and know that they can and will be dealt with in therapy. Because the patient's uncertainty about these matters prompts the call, one can presume that behind the urgent need lies a further level of difficulty in the therapeutic alliance. As the therapeutic alliance consolidates and becomes more effective, such needs diminish. For patients who seem unable to communicate otherwise with the therapist, the underlying therapeutic misalliance and associated transference distortions must be brought into focus and worked on. In any case, such misuse of the telephone can become an occasion for meaningful work on the therapeutic alliance.[8]

Payment of the Fee

Arrangements for payment of the fee, the amount of money, and the manner and schedule of payment are contractual issues also open to mutual negotiation. Freud (1913) stipulated that payment of the fee involved real and neurotic issues related to both sexuality and power. He recommended monthly billing and advised against allowing a balance to accumulate or giving low-fee or free treatment.[9] These can be tricky issues for beginning therapists (Adler and Gutheil 1977; Pasternack 1977) or even more experienced practitioners who shift from one practice setting to another (institutional or training settings to private practice). The specifics are less important than the negotiations that create them. The therapist should have a thoughtful policy about setting of fees with each patient, taking into account the therapist's financial requirements—the laborer is worthy of his hire—and the patient's financial circumstances and ability to pay.[10] A systematic approach to billing and receiving payments is helpful (Kanter and Kanter 1977).[11]

One issue of some importance is charging for missed appointments—another of Freud's (1913) recommendations. Patients may have many reasons for canceling an appointment—business or personal—but their responsibility for attending therapy sessions remains in effect as long as they remain in treatment. Eissler (1974) described two approaches to this problem: the "rule of indenture," by which the patient is responsible regardless of circumstances, and the "gentleman's agreement," which allows a degree of individual discretion. Reasons for charging for missed appointments are multiple, including the labor-intensive nature of the therapist's business and the financial loss for him from such missed appointments if not charged. Payment of the fee can easily become an arena for acting out. More significant, however, are the countertransference implications. While there is room for both firmness and permissiveness (Allen 1971), negotiation and firmness around the fee carry important messages in consolidating the alliance, particularly countering the narcissistic illusion of being special and privileged. Kindness or retreat from firmness may imply that the analyst "has guilt feelings, that he is masochistic, that he is in love with the patient, that he wants to bribe the patient to love him, that he is afraid of the patient and that he is afraid of being considered greedy" (Haak 1957, p. 194). Such an accommodating attitude can effectively inhibit the patient's expression of hostility as well, resulting in displacements that will be detrimental to the therapeutic effort.

Charging for missed appointments to my mind removes a potential source of countertransference resentment of the patient. By the same token, it removes this arena from the reach of the patient's manipulativeness or need to punish the therapist for one or other reason. Charging for missed appointments is also a way of reinforcing the therapeutic contract—if the patient chooses to skip an appointment, for whatever reason, he remains responsible for it. At the same time, another part of the alliance is respectful of the patient's freedom to decide not to make use of his appointment. Thus, the issue as far as I am concerned is never the patient's right to make that choice, but the therapeutic concern falls rather on the patient's motives, conscious and unconscious, and their implications for the therapeutic process and relationship. Furlong (1992) has extended this view to include issues of presence and absence, separation and attachment; in this view, payment for the missed session can be viewed as a psychic marker serving to maintain the analytic space that has been vacated and left behind—"a symbol of psychological movement which does not sap the Other's vitality, and the trace of the unconscious desire of the Other" (p. 716). Thus, the therapeutic option favors firm maintenance of the frame over flexibility.[12]

A different issue arises around problems related to changing the fee. Reasons may justify raising or lowering a fee. It is not unreasonable to modify the fee schedule in the face of inflationary pressures or when exceptional circumstances arise—as, for example, when the patient's earning power increases or diminishes significantly. Such modifications, in the spirit of the alliance, should be matters for mutual negotiation. Raising the patient's fee arbitrarily has its risks and may constitute a violation of the alliance. Smith (1993) provided a clinical example of the difficulties encountered in raising the fee. His patient responded with displaced anger and acting out around payment of the new fee. Smith traces the reverberations of the change in the analytic process and the influence of transference and countertransference interactions. But a focus on the alliance and the therapeutic contract might prompt questions about how the change was decided on and implemented. The agreement was that the fee would be raised or lowered according to the patient's income, but how was the negotiation over raising the fee carried out? The patient's response might suggest that the issue was not settled to mutual satisfaction, so that a question could arise whether the requirements of the alliance had been satisfied by the conditions of the negotiation. If not, transference and countertransference perturbations could be expected, whether or not therapeutic mileage could be gotten out of them. A similar case in my own experience led to angry recriminations and an efflorescence of negative transference reactions.[13]

A case came to my attention in which the therapist moved from a hospital-based to private practice—a not uncommon phenomenon. The decision to raise the fee accordingly was made unilaterally and presented to the patient as a fait accompli. The patient was understandably outraged, felt that he was paying the maximum he could afford even with an extra job, and threatened to break off the therapy. The situation was complicated by the therapist's conjoined effort to reinforce the therapeutic frame that he had been lax about—limiting telephone access, changing rules for extra appointments, and so on. These unilateral changes left the patient feeling violated, devalued, frustrated, and angry—to some extent attributable to his entitlement but also in some degree reflecting his resentment at the authoritarian treatment he was getting. The question in this case was not whether the changes were proper and therapeutic or not, but whether the manner in which they were implemented was inconsistent with a good therapeutic alliance. It was clear in the patient's mind that if the therapist had taken the trouble to discuss these matters and his reasons for wanting to make the changes, the patient would not have found them unreasonable.

In sum, financial arrangements for charging and paying the fee provide a significant boundary for the therapy and the therapeutic relation that has both material and symbolic implications. No other material or financial transactions are called for by the alliance. Giving gifts on the part of the patient or the analyst (Freud's behavior with the Rat Man and the Wolf Man to the contrary not withstanding) or offering services beyond those inherent in the therapeutic contract is not consistent with the alliance. I regard gifts from patients as usually reflecting a transference fantasy (Rothstein 1986; see discussion in chapter 7). Dealing with matters of gifts and rendering of services beyond those entailed in the treatment are not so much matters of contractual agreement as appropriate limit-setting and boundary maintenance on the part of the therapist.

Self-Disclosure

Considerations regarding self-disclosure call for appropriate boundaries. The therapist must keep in mind that the therapy is for the patient and only for the patient. Considerations of self-gratification or acting out of inner needs and conflicts on the part of the therapist are not part of the therapeutic frame nor of the therapeutic process. Within that limit, use of the therapist's own experience as a basis for interpretations is entirely appropriate, but beyond that perspective a boundary can be crossed and the frame violated. Interaction between therapist and patient has moved from the therapeutic alliance to the real.[14]

Physical Contact

Similar considerations come into play with regard to any form of physical contact. There is no form of physical contact called for by the therapeutic frame. Boundaries regulate the appropriately shifting distance between therapist and patient (Bouvet 1958). Incidental physical contact, however, may not infringe on the therapeutic arena—as, for example, a cordial handshake at the door as the patient enters or leaves the consulting room, or when the therapist's foot accidentally brushes against the patient's in shifting position. This latter incident is entirely accidental and trivial. The handshake is neither accidental nor trivial.[15] As Gutheil and Gabbard (1993) note, "From the viewpoint of current risk-management principles, a handshake is about the limit of social physical contact at this time" (p. 195). If the patient initiates the contact, it may not have any further meaning than a cordial and friendly gesture; then again it may. The patient may be acting out some inner need through the behavior; the therapist may do no more than note it mentally, but it may also become material for therapeutic discussion. In my view, for the therapist to initiate the handshake is a crossing of boundaries that does not belong to the therapeutic frame. Any other forms of physical contact between therapist and patient are clear violations of the frame and should be dealt with as such. Expressions of physical affection are clear violations of the therapeutic frame and cross the line into ethical, if not legal, culpability (Weiner 1972).[16] As Lester (1993) notes, certain regressive transferences can generate ambivalent sadomasochistic struggles to control the analytic distance, resulting in countertransference pulls either to succumb to the patient's regressive demands or to punitively re-establish the analytic frame.

Important Decisions

Delay in making important decisions during analysis is not an ironclad rule. Life circumstances at times make such decisions necessary—even during analysis. The point of this aspect of the frame is to provide a hedge against acting out or making such decisions impulsively or as a result of neurotic motivations.

The delay factor urges the patient to explore and reflect adequately on the options, implications, and consequences before coming to a decision. This perspective is congruent with the analytic approach in which the emphasis is put on exploration and understanding as preceding and essential for adaptive and constructive action.

Deviations

Deviations from the framework can occur by reason of circumstance or they may have a motivational component. Accidental occurrences do not necessarily rule out motivational factors. A patient may arrive late due to a breakdown in the transit system, but the therapist might wonder whether this circumstance serves some hidden countertherapeutic purpose. Once is an accident, more than once might mean something else. One such patient came habitually ten to fifteen minutes for every analytic hour. There was always an excuse—weather, important telephone calls, other interfering demands, and so on. One morning he arrived twenty-five minutes late—the streetcar had broken down. But the so-called accident fit into a more general pattern of resistance to the analysis. What mattered was not the individual accident and its circumstances, but what it meant to the patient—an opportunity to act out his resistance to the process.

I am reminded of an oft-told story about Voltaire. Known as he was for his philosophical bent and his unorthodox views, a friend approached him to invite him to an orgy. Voltaire thought for moment, and replied, "I am a philosopher and a philosopher should be open to all forms of human experience. Yes I will come." Some months later, the same friend approached the philosopher with a similar invitation. Voltaire mused thoughtfully, and then declined. When asked why, he replied, "Once a philosopher; twice a pervert!" Regarding terms of the analytic frame, once an accident; more than once a deviation.

Regardless of circumstances, deviations alert the analyst to defects or failures in the alliance. Some analysts recommend confrontation of such deviations, countermanding the behavior and forcing the patient to stop it (Levenson 1992). I find this suggestion to lean in an authoritarian direction. It is not the part of the analyst to interdict or permit any acting out that deviates from or undermines the alliance. My own view is that the analytic task is to seek understanding of the behavior, leaving it up to the patient to decide on his own behavior. As Anna Freud (1954a) noted, a patient's misuse of a ground rule provides an opportunity for supporting it through interpretation and understanding rather than modifying it.

Deviations from the basic frame always carry therapeutic risks which are at times to be avoided and at times are required in the interest of dealing with a therapeutic crisis (Greenacre 1954). Any modification in the nature of the relation between therapist and patient runs the risk of contaminating the transference. Even minor modifications of neutrality—overprotectiveness, excessively nurturant support, and sympathy for the patient's suffering—may incur a cost in terms of contamination of transference or deviations from alliance. Greenacre (1959) further observed that even supportive modifications of the ground rules and frame can have adverse effects of weakening the patient's ego-functioning and critical capacity, leading insidiously to a more narcissistic alliance and to reinforcement of the patient's efforts to seek even greater deviations in the frame. Thus, in the example provided by Jacobson (1993) of extending the end of the hour, the therapeutic crisis may have justified the deviation, as he suggests, but in terms of the alliance and the multiplicity of unconscious meanings, at what cost?

I shall discuss problems of management of misalliances in chapter 16, but I am emphasizing here that observable deviations may reflect a distortion or perhaps disruption of the therapeutic alliance and call for some form of corrective response from the analyst, not necessarily interdiction. Consequently, I would not agree with Levenson's dictum: "I am saying that deviations in what I would define as the frame are mistakes, wrong, interfere with therapy and should be stopped. An authoritarian frame begets an egalitarian treatment. Paradox? Why not? Paradox is at the very heart of psychoanalysis" (p. 560). The idea that an authoritarian frame can produce an egalitarian relationship does not compute. Authoritarianism begets authoritarianism, dominance begets submission; it does so in all other human contexts and we cannot count psychoanalysis as an exception. The idea that the analyst sets about correcting the distorted version of reality or truth presented by the patient and substitutes for this neurotically motivated and deceptive view a better, truer, and higher version of the truth derived from the wisdom of the analyst does not correspond to any version of analysis that I know (with the possible exception of more extreme and dominating forms of Kleinian interpretation).

A more balanced view of the collaborative effort at understanding required by the therapeutic alliance is better considered in reference to the analyst's authority and its role in the analytic process (see chapter 12). Rather, analyst and patient have to find a way to work together to evolve a mutually meaningful and satisfactory understanding of the patient's life experience and its adaptive and defensive implications. It is not a question, therefore, of the patient's truth or the analyst's truth (Levenson 1992), but of an analytic truth that both are seeking. The analyst has no superior wisdom or clarity of vision—what he has is a method of exploration and understanding, and his task is not to provide answers but to engage the patient in a process of discovery. There is a further valid question that can be asked regarding the therapist's theoretical underpinnings and clinical experience and the role they play in the therapeutic process.[17]

CHAPTER TEN

Empathy and Alliance

The interactional perspective in psychoanalysis has gained increasing acceptance as being integral to therapeutic and theoretical consensus. The problem on both levels centers on difficulties in bringing disparate perspectives together in a coherent form that allows intrapsychic and interactional frameworks to be utilized in mutually reinforcing ways in clinical analytic work. Until Kohut (1959, 1971, 1977, 1984) elevated it to the centerpiece of his clinical approach, empathy held a respected place in clinical analysis that was more assumed than articulated. Significant exceptions were the contributions of Sullivan (1956) and Fromm-Reichman (1950), who emphasized the critical role of empathy in the treatment of even the most severely disturbed patients. One aspect of the problem relates to a clearer conceptualization of interactional and interpersonal dimensions contributing to the psychoanalytic dialogue.

I have addressed these issues in a preliminary way in previous discussions (Meissner 1992 and above), and in this chapter I shall argue that empathy is a central component of the therapeutic alliance and that it plays a specific role in the therapeutic interaction in psychoanalysis and all forms of psychotherapy. More to the point, I shall argue that empathy can be conceived of only inadequately as an intrapsychic process, and that both analyst and analysand contribute to it in meaningful ways. Empathy in the analysand in particular has been relatively neglected in psychoanalytic literature (Jacobs 1974).

The Meaning of Empathy

The nature of empathy and its role in the psychoanalytic process have been thoroughly discussed by various authors (Basch 1983; Beres 1968; Beres and Arlow 1974; Buie 1981; Greenson 1960; Kohut 1959, 1971, 1977; Lichtenberg et al. 1984; Olden 1958; Shapiro 1974). It has been described as generative empathy (Schafer 1959), coenesthetic communication (Spitz 1965), vicarious introspection (Kohut 1959, 1965), emotional knowing (Greenson 1960), resonant cognition (Kelman 1987), and even projective identification (Ogden 1979). Empathy is not based on observation, although it may intersect with observational data. Rather, it involves other forms of communication between analyst and analysand deriving from their capacities to know something about each other on the basis of their respective subjective experience of the interaction.[1] It can be distinguished from sympathy, which connotes condolence or pity (Greenson 1960)—sentiments not congruent with the alliance—and can assume various forms or varying degrees of distance from the object (Shapiro 1974). Empathy based on the community of human experience involves relative distance as it may not be personal, individual, and immediate but rather reached through conscious subjective construction.[2] Empathy can assume a more existential and immediate form, occurring more intuitively and unconsciously and reflecting earlier, more instinctual, largely affective components. In its regressive extreme, empathy can lean to diffusion of boundaries between subject and object and weakening of reality testing.

The developmental roots of empathy lie buried in the preverbal affective attunement between mother and child (Basch 1983; Harris 1960; Stern 1985; Winnicott 1971). The preverbal quality of empathic experience prompted Rayner (1992) to apply Langer's (1942) distinction between presentational and discursive symbolism: the former is visual, auditory, or kinesthetic, but essentially preverbal; the latter is exclusively verbal. This sort of preverbal affective attunement with another involves a degree of self-transformation (Bollas 1987) bordering on the aesthetic and is central to empathic attunement to the subjective experience of the other. Analyst and patient develop a "private language" of allusions, cryptic references, symbolic gestures, and other forms of privileged communication to which outsiders have no access and which become reflections of increasing mutual adaptation (Schlesinger 1994). Along this vein, Havens (1978, 1979) explored the empathic use of language in psychotherapy (e.g., use of pronouns to increase or diminish empathic distance between therapist and patient). Empathic statements are active in searching out the other, passive in supporting and echoing the patient's thoughts and feelings. Empathic statements are accepting and therefore validate the patient's feelings, allow expression of uncomfortable feelings, and bring into play a containing and integrating force that opens the way to more benign superego reactions.

Developmental contributions to the capacity for empathy are not limited to infantile forms of emotional attachment and encompass the full range of developmental achievement.[3] Preverbal attunement must be complemented by developmental attainments from other levels, including oedipal and postoedipal phases, as a basis for empathic resonance with later developmental dimensions of the other's experience and as a necessary contribution to self-object differentiations.[4]

Empathy as Trial Identification

Classic analysis, with antecedents in Freud (1912–13, 1915b), interpreted empathy as a form of trial identification allowing the analyst to understand the subjective experience of the patient. This view bases empathy in the internal experience of the analyst, a perspective I find constraining for the interactional perspective I am developing here. Moreover, basing empathy on a form of identification raises difficulties insofar as it is not identification in the sense I have come to in previous writings (Meissner 1970, 1971, 1972, 1981).[5] If identification connotes a form of internalized structural modification in the self-organization, empathy remains a phenomenon of a different order. It is experiential and transient, a cognitive-affective form of experiencing that attunes the subject to communications from another leading to some intimation of the state of mind or inner experience of the other. In this sense, rather than internalization, it is a complex form of affectively attuned perception and awareness that does not imply anything structural or necessarily internalized. Whatever the content of experience intuited from another, it is in the form of an action or activity that internalizes nothing from the other in the process.

This view runs counter to more traditional views of empathy as a form of "trial identification" (Basch 1983; Beres 1968; Beres and Arlow 1974; Fliess 1942; Greenson 1967; Levy 1985; Olinick 1969, 1975; Olinick et al. 1973; Reich 1966; Schafer 1959; Weigert 1954a).[6] Poland (1974) extended Racker's (1957) view of concordant and complementary identifications to empathy[7] and concluded, "The wish to understand the patient leads to the analyst's readiness to 'put himself in the patient's shoes.' With this sense of 'I am like you,' the analyst tends to identify part for part with the patient, e.g., 'My urges are like your urges, my ego like your ego, my superego like your superego.' It is this quality which is referred to as concordant identification" (pp. 285–286). Or, as Olden (1953) puts it, empathy is "the capacity of the subject instinctively and intuitively to feel as the object does" (pp. 112–113). However, it seems to me that this exaggerates the case. My state of empathic attunement with my patient is not synonymous with any experience of myself as simply like the patient, but involves a sense of self as like but unlike the other. Empathy may enjoy its best degree of validity when the experience is discordant rather than concordant.[8] Empathic attunement requires a capacity for self-decentering that allows one to be open to the experience of another. The concordant variant is more at risk of seeing (or mis-seeing) the other as like me than of seeing myself as like him. Likewise, viewing empathy as a form of projection (Beres and Arlow 1974; Berger 1984), despite its antecedents in Freud (1905b; Pigman 1995), has its difficulties. To the extent that it is projective, it is not empathic; rather than attuning to the self-experience of the object, it attunes the object to one's own self-experience. The reliance on overblown assumptions of our empathic astuteness are not only risky but are an open invitation to countertransference distortions (Langs 1976), particularly of a narcissistic variety.

This consideration raises a sticky theoretical problem vis-à-vis object relations and their role in self-other experience (Meissner 1979a). The theoretical issue is that the concept of trial identification is cast in terms of the classical one-person metapsychology. *Object relation* in that usage is equivalent to *object representation,* so that, by implication, attunement to the other is filtered through a subjectively internal representation of the other. This raises the problem of how and to what extent one can grasp the reality of the other. The point is neatly focused by Brice (1984) in his discussion of Buber's I-Thou and analytic object relations:

> This theoretical lacuna is especially evident throughout the psychoanalytic literature on empathy. Analysts have described empathy in various ways: as a trial identification based on the analyst's projective identification with the patient (Fliess 1942); as a regressive phenomenon based on the analyst's internal model of the patient (Greenson 1960) or on his fusion of self and object images (Olinick 1969), and conversely, as a phenomenon which depends on his conflict-free internalizations of and externalizations onto the patient (Schafer 1959). The patient, as the other that he or she is, does not appear in these accounts. The analyst: (a) incorporates an image of the patient, in which case the patient's experience becomes the analyst's own and the exclusivity of the patient's experience is lost; (b) fuses with his image of the patient and theoretically disappears, making a true meeting with the patient impossible; or (c) searches his "repertoire" of emotional experiences for one similar to that of the patient's, thus empathizing with himself, not with the patient. (p. 120)

Varieties of Empathic Experience

But our understanding of empathy is not constrained to the dichotomy of perception versus identification. Paul's (1967) definition sidesteps this objection: "Empathy is an interpersonal phenomenon that occurs when the empathizer, or subject, recognizes that he shares kindred feelings with another person, the object" (p. 153). True empathy, then, can attune to the experience of another and recognize similarities with one's own subjective experience, while keeping adequate perspective on differences (Treurniet 1983). The more closely aligned the analyst and patient are—biologically, psychologically, and culturally—the more likely it is that their unconscious affective communications will be mutually attuned and responsive (Basch 1983).

Freud (1915b) related empathy to unconscious communication between analyst and analysand: "It is a very remarkable thing that the *Ucs.* of one human being can react upon that of another, without passing through the *Cs.* This deserves closer investigation . . . but, descriptively speaking, the fact is incontestable" (p. 194). Whether the communication takes place on the unconscious or conscious level, it involves a complex process of interpersonal cuing and metacommunication. It may reflect complex forms of nonverbal communication, more affective than cognitive, including more or less conscious components.

Buie (1981) describes four subcategories of empathy in the analyst's experience of the therapeutic interaction: conceptual empathy, self-experiential empathy, imaginative-imitative empathy, and resonant empathy. Conceptual empathy arises from experiences with others or oneself, as well as more general experiences based on the creative symbolism of myth, art, and religion. Such empathy involves integration of specific self and object representations: the analyst may construct a conceptual model of the patient that includes a more elaborate, accurate, and individualized impression based on data gathered in the course of analysis (Greenson 1960, 1967; Kernberg 1993; Peterfreund 1975).

Self-experiential empathy derives from the analyst's memories, affects, feelings, impulses, superego, and other complex expressions of the analyst's inner world. They provide the basis for empathic attunement to the inner world of the patient, particularly affective dimensions of the patient's experience. Empathic attunement may also come through imitative use of the analyst's imagination, yielding a vicarious experience derived from sympathetic and imitative responsiveness to the patient's description of his own experience. Similar forms of empathy come into play in attending a moving drama or reading an engrossing work of fiction or poetry.

Empathy can also be based on affective resonance, described as a "primitive form of affective communication that has been called 'contagion,' in which a strong affect in one individual simply stimulates the same affect in the others" (Furer 1967, p. 279). As Buie (1981) cautioned, empathically derived affective experience may not mirror the inner experience of the object. The inherent limitations of empathic understanding do not prevent its serving as an invaluable guide in the work of therapy, but it cannot be relied on without some degree of verification from other analytic data (Margulies 1984). Absolute verification is impossible, but consistent effort to sharpen and confirm empathic impressions can significantly improve the accuracy and effectiveness of empathic understanding (Buie 1981; Meissner 1991).

Empathy in the Therapeutic Alliance

As Chessick (1985) notes, empathic attunement to the affective experience of another, especially to unconscious aspects, is one of the most basic and difficult skills required of the psychoanalyst or psychotherapist. Rayner (1992) has commented, "to be therapeutic, the analyst must be authentic, or speak from his true-self. This honesty is an emotional state and must somehow become recognized by the patient" (p. 39). Equally pressing is the patient's capacity to be authentic and that this emotional state be recognized by the analyst. This communication is mutually interactive and takes place on a preverbal and often infantile level, often under the influence of unconscious determinants. It is another case of *cor ad cor loquitur,* of the grounding of the I-Thou that Buber (1958) postulated as essential to any meaningful interpersonal relation.

It should also be clear that the affective attunement and communication involved in empathy does not contradict the reserve and emotional continence required by analytic neutrality (Poland 1984). Empathy does not call for softening of analytic anonymity, nor does it sustain any need for self-revelation—both potential variants of misalliance. Rayner (1992) puts the matter this way:

> The question posed for technique . . . is, thus, not whether the analyst should *aim* to reveal his private feelings—the answer to that is still, no. Rather it is, how much vocalization of feeling arising out of attunement to the patient is optimal for the patient to use? Perhaps, as just suggested, the analyst should never aim to express his feelings, but they may emerge in small doses from his position of continence and be detected by the patient. If the analyst is then not too guilty and jumpy, an atmosphere may exist where the patient can use his awareness of the emotionality. Sometimes the patient's fantasy will distort his reading of the analyst, sometimes not. This seems to be a natural fact of the analytic dialogue which can be used or misused. (p. 52)

This dynamic puts empathy at the heart of the therapeutic relation and specifically of therapeutic alliance. The point was made by Schlesinger (1981): "Responding empathically to a patient is only possible when the therapist can split himself into transference figure and therapeutic ally. Empathizing in this sense is not a capacity of transference figures who, after all, are figments of the patient's imagination and whose moods are defined by the transference scenario. The transference figure does not have independent freedom of movement. The therapeutic ally, however, can move independently. If the therapist (therapeutic ally) can separate himself from the transference figure, he can comment on the interaction between the transference object and the patient. The ability of the therapeutic ally to comment from several positions amounts to the ability to respond empathically" (p. 413). I should add that the same proposition can be made for empathic involvement of the patient mutatis mutandis.

Empathy in the Analyst

Empathy is a sine qua non of analytic work. For the analyst, it is one of the basic sources of analytic data providing information concerning the patient's inner mental state (Basch 1983; Meissner 1989, 1991). It provides the essential basis of analytic tact in the technical implementation of any intervention on the part of the analyst (Poland 1974, 1975). At the same time, from the point of view of the patient, it offers a channel of information about the analyst.

Olinick's (1976) comments on the relation of empathy to the analyst's work ego are to the point:

> Empathy is a phenomenon of two persons transacting; it entails processes both between and within each of the participants. It is a way of learning to know the other person by means of a rapid collating and organizing of apparently disparate data into a harmoniously corresponding system. To accomplish this . . . the empathizing analyst must enable an integration of his own external and internal perceptions. He does this by utilizing his regressive thoughts, reveries, and perceptions as they emerge during his evenly hovering attention; he associates to them in the context of what he already knows about the patient, consciously and otherwise, and discerns through clinical judgment and experience whether this meets the objective test of veracity and validity. By means of the empathic experience, the analyst is able to evolve in a creative way a working model of the patient out of seemingly incongruous internal and external perceptions. (pp. 10–11)

Put in these terms, empathic experience is not the same as any form of introjection or identification, but it does call on more mature integrative and synthetic functions of the self, involving id, ego, and superego. The attunement pertains to intrapsychic and interpsychic spheres for both participants and brings them into a meaningfully shared realm of experience. A point further advanced by Olinick (1976) is that this empathic attunement and resonance takes place within the realm of transitional experience described by Winnicott (1953). Olinick (1976) comments further: "These processes between inner and outer reality partake of both intrapsychic and interpersonal functions; they operate between primary and secondary process, having their origin in the period of separation and individuation from the mother-child matrix of infancy. As factors in progressive development, the transitional processes have much that is valuable and durable. They may lead to the developing of sound relationships, reality-orientation, imaginative living, and creativity" (p. 11). The emphasis usually falls on the role of empathy on the part of the analyst and its contribution to work of the analysis. Freud (1921) regarded empathy as central to the interpretive process since it provided access to another's mental life. It plays a role in formulating interpretations and shaping the timing and manner of interpretation (Kohut 1980; Levy 1985). It helps the analyst attune himself not merely to the analysand's conscious experience, but to unconscious experience as well—to what is avoided, repressed, fantasied, and desired—and to the developmental level congruent with the patient's experience (Gedo 1979, 1988;

Gehrie 1993; Modell 1988b). A balance of empathic and other avenues of analytic inquiry have much to recommend them. This compatibility of empathic impressions with other sources of information about the patient helps to distinguish empathy from projection, and it is important to keep the two separate clinically, since the former is a central capacity contributing to the alliance, while the latter is defensively motivated and linked to countertransference rather than alliance.[9]

But the analyst is also called on to empathize not only with the patient's negative transference resistance, but also despite the radical divergence in background and experience that arises (Beres and Arlow 1974)—for example, in cross-gender or cross-racial or cross-cultural analyses. In reference to therapy with borderline patients, Kernberg (1979) observed: "Empathy, however, is not only the therapist's intuitive emotional awareness of the patient's central emotional experience at a certain point; it must also include the therapist's capacity to empathize with what the patient cannot tolerate within himself. Therapeutic empathy, therefore, transcends that involved in ordinary human interactions and also includes the therapist's integration, on a cognitive and emotional level, of what is actively dissociated or split off in borderline patients" (p. 300). The analyst may be called on to address failures of empathy in the analysand (London 1985), or even not to provide empathic mirroring or support for the patient (Gedo 1977). The empathic process may, in turn, summon a degree of regressive attunement in the analyst for him to be in touch with the affective tone in the patient (Jacobs 1991). But again, this does not call for structural regression so much as topographical regression (Modell 1968). Empathy is a form of cognitive and affective communication and receptivity in relation to other humans; its determinants are multiple and complex but cannot depend on projection and need not depend on internalization. It is an experienced component of all meaningful human relationships. Internalizations, including identifications, contribute to the development, not to the actualization, of empathic capacity. The extent to which introjective dynamics (Meissner 1978) can enter into and interact with the empathic process varies, but they are by no means synonymous.[10]

Limits

Even so, empathy has its limits. The current overemphasis on empathy in psychoanalysis puts the analyst at risk of overestimating his capacity to know and understand the inner mind of the patient empathically, and undervaluing other sources of information about the patient (Good 1994; Meissner 1991).[11] Even more subtly, reliance on empathic mirroring may undermine the mutual effort toward collaborative investigation. Some patients may experience overly empathic responses as intrusive, as though the analyst could read their minds, a breach of separateness and distance that can be threatening and dangerous (Spence 1993). Risks arise with regard to premature closure, premature or inaccurate consensus on the meaning of the patient's experience (thus blocking access to unconscious fantasies or transference material), or interference with the patient's working through his own integration of the meaning of his experience (Goodman 1992; London 1985; Moses 1988; Stern 1988). And for some patients, particularly those with more primitive personality structures, empathic understanding may consciously or unconsciously feed fantasies of merger or union with the analyst, pose the threat of being devoured or penetrated, and thus provoke defenses of denial or avoidance of such understanding (Rycroft 1958).[12]

Nonetheless, not all analysts possess the same or an optimal degree of empathic capacity. Some analysts bring a high degree of empathic attunement and intuitive gifts to their analytic work, while others must make do with capacities of a more modest sort. Analysts who possess this gift in abundance must be wary of excessive reliance on it without the buffering support and confirmation drawn from other sources of information about the patient's internal states of mind. By the same token, analysts who are not as endowed in this area must rely more on historical, observational, verbal, and experiential/introspective sources of analytic data about the patient's inner life (Meissner 1991). No analyst worthy of the name is entirely devoid of empathic sensitivity, but for some it is not a strength of their analytic style.

Empathy in the Analysand

The role of empathy in the analysand and its place in the psychoanalytic and psychotherapeutic relation has been generally neglected. Insofar as empathy is an essential ingredient in the therapeutic alliance, it is essential not only from the side of the analyst but from the side of the patient as well. As Chessick (1985) observed: "If the therapist can not get himself or herself into the shoes of patients and somehow give them the feeling that he or she really understands where they are coming from intrapsychically—their self states—and what is important to them, then the patient cannot respond to the therapist as someone who is useful to them as a selfobject in resuming their development. Either there will develop a misalliance with a collusion, or the therapy will break up" (p. 40). To which I would add that unless the patient can get himself into the shoes of the therapist, possibilities for meaningful alliance will also be limited. Without a degree of empathic attunement from the patient, any therapeutic alliance is meaningless and futile (Greenson 1960; Makari and Shapiro 1993; Poland 1974)[13]

The forms of empathy in analyst and patient differ only with respect to their roles in the analytic relation. Following Buie's (1981) categorization, the analysand also constructs a conceptual model of the analyst, based on the flow of interactional experiences arising between them. The referents of such conceptual empathy are immediate, subjective, and personalized, and may reflect some functional model of personality and character in the patient's mind. To the extent that they can be contaminated by projective elements, they become less empathic. The patient's operative model of the analyst usually does not have the contextual refinement or the analyst's theoretically based understanding and sensitivity. The patient's empathy can also be self-experiential, or it may take place through imitative imagination or by way of affective resonance, as in the analyst. The effectiveness of such empathic involvement depends on the degree to which the experience is objectively rather than subjectively derived.

However, in conjunction with demands of the alliance, the patient's empathy comes into play in terms of his capacity to relate to the analyst as a helpful, positive, well-intentioned, supportive, and effective practitioner of his therapeutic task. There may be other reasons why a particular patient decides to engage in therapy with a particular therapist, but among them must be reckoned a sense of comfort, of confidence in the analyst sufficient to allow the neurotic defenses to yield and the therapeutic process to begin. The patient must be sufficiently empathically attuned to the person of the analyst in his function as helper and healer to establish and maintain the therapeutic involvement.

The further vicissitudes of the analytic process depend on the degree to which such empathic resonance can be meaningfully sustained in the face of transference erosions and distortions of the object representation of the analyst in the course of the analysis. This consideration comes into play in the face of the analyst's mistakes or empathic lapses in the course of the analytic work. Just as there are inevitable lapses in parental empathy (Arlow 1979), there are inevitable lapses in therapeutic empathy—every analyst, experienced or not, makes mistakes.[14] As Chused and Raphling (1992) write: "Mistakes are inevitable—in analysis as in life. However, analysis is a process in which one explores rather than denies the inevitable. When an analytic mistake is probed, often the unspeakable, the shameful, and the forbidden are revealed. The affective distress, consciously associated with the mistake, can then be related to the unconscious conflictual wish or fantasy that motivated the mistake. Analysis, at its best, is a therapeutic process in which mistakes are put to good use" (p. 115). While the focus of their discussion is on vicissitudes of the analyst dealing with and integrating his mistakes, the unspoken supposition is that working through the implications of any mistake on the part of the analyst requires a degree of empathic resonance on the part of the patient that allows him to remain in affective and therapeutic touch with the analyst's best intentions. In this sense, the alliance provides a degree of latitude and security within which both partners are able to make errors without disrupting the analytic process (Levenson 1992).

Many authors stress the difficulties created by empathic failures of the analyst (Kohut 1984; Langs 1976, 1982; Schwaber 1979). Whatever deleterious effects result from such inevitable failures, their correction and therapeutic resolution depend on restoration or maintenance of the empathic connection of the patient to the analyst. At times acknowledgement of empathic failures is called for, consistently with the alliance, but a too easy or too ready tendency to admit such failures may bridge over into masochistic countertransference territory and provide grounds for further resistance (Treurniet 1983).[15] In this connection, Levenson (1992) makes a useful distinction between technical errors and failures in maintaining the frame; the former can be explored and analyzed, the latter are better simply stopped.[16]

Empathy versus Transference

The form of empathy that contributes to alliance is distinct from transference reactions: the patient's empathic operative model of the analyst reflects something of the inner world of the actual analyst. Models based on transference distort perception of the analyst and any appreciation of the analyst's inner world. Elements of displacement and projection that undergird transference distortions undermine empathic attunement. Consequently, just as the analyst's countertransference distortions can interfere with his empathic attunement with the patient, the patient's transference derivatives may get in the way of his empathic contact with the analyst. The patient's lack of affective attunement can be placed at the service of transference gratification or the need to undermine the alliance (London 1985). Some patients resist empathic understanding and avoid being understood due to unconscious associations with power and control (Greenson 1960). How much of the analysand's experience of the analyst depends on transference components and how much on valid and realistic apprehensions of the analyst remains a nagging issue throughout the course of any analysis. As Poland (1974) noted: "Just as the role of empathy must be considered in the context of the total psychology of the analyst, so too must it be viewed regarding the patient's empathic capacities. Empathy serves the analyst as a perceptual mode for knowledge of the patient in the service of the goal of insight; empathy with the analyst is often used by the patient in the service of his efforts to obtain transference gratification and to guard against the experience of anxiety" (p. 296).

In this sense, empathy lies exclusively in the alliance sector and not in the transference sector. Transference is by definition an impediment and interferes with empathic resonance. Transference substitutes something else for the empathic grasp of the analytic object, the transference distortion implying that it injects into the analytic relation a set of images, impressions, and affective responses attributable to a different set of objects than the analytic one. Nor is there any contradiction in the patient experiencing transference derivatives while preserving an empathic connection with the analyst. This form of analytic split preserves the discrimination between fantasy and reality, between affectively toned and fantasy-related experience of transference on one hand, and continued contact with and rudimentary awareness that the analyst does not quite fit the paradigm and that the reality of the analytic situation remains at variance with the tone and imaginative content of transference on the other.

In most patients, a reasonable degree of empathic attunement is readily available and remains comparatively stable throughout the analysis. There are some patients, however, whose capacity for empathy is compromised or so overrun by the forcefulness of their transference experience that transference fantasy and the person of the analyst become one. In some of these patients, the analytic process is overwhelmed by a profoundly negative transference impervious to any objective clarification or interpretation. But one of the basic problems is the inability of the patient to gain any empathic attunement with the analyst. More often than not, any possibility for empathy is erased by transferential projections derived from the patient's own internalized and pathological introjects and self-images.

The brand of empathic selectivity that can attune itself only to certain aspects of the object has been described strikingly in certain borderline patients (Krohn 1974; Meissner 1984a), who demonstrate a remarkable sensitivity to latent and unconscious impulses and motives. They seem unusually responsive to unconscious fantasies and impulses and to more primitive superego tendencies in others. Any positive aspects of the functioning of the other, however, are held in distrust, so that any integration of the enduring, consistent, and constructive aspects of objects becomes unlikely. Primitive and drive-related aspects of the object's functioning are taken as valid and genuine, while positive aspects of character, self, and personality are regarded as fake or untrustworthy. Such patients also tend to regard elements of their own ego-functioning, character style, and self-organization as unreal or phony. This empathic selectivity makes a point relevant to the analyst as well, namely, that the empathic resonance in therapeutic alliance cannot be partial but must embrace the full scope of the patient's self-system and personality. Empathy on both sides of the analytic couch includes potentially conscious intentions and unconscious motives, drive derivatives and ego states, as well as the affective tone and superego expressions in the personality of the other member of the dyad.

But the relative capacity for meaningful empathy is not simply a function of the level of psychic structure. Impediments to empathic experience are not found only in primitive character disorders. Reasonably healthy and neurotic patients can at times show similar difficulties. Often enough, the analyst may think that the patient is resisting, but any attempt to work directly on the "resistance" will more likely be experienced by the patient as confirmation of his distorted view of the analyst. The issue lies rather in the therapeutic alliance and the patient's inability to connect with the analyst in any empathic way, or the reverse. When such difficulties are at work, the outcome is more than likely to be therapeutic impasse. Whatever approach an analyst or therapist might choose, no technical maneuver can create empathy where none exists. The ultimate determinant of therapeutic outcome, even resolution of a therapeutic impasse, lies in the patient. The prospects depend on mobilization of resources in the patient to gain a more empathic footing in the analysis.

Empathic Listening

The capacity for empathic listening has been the hallmark of the physicianly healer (Pickering 1978), and particularly the psychological healer, throughout the history of the healing professions. As Jackson (1992) notes, "The psychological healer, in particular, is one who listens in order to learn and to understand; and, from the fruits of this listening, he or she develops the basis for reassuring, advising, consoling, comforting, interpreting, explaining, or otherwise intervening" (p. 1623). A primary need of the sufferer is for someone to listen to and understand his pain. The simple experience of accepting, nonjudgmental, empathic, and sympathetic listening can bring psychological relief (Stolorow 1993). The "talking cure" was effective because it was received by an empathic listener. Freud (1912) expressed this in terms of "evenly-suspended attention" (p. 111) and turning "his own unconscious like a receptive organ towards the transmitting unconscious of the patient" (p. 115). Reik (1948) referred to the analyst's "third ear," which allowed the analyst to attune himself to the patient's subjective experience and facilitate more meaningful communication between sufferer and healer. Not only is an empathic stance essential to alliance, but listening from the vantage point of alliance facilitates the analyst's and the patient's empathic listening.

This idea brings the present reflection into contact with the role of empathy as described by Kohutian self psychology.[17] Empathy in the psychoanalytic process was one of the major themes in his work (Kohut 1971, 1977, 1984). In his usage, empathy was not merely a channel for information gathering—his empathic introspective mode of observation (1959) or "vicarious introspection," which he regarded as the only tool at the analyst's disposal for knowing the inner state of another—but also a clinical technique involving the analyst's immersion of himself in the patient's subjective experience and communication of his understanding of the patient's experience in a reflective and nonjudgmental manner (Goodman 1992).[18] In Kohutian usage, empathy involves supplying the patient's selfobject needs for missing structure or function, and empathic failure implies a failure to supply such functions (Schwaber 1979). Schwaber's (1979) description is apt: "The 'empathic' point of view may then employ a particular focus of the analyst's attention and perception which is tuned more sharply to how it feels to be the subject, rather than the target of the patient's needs and demands, to the subtleties of the analyst-patient interactive vicissitudes, to the more immediately perceived, closer to awareness, expressed state of the patient, in utilizing this kind of analytic responsiveness, creates and recreates an emerging self" (p. 472). In these terms, empathic mirroring has acquired a place in the armamentarium of analytic techniques, if only to communicate to the patient that affect has been received and shared with the analyst. Rayner (1992) suggests that such preverbal, affect-attuned exchanges might serve as necessary precursors for meaningful verbal communications.[19]

Kohut's formulations have spawned an active debate regarding the place of empathy in psychoanalysis—rational understanding and insight versus emotionality and affective attunement on one hand, and a theory of affects and affective communication versus a romanticized and quasi-mystical approach on the other (Bornstein and Silver 1981; London 1985; Makari and Shapiro 1993; Strenger 1989). The debate centers around the nature of empathy: is it a special mode of perception or source of data allowing the analyst to resonate with the patient's state of mind? Or does it also possess a curative function that mobilizes growth potential of the self? While there is general agreement that empathy is required in understanding patients and provides an important component of the analytic relation, disagreements arise around the extent to which empathy can be relied on as a source of knowledge and as a technique. Blum (1981), for one, asserts that empathy devoid of interpretation and insight is ineffective. He wrote: "Empathy, which involves subliminal perception and unconscious cues, is complementary to natural-science type observation. The patient is known to be bereaved or depressed through empathy, but also through observations of the patient's stooped posture, depressed facies, frown, etc. The trial identification, nonverbal affectomotor communication, and other ingredients of the complex 'empathic process' have to be filtered through the secondary process and integrated into analytic understanding. . . . Empathy, like love, is not enough and will not, in itself, achieve analytic resolution of unconscious conflict, reintegration of the repressed, or insightful change of the personality" (pp. 53–54).[20]

Ferenczi (1919) put his finger on the nub of the tension between empathic participation and scientific observation. He wrote: "Analytic therapy, therefore, makes claims on the doctor that seem directly self-contradictory. On the one hand, it requires of him, the free play of association and phantasy, the full indulgence of his own unconscious . . . [in order to] grasp intuitively the expressions of the patient's unconscious that are concealed in the manifest material of the manner of speech and behavior. On the other hand, the doctor must subject the material submitted by himself and the patient to a logical scrutiny, and in his dealings and communications may only let himself be guided exclusively by the result of this mental effort" (cited in Makari and Shapiro 1993, pp. 992–993). Reich (1960, 1966) made the ability to shift between participant and observer perspectives central to the analytic process and a discriminating note separating empathy from countertransference. Yet the unasked question remains—does the patient's empathy exercise some curative role in the psychoanalytic process and how (Rayner 1992)?

The empathic mode of listening shifts the analyst's orientation to the patient from one that is objective to one that is better attuned to the patient's subjectivity (Basch 1986; Schwaber 1981a, 1981b). Empathy, then, becomes less a content or form of communication than a stance of the listener toward the object, whether that be the analyst joining the patient in his analytic encounter with the variety of transference imagos, unconscious fantasies, and projections populating the analytic field (Schlesinger 1981, 1994a, 1994b), or the patient joining the analyst in the effort to explore and understand the complex terrain of their mutual adventure and the depths of the patient's psychic life. Or is it a form of emotional sharing deriving from the mother-child symbiosis and functioning in a more emotional-romantic modality of analytic experience (Shapiro 1981)? Schwaber (1981a, 1981b, 1983a, 1983b) extended Kohut's mode of empathic listening as the primary method of psychoanalytic observation and data gathering. One can argue with Schwaber's assumption that such empathic listening is as central or exclusive as she suggests, but it remains important in the more complex process of analyst-patient interaction and is a central contributing component of therapeutic alliance.[21]

Therapeutic Role

Kohut (1984) described the role of empathy in terms of a two-phase model: the first phase was based on the analyst's empathic bond with the patient allowing access to an understanding of the patient's inner life; in the second phase the fruits of this understanding were conveyed to the patient through primarily dynamic and genetic interpretations. The process was meant to deepen the patient's empathic acceptance of himself and to strengthen his trust in the empathic bond with the analyst. Kohut states his case clearly: information does not cure, empathy does. Thus, experience of an empathic bond with the analytic selfobject sets the stage for transmuting internalizations that contribute to development of structure. In the second phase, empathy takes the form of communication of empathic understanding rather than the previous form of archaic affective attunement. This point of view omits the patient's empathy and its role in the analytic process. The analyst's empathic attunement is of little moment without a complementary attunement on the part of the patient to the benign and therapeutic intentions of the analyst. The analyst cannot be experienced as trustworthy without the patient being empathically attuned to that part of the analyst's self.

The debate has raged among adherents of the self psychology perspective between those who view empathy within the selfobject relationship as playing a central reparative role (Bacal 1985; Friedman 1986; Kohut 1984; Ornstein 1974; Stolorow 1983, 1986, 1993; Stolorow, Brandschaft, and Atwood 1987; Stolorow and Lachmann 1980, 1984; Terman 1989; Wolf 1988) and those who see it as an essential mode of data acquisition and the basis for further explanatory or interpretive components (Bacal and Newman 1990; Basch 1984, 1986, 1988; Chessick 1985, 1989; Goldberg 1978, 1988; Levine 1983; Lichtenberg 1983a, 1983b; Post 1980). For the latter theorists, the empathic bond is an integral aspect of the interpretive effort, even becoming an object of analytic scrutiny and exploration.[22] When he feels accepted and understood, the patient is more likely to want to communicate more about himself and his inner feelings, and the analytic relation is deepened—"more is said, more is heard, more is understood, more of a sense of being understood is experienced" (Jackson 1992, p. 1629). To which I would add—on the part of both participants who are both listeners and speakers.

Therapeutic Pitfalls

If empathy has its technical uses in the analytic process, it also has its limits. Use of empathy as an exclusive or primary source of information puts the analyst at risk of assuming he knows more about the patient than he does. He may also fail to consider adequately knowledge of the patient from other sources (Good 1994; Meissner 1989, 1991; Spencer and Balter 1990).[23] Excessive reliance on empathic mirroring can result in premature closure or false consensus on the meaning of a given experience, or it can get in the way of the patient's effort to integrate his experience for himself, or it can block further emergence of unconscious fantasy or transferential material (Moses 1988; Stern 1988). In addition, persistently validating comments from the analyst may reflect a form of deception and self-deception and may be sensed by the patient as a self-protective strategy. The unremitting focus on the patient may come across to some patients as a form of self-hiding (Slavin and Kriegman 1992). The empathic stance may also rest on a developmental perspective that nudges the analyst into a parenting role, so that, as Mayer and Spence (1994) note, "Once this stance is adopted, empathy, mirroring, and corrective experiences tend to be used in place of analysis and interpretation, and because a particular role is being enacted, the transference is clouded and other, projected roles become more difficult to discover" (p. 811). Therefore, to the extent that empathy has a therapeutic role, it must be qualified and complemented by other therapeutic stances of the analyst and other forms of analyst-patient interaction.

The advocates of empathic analytic listening are anxious to keep open the channels to the patient's inner world and seem to regard any theorizing or hypothesizing as potential interferences in this process (Baranger 1993; Schwaber 1981a). There is a dilemma here: if an analyst can only hear what the patient can express in terms of his theoretical orientation, his listening is not empathic; yet if he listens to the patient's productions without a theoretical orientation, he can make no analytic sense of them. To echo Kant, theory without data is empty, and data without theory are meaningless. The situation is complicated by the simple fact that there can be no analytic data without interpretation of some kind. As Leavy (1993) commented, "surely Schwaber and other followers of Kohut would agree that their theoretical model is exercised in their therapeutic and analytic actions, quite as much as that of any other school" (p. 416).

The situation is complicated by the intersection of subjectivities involved in the analytic relation (Schwaber 1983a, 1983b, 1986) and the nuances of subjective engagement by the analyst in encountering the analytic surface and the analytic space (Poland 1992). Analytic listening is immersed in multiple and shifting perspectives that modulate continuously with the flow and quality of clinical material (Gardner 1991). As Brenneis (1994) notes, "It is possible that analytic listening can no more be separated from thinking than perception can be separated from selection and translation" (p. 32). Agger (1993) makes the point well: "We become listeners with multiple ears. What we hear tells us about the coordinates of another person's mental experience of his or her life. We listen to the rise and run of a particular narrative from the economic, dynamic, genetic, and structural viewpoints to locate ourselves empathically so as to substantively assist with that individual's voyage of self discovery" (p. 405). The conceptual and theoretical component may express itself in Brenneis's (1994) "state of shaped expectancy": "I have been absorbing *and* sorting simultaneously. I have attended to some things more than others, but I have also drawn conclusions from what I have heard, conclusions based on a gradual building up of clusters of what my mind has linked. These clusters are like seed crystals which imperceptibly accumulate material of similar structure" (p. 39).[24] A useful balance regarding the role of the analyst's expectations and conceptual orientation in the listening process has been struck by Renik (1993, 1995b), who writes:

> I am certainly against privileging the analyst's point of view, and I think it is of the utmost importance to respect the patient's autonomy within the ana-

lytic relationship (in fact, I would say *insist* upon the patient's autonomy, inasmuch as some patients are all too disposed to abdicate it), and I think an analyst's job is to maximize the patient's exploration of his or her own psychic reality; but I do not believe that these objectives are best achieved by trying to diminish the subjectivity of the analyst's participation in analytic work.

It seems to me we have come to recognize that an analyst's contribution to a clinical analysis is constantly and irreducibly subjective, and that therefore the best way to avoid coercive influence and exploitation is not to ask the analyst to engage in the impossible task of trying to set aside his or her own values and constructions of reality, but rather to make them as explicit as possible within the treatment, putting them forward as matter for mutual consideration. Then every effort can be made to identify and question ways in which the analyst is idealized and his or her assumptions and values given undue authority by the patient. (1995b, p. 85)

Stone (1981) raised some old ghosts by comparing Kohut's use of empathy to Ferenczi's experiments with supplying patients with the acceptance and love they had missed as children. For Kohut, supplying the appropriate empathy in the analytic process would remedy the lack of maternal selfobject empathy in childhood. As Stone notes, whether or not empathy can claim the effects Kohut suggests, its contribution to the therapeutic alliance is secure. He wrote: "I do believe that the patient must feel the analyst's support, sympathetic understanding of his painful predicament, and long-term physicianly commitment to the therapeutic task, despite the stringent limitations of expression imposed by technique on a unique personal relationship" (p. 115).

Empathy as Alliance Building

I have argued that empathy is essential to therapeutic alliance and that the alliance requires mutual empathic involvement of both patient and analyst. Regardless of its inherent reparative function, the interpretive aspect of the analytic process would lack significant effect without an empathic bond between both parties: the analyst's empathic attunement guiding his interpretive stance in both form and content, and the patient's empathic attunement accepting the analyst's communication as coming from a well-intentioned, caring, and constructive source.

The role of empathy in facilitating alliance may take precedence over other interventions. A rather narcissistic and sexually promiscuous young man was facing the fact that his girlfriend of some years had decided to leave him. Despite his defensive maneuvers, he was beginning to feel a sense of loss and narcissistic injury. His revelation of these feelings to his female analyst was guarded and tentative, reflecting negative elements in his complex transference reaction to her and the fragile status of the alliance. His early fantasies of her as a mad scientist who would take away his brain and store it a locker and thus exercise some magical power over him were related to his experience with a controlling, manipulating, openly seductive, and constantly disappointing mother. Loss of his girlfriend closely followed a six-week hiatus in his analysis occasioned by the analyst's illness. He was caught between feelings of loss and the pain associated with it and his need to fend off the pain and sense of vulnerability he found so narcissistically wounding.

The analyst's intervention took the form of a somewhat dispassionate inquiry into the meaning of his loss, resulting in a series of intellectualizations and rationalizations that seemed to fit his defensive need at the moment. The question "What might her leaving mean to you?" was not inappropriate or improper, but we could question whether that was what was most needed at the moment. A more empathic comment could have indicated that the analyst was in touch with the patient's pain and his need. By approaching the situation from the vantage point of the observer and emphasizing understanding, the analyst drew the patient away from his sense of pained vulnerability and hurt. If the deeper understanding of the meaning of his experience is a pertinent and legitimate subject which the analytic inquiry would come to at some point, perhaps a question that was more to the point at this juncture would have enabled the patient to accept painful feelings of the moment. An empathic stance would have contributed needed support to the alliance, since the patient could not be sure whether the analyst was on his side or whether she would play the part of his mother. The actual question may have veered in the direction of the less-than-empathic mother who was not altogether accepting of his feelings of weakness and vulnerability. The analyst's intervention may have reflected some countertransference dynamic, possibly related to concern and some guilt for having interrupted the analysis. As it was, the patient was deprived of empathic support that he may have needed to look more deeply into his pained and disappointed feelings and his underlying narcissistic rage. He could not at that juncture entertain any degree of empathy with the analyst's good intentions or the purposefulness of her question. Only when he had developed this capacity might the patient become more open to inquiry about the meaning of his experience and its implications for self-understanding.

Alliance and Interpretation

The mutual empathic attunement of analyst and analysand makes interpretation possible and allows for its potential mutative effect on the analysand. This emphasis strikes a quite different note than the classical view of Strachey (1934) on mutative interpretation, without foregoing his perspective. But the accent shifts to the alliance in that interpretations having mutative force are related to optimizing of the empathic interaction rather than to evolution of transference. It also strikes a different chord than the Kohutian emphasis; here empathy does not cure but facilitates the alliance that will sustain the effects of further interventions.

While transference vicissitudes and alliance factors are intertwined, the interpretive process takes place in the alliance sector of the analysis. Alliance and interpretation do not play any therapeutic role without mutual empathic attunement. As to whether empathy in itself exercises a curative effect, my sense is that empathy more reflects an underlying curative process taking place through therapeutic alliance and that, if the reparative effect takes place, it is a function of the reciprocal interaction within the mutually empathic bond between analyst and patient.[25] In this context, then, inevitable empathic failures, whether of analyst or patient, are not necessarily countertherapeutic. The analytic ideal is not absolute mutual empathy, but optimal empathy—a perspective allowing for empathic defaults that leave room for potential and/or emerging separation and individuation, which are integral to the analytic process. Without such separation and the aggressive assertion of individuality accompanying it, the truly mutative internalizations and identifications that analysis seeks to facilitate would not be possible (Meissner 1981).

CHAPTER ELEVEN

Personal Qualities in the Alliance

The alliance concept, as developed here, includes not merely structural aspects of the analytic situation, but also personal qualities of the participants as they experience the vicissitudes of the analytic process. These qualities are in the first place characteristic features of the individual personalities of both analyst and patient, and, second, they reflect their mutual interaction. I have commented on the developmental underpinning of some of these qualities (trust, autonomy, and so on) in chapter 8, but in this chapter my focus is on their evolution and interaction in the course of the analytic or therapeutic process. As these aspects of alliance have a developmental ontogeny, so do they develop within the analytic process. While epigenetic sequencing of these components of the alliance cannot be laid out as elegantly as in the Eriksonian schema, they form a relative progression in the course of an analysis: trust seems to take priority over autonomy and comes into focus usually as the more dominant element in early phases of analysis, for example. Also, I shall describe the evolution of each component as the patient moves through stages of the analytic process: trust evolves from that required and characteristic of the opening phase (more closely linked with dependence), into a more developed form that interacts with other qualities of the alliance relation and the interpersonal context of the analysis. The same is true of other components mutatis mutandis. In the present chapter, I shall focus on those parameters related to the Eriksonian schema—trust, autonomy, initiative, and industry; in the following chapter, I shall concentrate on other personal factors that imbricate the therapeutic alliance—authority, freedom, and responsibility.

Trust

The earliest formulations of the concept of therapeutic alliance put excessive emphasis on early infantile origins of the capacity for alliance, especially development of basic trust. Zetzel (1956, 1965), for example, made infantile trust the core element of her view of alliance. But objections quickly arose that this primitive developmental perspective was too restrictive (Arlow and Brenner 1966). As Curtis (1979) put it: "Zetzel's hypothesis that the psychoanalytic situation uniformly recreates the earliest mother-child relationship seems an unduly broad generalization based more on analogy than on clinical data in each case. While turning to another person for help may have some of its genetic roots in the mother-child relationship (as, for that matter, every human relationship may have), it does not follow that it is the only derivation of the capacity to trust and to cooperate with another person, given the many complicated object ties and experiences encountered in development" (p. 172). Curtis labeled reduction to early developmental strata as a form of genetic fallacy (Hartmann 1939) and regarded Zetzel's recommendations for early interpretive intervention as analogous to the Kleinian penchant for early and deep interpretations—both intended to alleviate anxiety and establish trust.

Part of the problem lay in Zetzel's somewhat simplistic reliance on trust as the defining characteristic of alliance; had she paid more attention to other developmental attainments—autonomy, initiative, responsibility, and so on—her perspective may have broadened accordingly. Despite these objections, similar views of the alliance persist, largely reflecting the tension and ambiguity between seeing the alliance as excessively rational and continuing to claim a place in it for prerational components. Treurniet (1993), for example, opines that analysands know unconsciously that the alliance relationship refers back to the beginning of life; he cites Bollas (1990): "The increased sense in infancy that one is inside a container that is alive, psychic . . . and consequential. To varying degrees this alliance—*the experience of being inside a process to which one contributes*—will indeed be transferred to the clinical space as the patient reconstructs his experience of being contained . . . by the other" (p. 879). In my view, this primary infantile sense of relation is more transference than alliance and is more consistent with the "primary relationship" (de Jonghe et al. 1991) than the therapeutic relation.

Many patients come to analysis with at least an implicit sense of trust in the analyst and the analytic process. Many, however, do not. For patients to whom trust comes easily, part of the analytic work is to enable them to find a more balanced position that avoids difficulties of naivete and willing compliance, or unwillingness to evaluate or criticize the analyst's contributions. Excessively infantile trust tends to avoid certain key responsibilities that are part of the patient's functioning in the analytic context. Dependence and openness to influence from another, which is associated with trust, must eventually yield to a trust that is more limited in time, space, and quality and more consistent with an evolving alliance (Levine 1972). In contrast, for many patients issues of trust lie close to the core of their psychopathology, and they experience considerable difficulties in engaging themselves in the analytic relationship. Such patients—for example, those with severe narcissistic, paranoid, or masochistic difficulties (Doroff 1976; Kernberg 1968, 1970, 1974; Meissner 1978)—must be helped to unearth and resolve at least some sources of their mistrust in order to facilitate analytic work.

In such cases, establishing and maintaining a sense of trust becomes an objective of the analytic process requiring at times considerable effort. This can be accomplished by firm adherence to terms of the alliance, not only contractual factors and boundaries, but also to personal factors. Central to that endeavor is the analyst's self-trust and his persistent trustworthiness in his dealings with the patient. As Stone (1981) noted: "Even the patient's capacity for 'basic trust' may have evolved in relation to adequate considerateness, reliability, empathy, and a controlled but manifest interest. . . . The 'love' implicit in empathy, listening and trying to understand, in nonseductive devotion to the task, the sense of full acceptance, respect, and sometimes the homely phenomenon of sheer dependable patience, extending over long periods of time, may take their place as equal or nearly equal in importance to sheer interpretive skill" (p. 114). The patient, then, brings his capacity for trust into the analysis, but it can be reinforced or discouraged in the interaction with the analyst. By the same token, if the patient seeks gratification rather than analysis, or cannot accept the frustration of his sexual and aggressive wishes, the analyst cannot create trust where it is rejected or resisted by the patient (de Blecourt 1993).

Even though trust takes its origins from basic levels of early infantile mother-child experience, the trust that is essential to therapeutic alliance is not simply that. In my view, basic infantile trust is another form of transference—or at least not easily discriminable from unobjectionable positive transference (Stein 1981)—and is not the optimal trust desirable for the therapeutic alliance. Infantile trust may serve as a starting point for a more mature form of trust that can be meaningfully integrated with increasing degrees of autonomy and responsibility. Trust, in this view, develops, allowing for increasing degrees of circumspection, independence, and judgment. If the work of analysis in the early stages rides on a certain degree of trust in the analyst on the part of the patient, the ultimate trust toward which the process aims lies more in the patient's capacity to trust in himself in taking control of his own desires, wishes, hopes, and purposes.

This progression is paralleled in the analytic process. As the therapeutic alliance emerges out of the narcissistic alliance, the element of trust undergoes a corresponding differentiation which maintains the rudiments of basic trust and organizes them in a form of secondary elaboration in the manner of its functioning and structure.

Mehlman (1976) believes that this form of secondary trust develops in a genuine therapeutic alliance:

> The failure of secondary trust or premature closure and solidification deprives the individual of the possibility of subsequent modifications developmentally (for instance of the superego) and makes the development of a genuine therapeutic alliance by definition relatively more impossible, since the kind of relating we are talking about in a therapeutic alliance is a late development in a relatively mature system and no longer subject only to primitive object relationships. The insistence upon the primitive usage of the parental object in avoidance of this progress, altogether representing an avoidance of closure (accepting an oedipal reality, for instance), also makes the development of a genuine therapeutic alliance impossible.
>
> The development of trust, then, has its ontogeny, just as does narcissism. Basic trust would seem to be a necessary antecedent to the earlier establishment of sufficient object relationship to enable these early ego introjects to take place at all. Secondary trust or its failure has to do with subsequent traumata that necessitate the child's becoming his own parent far too early and is probably a great deal of what we struggle with in developing a therapeutic as opposed to a purely narcissistic alliance. One could rephrase this by saying that premature closure calls a halt to the process of development that brings narcissistic need and therapeutic need closer together. We would hope by the later stages of treatment that the two had begun to approximate each other. (p. 24)[1]

As we have seen, the patient's capacity for basic trust lays the ground for the patient's reorganization of narcissistic defenses to an extent that allows him to place himself in a relationship of dependence on the analyst. While it involves a reorganization of the patient's narcissistic defensive organization, the narcissistic alliance does not change the basic pathogenic configuration. It merely sets the conditions within which the patient is able to submit to the eliciting conditions of the analytic process, leading to emergence of transference elements and evolution of transference neurosis.

A transition, however, must be made from this initial level of narcissistic defensive alliance to a genuine therapeutic alliance. The critical element is transformation of basic trust into a more elaborated and secure sense of secondary trust. What makes this transition possible is empathic responsiveness of the analyst, who senses the locus of the patient's narcissistic vulnerability and provides sufficient support and reassurance for the patient to enter more deeply into the relationship without threat of further narcissistic injury. It is at this critical juncture that the characteristics and sensitive empathic response of the analyst play a key role (Greenson 1960; Olinick 1975; Poland 1975; Schafer 1959). If the analyst's demeanor in the analytic situation does not respond to the patient's sense of narcissistic need, the patient will react by premature closure, cutting off any emerging sense of further or deeper reliance on the analytic object.

Transition to a more genuine therapeutic alliance is possible only to the extent to which the patient can move to a position of sustained openness and receptivity with regard to the analytic object. For most analyzable patients, the level of secondary trust is sufficiently established to allow this transition to occur almost inadvertently. But in those patients in whom premature closure of basic trust has constituted a developmental problem, interaction with the analyst at this juncture consists of an initial reworking of the developmental defect to allow the analysis to progress. Mehlman (1976) wrote:

> It is this secondary trust which I believe must be revived or maintained if a therapeutic alliance is to be established. Needless to say, this state may well represent the end stage of many analyses, rather than the beginning and represent in those obsessional patients I mentioned the repair and amelioration of a secondarily disturbed object relationship which also prevents the establishment of close and loving *adult* relationships involving this very same sort of trust. The degree to which this openness is *not* established would also seem to determine how little beyond the situation of basic trust going on to transference development, transference flooding, and private efforts to control the patient will go. This failure would appear to be intimately involved in the inhibition of the development of the therapeutic relationship which . . . is not only the cause of but also the remedy for this kind of narcissistic emergency in therapy.
>
> It is at this juncture that the sequence of transference flooding or crisis, mobilization of defensive need, narcissistically protective resistance, analysis of the resistance and enhancement of the therapeutic alliance may be seen. On the basis of the narcissistic alliance on which the transference is based, a struggle is joined and not broken off, and the sequence of therapist interposing himself between the patient and danger by joining the patient in his struggle with it becomes the intermediary from narcissistic defense to therapeutic alliance. (p. 22)

Therapeutic alliance thus becomes the essential vehicle for further progress in the analysis. But therapeutic alliance itself is not simply established and maintained during emergence and resolution of the transference neurosis. Rather, the therapeutic alliance itself undergoes dynamic change. Moreover, at each stage of the analytic process, the status of the therapeutic alliance sets limits within which analytic regression takes place, as well as the extent to which the ego can tolerate emerging infantile derivatives and their attendant anxieties.

Emergence of the transference neurosis occurs gradually as a rule, and each step of the regressive revivification of transference elements is correlated with a deepening and a consolidating of the therapeutic alliance, even as it challenges the alliance. There is a reciprocal relationship between the predominance and intensity of transference elements in the therapeutic relationship and the operation of alliance factors. The more the relationship with the analyst is contaminated by transference factors, the more difficult it is to maintain a stable and effective therapeutic alliance. Consequently, constant effort must be made to maintain the therapeutic alliance during stages of analytic regression, as it may be eroded by the emergence of infantile derivatives in the transference neurosis (Dickes 1967).

During this phase of analytic regression and emergence of transference neurosis, trust becomes a key element in the therapeutic alliance. As regression takes place, the patient's trusting relationship with the analyst, particularly in terms of the differentiation and consolidation of secondary trust, must be continually reinforced and sustained. As transference elements deepen and reflect successively more regressed aspects of the patient's functioning and personality organization, the therapeutic alliance is increasingly threatened and undermined. This effect is primarily buffered by the capacity of the analyst to contain the patient's anxiety and protect the critical areas of narcissistic vulnerability.

So far I have discussed only the first epigenetic phase, having to do with elements of trust. To reiterate: essentially the function of secondary trust within the analytic process is to maintain a condition of openness to the analytic influence and a willingness to commit oneself to the analytic process. This trust involves a certain willing dependence on the analyst and on the analytic process, along with a sense of reliance and hopefulness that the process has meaning and will eventuate in a good therapeutic outcome. This sense of reliance on the other is an important factor in initiation of the analytic process, but if the patient remains locked in this state of willing dependence and trusting reliance, the analytic process will stalemate and therapeutic progression will be short-circuited. The not infrequent hysterical willingness to trust may be as much of a block to forward motion as the obsessional's premature closure of trust and the corresponding failure of secondary trust. In other words, excessive trust or excessive mistrust impedes the patient's capacity to enter the next phase of epigenetic development. As the analysis progresses, the element of trust must differentiate and become integrated with other emergent qualities of the therapeutic alliance. As in the epigenetic sequence in childhood, trust is not lost or eliminated in the move to the next developmental stage, but rather serves as a foundation for emergent qualities involved in the resolution of later developmental crises.

In most analyzable patients the issues of trust are sufficiently resolved so that the therapeutic alliance can be sustained and movement to subsequent phases is not impeded. Nonetheless, in many patients—and this is clearly the case in narcissistic disorders and other forms of more severe character pathology (Meissner 1988)—reworking of elements of trust is an important aspect of the therapeutic process. Resolution of infantile determinants impeding development of a genuine sense of trust presents some of the most difficult and problematic questions confronting psychoanalysis today.

Autonomy

As a quality of personal self-organization, autonomy connotes other capacities described by philosophers, such as reason and free will. Kant, for one, regarded rationality as an essential attribute of the human person, so that autonomy, which he regarded as freedom from internal constraint, came to imply freedom to be rational. In contrast, J. S. Mill interpreted autonomy as freedom from external constraint, thus making freedom the essential ingredient. Others regard the notion of autonomy as requiring both the capacity for reasonable decision making and freedom (Ost 1984). As the patient enters the analytic situation, he must do so freely. Requirements for informed consent are largely concerned with this form of autonomy. The patient's commitment to the analytic process is of his own volition and in this sense autonomous. This satisfies Mill's criterion for autonomy, but not Kant's; freedom from internal constraint is open to question and for the most part in doubt.

Within the professional relation between therapist and patient, two prevailing models impinge on the question of relative autonomy in their interaction. The first model, based on authoritarian principles, provides for autonomy of the therapist. The distribution of autonomy is thus defined by the relative autonomous functioning of the treater and by the subordination and dependency of the treated.[2] The second model is contractual, as implied in the discussion of the therapeutic contract. This model is egalitarian, regards informed consent not only as an entrance requirement but as a continuing component of the therapeutic process, and respects and supports patient autonomy (Agich 1985). This second model is consistent with therapeutic alliance; the first is not.

Autonomy is essential to an effective analytic process as well as being one of the capacities continually fostered by the process itself. The alliance is a major aspect of the analytic structure contributing to authentic autonomy in the patient. Levy and Inderbitzin (1992) bring this connection into sharp relief in their discussion of neutrality:

> In all the analyst's interpretive efforts, an overriding aim is expansion of the analysand's ego autonomy from id, superego, and reality, including the

> reality of the analyst's influence. While such autonomy is always relative, the analyst attends especially to the patient's capacity for independent (autonomous) self-observation and steadily interprets the intrusion of conflict into this central ego function with an eye toward facilitating post-treatment self-analysis. . . . Psychoanalysis promotes autonomy by virtue of its expansion of the analysand's ability to recognize these intrapsychic conflicts and to utilize the signal function generated by disphoric affect to activate self-observing capacities rather than automatically resort to regression and defense. (p. 1010)

Autonomy plays a central role in the ego-psychological view of the analytic process. The ego in that view was the intermediary of autonomy (Loewenstein 1972)—the basic rule, for example, accentuated the conflict between autonomous and defensive functions, enhancing certain autonomy functions (e.g., self-observation, verbalization) and inhibiting others. As Loewenstein (1972) commented, "Only patients with some degree of integrity of the ego are accessible to psychoanalytic treatment. This means intactness not alone of some defenses, but also of autonomous functions. The very prerequisites of the analytic situation hinge upon them. The autonomous ego is the medium through which patients communicate to the analyst what they observe in themselves" (p. 5). Fair enough, but the communicating ego is never simply autonomous; to steal a leaf from Lacan, often enough it is not the autonomous ego speaking, but the unconscious or superego using the voice of the ego. As Loewenstein recognized, the analytic task requires both the use of autonomous functions and their relaxation to honor the demands of the analytic process.[3] While alliance between autonomous functions of both patient and analyst are essential to analysis, the dangers of collaborative reinforcement of pseudo-autonomous functions can lead to misalliance and an inhibition of true autonomy resulting from enhancement of defensive functions.

As previously discussed, the autonomy involved in alliance is self-autonomy, a concept receiving growing recognition (Sutherland 1993). Insofar as the alliance is a form of object relation, it involves a relation between two individuals, between two separate selves, thus bringing into play relational components of the respective self-systems. Authentic autonomy, in this sense, is not a form of hyperindependent (read "schizoid") isolation but instead entails the capacity of the individual to be meaningfully related while maintaining the integrity and functional capacity of the autonomous self (Modell 1993).[4] The autonomous self, therefore, is better able to engage in interpersonal relations and mutual dependence than the nonautonomous self.

Autonomy is not the same as independence. Autonomy occupies a balanced middle ground between excessive independence on one side and excessive dependence on the other. Thus, there is no contradiction between autonomy and independence nor between autonomy and dependence. In clinical terms, the phenomenon of a hyperadequate or hyperindependent façade covering an underlying fragile and threatened self-autonomy is familiar enough. By the same token, a combined maturity of dependence and relative intrapsychic autonomy is a worthy therapeutic objective for many patients. Transference in its many guises always undermines autonomy of the self (Blum 1971b), and when it engages the analyst in a transference/countertransference interaction, it effectively undermines the autonomy of both patient and analyst.

Autonomy, as with other dimensions of the alliance, is both a goal of the analytic process and a requirement for its working. Whether considered in reference to the autonomy of specific ego functions (Beres 1971) or of the self (Meissner 1986a), autonomy may be fragile as the patient undertakes the analytic process, making him excessively dependent, suggestible, and anxious to gain acceptance and recognition from the analyst. The therapist's primary responsibility is to safeguard the patient's autonomy, and this is done by adherence to the frame and the ground rules (Greenacre 1954, 1959). To the extent that autonomy is lacking, the bases for the analytic process, at least as it begins to take hold, lie more in the sectors of trust and dependency. These rudimentary factors of the alliance, along with at least a minimal acceptance of the analyst's authority, allow the process to begin. The tension between the more nurturant, accepting, and holding stance that encourages dependence and union on one hand, and the more distant, observing, separate stance that facilitates a greater degree of individuation and autonomy in the patient on the other remains inherent in the analytic process. Any parental model operative in analysis and directed toward facilitating psychological growth in patients would include empathic support and closeness, which can contribute to security and trust, and a more objective, individuating approach facilitating to a greater degree the development of autonomy (Sandbank 1993).

As the analysis progresses, however, the status of autonomy changes so that by degrees the patient can come to claim a more authentically autonomous stance within the analytic relationship. Rangell (1992) expresses this development in these terms:

> Both patient and analyst continue to play their key parts, which change in quality and quantity, in degrees of activity and passivity, during the course and various phases of the analytic process. From the patient's side, alongside the alliance, at first leaning on it and increasingly independently, the key agent of change, as the experience of the analysis, its insights and affects, proceeds and gains momentum, is his autonomous ego. Autonomy is always relative, restricted within channels on both sides, instinctual pressures on

> one, and superego and external forces on the other. The course of the analysis, however, continuously enlarges its scope and functioning, increasing the ratio of the autonomous ego compared to ego aspects which are passive and reactive, constricted between restraining forces on its flanks. (p. 420)

One of the functions of interpretation is enhancement of the patient's autonomy (Stewart 1963), since it draws some part of the patient's autonomous understanding and judgmental capacity into play—at first more receptively, and gradually more independently of the analyst's input. This is one index for gauging progression in the analytic work. If movement toward greater and more reliable autonomy does not take place over time, something is not right. The emphasis here is on authentic autonomy and not on hyperindependence, which is both a form of misalliance and a potential source of major resistance.[5] To the extent that the patient is able to integrate issues of trust, he is capable of moving on to a stage of emergent autonomy. Within the framework of a positive trusting relationship with the analyst, the patient begins to establish areas of autonomous functioning. The ontogeny of autonomy within the analytic process is a subject worthy of study, and little attention has been paid to it thus far. Perhaps the most pertinent work in this area is the contribution of object relations theorists dealing with the progression in the analytic work from dependence to independence (Winnicott 1965). The analogy to the toddler's testing of autonomy in the process of separation-individuation (Mahler et al. 1975) is also relevant.

The emergence of autonomy within the analysis implies that the patient is ready, willing, and able to enter into the work of the analysis and to take responsibility for it. This is quite different from the earlier attitude of trusting dependence. The emergence of autonomy implies that the patient is an active agent in the analysis and that he contributes to its forward movement in important and significant ways. It is in this context that the patient takes responsibility for meeting appointment times, paying his bills, producing material, and working effectively and productively within analytic hours, reporting dreams, and so on.

The process of establishing and maintaining autonomy is a delicate one that requires careful attention on the part of the analyst to the needs of the patient. The analyst must be careful to respect the patient's emerging autonomy and not to subvert it with implicit demands for analytic subservience or compliance. The line between signs of the patient's resistance, which need to be analyzed and interpreted and effectively diminished, and aspects of the patient's growing autonomy, which need to be supported and sustained, is often a difficult one to tread. Within a given analytic context, the patient's missing a therapy hour may express important resistances, but it may also indicate emerging autonomy. The therapist must take a careful reading of the state of the patient's defenses, the status of the alliance, and the level to which the analysis has advanced and must situate the patient's behavior within the complex context of the overall analytic progression.

In addition, genuine autonomy allows for acceptance and acknowledgment of autonomy in others. Thus it is important for fostering the patient's autonomy that the therapist's own autonomy be genuine and well-integrated. The critical question here is the extent to which the patient's modified dependence and emerging independence are a source of difficulty for the analyst. It is too easy to interfere with the patient's growing autonomy. Excessive quickness to interpret on the analyst's part, for example, can deprive the patient of an area of hesitantly emerging autonomous functioning. The safeguard for the analyst's functional autonomy in the analytic relation is the alliance.

Here, too, any deviation from genuine autonomy in the direction of excess or deficit, by analyst or patient, will affect the analytic process. If the patient prematurely asserts excessive independence of the analyst, the alliance is disrupted and one can presume that this retreat to hyperindependence is serving defensive needs. On the other hand, if the patient is overly compliant and fails to exercise his independent judgment at the appropriate phase of the analytic process, the alliance also suffers. At a certain phase in development of the therapeutic alliance an appropriate balance between the relative autonomies of patient and therapist must be obtained for effective progression of the analytic work. A patient may come to the threshold of a more autonomous relationship with the analyst and then may retreat to an earlier position of accepting trustfulness and nonconfronting dependence that is defensively motivated and forms a type of resistance within the alliance.

Gender differences may affect the patient's autonomous functioning. These may be in part matters of cultural conditioning in gender role definition, but they may also ride on an underlying biological disposition. Autonomy frequently plays a different role in the lives of men than in the lives of women. The problem for men is usually to avoid losing a threatened autonomy; for women the problem is more often how to attain autonomy without jeopardizing important personal relationships. Intimacy can pose particular threats to men with fragile autonomy insofar as it connotes opening themselves to the needs, demands, and expectations of another—especially a woman who gives rise to the additional threats of dependence, responsibility, and commitment. For many such men, the issue is less castration anxiety than the preservation of a narcissistically invested sense of self. Women are less troubled by intimacy and responsible commitment to a significant other, but the problem is how to have the relationship without giving away the store. This inherent orientation can at times look masochistic or developmentally deficient. Levenson (1984), for example, wrote: "For the majority of daughters, however, I believe that the constraints and prohibitions I've described result in ego functioning limited enough to be diagnosed as a developmental deficiency. Since their egos are built on an inadequate and guilt-ridden separation and individuation, with a consequent unresolved, primitive identification with the mother, and a guilty, gender-incongruent identification with the father, daughters' autonomous functioning is, at the very least, fragile and easily undermined" (p. 534). This may overstate the case, and certainly could not be taken as true of all daughters, but it may come close to the mark in enough cases to make the issue of autonomy central in the therapeutic process. If autonomy can be sacrificed for the sake of a relationship in the everyday lives of such patients, there is no need to think that the same may not transpire in the therapeutic relationship as well.

Initiative

Initiative is another dimension of alliance that develops during the analytic process in more or less epigenetic fashion. The patient who seeks help and self-understanding exercises a degree of initiative in so doing, but his initiative may be contaminated by infantile derivatives of various kinds. Initiative changes its shading as the analysis progresses, however, and the patient assumes increasing degrees of responsibility—bringing in material for the analytic process to work on, associating and processing the material, even interpreting. True initiative facilitates the work of the analysis in collaboration with the analyst, without undermining or subverting the contributions of the analyst. Otherwise, initiative can become a deviation that expresses a misalliance and serves as a resistance to the process—as, for example, when the patient assumes or insists on his own initiative to the exclusion of any from the analyst, thus subverting and negating the analyst's efforts to interpret. Likewise, failure or lack of progressive development in initiative during the analysis can signal an underlying misalliance and related transference difficulties.

Given a persistent and differentiated sense of trust and a relatively stabilized sense of genuine autonomy, the patient is gradually more able to express his own initiative within the analytic process. Initiative in this context essentially involves willingness to undertake, on his own recognizance, as it were, the interpretation and application of his own therapeutic material. Enhancement of the patient's initiative opens the way to increasing spontaneity and playfulness, making participation in the analytic process more gratifying and more interesting for patient and analyst. The model of play that Winnicott (1971) proposed for the analytic process does not materialize without the capacity for initiative in both patient and analyst. Initiative in this sense also includes a willingness to undertake change in attitudes, beliefs, values, and behavior, both within and beyond the analysis. The critical question at this juncture is whether the patient can undertake this initiative without the risk of rejecting, deflating, or attacking the analyst. Here a vital element is the narcissistic resiliency of the analyst, who must tolerate and even encourage the patient's initiative within limits of the analytic work. One vehicle by which the analyst encourages and facilitates initiative in the patient is through his own capacity for spontaneous interchange with the patient—partially by eliciting responses from the patient, but also by way of presenting a model of analytic activity for possible internalization.

For many patients this is a crisis point in their developmental experience, since so often the emergence of the child's individuality and self-assertion and the undertaking of critical initiatives in various areas of life experience have somehow come to mean rejection, defeat, or attack on the narcissistic vulnerability of the parents. As Markson (1993) comments:

> It is important for the analyst to respect and to legitimise these manifestations of strength and will when they appear in the transference. The signals of emerging selfhood are easily disrupted; they may often seem maladaptive in their nascent form and be mistaken for resistance. They are, however, essential for the development of entitlement and efficacy; they represent an attempt to have an effect on the environment in an active way and come to replace passive attempts to influence the world through the coercion of suffering and victimhood. . . . With a favourable outcome the patient will no longer experience ordinary initiative or assertion as ruthlessness. Guilt is significantly attenuated in this way. To facilitate this change requires interpretive work; it also requires the analyst to create an atmosphere in which initiative is recognised, tolerated and welcomed, even though it may be unpleasant in its emerging forms. (p. 938)

The negotiation here is sensitive in that it requires not only acceptance of the patient's initiative but also integration within the analysis in such a way as to extend the analytic work as a collaborative effort between the analyst and the patient. The patient's initiative must be exercised in a manner congruent with the position of the analyst and the ongoing requirements of the analytic process.

Industry

Closely related to issues of autonomy and initiative is the question of industry. In Erikson's (1963) terms, the sense of industry has to do with the child's application of emergent skills toward achievement of recognized goals. A deficit of industry, stemming from discouragement of the child's use of newly acquired skills, leads to an abiding sense of inferiority. One objective of the analytic process in this regard is that the patient gain a sense of reliable skill in the application of analytic insights and in internalization and utilization of the analytic frame of mind as a permanent possession. This is what is generally intended by references to internalization of the analytic process as one of the therapeutic outcomes of analysis.

Emergence of a capacity for effective working within the analysis rests on increasing autonomy and a more comfortable assertion of initiative in collaboration with the relative autonomy and initiative of the analyst. Analyst and patient together advance the analytic process. Industry then connotes the patient's increasing capacity to engage in this collaborative effort and to contribute to this mutual process effectively on his own terms and following his own initiatives. This capacity comes to fruition in the process of working through, when it is no longer a question of recovering unconscious material so much as a process of reworking old ground and finding different connections and associations, thereby consolidating the gains of the previous analysis.

CHAPTER TWELVE

Personal Factors: Authority, Freedom, and Responsibility

The personal factors discussed in this chapter also have their respective ontogenies, but they have been paid little direct attention in the developmental literature and remain more or less implicit in analyses of growth to psychological maturity. Nonetheless they are essential components of therapeutic alliance. As was the case for personal factors considered in the previous chapter, these elements also undergo development within the analytic process, extending from the beginning of analysis to its termination and beyond.

Authority

The issue of authority is inherent in the therapeutic relationship. Analyst and patient play different roles in the analytic drama. From the beginning of their mutual involvement, the analyst wears the mantle of authority based on his professional role and expertise; as he enters the analytic situation, the patient dons the mantle of one needing and seeking expert assistance, support, and caring. The analyst is invested, by reason of his training and experience, by society and by the patient, with expert power that gives him a unique authority. This authority is based on reality and on the patient's transference, reflecting residues of parental power and reinforced by the relative inaccessibility and anonymity of the analytic situation.[1] A continual interplay between the essential mutuality and asymmetry of the analytic relation gives rise to an alternation of views of the analyst, as in some sense like the patient on one hand, and as a possessor of superior knowledge, power, wisdom, and judgment on the other (Hoffman 1994). The physicianly model plays a part here, complete with overtones of paternalism and authoritarianism. In some measure, this configuration is built into the analytic relationship and cannot be expunged. In some degree, dynamics of this aspect of the therapeutic relation reflect transference issues that may have a particular cast in individual cases but that play some part in all analyses.

However one conceives authority—I see it as a relation obtaining between analyst and patient as an essential part of the therapeutic relationship—the balance of elements constituting the authority relation are constantly evolving during the course of the analytic work. In a sense, an objective of the analytic process is to shift the balance and quality of the authority relation so that the analyst becomes less the "authority" and more an egalitarian participant in the process of discovery and understanding. As the analysis moves forward, his professional understanding gives way to increasing uncertainty and a more probing encounter with the unknown in which both he and the patient become collaborating investigators (Newton 1973; McLaughlin 1993).

Authority as Relation

The relationship between authority and power has been a dominant motif in almost all approaches to the concept of authority, whether philosophical, theological, or sociological. A gradual shift has been taking place from the notion of authority as power to that of authority as a relationship between two or more persons by which one party lays claim to the cooperation or subservience of the other party and the other party accepts this claim. Obviously the relationship involves power, but the shift in emphasis also entails a modification in the concept of power from that of a capacity resident in the power-bearing person to that of power as a relational phenomenon. Both the bearer of authority and the recipient of authority contribute to the functioning of authority. The relationship is dynamic and reciprocal, so that one cannot presume compliance with authority on the grounds that the bearer of authority possesses a certain amount of power or that he holds a particular office or position.

The relational point of view provides a broader and more flexible context for the exercise of authority. The approach in terms of power and power relationships tends to emphasize the role of the one exercising power in the authority relation, thus lending itself to overemphasis on the exercise of authority in terms of the formal, asymmetrical structure of the relation as well as isolating it from dynamic processes going on concurrently, which inevitably modify and channel the influence of authority within the analytic dyad. Another view of authority based on a communications model offers a more radically situational approach in which more formal and structural aspects of authority tend to be dissolved and authority comes to depend upon the acceptance of the individual participant.

The relational view, then, respects the demands of a formally structured system and brings into clear focus dynamic processes, at conscious and unconscious levels, which determine the response of individual participants to authoritative directives or requirements.

The emphasis on relation makes it possible to consider authority as involving more than a relationship of power. From the point of view of the subject, acceptance of authority rests on more than the inherent dependency of the power relationship. Acceptance of authority must be based on a more comprehensive view of the subject's motivation. The conception of authority as based simply on power is adequate for considering only the paternal or unifying functions of authority. The volitional or motivational aspect of the function of authority is not adequately explained on the basis of power. Since authority is rooted in man's social nature, it seems reasonable to conceive of authority as based not only on human capacities for submission but also on other basic human needs and capacities. In other words, acceptance of authority cannot be ascribed merely to the power-dependence dimension. There must be other dimensions, which we can denominate diversely as gratification, self-fulfillment, or self-enhancement. Participation of the patient in an activity of collaboration with an authority figure (the analyst) ultimately depends on a spectrum of motivations making it psychologically rewarding, and in some sense fulfilling, for him to participate in the analytic process. The exercise of authority and the reciprocal response are determined by complex human motivations. These fundamental and often unconscious motivations often disrupt legitimate functions of authority such that we cannot adequately understand the operations involved in the authority relation unless we bring these forces into view.

If these basic motivations are grouped under the rubric of personal interest, then as a general rule personal interest is an essential component of the progression to greater maturity, both developmentally and therapeutically. Successful implementation of authority, therefore, must respect the demands of personal interest in the analytic context, but personal interest is not equivalent to personal wishes. In other terms, the exercise of authority must always respect individual freedom, but individual freedom does not imply total lack of constraint and must be understood in reference to personal responsibility as well as cooperative obligation. Moreover, successful exercise of authority not only respects personal interest, but also fulfills the demands and obligations of the responsibility allied with acceptance of authority—whether of the patient or the analyst. The balance required for the authority relationship is delicate and complex: an overemphasis on the power dimension without concern for the personal interest and needs of the individual may well result in rebellion, and an overemphasis on personal interest at the expense of the directive exigencies of authority and responsibility will result in the frustration of common goals and objectives.

Authority in the Alliance

The therapist's expert authority, associated with his professional role, can be distinguished from his managerial authority, associated with his responsibility to structure the therapeutic situation and set conditions for the therapeutic process (Newton 1973). Expert authority is related to professional status and is legitimized by society. Managerial authority, however, derives from the contractual agreement between therapist and patient, by which their respective roles and functions are defined. With respect to expert authority, there is an imbalance in the therapeutic relation, since society invests the therapist with a specific kind of authority and takes certain steps to ensure the therapist's proper training and competence. There are no such provisions for the patient role. The dilemma thus arises—how can an egalitarian and collaborative relation develop between participants of unequal status and authority? An essential tension results, owing to the need to transform an essentially unequal and asymmetrical relation into a mutually egalitarian one that pervades every analysis (Hoffer 1993).

Part of the therapeutic task in analysis is enabling the patient to shift this balance of power in the analytic relation. The therapy begins with an imbalance of power that must be acknowledged as such. The effort to achieve empowerment and a balance of authority in the analytic relationship requires appropriate modulation of the analyst's own power needs and investments and a careful assessment of authority issues—including conflicts and characteristic positions of dominance and submission—in the patient's adaptation to authority figures (Faigon and Siquier 1992; Puget 1992).[2] The authority relation thus involves elements of transference, along with elements belonging to the real relation and the alliance.[3] To the extent that transference elements from previous authority relations and figures play a role in the analytic relation, they have the potential to distort the authority relation and draw it away from a secure base in the alliance sector. A particular risk is defensive use of the analyst as an externalized superego or authoritarian regulator of the patient's impulses and wishes (Levy and Inderbitzin 1992).

Reality factors and the imbalance they bring to the relation cannot be eliminated or ignored, but in the process of developing the analytic relation they must be integrated with the alliance. This includes not only the analyst's possibly greater age, knowledge, and expertise, but also personal characteristics, e.g., tendencies to paternalistic or authoritarian attitudes,[4] as well as gender. The authoritative function of the female analyst may differ from that of the male analyst—as a matter of personal, and social and cultural patterns and even stereotypes—resulting in a somewhat different shape to the authority relation, but the dynamics remain comparable. The pattern variants may influence the interplay of erotic and idealizing transference derivatives and make them more likely to be directed toward males as power figures than females. If women are seen as powerful, they are less likely to evoke erotic and idealizing responses (Benjamin 1994; Person 1988). But the authority relation involves more than these transference manifestations.

The analyst becomes the primary authority figure in the patient's mental horizon as the analytic process becomes established. To the extent that the therapist has expert knowledge of the analytic process and assumes responsibility for its maintenance and integrity, he fulfills his authoritative role. But the patient is inevitably in a privileged position in that he is the purveyor of his own inner world and the ultimate discriminator of his own life experience and history. He has primary access to his own psychic reality that the analyst does not and cannot have. Neither have privileged access to any other reality, so that neither has the authority to determine reality. Access to reality requires that their respective authorities be conjoined and integrated.

Countertransference elements can also contaminate the authority relation in the alliance. To the extent that the analyst enters the therapeutic relationship assuming that the patient is sick, unrealistic, distorting, or developmentally impaired, he can take on an authoritarian role and treat his patient in a demeaning and infantilizing manner. The authoritarian gradient thus introduced gives the analyst the high ground and the patient must take the low ground—an arrangement well calculated to allay any anxieties the therapist may experience and to enhance his faltering narcissism. The analyst has his own need to be needed, and authoritarian assumptions of this sort reinforce the perception of the patient as needing the therapist to straighten out his life and correct the failures in his interpersonal sphere. Obviously such an imbalance does little beside sustain if not elicit the patient's transferences along with the analyst's countertransference and undermines the therapeutic alliance. The analyst can also end up in the submissive position on the basis of his need for gratification from the patient (Olinick 1959).

The authority relation is embedded in a context of more or less egalitarian participant observation involving both analyst and patient in a dialogue based on attitudinal interactions (Betz 1970). The respective positions of analyst and patient shift as the therapeutic dialogue progresses, from an early level of receptive interest in a search for understanding to more complex interactions as the therapist begins to engage the patient's more characteristic and self-defining attitudes. The therapist's counterattitudinal reactions gradually introduce questions and doubts for the patient about his own habitual patterns. The responses move from acceptance to questioning, toward a revised appraisal of the self that may provoke anxiety or defensiveness but may also lead to relinquishment of maladaptive patterns and integration of new adaptive configurations. The more that authoritarian attitudes give way to more authoritative or even egalitarian attitudes, the less difficult is modification of the patient's self-directed attitudes.[5]

The patient moves from looking to the analyst for guidance or interpretive input to greater activity and responsibility for uncovering, sorting out, and integrating his own psychic experience and analytic productions. As Gargiulo (1989) points out: "When the analyst stands over against the patient, as the powerful knowing other, he perpetuates the anxious ego and / or asks the patient to submit to ideology. Ideally both 'the analyst and his knowledge' have to be learned (incorporated?) and then forgotten by the patient in order for the patient to recognize authority without submitting to it" (p. 155). The analyst and patient gradually come to occupy a middle ground in which both contribute, share, and collaboratively process analytic material and so gain a deeper understanding and resolution of neurotic difficulties. As Fogel (1993) puts it, "The authority the analyst had temporarily assumed in the patient's psychic economy could then be replaced by the patient's own authority and autonomy" (p. 586). This also applies beyond the analytic context. Part of the process involves the internalization of authority as a result of identification with the analyst (Benjamin 1994).[6] The patient comes to claim as his own a degree of personal authority that he has previous lacked or conflictually undermined. The emergence and maturation of such a sense of authority—a fundamental acquisition of the self—is an important developmental achievement in the analytic process.

The analyst's role, along with physicians in general, stamps him with the authority of the teller-of-truth (Weir 1980). But he must be able to disengage from the patient's wish to look to him as the giver of truth or answers (Webb et al. 1993).[7] The further paradox in all this is that, along with this progression in the analytic process, the analyst never entirely divests himself of his authority and his role as expert participant in the process and as manager of the analytic situation.[8] In addressing the tension between intersubjectively derived egalitarian viewpoints and a view that respects the degree of the analyst's authority, Schafer (1995) observes:

> Those who adopt an absolutist position on intersubjectivity are making claims about knowing, facticity, or reality testing that they cannot totally support in practice. Here I would point especially to those self psychologists and interpersonalists who claim that the analyst is not, and should never try to be, the ultimate authority in the clinical dialogue on what is real, true and correct, or else fantastic, false, or distorted; in other words, to those who claim there can only be encounters of two subjective realities in what is implicitly a completely solipsistic universe. This claim contains a paradox. For it is the analyst who keeps the record and the frame of the analytic work; it is the analyst who steadily tries to affirm and integrate and safeguard the treatment and the analysand. (p. 231)

This comment addresses therapeutic alliance as proposed in the present study and articulates specifically the role of the analyst's authority. It does not, however, speak to the role of the analysand's authority.

Freedom

The concept of freedom has had an uncertain place in analytic thinking. Its conceptualization in psychoanalytic terms has only gradually been clarified and articulated as an aspect of autonomous psychic functioning (Hartmann 1966; Holt 1965; Knight 1946; Lewy 1961; Meissner 1984b; Waelder 1936; Wallace 1985; Weisman 1965). Nonetheless, freedom is an essential ingredient in the patient's participation in the analytic process as well as a core component of the therapeutic alliance. Unless the patient freely chooses to enter the analytic process and willingly engages in it, there is no possibility of a sound therapeutic alliance. The same is true from the side of the analyst, but therapists are more ready to recognize that participation in the process as professional healers is of their own choosing and determination. They do not treat the patient unless they decide to do so; any coercion would be regarded as countertherapeutic.

Even when the patient undertakes the analytic effort of his own choice, there is little difficulty in recognizing neurotic constraints limiting and contaminating his basic human freedom. Part of the work of the analytic process is helping the patient recognize these limitations on his basic freedom, to understand the reasons for them, and find a way to free himself from them. As Jacobson (1993) notes, "The desired move ahead toward greater freedom and richer satisfactions brings with it the threat of having to alter or leave past bonds which, unsatisfactory as they may be, are familiar known quantities, are felt in some way to offer safety, and often represent all the individual has ever had" (p. 546). And, as Segal (1989) comments: "Freedom of thought—and at best, I think we still have a very limited freedom in this respect—means the freedom to know our own thoughts, and that means knowing the unwelcome as well as the welcome, anxious thoughts, those felt as 'bad' or 'mad,' as well as constructive thoughts and those felt as 'good' or 'sane,' and being able to examine their validity in terms of external or internal realities. The freer we are to think, the better we can judge these realities, and the richer our experience. But like all freedoms, it is also felt as a bind in that it makes us feel responsible for our own thoughts. And formidable forces, external and internal, mitigate against this freedom" (pp. 62–63).

Even within the analytic process freedom has a somewhat ambiguous role to play. As Spruiell (1983) commented: "From the beginning of an analysis, the patient is set a seductive, but for any length of time, impossible task: to come close to telling *everything*—without self-criticism, tendentiousness, or censorship. We assume with him that he does not have freedom to convert his impulses into motor action during sessions, but he does have *absolute* freedom verbally; we overtly and covertly encourage that freedom. Then we wait for him to fail, as he surely will. Much of the work is involved in showing him how he fails to allow himself freedom and discovering the reasons for his keeping himself in bonds" (p. 10). Even constraints imposed by the patient's transference impose limits on his capacity to enter into the analytic relation and utilize it to his best advantage.[9] The analytic work entails a gradual process of resolving these constraints and helping the patient gain increasing degrees of freedom not only from external constraints, but more particularly from internal defenses, anxieties, and inhibitions impinging on his capacity for a fulfilling human existence.

Freedom is one of the inherent values of mature personal identity toward which analysis aims (Puget 1992). Freud's (1925) reference to "freedom from the consequences of repression and, with it, from the compulsion of the pleasure principle" (p. 239) points, as Smith (1991) notes, to a level of "development and organization of higher-level structures that provide the capacity for judgment and, in general, for a relative degree of autonomy from compulsion—that is, it is a reference to freedom from being at the mercy of either the drives or the external environment (Rapaport, 1957)" (p. 82). Or, as Freud (1923) put it on another occasion, the therapeutic aim of psychoanalysis was "not . . . to make pathological reactions impossible, but to give the patient's ego *freedom* to decide one way or the other" (p. 50).

The sector in which this development toward increased freedom takes place is the therapeutic alliance, just as countertransference suppresses freedom (Fenichel 1941). We have long recognized that patients gain greater freedom in the course of analytic work in relation to the resolution of neurotic inhibitions and repetitions, among other things. But the gain in freedom may be seen as negative, as the result of removing obstacles posed by neurotic defenses and transferences. The view from therapeutic alliance, however, asserts the positive component of that process, that the experience and working through of the therapeutic alliance fosters growth to greater freedom (Ramzy 1961). As Benjamin (1994) notes, "Still, the analyst's self-mastery becomes the basis for the patient's freedom: [citing Freud] 'She has to learn from him to overcome the pleasure principle . . . to achieve this overcoming of herself . . . to acquire that extra piece of mental freedom that distinguishes conscious mental activity' (1915a, p. 170)" (p. 541).

Responsibility

Responsibility is an essential component for both analyst and patient in the therapeutic alliance. The patient must take responsibility for the negotiated terms of the framework, including coming to the determined hours, coming on time, paying the fee in a regular and responsible manner, producing material for the analytic process to work on—particularly through free association, but also in terms of his openness about thoughts, feelings, fantasies, and other mental processes that come to conscious attention during the sessions. In analysis, he is called on to take responsibility for his symptoms and psychic productions—dreams, associations, feelings, fantasies, wishes, and so on. On responsibility for dreams Freud (1925b) commented: "Obviously one must hold oneself responsible for the evil impulses of one's dreams. What else is one to do with them? Unless the content of the dream (rightly understood) is inspired by alien spirits, it is a part of my own being. If I seek to classify the impulses that are present in me according to social standards into good and bad, I must assume responsibility for both sorts; and if, in defense, I say that what is unknown, unconscious and repressed in me is not my 'ego,' then I shall not be basing my position upon psychoanalysis" (p. 133). The patient must also actively try to understand and put in perspective material that comes into focus in the course of analytic work. Also, perhaps most telling of all, the patient must take responsibility (along with the analyst) for the changes analysis leads to (Halleck 1982) so that the final outcome is a product of their collaborative effort. This aspect of the therapeutic alliance calls into play the work ego of the patient, in a sense (Gray 1990). Responsibility in this sense is a correlate of rather than the converse of the patient's free engagement in analysis.[10] The transference-dictated assumption that the analyst bears the responsibility for maintaining the analytic effort—a not uncommon persuasion—is, in this view, contrary to the therapeutic alliance.

The analyst's assumption of his analytic responsibilities plays a central part in the analytic process. The analyst's responsibility can be cast in both negative and positive terms. As Poland (1978) noted: "It is easier to speak of what the analyst's responsibility is not than of what it is. The analyst cannot himself keep the suicidal alive nor make the sick well; therapeutic zeal has been exposed for its unconscious origins and its antianalytic effect. The analyst must inhibit his wish to heal in order to analyze, assuming a stance of temporary partial goallessness for the sake of the long-range analytic goal. The analyst must master personal underlying motivations, never allowing reaction formation to substitute for aim inhibition" (p. 187). On the positive side, his responsibilities include being there, being on time, attending to maintenance of the analytic framework, preserving the regularity and integrity of the analytic situation (Langs 1973b; with particular regard for maintaining conditions for confidentiality), listening carefully to the patient's productions, trying to understand them, conveying what seem to be useful understandings to the patient when appropriate, dealing with the patient in terms that are respectful, ethical, and professional, avoiding countertransference traps and technical errors to the best of his ability, and using his skills and knowledge in the best interest of the patient. . Without addressing technical implications, I would say that much of the analytic effort is frequently devoted to facilitating the patient's capacity to engage more effectively in his appropriate responsibilities in the analytic work and in monitoring and sustaining the analyst's own fulfillment of his responsibilities in the process—in terms of living up to and not exceeding them.

One bone of contention has to do with limits of the therapist's responsibility. Those who appeal to a medical model tend to overstate those responsibilities in terms of the alliance. Voth (1972b), for example, wrote: "Guided by this concept [the medical model], the physician is required (1) to induce change in his patient and to help his patient achieve the highest level of health which the life circumstances of the doctor and patient, and conditions within the patient and doctor, will permit; and (2) to protect his patient and those affected by him from the patient's illness, in particular from destructiveness and self-destructiveness during the course of the treatment" (p. 69).

From the perspective of therapeutic alliance, every item in this statement is open to question, yet from the point of view of the medical model and the medicolegal context in which it is framed, it makes perfect sense. For better or worse, society and the medicolegal forces within it force physicians (and, in consequence, therapists) into undertaking responsibilities that are not congruent with the demands of the alliance. With respect to countertransference aspects of this approach to analysis, the analyst's therapeutic effort requires a view of the patient's psyche as involving forces or energies beyond the range of the patient's capacity to assume reasonable responsibility, or that the encounter with defenses protecting him against fear of change inevitably result in an experience of opposition or struggle for the analyst. Rather, the analyst's investigative and other personal motives become congruent with his public role as professional helper, and this integration influences his knowledge and manner of dealing with the patient and reflects in some degree his need for both professional and personal mastery. Such needs reflect values inherent in our culture for persons trained as members of the helping professions, especially medicine and its affiliated subspecialties in which some variant of paternalistic philosophy is operative. To this extent, then, cultural influences can reinforce countertransference dynamics that contribute to more authoritarian and controlling tendencies in the analyst. This trend and the personal needs it involves are rationalized by a professionally reinforced ideology that the analyst is responsible for bringing order and intelligibility to the therapeutic interaction and for bringing about change in the patient. However, to the extent that the analyst or therapist has resolved his own needs for mastery and dominance, engagement with the patient around these issues need not evoke an experience of struggle.

The medical model may have greater application for psychotic patients in the mental hospital than it does for neurotic, narcissistic, or personality disordered patients who are not in the hospital. I question whether the therapist can be responsible even for the patient's self-destructive impulses. The basic responsibility for keeping the patient alive belongs to the patient. If the therapist has any responsibility, it is helping the patient take responsibility for keeping himself alive. To act otherwise is to undermine the patient's autonomy, freedom, and responsibility. It is the therapist's responsibility to assist the patient in gaining some understanding of his life and behavior and in attaining a degree of freedom that will allow him to change or not to change as he sees fit. A comparison of the medical model with the alliance makes it clear that the former is steeped in paternalism and regards the patient as lacking any capacity for responsibility or reasonable choice. Writing on the question of responsibility in health care, McCormick (1978) wrote: "When an individual puts himself in a doctor's hands, he engages the doctor's services; he does not abdicate his right to decide his own fate. Patients retain the right to refuse a physician's advice, however ill-advised they might be in doing so. . . . What I fear is that a system that increasingly reinforces the notion of physicianly mastery over patients will at the same time undermine those altogether balanced perspectives within which patient choice ought to occur" (p. 36).

Insistence on the patient's acceptance of his appropriate responsibility for participation in the healing process carries with it an attitude toward the patient that is in itself therapeutic. The therapist's insistence on the patient's freedom can open the possibility for choosing more adaptive and functional patterns of behavior. This attitude implies an expectation that the patient shift from the position of infantile dependence toward increasingly mature and adaptive functioning and undercuts any supposition of incapacity in the patient. As Levenson (1992) puts it, "the cardinal mistake in psychoanalysis is to assume that the patient is sick, distorting, developmentally impaired. The reification of the patient *qua* patient has the effect of protecting the therapist against his or her own anxiety, fosters a subtle disdain for the patient, and reinforces the assumption that the patient needs the therapist to explain the patient's life, or to rectify failures in relationships in the patient's earlier life" (p. 569).

At the same time, the pressure on the patient to assume appropriate responsibility has to be measured against the patient's capacity to respond. Overemphasis on responsibility to some patients can have a discouraging effect. By and large, emphasis on responsibility with depressed patients can reinforce their sense of inadequacy or failure, but part of their difficulty lies in their reluctance to accept the reality of their lives and take responsibility for changing or improving it. Similarly, passively tolerating the patient's failures to meet responsibilities, especially those specified by the therapeutic contract, or accepting or failing to question excuses, can also have deleterious effects. If the therapist vacillates or is inconsistent in dealing with these matters, the therapeutic effects can be even more compromised (Halleck 1982).

Judgment is also helpful with regard to what the patient should be held responsible for and what not. Responsibility for his or her role and participation in the analytic process should be consistently reinforced (Kaiser 1955). Can the patient be held responsible for his resistances? Some would argue that, if the patient resists, it is up to the doctor to take responsibility for removing them so that therapy can progress. But, from the perspective of alliance, it is relatively easy to overstep the bounds of the alliance and take responsibility for engaging in the work of the analysis away from the patient and place it in the analyst's hands. This creates a significant misalliance, according to which the patient is no longer responsible for his impulses and unconscious defensive responses. Such a misalliance is both countertherapeutic and destructive. In the best of all therapeutic worlds, the patient should be held responsible for his participation in the process. If he does not meet these responsibilities, the therapist's task is to help him find out why and clarify the implications and consequences—no more.

The question of what the patient can be held responsible for outside the consulting room is more complex. Responsibility is not a black-and-white, either-or quality, but rather is a matter of degrees, and some patients are more capable of taking responsibility than others. But the criteria and goal of responsibility are the same for all patients. The patient is not responsible for others' behavior or for events and trends beyond their control. But they are responsible for how they react to or adapt to and deal with such events. Similarly, patients cannot be held responsible for feelings they experience—not in the ordinary sense of direct control—but it is not unreasonable to expect them to be held responsible for what they do with such feelings. They can and should take responsibility for such choices and their consequences.[11] Even unruly feelings cannot be disowned as though one did not have to assume ultimate responsibility for them. Consistent with Freud's view, no one else can assume responsibility for the patient's feelings. The understanding toward which analysis aims is not the basis for excuses (Halleck 1988), but should lead toward greater capacity for responsible action.[12]

CHAPTER THIRTEEN

Ethical Dimensions: Confidentiality

Ethical considerations enter into all phases and aspects of therapeutic alliance, and for both the patient and the analyst. Freud's (1915a) emphasis on moral standards and his commitment to truthfulness cast analysis in an ethical mode—a form of ethical therapeutics (Rieff 1959).[1] When Freud (1940) proposed the "analytic pact," he meant it to include an ethical code: "With the neurotics, then, we make our pact: complete candour on one side and strict discretion on the other" (p. 174). Even the fundamental rule serves as an ethical imperative, analogous to freedom of thought or freedom of speech (Breggin 1971), its purpose being personal liberation from internal neurotic constraints.

Nothing destroys the atmosphere of trust and security more quickly or surely than unethical behavior on the part of the analyst. If the patient is expected to approach the analytic situation with complete candor and honesty, it is incumbent on the analyst to match these qualities in his own behavior. Ethical issues are involved in the setting and arrangements for payment of fees (including issues of ambition, competition, greed, fee-inflation, self-interest, and their attendant narcissistic undertones), principles and practices for making appropriate referrals (is the patient better served by someone else, by a different therapeutic approach?), selection of patients (relatives, friends, other social or professional contacts?), failure to deal effectively with difficult matters out of fear of losing the patient or scaring away potential referrals, and tailoring therapeutic options according to the nature and degree of financial support, and so on (Appelbaum 1992). I regard the ethical dimension of the therapeutic relation as another perspective specifically of alliance. Ethical considerations contribute specific criteria that are expected to govern the behavior and participation of both analyst and analysand within therapy.[2]

Any ethical deviations are contrary to the interests of the alliance and will inevitably undermine and distort it. All negotiations and interactions between analyst and patient must be conducted openly, honestly, without deception of any sort. From the side of the patient, this requires honesty, no effort to deceive or mislead the analyst, and fairness in dealing with the analyst, particularly in meeting responsibilities related to the therapeutic framework. From the side of the analyst, it implies observance of more than the ethical codes of professional conduct to which he may be bound; the analyst is held to a higher standard.[3]

Confidentiality

Confidentiality is essential for preservation of trust in the analytic relation and therapeutic alliance (Levine 1972). Confidentiality is protected by the ethical codes of all health professions and its importance is generally accepted. Szasz (1962) drew distinctions among confidentiality (which he regarded as the therapist's obligation not to use information gotten from the patient against the patient's best interest), privileged communication (the legal right of the patient to exclude the therapist from testifying about his treatment), and privacy (the exclusive nature of the therapy situation and the contractual agreement that the therapist will not divulge any information from the therapy to others). Analysts fairly consistently advocate confidentiality and privacy, allowing for certain exceptions.[4]

But in contemporary society, confidentiality is rapidly becoming an endangered species. Confidentiality of the relationship between the analyst or therapist and his patient is subject to increasing inroads from governmental agencies, insurance companies, credit bureaus, educational institutions, industry, and even the news media. Legal exceptions and intrusions on the principle of confidentiality include provision of information for involuntary commitment, obligations to report threats of violence or child abuse, waiving of plaintiff rights in cases of emotional harm, access to records of parents in child custody cases, access to records of victims granted to criminal defendants, and so on. All these institutional entities pressure the therapist to divulge information regarding the mental and emotional condition of his patients. As Senator Sam Ervin (1975) told the Conference on the Confidentiality of Health Records sponsored by the American Psychiatric Association, "The psychiatrist must steadfastly resist these demands if psychiatry is to remain armed with its most potent weapons for combating mental illness—the confidence and cooperation of patients."

In psychotherapy or psychoanalysis, complete honesty and open communication is absolutely necessary. Establishing a confidential relationship is critical to an effective therapeutic alliance; practically speaking, the psychotherapeutic relationship and effective treatment cannot obtain unless such confidentiality is a part of the structure of the situation (American Psychiatric Association 1973, 1987; Panel 1972). Thus demands for confidentiality in the therapeutic relationship will come into conflict with more or less legitimate demands of social agencies for information (Dubey 1974; Hinkle 1977; Lipton 1991).

Threats to Confidentiality

Therapists communicate confidential information about patients in several ways. Each of these avenues of communication can be legitimate and ethical, but each is also open to specific abuses that vary considerably in import from one to another. Among risks to confidentiality are verbal communications between therapists, scholarly writing about patients, written records, and requests of insurance companies or other agencies for information about patients. In all these cases, questions remain as to who has the right to determine what information is released and to whom it belongs—the therapist or the patient (Panel 1972). The answers are not simple.

Teaching and Health Care

In the context of teaching conferences or supervision, a great deal of information about the therapist's experiences with patients can be communicated, not only about the therapist's own patients but also about those of other therapists whose work he has supervised. In addition, more casual conversations among mental health workers, often refer to individual patients—a legitimate communication between professionals. It can include conveying important information to other members of a health-care team who are concerned with ongoing care of a particular patient.

Even in these legitimate contexts, however, there are limits to what can be ethically communicated.[5] In contexts where identity of the patient is essential and commonly known, there is little need to delimit identifying information, but highly personal or embarrassing details about the patient's psychosexual or fantasy life often are not germane to the subject under discussion, nor are they necessary for other professionals to carry out their work.

The therapist consequently must exercise considerable judgment and discretion in discussing material that has intimate relevance to the inner life of the patient. If he unnecessarily divulges such sensitive information, he is violating confidentiality and unnecessarily exposing the patient to the possibility of harm. Generally in such contexts information can be supplied in relatively general descriptive terms and critical details of the patient's life situation disguised so that identity of the patient is concealed, while important aspects relative to the teaching context can be explored and discussed.

Telephone Requests

Frequently the therapist is asked for information about his patient via a telephone request. Responding to such requests for information assumes that the therapist has the information in question, that the request is legitimate, and that the decision to communicate lies with the patient (Mariner 1967). The risks of violating confidentiality in such a context are significant. A therapist should exercise great caution and have some assurance that the person at the other end of the line not only is who he says he is but also has some legitimate and purposeful need for the information requested. I recommend the precaution of not communicating anything to another professional over the telephone without some prior agreement with the patient that such communication has his approval. But, as there is no practical way for patients to monitor such communications, the therapist has a responsibility to use careful judgment in what he communicates about the patient, and to whom he communicates it. The therapist should know what purpose the information requested is to be used for and tailor his communication to meet that purpose—no more. My own practice is to communicate nothing about my patients—past, present, or future—over the phone. The only exception is consultation with other therapists whose identity and professionality is known to me.

Casual Conversations

Conversations between two therapists about a patient are frequently legitimate and often necessary. But there are other situations in which any form of communication about patients is quite illegitimate and cannot be condoned. Talking about one's patients at a cocktail party or among friends is an egregious and outright violation of confidentiality, especially when the information communicated is sensitive (Levine 1972). Such trivial communication about highly personal facts of patients' lives is inexcusable, but it happens too frequently. It can be particularly difficult in a small community where entangled personal relationships are the rule rather than the exception (Beskind et al. 1993).

Scholarly Communication

Scholarly articles, books, papers presented at conventions, and talks given at meetings are all examples of legitimate professional communication. The need of a scientific profession to gather and communicate information in the interest of advancing the science tends to hold the demands of confidentiality in balance. Scholarly communications promote that goal, so the professional has an inherent right to communicate about even confidential information gained from his patients (Slovenko 1976). The tension between protection of the patient's right to confidentiality and privacy and the scientific right of the analyst to contribute to research and teaching was clear in Freud's mind (1905a). There is a corresponding responsibility to communicate in such a way that the information does no harm to his patients (Lipton 1991). Consequently every device for concealing identity of the patient should be applied so that anyone reading the case material would be unable to identify the patient unless he had prior knowledge of the case.

As Lipton (1991) notes, use of short clinical vignettes or brief clinical descriptions probably do not warrant explicit approval from the patient, but any extended account might. The approach to this problem is best made from the perspective of the alliance: what use and what negotiation best conforms to the interest of the therapy? It seems obvious that in cases of extensive use antecedent approval should be gained at least verbally from the patients whose material is so employed, but there have been cases where conflicts have arisen over the publication of patient material. In ethical terms, the scientific author would have the right to publish material about a patient as long as he had taken reasonable and adequate safeguards to preserve the patient's identity, this even without the patient's approbation or with his opposition. Such forms of communication in legitimate scientific channels do not violate the patient's confidentiality. When such safeguards are not effected, however, the patient's confidentiality would be placed in jeopardy by even legitimate channels of communication, and he would have every right to withhold approval. Publication of such material would, of course, be a violation of confidentiality.[6]

An author who publishes confidential information legitimately and ethically still may be sued by a patient who believes his confidentiality has been breached. Many patients, especially narcissistic patients, harbor a wish-fantasy that the analyst will write about them—a fantasy of being special, important, and engaged in a creative collaboration with the analyst (Berezin 1957; Stein 1988). We recall the Wolf Man's pride in regarding himself as one of Freud's favorite and special cases (Gardiner 1971). Countertransference traps loom large, as Lipton (1991) observes: "To report a case can be a powerful stimulus for countertransference enactment. And to report a case verbally can be more dangerous than to report it in writing. In addition to the betrayal of trust is the possibility of acting out sadistic, masochistic, exhibitionistic, aggressive, or narcissistic needs. We may be unduly influenced by identifications or rivalries with supervisors, colleagues, or our own analysts; by needs to publish for academic career ambitions; or by excessive fears of power struggles about who is controlling the analysis and anxieties regarding the consequences of losing our patients' love" (p. 984).

Medical and Insurance Records

Keeping records is a particularly sensitive area. Records are kept in all mental health facilities and are a particularly vulnerable source of information about patients. Questions of how such records should be kept and who should have access to them are difficult issues. Security arrangements of most institutions for limiting access to them to specifically authorized personnel are generally highly permeable (Noll and Hanlon 1976). Use of fraudulent methods to gain access to sensitive information contained in health records is a widespread practice in which patient confidentiality is severely abused. If the treating therapist is to respect his patient's confidentiality, he will put into the record only such information that he presumes will be available to any social agency wishing to have access to it. Any information that could be used to harm the patient or act against his best interests, consequently, cannot be included in such a permanent record.[7]

Increasing concern over threats to confidentiality has been caused by corporate and governmental agencies' increasingly central role in most patients' lives. In order for such agencies to carry out their important social functions, they require access to personal information about individual patients. Not only insurance coverage is in question, but also the patient's credit rating, as well as evaluative and control functions of health-care and governmental agencies (Lipton 1991). Information about the individual patient has become an increasingly valuable commodity, which probably in part explains the increasing incidence of use of illegitimate means to gain access to such information. As things now stand, in a world of mushrooming technology for information storage and retrieval, the individual practitioner or individual patient can control only the information introduced into the system. Once information is put into the computers, the therapist has very little control over what use will be made of it.

Insurance Forms

One of the most difficult and touchy areas for potential abuse of confidentiality is medical insurance—the therapist's filling out the insurance form, and providing information about patients to the insurance company so that claims can be processed. Insurance providers and managed care systems have increasingly demanded access to patient records and other personal information. Such entities are bound by no code of professional ethics, and laws regulating disposition of information are inadequate or nonexistent. There are several points in dealing with insurance companies where confidentiality is placed in jeopardy. Failure to disclose prior psychiatric treatment is grounds for the insurance company to invalidate the contract. At the same time, therapists actively distrust the use that insurance companies make of such confidential information (Lipson 1974).

Most applicants for life insurance are required to sign a form authorizing the company to seek information from any licensed therapist, medical practitioner, hospital, clinic, or any other source about the patient's health status. Many such forms also specify that a photocopy of the authorization has the same validity as the original. Such general forms, without specifications as to what information is to be given, to whom, and for what purposes, is equivalent to the patient's signing over his right to privacy. The authorization becomes a fishing license for insurance companies to gather any information about the subject from whatever source and in whatever manner. Ethically speaking, such authorization forms cannot be taken at face value. Often the patient signs such forms without realizing their implications and under the implicit threat that his application for insurance will not be accepted unless he signs. When the therapist receives such a request for information and an accompanying authorization from the patient, such an authorization is ethically meaningless. In my opinion the therapist has no right to divulge any personal information about the patient unless he has obtained specific authorization from the patient to cover specifically this information for this specific purpose, to be communicated to these specific persons. Only when the implications of such a provision of information have been explored and thoroughly understood and endorsed by the patient does it become legitimate.

Requests for information to aid claim evaluation often ask for a diagnosis. The therapist must provide a diagnosis that will satisfy insurance adjusters without proving unduly damaging to his patient and balance the patient's need for confidentiality against the insurance company's right to legitimate information (Chodoff 1972; Slovenko 1976). An important principle is that information about the patient is not the property of the therapist, even though he has obtained it and formulated it by talking to and observing the patient.[8] The information belongs to the patient, and only the patient has discretionary power over its use and distribution. Therefore, insurance forms should include only such information and such diagnostic specifications to which the patient has agreed, and they should be filled out with the patient.

Filling out insurance forms can have the subtle effect of turning the therapist into an agent of the company who equivalently carries out a negotiation with the patient for the sake of the company. The possibility of this distortion needs to be clarified in any dealings with the patient in reference to insurance. It must be made absolutely clear that the therapist is not an agent of the company, that the therapist is in no way in the position of passing judgment on or evaluating the patient for the company, that the patient's contract with the company to cover costs of treatment are between the patient and the company and have nothing to do with the therapist (Meissner 1979b). The responsibility for negotiating for payment of treatment remains the patient's and is an essential component of his participation in the therapeutic contract. Any arrangement that mitigates or minimizes that portion of the patient's participation undermines the grounds on which therapeutic change can be mobilized.

Occasionally filling out standard forms does not satisfy the insurance adjusters' lust for information, and additional and more detailed information will often be requested about the patient's condition and treatment. The therapist then will be called upon to write a letter explaining in greater detail the patient's difficulties and the rationale for treatment. When I am required to write such letters I write them with the patient—exploring with the patient sentence-by-sentence how much information is relevant, how much the patient wishes to tell the company, and about what. I insist on the patient's reading and approving the final copy of such a letter. When it is typed in its final form and signed, I hand it to the patient in an open but stamped envelope and assign him the responsibility for sealing the envelope and putting it in the mailbox. It is, after all, his letter, and I am merely the instrument of his purposes in carrying out the negotiation with his insurance company.

The process of insurance companies' seeking to extract information from the psychotherapeutic context does not stop there, however. There have been occasions on which insurance companies have asked for photostatic copies of all of my personal notes and records about a given case. I would contend that the insurance company has no right to such privileged information and that such a request is an outright and blatant violation of the patient's right to confidentiality.

Insurance companies will also request photocopies of institutions' medical records for purposes of processing hospital or clinic treatment claims (Halpert 1985). The policy of such a blanket release of information under any circumstances must be considered ethically wrong and a gross violation of the patient's confidentiality. In any such record, a considerable amount of personal detail is relatively sensitive and has nothing to do with the information needs of the inquiring agency.

Distribution and Use of Information

Hovering in the background of these considerations regarding availability of information is the larger question of what happens to that information once it gets into the hands of the insurance company. With the increasing propensity to gathering information and the constantly growing capacity to store, retrieve, and distribute it, there is understandable anxiety over the erosion of personal privacy (Halpert 1985). It is by no means an impossibility that such a data-retrieval system could become the heart of a governmental surveillance system capable of keeping tabs on the lives of virtually all citizens. Already Social Security numbers are serving as standard lifelong identification for tax, banking, education, Social Security, military service, and many other purposes. More than one government agency has publicly acknowledged in the very recent past that it has collected such data on politically active individuals. Collections of health data for such purposes are difficult to justify under any circumstances, but the permanent storage of such data in computer records could threaten individual rights. Mere assurance by an official of a government agency that the collection of information will not be used for repressive purposes is hardly a satisfactory assurance that such abuses will not take place. The Westin report (1977) found that individual health and medical data circulate from doctors' offices, clinics, and hospitals to the files of insurance companies, health care review committees, employers, educational institutions, the military, the police, credit bureaus, government licensing agencies, research studies, surveys, and other users. There already is a widespread disregard of confidentiality and a misuse of health data about psychiatric patients, homosexuals, women who have had abortions, and persons who have made rehabilitative efforts to overcome alcoholism or substance abuse.

Confidentiality is not an absolute right (Redlich and Mollica 1973). Legitimate social interests can lay claim to private data for a variety of purposes. Under ordinary circumstances patients will probably have little objection to such legitimate usages as long as the information concerned is not potentially harmful. It can readily be seen, however, that both therapist and patient cannot simply have in view their own transaction or the immediate transaction with whatever third party. They must look beyond the immediate sphere of communication to the broader implications of information distribution and utilization.

There may be times when the therapist himself must breach the ordinary limits of confidentiality, just as there may be times when the therapist may have to hospitalize a patient for the patient's own good. Such actions are part of the therapeutic contract according to which the therapist will undertake measures that are for the patient's benefit regardless of the patient's feeling or objection. Such actions, rare though they are, protect the patient from self-harm and must be presumed to be a part of the ethics of confidentiality, as is the therapist withholding or selecting information to protect the patient's best interest.

CHAPTER FOURTEEN

Ethical Dimensions: Values

Values and Personality

Values hold a central place in personality organization and functioning and directly influence behavior and experience. In addition, value distortions and conflicts come to play a significant part in many cases of neurotic and character pathology. Gedo (1979) has even proposed "that the personality as a whole is most fruitfully understood as a hierarchy of potentials for actions, i.e., of both organismic and subjective goals, as modified by a system of values" (pp. 11–12). In this sense, the value system becomes an intrinsic part of the individual's identity as an adult. In addition, the value system integrates a series of complex motivations connected with more primitive desires and drive derivatives but also involving components entirely separate from them (Zinberg 1967).

Despite the centrality of value systems in understanding personality functioning and deviation, analysis has paid little attention to them. An important factor contributing to this general reluctance may be the ambiguity surrounding the role of the psychoanalyst's own values as they enter into and impinge upon the psychoanalytic relationship, and specifically the therapeutic alliance (Klauber 1968). The analyst brings to the analytic encounter certain values, in part personal and in part professional (Ticho 1972), that govern the character of his analytic work to some degree. He cannot avoid the influence of these values within the analytic process and on the patient.

While a good therapeutic alliance dictates a position of value neutrality (with the possible exception of Hartmann's [1960] "health values"), these values will and do assert themselves simply by virtue of the fact that the analyst is engaged in the analytic process with his total personality, including his superego and ego ideal. The good analyst's participation in the process may involve value elements that he cannot be expected to exclude, nor would it be in the interest of analytic work and of benefit to the patient to do so. By the same token, ethical values of understanding, authenticity, the centrality of self-knowledge, and so on are embedded in the very structure of the psychoanalytic process and cannot be expunged without destroying its very nature (Meissner 1983).

The reader will note that I have not included cure or behavioral or structural change or even symptomatic relief as values of the analytic process. I would regard these instead as goals of the process that are not always even partially achieved (Bader 1994). Meaningful change should be one of the outcomes of analytic therapy, but for the patient who has developed adequate understanding yet experiences no significant or meaningful change, the inherent value remains understanding. Analytic objectives remain subject to Freud's dictum that analysis does not result in freedom from pathology, but in freedom of the patient to choose between the adaptive and the pathological.[1]

Granted these value dimensions of the analytic situation, the intent of analyst and process is not to impose any values on the patient, but rather to accept and work with the patient's own personal or cultural values and to help him assess them so as to integrate them in a less neurotic and conflictual life adaptation. Therapeutic alliance aims at attaining this objective and preserving the context within which such exploration and evaluation can take place meaningfully and objectively.

The Role of Values in Psychoanalysis

Debate over the role and function of values in psychoanalysis can be traced from Hartmann's classic monograph *Psychoanalysis and Moral Values* (1960)—more or less the standard for discussion of values. Hartmann's view was based on an ideal of scientific objectivity and attempted to place the issue of values on a more or less impersonal basis. He wrote: "The approach of the analyst as analyst is basically, so far as values are concerned, the same as he has become used to elsewhere in psychoanalytic psychology. His attitude is that of the psychological student of moral—or other—valuations and their interrelation with other individual or social-psychological phenomena. His objectivity is scientific objectivity, his truth is scientific truth" (p. 101).

This view, then, regarded psychoanalysis as a technology whose therapeutic aim was achievement of "health values" and diminishing of value conflicts. As Hartmann (1960) expressed it: "In the therapeutic situation something appears that we can account for only if we decide to make a distinction between the therapist's general moral codes and the one he is guided by in his therapeutic work which could be called his 'professional code.' In his therapeutic work he will keep other values in abeyance and concentrate on the realization of one category of values only: health values" (p. 55). Hartmann presumed that the analyst would keep his personal values in the background and engage in the analytic process only in terms of health values, or, as I would prefer to call them in this discussion, technical values. The question remains open and moot whether Hartmann's view of the role of values in psychoanalysis can be satisfactorily and unequivocally maintained.

Subsequent psychoanalytic thinking about values has inclined more in the direction of acknowledging non-neutrality. Even though most writers acknowledge Hartmann's formulation as a sort of analytic ideal, they question whether such neutrality is ever attainable or even advisable (Viederman 1976). Roazen (1972) stated that it is impossible to exclude values from the psychoanalytic situation. The psychoanalyst's values, both technical and personal, always influence the analytic process and may play an important role in the analytic outcome. Despite valiant attempts to remain neutral, the analyst can easily be drawn into taking sides, overtly or covertly, with one or another aspect of the patient's conflicts. By the very nature of the process, the analyst makes certain value judgments, that certain forms of behavior are self-defeating or self-destructive, pathological, or maladaptive. Such judgments are based on an implicit scale of values that come to bear in the analytic work and influence the analyst's responses and interventions.

Freud and Hartmann both presumed that, for the most part, there would be a certain congruence in value orientations between analyst and analysand. The assumption is questionable in the current context of analytic practice, partly because of its broadened scope, but also because of a diversification of acceptable value systems in Western society and culture and, naturally, among patients. This increases the potential for basic conflicts between patient and analyst regarding value orientations that may make analytic work at worst impossible, but at best may lead to meaningful analytic exploration and understanding. The opposite scenario may also play itself out, in the form of a certain blindness or collusion, whereby the analyst may fail to recognize and process significant value conflicts.

Value judgments seem to seep into the therapeutic process through every available pore. Value judgments can enter into use of clinical and diagnostic categories (Roazen 1972) and may be embedded in the very fabric of our clinical theory. For example, in the structural theory. without identifying the superego with moral values, we may be able to attach certain moral values to the superego, while a corresponding system of values, focused around issues of self-interest, may attach to the core of the ego (Ottenheimer 1972). Different theoretical approaches in psychoanalysis contain implicit value orientations, dictating corresponding attitudes toward patients and toward their pathology, and require adjustments in therapeutic rationale.

In this view, the analyst's values, both technical and personal, impinge on the analytic process. Despite ideals of objectivity and neutrality, the analyst's listening to the flow of patient material is not totally detached and dispassionate. Rather, he listens as a human being with convictions, social and cultural attitudes, moral and ethical values, standards of right and wrong, good and bad, healthy and unhealthy. It is unrealistic or illusory to believe that the analyst can engage with his patient on any other terms than would be dictated by these complex human factors.

What the analyst might choose to comment on, what he might decide to focus on in an exploratory effort at deepening understanding, or how he might react to a particular piece of information conveyed by the patient, all are potential media for conveying significant value judgments. Zilboorg (1956) observed that psychoanalysts, like other human beings, must have a philosophy of life, a system of values, not only as cultivated human beings, but more particularly in their roles as analysts, constantly walking a fine line between ontological issues on one hand and moral issues on the other, between judgments of fact and judgments of value.

This problem can become particularly acute when the patient's values are at odds with accepted social or cultural values. In such circumstances, the analyst may be caught between his attunement to and alliance with the inherent individuality of his patients and the values of the society in which he and they must live. In such conflicts, the good, the right, and the true rarely reside on one side of the question, and the wrong, the bad, and the false on the other. Rather, truth, merit, and justice can usually be found on both sides of the conflict. The question is whether the analyst does his patient a disservice by espousing one or another of these conflicting sets of values, or whether, at times, injection of the analyst's own values into the analytic process may advance that process and promote an adaptive analytic outcome.

Values Inherent in the Psychoanalytic Situation

There are inherent values built into the very nature of the psychoanalytic situation—whether they are envisioned as "therapeutic morality" (Hartmann 1960) or as "integrity" (Rangell 1981). They may be regarded as technological, in Hartmann's sense, but whether they can be reduced to "health values" and adequately distinguished or divorced from personal values remains open to question. First is the value of self-understanding, which provides a guiding principle for most technical efforts in the psychoanalytic process and calls for openness and candor in all aspects of the analysis, on the part of both patient and analyst.[2] But, more important, it focuses the primary direction of psychoanalytic inquiry on understanding rather than on evaluation or judgment. The neurotic superego stands ready to judge and to be judged. The analytic effort, however, seeks constantly to circumvent such judgmental obstruction to the analytic process and to understand the patient's behavior on whatever terms may be available at a given point—economic, dynamic, genetic, structural, or adaptive. As Kanzer (1972) noted, the analyst's observance of superego prescriptions governing his participation in the analytic process makes a significant contribution to progressive modification of the patient's superego functioning. Whatever the patient's behavior, thoughts, attitudes, fantasies, or feelings, analysis aims at understanding their meaning and their place and function in the patient's psychic life.

With respect to Hartmann's health values, does psychoanalysis in fact take a position about psychic health versus psychopathology, whether one is good and the other bad? An emphasis on self-knowledge and understanding precludes judgment or evaluation in this connection. The analyst's concern is restrictively focused on understanding the origins, contributing determinants, consequences, and implications of the patient's value orientation and behavior. Any attempt to evaluate would foreclose on that inquiry and its objectives. The whole debate over the psychiatric evaluation of homosexuality, for example, seems to miss the point: the psychoanalytic approach makes no judgment as to advisability or inadvisability, preferability, or morality of homosexuality but focuses on the inquiry leading to understanding of the roots, contexts, meaning, consequences, and implications of the patient's sexual preference.

The self-understanding I am describing here cannot simply be reduced to, nor is it synonymous with, insight. Even if insight is regarded as a goal of the psychoanalytic process, it must be with the reservation that insight of itself rarely if ever accomplishes much. Insight into a piece of behavior or symptomatology, or even into a pattern of character organization and functioning, carries a limited potential for resolving the patient's neurotic difficulties. By the same token, not infrequently patients improve and begin to function in a more adaptive fashion without any apparent related insight. Thus insight is part of the technical effort of the analytic process, but not an inherent value of the process itself.

The technical apparatus of analysis should not be confused with the value system governing and directing its procedures. Rather, the inherent values of analysis guide the analytic inquiry, without any inherent commitment to greater health or maturity or functioning. In this sense, then, values in this context cannot be reduced to Hartmann's health values. There is no guarantee that self-knowledge, serving as a sustaining ideal and purposeful objective, will bring with it any greater degree of psychic health, conflict-free functioning, or even happiness. We can only hope that the patient's increased self-knowledge may allow him to shape a more meaningful sense of his own existence and human worth.

A second value in the psychoanalytic situation is authenticity, that the patient's authentic self is basically good, adaptive, and constructive. Emphasis falls on both terms, *authentic* and *self*—including the patient's whole self, not only his instinctual life, drives, libido, aggression, and narcissism, but also the full range and implications of both ego and superego functioning, as well as the organization and integration of his psychic self (Meissner 1986a, 1993). The psychoanalytic perspective leaves nothing out. The emphasis also falls on the aspect of authenticity, namely on that self-organization, which is also valued as good and constructive, which most authentically expresses the harmonious synthesis of the wishes, goals, purposive directions, and attainments of all the psychological components of the personality. In this sense, libidinal wishes that violate the standards and objectives of ego and superego cannot be regarded as authentic. By the same token, superego directives imposing inhibitions that violate the direction, integration, and realistic satisfaction of instinctual components cannot be regarded as authentic. Only when these various components have been brought together in an integrated fashion, so that the objectives and needs dictated by each of the psychic agencies find their compatible and mutually reinforcing realization, can a fully authentic sense of self be achieved. As the level of internal integration is gradually achieved, the patient gains that increasing degree of internal freedom allowing him to become more authentically himself.

The value of authenticity assumes that in every human being there is a core selfhood that, if allowed free and unconflicted expression, would allow creativity, adaptation, and meaningfully productive and healthy living. The neurotic, who lives under the sway of internal contradictions and conflicts, has not achieved this level of authenticity and inner freedom. One of the primary aims of analysis is to enable patients, by way of resolution of neurotic conflicts and mobilization of internal psychic resources—leading to a greater degree of internal integration and building up meaningful psychic structures—to gain such internal authenticity and freedom.

A third value inherent in the analytic situation is the value of values. This may sound tautological, but I refer to a commitment on the part of the analyst and the analytic process to the proposition that values are a singularly important aspect of the patient's personality integration and functioning. More important, however, is the notion that the values themselves be authentic, that is, that they be the patient's own formed and chosen values, the norms and standards he chooses autonomously and adaptively. These values may not be congruent with those espoused by the analyst, but they are principles according to which the patient ultimately organizes and directs his life. In fact, the shaping and integrating of such authentic values are essential components of the patient's capacity to work through underlying neurotic conflicts and function more autonomously and adaptively and, consequently, form a primary goal of the analytic process. To the extent that analytic work achieves or abides by these inherent values, the outcome will be a greater degree of psychic health and adjustment. The benefit to the psychic well-being of the patient may vary considerably, for these values do not even imply such a beneficial or healthy outcome. Consequently, they must be regarded as transcending the issue of health values and as operating within an entirely different frame of reference.

The fourth value that can be added to the list of values inherent in the psychoanalytic process is the quest for truth. Psychoanalysis embraces and commits itself to the search for truth—the psychological truth that brings meaning and freedom from neurotic conflict and constraint. The quest for truth is related to self-understanding, but its scope and intent are somewhat different. The resources of a psychoanalytic methodology and its technical procedures aim at exploring and clarifying the psychological truth embedded in the patient's life experience. It is the search for hidden meaning, the quest for the latent truth behind the manifest ambiguity or disguise, that gives freedom. As Ottenheimer (1972) observed: "The value of the truth in the hierarchy of the analyst's values exceeds all other values of his own personal code. The truth in itself is, of course, neither good nor bad—it is. The so-called permissiveness of the analyst refers to his permission, even requests to express the truth. The value placed upon truth makes it possible for the analyst to be nonjudgmental and accepting, even if those truths reflect values which are normally not in the analyst's value system" (p. 243).

These values cannot be regarded in any sense as "health values," as they both prescind from and transcend the whole question of health or illness. We make an assumption that attainment of these values will result in a patient who is in fact healthier, happier, more accepting of himself, and better able to adapt to his environment, particularly his interpersonal environment. But we are by no means assured of this. For example, a patient may achieve a basic integration of values in an effective and meaningful way and opt for a homosexual way of life. The values themselves do not decide the issue one way or the other, and any attempt to decide the issue on other terms opens the door to the introduction of the analyst's personal values, which may contaminate the analytic work.

Technical Versus Personal Values

The question of the relationship between the analyst's technical values and personal values remains. Is it possible for the analyst to separate personal values from technical values such that he can effectively apply the latter in the work of analysis, even though his personal views contradict or diverge from them? My answer is, first, that he cannot make such a separation, and, second, that he must. I do not see how an analyst can be an effective analyst unless these values are for him not merely technical adjuncts to his work but matters of deep personal conviction. An important aspect of the analyst's participation in the analytic process is that the values inherent in the analytic effort are also his own deeply felt personal values. On this level, the nature of the analytic process does not allow separation of the technical and the personal.

But on another level the analyst must be clear about how his own values are congruent or different from the patient's and must carefully monitor his own reactions and interventions so that his personal values are not imposed on the patient and do not contaminate the analytic effort. Like the rest of humanity, patients can be venal, selfish, crude, sadistic, perverse, and even immoral. The analyst may have his own personal values, according to which he would disapprove of such behaviors. This leaves aside the more complex issue of how the analyst's personal values penetrate the analytic encounter and influence the nature and focus of his interventions. While any imposition of values is contrary to the analytic work, the pervasive influence of such values is not.

An example may help to focus some of these issues. Not long ago I was treating a borderline man in his mid-twenties whose life was dedicated to an unremitting guerrilla warfare with his harsh, punitive, and judgmental father. The struggle took the form of intense and inexorable challenging of all authority figures of whatever size and shape, carried out in a continual exercise of compliance and defiance. He got along with no one, was continually generating confrontations with nearly everyone in his environment, and lived in a hate-ridden schizoid world largely of his own construction.

On one occasion he arranged a casual social outing with a fellow student. When the fellow student failed to show up, my patient became enraged, located the other student's car in the school parking lot, and smashed all the windows with a brick. When the patient told me about the episode, I was somewhat shocked. Such behavior was hardly congruent with my own system of values. I commented that it was rather unusual behavior and wondered whether we might be able to examine it and see what we might make of it. I asked what the patient had been experiencing that might have led him to such a path of behavior.

After a little, the patient asked whether I wasn't shocked by his behavior. I said that I found it a little disturbing, but I wondered whether that was the reaction he had been expecting from me. Did he want me to respond by being shocked and offended? He agreed that he had, and this admission opened the way to a discussion of the provocative nature of this behavior and his telling me about it from the point of view of the father-transference reaction it reflected. In this provocative acting out and his conviction that I would disapprove, he was replaying a scenario he had enacted countless times with his own father.

My effort, as I look back on this experience, was not so much to suspend my own judgments as to what constitutes proper behavior, but rather to put them in the background and to respond to my patient in terms of the predominant values inherent in the therapeutic situation—seeking understanding and authenticity. I shifted the focus of inquiry to the underlying issues behind the behavior. Exploration of this episode, in addition to bringing to light the transference material, directed the patient's attention to the consequences and underlying assumptions of his behavior. In this case, the destructive acting out was an expression of his own feelings of impotence, lack of worth, and frustrated rage. The only resource he could muster in the face of all this was to act out in an infantile and destructive manner and thus reinforce his image of himself as worthless and impotent.

In this episode, the analyst's capacity to maintain the primacy of therapeutic values was both possible and therapeutically useful, but there are other circumstances in which such a course may be extremely difficult or fraught with other implications that would seem to jeopardize the therapeutic values. In some cases strong limit-setting measures may be called for to protect the patient from a course of dangerous acting out. However much we might desire to maintain essential therapeutic values, patients usually hold the trump card. A suicidal patient, for example, may force us to take whatever measures are necessary to protect him from his own self-destructive impulses. However, we would do so, specifically because the patient forces us to take such a course of action by refusing to exercise his own responsibility for his impulses and actions. But we also would be aware of the risk of violating basic therapeutic values and jeopardizing the therapeutic work.

To be clear about the implications of such a situation, hospitalizing a patient because of a serious threat of suicide violates the basic therapeutic values by preferring action to understanding, by interfering with the patient's life and taking away the exercise of his responsibility for himself and his actions. My own approach in such matters is to hold as firmly as I can to the therapeutic values, which dictate that the therapeutic effort should be directed to understanding the patient's wishes and impulses to kill himself, and to bringing the patient to a point where he can begin to accept responsibility for such impulses and, by implication, deal with them adaptively rather than acting them out self-destructively.

In discussing the therapeutic values inherent in psychoanalysis, I have not said that the analyst is responsible for keeping the patient alive, nor that the analyst is responsible for easing the patient's pain. These are not values inherent in any therapeutic process, and where they are called into play they reflect a subversion of the therapeutic process that often may become irremediable. Hospitalization of a severely disturbed suicidal patient may or may not signal the effective end of a therapeutic process, but it certainly reflects the degree to which the patient has succeeded in drawing the therapist out of his therapeutic posture.

Similar difficulties arise in other extreme circumstances where the therapist may be forced to diverge from the therapeutic value system. The Tarasoff case in California, for example, poses the question whether the therapist has the right, even the duty, to violate the patient's essential confidentiality by warning persons the patient might have threatened to kill. In such cases the therapist is forced to weigh the factors as best he can, measuring the need for maintaining therapeutic values and confidentiality against the possible implications and consequences of not forewarning potential victims or preventing the projected course of destructive action (Lipton 1991).

The situation is essentially the same in almost any context of potentially destructive acting out. The clinical judgment whether a patient's talk about his murderous wishes toward a particular person represents a meaningful and intended course of action is in itself difficult. The therapist cannot intervene whenever the patient talks about such thoughts, wishes, or fantasies. Such action would severely prejudice any communication from patients about such conflicted and disturbing impulses. But if the therapist is convinced that the patient's intention raises a real threat, the therapist must intervene. But here again, the more legitimate course of action might be hospitalization of the patient rather than warning of victims, on the ground that the patient is no longer capable of taking responsibility for his destructive impulses. The case would be similar to that of a severely suicidal patient, except that the object of the destructive impulse is someone else rather than the patient. The point of such examples is that, no matter how firmly one holds to the therapeutic values in any course of action, there are instances in which these values can be superceded by other considerations, particularly those that come from personal value judgments or that may be imposed by social forces.

There are other cases in which we make explicit and legitimate value judgments about a patient's patterns of behavior. I have in mind my experience with a young woman therapist whose masochism, more than being merely a drive-determined piece of instinctual pathology, had been incorporated into a system of values that made a value of and gave a powerful religious connotation to suffering and martyrdom. Her espousal of these values was profound and seemed to be expressed in nearly every facet of her life, both professional and personal. She carried out her professional work in ways that constantly left her in a position of disadvantage and self-torment. In addition, she had married a man who was both borderline and paranoid. As I listened to the seemingly endless flow of self-punishment, self-defeat, and self-torment, I felt that some form of intervention was called for that would bring her attention to the way in which she was dealing with her life.

I decided to confront the patient about the implications and consequences of her masochistic manner of dealing with her problems. I asked her to look at what she was describing, to consider what she was doing to herself in all of these situations: how she was continually putting herself in the position of being the helpless and impotent victim of circumstances, of the demands of her patients, of her husband, of her son, and so on. And in the face of all this, she would not acknowledge that there was anything she could do about it, anything she could do to stop it, anything she could do to change it. To my patient's credit, she reacted better than I had hoped to this confrontation. She did not react to my comments as though they were some form of superego castigation, as I was afraid she might; in fact, she was able to look at her behavior with some degree of objectivity and see how dramatically she was acting out a powerful identification with her long-suffering, self-sacrificing, masochistic mother.

The point of the example is not the therapeutic outcome, but the role of values as they enter the analytic situation. At issue was my value judgment regarding the masochistic pattern of her life experience, posing a basic conflict between my own inherent values and those espoused by the patient. But my intervention was not propounded on the basis of my personal value system, but rather it led me to make a judgment that this particular patient was ignoring the consequences and implications of her behavior in the service of a pathologically determined value system. My approach was not to say that her masochism was bad and should be got rid of, but rather that her masochism had certain consequences and implications that it was essential for her to begin to examine and evaluate.

The drift of the inquiry in this case, then, is similar to that in the case of the young man who broke his friend's car windows. In both cases, the therapist's personal values entered into the therapeutic process in such a way as to steer the process back into the channel of basically therapeutic values and toward addressing the patient's own value system in therapeutically effective ways.

A similar phenomenon can take place not only where there is divergence between the patient's and therapist's value systems but also where there is congruence. One particular patient, a teacher, was by religious upbringing and conviction Catholic. He was an intelligent man whose religion was sophisticated and theologically informed, so that much of what he had to say with regard to religious matters was congruent with my own religious convictions. But this patient was also a clearly narcissistic personality whose religious orientation had been brought into the service of his considerable narcissistic needs. The patient's basic narcissistic pathology left him prey to intensely perfectionistic needs and at the same time vulnerable to recurrent depressions. These underlying narcissistic needs had been elaborated into a conceptually sophisticated and religiously based system of values.

Here again, my own personal values unavoidably entered into the therapeutic equation, but in this case in a somewhat different fashion. The congruence in our value orientations required that I more self-consciously reflect upon my own system of values, including religious values, in order to focus on how the patient utilized his own similar values in ways that were pathological and self-defeating. My interventions, therefore, did not come to bear on the value system as such, but rather on the patient's use of his values in the service of pathological need. Here the technical approach, which would not differ substantially from my approach to the masochistic therapist, is not through confrontation of values, but by way of return to basically therapeutic values, which technically dictate an attempt to explore and understand the implications, connotations, and consequences of the manner in which the patient utilizes or expresses his underlying value system.

In this sense, then, one can postulate a hierarchy of values in terms of which the analyst works, and that the psychoanalytic value then takes precedence. In other words, if the analysand expresses or resolves on some direction or action morally repugnant to the analyst, the analytic emphasis falls on the continued inquiry and search for understanding the origins, determinants, consequences, and implications of such behavior and a commitment to the position that, as the patient gains such understanding, his attitudes, feelings, and values gain their own inherent authenticity.

Values and Countertransference

Finally, two general points must be kept in mind in any discussion of values in the analytic situation, which by their nature reach far beyond the scope of this present discussion. The first is that the whole area of values within the analytic situation is ripe territory in which countertransference elements may play themselves out. Analysts cannot hide behind technical or professional or even "health" values. We cannot pretend that our own personal values do not come into play within the analytic situation and have a powerful influence on the course of the analytic work and on the analytic process. Not only is it impossible for the analyst to keep personal values out of analytic work, but, as I have already suggested, there are times when it is not only therapeutic but mandatory that he include them.

Personal values, then, become an area for particular self-scrutiny and monitoring, so that analysts become not only more self-consciously aware of them, but also more explicitly attuned to the manner in which they enter into and determine the pattern of reactions to patients' productions and analysts' therapeutic interventions. I have proposed a hierarchical model to integrate personal and technical values. To the extent that the analyst's own personal values are brought into congruence in a meaningfully and personally integrated way with technical values inherent in the analytic process, the possibilities for countertransference contamination are minimized.

Values and Internalization

My last general point has to do with internalization of values in the analytic process. Internalization of values, particularly through identification (Meissner 1972, 1981), is one of the major parameters of therapeutic improvement and personality change effected by the analytic process. Internalization of values is a function of the therapeutic relationship, and, in terms of the hoped for, more adaptive, and more mature reshaping of the patient's personality, the significant identifications take place through the resolution of transference in the context of an effective therapeutic alliance (Meissner 1981).

Both personal and technical values are subject to internalization. To the extent that the analyst's personal values enjoy a degree of congruence with the inherent analytic technical values, this provides a framework for more meaningful and authentic internalizations on the part of the patient. It increases the potential for the patient to internalize these values in a more objective and impersonal context, allowing for integration with the patient's own psychic structure in a more authentic and creative fashion. Where the analyst's personal values have identifiably and independently become involved in the analytic interaction and the patient may have to some degree assimilated them, the risk is increased that some degree of unresolved transference will reflect contamination of the analytic process by countertransference involvements. Consequently, the monitoring and assessment of these value components must be a central part of every psychoanalytic process.

PART IV

The Therapeutic Alliance in the Analytic Process

The approach to the therapeutic alliance as an integral part of the therapeutic and analytic relation has implications for the clinical praxis of both psychotherapy and psychoanalysis. The theory of the therapeutic alliance and its role in clinical praxis are intimately connected. Moreover, the theory of the therapeutic alliance underscores the importance of our understanding the nature of the psychotherapeutic encounter and the elements in it which carry the burden of therapeutic effectiveness.

The implications of an approach rooted in the therapeutic alliance, as developed in these pages, can be focused around pragmatic issues connected with beginning the therapeutic process and establishing the therapeutic alliance (chapter 15). By the same token, management of the therapeutic alliance, particularly when threatened with disruption or distortion by impasses or in the guise of therapeutic misalliances (whether acute or chronic), requires application of understanding of the therapeutic alliance and what goes into its construction and preservation, and, when necessary, reconstitution (chapter 16). In addition, the role of the therapeutic alliance is discussed with respect to some of the essential aspects of the analytic process that can be identified as influencing the therapeutic outcome, specifically interpretations (chapter 17) and internalizations (chapter 18). Basing interpretations on the therapeutic alliance focuses on the beneficial influence of the interpretive process, specifically in locating the conditions subserving the development and integration of meaningful interpretations. The emergence of internalizations, in contrast, tends to be a matter of unconscious influence and assimilation that is interwoven with other components of the therapeutic process and has a decisive impact on the eventual therapeutic outcome. Correspondingly, the approach to the therapeutic alliance affects the pragmatic methods of working through the termination, with special emphasis on what role the therapeutic alliance has in making termination potentially successful (chapter 19).

CHAPTER FIFTEEN

Establishing the Therapeutic Alliance

Therapeutic alliance, far from being a static or unitary phenomenon, has a development within any analysis that can be traced through the analytic progression. Our major concern in the process approach to therapeutic alliance is to delineate some of the dimensions of this progression. But, first, if therapeutic alliance has a developmental progression, what is the starting point of the therapeutic alliance?

Another way of phrasing this is to ask: What are the minimal conditions that allow for setting up and putting into play basic constituents of the analytic situation? (This inquiry is not about structural requisites for therapeutic alliance, factors whose contribution to the analytic situation has already been considered.) Rather, we are concerned with basic conditions necessary to get the analytic process under way. The minimum conditions for the patient's initial contact in the therapeutic situation are hardly different from the terms that bring any patient to seek assistance and alleviation of pain from a helping person (Friedman 1969). These conditions obtain generally in the doctor-patient relationship throughout the whole range of medical practice. As Rangell (1992) comments: "The first agent to bring about the beginning and early stages of the psychoanalytic process is the combined effort under the analytic alliance. This bond, which is not there *de novo* but gradually builds, is between the analyzing function of the analyst, practised as a component of his psychoanalytic theory, and the patient's rational ego, his capacities of observation, discrimination, judgement, and decision-making. Every patient fulfilling the criteria for analysability has a sufficient degree of rational ego available to undertake the task, however compromised his ego functioning is on other scores" (p. 420).

Patients come because they are in distress, because they are in pain, or because they realize that they are suffering from a condition that places them at significant risk. They seek alleviation of their distress, relief from their pain, or correction of the maladaptive condition. They place a certain fundamental trust in the helping figure. The process of coming to a therapist or analyst and submitting oneself to his care implies a basic willingness to accept his competence to cure (Jackson 1992).

There is a rational and an irrational side to this willingness (Greenson 1967). The reasonable component has to do with the therapist's training, knowledge, experience, and competence, as well as the objective necessity for therapeutic intervention. The irrational component, however, embraces symbolic elements, sometimes magical expectations, superstitious beliefs, preformed transference elements, wishes, narcissistic defenses, as well as the basic capacity for entrusting oneself to the care of another human being. The analyst offers himself as a trustworthy object for the patient's dependence by his constancy, sensitivity, and empathic attunement. As Freud (1913) indicated: "It remains the first aim of the treatment to attach him [the patient] to it and to the person of the doctor. To ensure this, nothing need be done but to give him time. If one exhibits a serious interest in him, carefully clears away the resistances that crop up at the beginning and avoids making certain mistakes, he will of himself form such an attachment. . . . It is certainly possible to forfeit this first success if from the start one takes up any standpoint other than one of sympathetic understanding" (pp. 139–140).

The issue of establishing a trusting relation and its relation to issues related to the narcissistic alliance are endemic in one or other degree to every analytic process. I shall discuss this dimension of establishing the therapeutic alliance first, and then explore some technical difficulties entailed in the transition from the initial narcissistic alliance to a more firmly established therapeutic alliance. We can then examine some of the technical aspects of setting the analytic stage, i.e., structuring the analytic situation in terms of the therapeutic alliance. Although the vicissitudes of the narcissistic alliance and its metamorphosis are involved in every analysis, the need for structuring the analytic situation may vary considerably given the needs and capacities of the individual patient.

The Narcissistic Alliance

Following Mehlman's (1976) clarifying suggestions, a critical element in this context is that the narcissistically vulnerable patient includes the relationship with the analyst in the armamentarium of protective elements, a quality enabling the patient to reorganize the narcissistic defensive organization to include the analytic relationship akin to Zetzel's (1970) "basic trust." Mehlman (1976) described the initial therapeutic rapport as a "narcissistic alliance which is rooted in basic trust." In her original discussion of the therapeutic alliance, Zetzel (1956) linked elements of basic trust to successful negotiation of the early maternal one-to-one object relationship, in much the same terms as Erikson (1963).

Here a basic discrimination must be made. The patient must carry into the treatment context a capacity for narcissistic alliance. If, however, archaic narcissistic elements dominate the personality, this capacity may be seriously impaired. Such patients may be so involved in the demands instituted by the grandiose self or the need to maintain narcissistic equilibrium by attachment to an idealized object (Kohut 1971) that even the first step of the narcissistic alliance becomes problematic. In some cases, grandiosity of the self cannot tolerate any dependence on a helping object, or the need for an idealized self-object generates such magical and illusory expectations that effective alliance is subverted and brought into the service of the patient's narcissistic needs (Meissner 1977). Establishing any degree of trust with such patients may be extremely difficult, but not impossible, for a consistent respect for their vulnerability and a recognition of their need not to trust may in time undercut their defensive need. Analysis with such patients, which may seem either impossible or possible only with limited goals, may prove feasible insofar as psychotherapy is able to sufficiently modify the patient's narcissism to permit a narcissistic alliance to emerge.

This first trusting rapport or narcissistic alliance provides the basic root out of which therapeutic alliance will develop. Nourishing these rudiments of therapeutic alliance depends in large part on the empathic and intuitive responsiveness of the analyst from the first contact with the patient. Zetzel's description of this process, in terms of working through primitive one-to-one issues in relation to primary objects, is very much to the point insofar as the model of that early parental interaction is operative from the very beginning of the therapeutic interaction.

The therapist is called on to respond to the patient's willingness to include the therapeutic relationship in his narcissistic defensive organization in a way that is sensitive to the areas of narcissistic vulnerability, minimizes anxiety, and shores up the patient's faltering narcissism. Commenting on this process, Mehlman (1976) observed:

> In order to begin any kind of reasonable rapport, we are forced to allow to exist whatever latent willingness to trust in our charisma there is or whatever non-rational positive motivations already exist. Indeed, the appeal to reason so often only aggravates the situation, and the patient's initial comfort or fright can be said to be dependent on a variety of inarticulate factors which the successful practitioner intuitively responds to. He does a series of things that can be summed up by saying that he determines what the locus of the immediate narcissistic crisis or problem is, addresses himself to it, intuitively or cognitively, and in the process avoids *adding* to the fright and actually *diminishes* it sufficiently to allow the patient to include

> him *irrationally* as part of the adaptive-defensive system already operating. (pp. 15–16)

The sense of basic trust is established in the mutual responsiveness between mother and child (Erikson 1963). Similarly, the therapist's capacity to respond empathically and intuitively to the patient's sense of vulnerability and individuality contributes maximally to establishment and evolution of the therapeutic alliance.

Even at this initial level, alliance issues are quite different from those of transference. The distinction was adequately drawn in Zetzel's (1956) original formulations, but because our consideration of narcissistic issues may give rise to some confusion, the narcissistic alliance is to be clearly distinguished from forms of narcissistic transference. In describing formation of alliance in the narcissistic personality disorders, Kohut (1971) wrote:

> The observing segment of the personality of the analysand which in cooperation with the analyst, has actively shouldered the task of analyzing, is not, in essence, different in analyzable narcissistic disorders from that found in analyzable transference neuroses. In both types of cases an adequate area of realistic cooperation derived from positive experiences in childhood (in the object-cathected and narcissistic realm) is the precondition for the analysand's maintenance of the therapeutic split of the ego and for that fondness for the analyst which assures the maintenance of a sufficient trust in the processes and goals of analysis during stressful periods.
>
> The idealizing transference, on the other hand, and the mirror transference are the objects of the analysis; i.e., the observing and analyzing part of the ego of the analysand, in cooperation with the analyst, is confronting them, and, by gradually comprehending them in dynamic, economic, structural, and genetic dimensions, attempts to achieve a gradual mastery over them and to relinquish the demands that are correlated with them. The achievement of such mastery is the essential and specific therapeutic goal of the analysis of narcissistic disorders. (p. 207)

Thus development of the therapeutic alliance is as essential to establishing the analytic situation for Kohut as for any form of analysis.

Early Distortions

After realignment of the patient's narcissistic defensive organization has taken place and the narcissistic alliance is allowed to emerge, a basic trusting rapport and dependency on the analyst sets the stage for the transference neurosis to develop. It is owing to the narcissistic alliance, then, that the patient makes himself subject to the regressive influences of the analytic situation and the analytic process is set in motion. Emergence of the transference neurosis is an expectable consequence. Highly developed and rigid preformed transferences may interfere with establishment of narcissistic alliance, however, and may indicate the operation of massive, pathogenically organized narcissistic defense systems. (This is often the case in psychotic or severely borderline patients.) Narcissistic alliance may also be undercut by the effects of the analytic regression, which may precipitate a measure of traumatic anxiety or fragmentation of the patient's self. The latter circumstance may force the patient into more primitive narcissistic defenses undermining rudiments of basic trust and not sustaining even a narcissistic alliance.

This initial phase of establishing the therapeutic alliance may vary considerably from patient to patient in its form of expression or in the length of time it takes. It is unusual in my experience for patients to enter the analytic situation in such a way that the alliance is easily or readily established. More often than not, it takes specific work to accomplish this first step. Some patients may negotiate this phase in a very few sessions; others may take years to work through it. In one exceptional case, a young woman with rather severe obsessional tendencies and considerable narcissistic vulnerability spent the first several years of her analysis coming late, often missing all but a few minutes of her session. Sometimes she missed appointments altogether. This woman spent long hours on the couch in silence, addressing significant material only in the most guarded terms, and then only when she felt that she herself already understood the material, so that I would not be able to surprise her with anything she hadn't already thought of.

This imperiling of the narcissistic alliance emerged more dramatically in a patient whose analysis I have discussed in detail elsewhere (Meissner 1978b). This man was in his early twenties and had been referred for analysis because of his complaints of impotence, his phobic anxieties, and his persistent depression. The initial evaluation and arrangements for the analysis were made before summer break, but the patient did not begin analysis itself until late fall.

The intervening weeks provided ample opportunity for mobilization of the patient's anxieties about entering analysis and for emergence of powerful preformed transference elements related to his obsessively anxious, intrusive, and controlling mother, as well as to his perfectionistic and sadistically demeaning older brother. In his first hours on the couch, the patient's intense anxiety and fears of being hurt, attacked, or, as he put it, "shot down" pervaded his reaction to the analytic situation. He felt helpless and vulnerable, and I became a powerful monster who was certain to pounce on him and tear him to shreds. The only alternatives were, as he saw it, to submit himself in total obeisance and placating submission to the will of the analyst, or to take flight. For several hours he hovered on the brink of fleeing from the analysis, and it was only by dint of reassuring and clarifying interventions on my part that the impulse to flee was short-circuited and the patient was able to moderate his persecutory anxieties. His alliance nonetheless remained a tenuous one through a significant part of the analysis and rested primarily on a narcissistic foundation. It was only when the transference wish to submit himself to an idealized but powerfully destructive object was clarified, and when he began to realize that I was not going to respond to his expectations of sadistic attack, that he was able to move from an essentially paranoid position to the beginnings of a narcissistic alliance.

Capacities contributing to the narcissistic alliance derive from critical internalizations early in development in the interaction with parental objects, particularly the mother. The rubric of "basic trust" does not do justice to the reality any more than it does justice to the full understanding of the elements that initially contribute to narcissistic alliance. Included are elements related to optimal symbiotic union with the mothering figure and those contributing to optimal distancing and separation from that symbiotic union. If, at this early stage, the child is overwhelmed by the threat of separation, loss, and annihilation, and experiences pressures of severe anxiety and ambivalence, the balance of internalizing processes may shift away from constructive, positive identifications toward defensive, drive-dependent forms of introjection.

The capacity for alliance reflects the influence of these early identifications, particularly with the mother, but not exclusively so. Early experiences of good mothering and of interaction with an adequately responsive need-satisfying object lay the groundwork for more positive and ego-building introjections and/or identifications. With these internal modifications comes a gradually more consolidated capacity for basic trust, which allows further adaptive capacities to emerge in the parent-child interaction.

To some degree the analytic interaction, particularly in the initial stages of the alliance, both expresses and relies on these fundamental psychic capacities and that it calls into play these internalized structures and their object-related aspects. By the same token, not infrequently these capacities are impaired because of the early contamination of object relations and the resulting acquisition of defensively organized and ambivalently motivated introjects. The analytic task then becomes one of working through the bases of these pathogenic introjects so that a more constructive and adaptive introjective alignment can replace the pathogenic one and thus provide the basis within the analysis for the emerging therapeutic alliance. As I have indicated, in more primitively organized personalities—the borderline and narcissistic disorders—this effort may constitute a major focus of the entire analysis. In the more ordinary run of analytic experience, however, this work belongs primarily to the initial phase.

The resolution of the early developmental crisis weighting the psychic factors on the side of basic trust is accompanied by a predominance of constructive and relatively nonambivalent and nondefensive identifications (Meissner 1972). In contrast, if the crisis resolution leans in the direction of basic mistrust, internal processes are caught up in the vicissitudes of ambivalence and defensive pressures. Introjective processes are then mobilized so that the external relationship with a bad or less-than-good object becomes an internally possessed sense of evil or defectiveness. Thus, from the very start of the narcissistic alliance, the analytic process begins to tap fundamental roots of the introjective system and mobilize them.

The Place of Holding in Establishing the Alliance

For some patients, whose capacity for therapeutic alliance is minimally developed, initial involvement in the analytic process is complicated by their need for maintaining an isolated, noncommunicative stance. In many such cases, the most that can be hoped for in terms of development of an alliance is some form of holding (Modell 1976), but at times the discrepancy between the therapist's holding framework and expectations and those of the patient are sufficient to frustrate any engagement on these terms. Whatever holding framework the therapist may provide is met with rejection, disdain, or sabotage (Goldberg 1989). The patient's attacks on the analyst's verbal-symbolic frame of reference—reminiscent of Bion's (1977) attacks on linkage or Balint's (1968) "basic fault"—may require the analyst to find an emotional and psychological position, in nonverbal terms, that will allow the patient to enter a common ground for potentially shared experience. Any effort to deal with the patient's reluctance as resistance or by interpretive interventions is doomed to failure.

As Modell (1976) indicated, for more primitively organized patients this phase of establishing even the narcissistic alliance may take time—he estimated as much as a year—and can create a variety of countertransference vicissitudes for the analyst, who can hardly fail to become bored, frustrated, or impatient. He observed:

> Although the analyst in the initial period may have a feeling that nothing is happening, we believe that the analytic process is set in motion by the holding environment and the tie to the analyst himself. During this period there cannot be said to be a therapeutic alliance, for this requires a sense of separateness that has not yet been established. Instead of a therapeutic alliance, we see a magical belief reminiscent of what has been described in borderline patients as a transitional-object relationship—the object stands between them and the dangers of the real world. It is as if the patient really believes . . . that there is no need for him to obtain anything for himself—

> there is a denial of the need to work. Implicit here is the belief that the analyst can rescue the patient in spite of himself and that the analyst has sufficient power to preserve the analysis in spite of the patient's efforts to sabotage it. (pp. 295–296)

The analyst has few resources but to wait and hold. Even in more classical cases, the potential remains for periodic regressive abandonment or distortion of the therapeutic alliance, forcing the analyst to retreat to a holding pattern until the patient sufficiently reconstitutes and the therapeutic alliance is repaired enough to allow exploration and interpretation of the patient's regressive episode.

When premature and especially negative transference distortions emerge early in therapy, most therapists agree that it is important to deal effectively with them. Primitive and immediately aroused transferences that come into play early in the treatment process (not only as resistances but also as factors undermining establishment of a therapeutic alliance) are not immediately or directly open to interpretation. Kernberg (1976b) recommends direct interpretation of these transference distortions in the here-and-now of the therapeutic interaction, at the same time warning against premature genetic reconstructions. I would prefer to deal with these early distortions of the therapeutic relationship as deviations within the alliance sector rather than as transference distortions. To the extent that early, premature, or precipitous transference paradigms undermine the therapeutic alliance and can be effectively focused and clarified, this helps to clear the way for establishing an initial therapeutic alliance. But dealing with transference elements does not guarantee the establishment of a therapeutic alliance. It seems more useful to regard these early distortions directly in alliance terms and to deal with them on that level.

I would further question whether such early transference interpretations actually contribute to therapeutic alliance, or whether they contribute only to a form of transitional relatedness responding to an underlying need to re-create the lost sense of relatedness to the mother (Feinsilver 1983). Emphasizing alliance factors would mean focusing on and dealing with those factors that interfere with and distort the structure of the therapeutic relationship in the here-and-now. The therapist's concern centers on establishing parameters of the therapeutic situation, particularly those elements involved in the therapeutic contract and in the engagement with the patient in the collaborative work of therapy. In the face of the patient's demanding and clinging behavior, the therapist would attend to management of extratherapeutic contacts and aspects of the patient's involvement in the therapeutic effort, including matters of absences, coming late, or difficulties in payment of fees, and with the ongoing utilization of the therapeutic context.

From Narcissistic Alliance to Therapeutic Alliance

The narcissistic alliance provides a minimal basis for the analytic process, but hardly a satisfactory one. Even within a self psychological perspective, a primarily narcissistic basis[1] falls short of the mark. While "selfobject" needs are respected and empathically responded to, they must give way to more evolved forms of therapeutic alliance. The movement from such a narcissistically fragile position to formation and consolidation of therapeutic alliance becomes a primary concern in establishing the psychoanalytic situation (Zetzel and Meissner 1973). The patient's capacity for object relatedness plays a significant part in this development. The patient places himself in a position of dependent reliance and trusting involvement with the analyst (Friedman 1969). For this to occur, there must be a certain capacity for basic trust and a certain willingness to open oneself to the risk of narcissistic injury. From the analyst's side, facilitation of the patient's shift to a more therapeutic form of alliance demands empathic responsiveness to areas of sensitivity and narcissistic vulnerability in the patient (Kohut 1977).

For many patients, the task of establishing the therapeutic alliance encounters few and minor difficulties, insofar as those patients bring a better developed capacity for alliance to the analytic encounter (Greenson 1965). For other patients, the shift is complex and difficult, particularly in cases of narcissistic character pathology and other forms of narcissistic impairment where more archaic expressions of narcissistic pathogenicity are operative. In such cases, the shift to a more genuine therapeutic alliance may not be possible or may be so difficult as to preclude effective analytic work. Whatever alliance evolves may continue to emerge along narcissistic lines, so that the alliance that would develop in the course of analysis is determined more by narcissistic needs and vulnerabilities rather than by genuinely therapeutic and growth-facilitating concerns. This can become a kind of narcissistic misalliance, which may allow for continuation of the analytic process but severely constrains the potential for effective therapeutic work and for achieving a good analytic result. This may, in fact, have been the problem Freud and Brunswick faced in their attempts to treat the Wolf Man (Meissner 1977, 1979c).

Impediments to Establishing the Alliance

The analytic situation is a unique and somewhat strange experience for all patients, and one that is heavily weighted with expectations and hopes. A significant degree of anxiety may attach itself to this initial strangeness, as well as to the pull toward regression. More often than not the analyst must provide a greater degree of structure to cushion the patient's anxiety and to stay the regressive pulls of the analysis for adjustment to take place. This may be particularly necessary with patients who have suffered early object deprivations. As Fleming (1972) observed:

> Object deprivation in childhood tends to perpetuate an intense and immature ego-object-need which distorts the reality of later object relations in the service of trying to restore a sense of the presence of the object needed for development. The parent-loss patient requires special responses from the analyst in tune with the level of object need to aid in the functioning of an observing ego and to interrupt the transference defenses against grief and mourning. The analyst's empathically symbiotic responses provide a temporary substitute for the "coordinates," necessary for "refueling" throughout childhood and adolescence, a diatrophic alliance for continuing growth that was prematurely interrupted by early parental loss. (p. 45)

The analyst can provide such structure by adopting a relatively greater degree of activity, by delaying the patient's advance to the couch or by a more active, if tempered, pacing of interventions in the early stages of analysis. Titration of such activity is a function in large measure of the patient's capacity for a therapeutic relationship with the analyst, determined in part by the patient's capacity for object relationship. The analyst's responsiveness in this context is dictated by sensitivity to issues of separation and object loss, as well as by the need to establish and consolidate the analytic situation, which takes precedence over inducing analytic regression. The latter concern assumes increasing prominence as the analytic process moves forward.

A possible example of the therapist, intervening in active fashion to establish the alliance in the face of the patient's wish to change the basic procedure of analysis, is provided by Freud's experience with the Rat Man (1909), who sought an exemption from the fundamental rule in his first analytic hour, thus seeking to modify the analytic frame. Gedo (1995) comments on Freud's response: "You will recall that Freud did not treat this request as simply another link in a chain of associations, to be met with expectant silence; rather, he chose to intervene in a noninterpretive manner, instructing his patient to consider that assenting to the analysand's request would constitute a procedural violation that was likely to defeat their therapeutic aim. In other words, he met this resistance to adhering to the analytic compact not through an interpretation of defensive motives, but by confronting the basis of the demand in poor reality testing. This classic example demonstrates that even patients well suited for psychoanalysis require orientation and instruction in its methods if they are to profit optimally from their treatment" (p. 351). Whether the confrontational mode was optimal and whether one regards such alliance directed interventions as instructional or not remains open to question, but I would emphasize that

Freud recognized the necessity of constructing an optimal working arrangement in order for the analytic process to proceed. Not only addressing such issues as they arise, but approaching them in a spirit of open discussion and consideration of options, implications, and consequences is beneficial for the institution of a good alliance.

A major risk in this phase of the analysis is that attempts to stabilize the therapeutic alliance may be excessively contaminated by transference elements. Frequently enough, the analyst has to deal with precipitant transference reactions, which may distort the analytic relation and interfere with establishment of the therapeutic alliance. These early transference reactions can be distinguished from the later emergence of a transference neurosis by the fact that they tend to take the form of generalizations from previous object-related experiences, particularly relationships with parental figures, authority figures, or even other professional personnel. The analyst must be particularly sensitive to possible negative transference reactions that can develop early in the process and may remain unspoken and unacknowledged, but positive transference elements may also contribute to undermining or impeding the therapeutic alliance (Jacobs 1991). Patients should be encouraged to express any feelings they may have about the analyst, even at this early stage, not only because it is congruent with the basic rule of free association, but because they reflect dynamics of the therapeutic alliance and possible transference components. In some patients, however, this tendency to precipitous transference reaction is exaggerated and correlates with a general tendency to projection in their interpersonal relations, which is associated with higher degrees of narcissistic vulnerability and predominance of narcissistic issues in the pathology.

Emergence of such projections in the analytic interaction is difficult to deal with and makes establishing the analytic situation a complex task. In extreme cases, such transference distortions can lead to a transference psychosis and may necessitate interruption of the analysis. Even projective distortions of minor degree, however, call for a specific response from the analyst to shift the balance in the analytic interaction back toward therapeutic alliance. Efforts can then be made to minimize regressive pulls and to emphasize more realistic elements in the analytic situation. Care must be taken to consolidate the therapeutic alliance so that the increasing pressure toward regression will not mobilize the patient's anxiety to an excessive degree. The precipitous emergence of these anxieties, usually linked to underlying narcissistic vulnerability, gives rise to projective tendencies.

An important condition for the therapeutic alliance is that the initial narcissistic alliance not be precipitously distorted by the emergence of narcissistic transference elements. In typically neurotic patients, this risk is minimal insofar as these patients are generally capable of engaging in a meaningful relationship with the analytic object without narcissistic vulnerability looming too large. Narcissistic issues remain in the background, although they may gradually become operative under pressures of analytic regression. For other patients, however, in whom narcissistic pathology plays a more predominant part, the tendency to shift to the level of narcissistic transference, bypassing issues of therapeutic alliance, can be a complicating factor. I shall have more to say about emergence of the narcissistic transference later, but at this point I would stress that in such cases establishing a meaningful therapeutic alliance is a major issue in the initial stage of the analysis and may remain a critical dimension of the analytic work throughout the entire course of analysis.

Correlated to establishing the therapeutic alliance in the initial phase is overcoming the patient's initial anxiety and resistance. For all patients entering psychoanalysis, certain basic anxieties are intensified because of the importance the patient attaches to the undertaking. It represents a serious and often burdensome investment of time, effort, and financial and emotional resources. In addition, patients often come to analysis after a series of therapeutic frustrations, and this places their self-esteem in further jeopardy as they undertake what must seem to them a radical, if not desperate, procedure.

The basic question is whether the patient can become engaged in a trusting, dependent, and therapeutically productive relationship with the analyst in the face of this elevated titer of narcissistic vulnerability. It is important, therefore, that the analyst be present in the interaction with the patient as a relatively constant, confident, reasonably optimistic, and professionally competent object. These qualities in the analyst set the stage for the shift from basic trust to forms of secondary trust and provide the patient with some degree of reassurance.

Frequently, in initial stages of negotiation of the analytic contract, patients evaluate these aspects of their potential analyst. Ample opportunity should be provided for patients to make such assessments, particularly in face-to-face interviews before beginning analysis. Determination of these issues not only sets the stage for emergence of the therapeutic alliance, but also allows for and to some degree induces the initial dependence which the patient must be able to tolerate in order to enter into the analytic situation and to enjoy some degree of openness to analytic influence. Beyond these qualities in the analyst, however, is the important initial work of identifying and empathically working through the patient's early resistances and anxieties in order to foster engagement in the analytic process and in a meaningful therapeutic alliance.

The opening phase of the analytic process involves a complex interaction between analyst and analysand, and this fundamental work cannot be taken for granted in the further progression of the analysis, but it must be continually reinforced, refocused, rearticulated, and developed throughout the analysis. The psychoanalytic situation is not definitively established in the opening phase, but rather requires constant effort toward consolidation and reinforcement. The opening phase only accomplishes the first, major steps in this direction.

I am emphasizing the importance of the therapeutic alliance since it provides the buffering and sustaining dimension in the analytic process that allows other aspects of the therapeutic relationship to develop. The patient's tolerance for dependence within the therapeutic relationship contributes to the therapeutic alliance at the same time that it elicits and fosters the transference neurosis or its equivalent. To the extent that the therapeutic alliance has been consolidated, subsequent emergence of the transference neurosis can become potentially therapeutically productive.

For many patients, the buffer of the alliance permits them to tolerate the beginning transference neurosis. These, however, tend to be patients in whom maintenance of structure has primary importance and for whom analytic regression may carry the risk of overwhelming anxiety or constitute a threat to underlying narcissistic vulnerability. In other patients, the propensity to plunge into a transference relationship reflects an ease of transference mobilization that may derive from underlying character or structural defects. Here the risk is of precipitous engagement in the transference neurosis without the safeguard and point of analytic purchase provided by a relatively stable therapeutic alliance. This is particularly true for patients with more primitive forms of character pathology, especially borderline personalities in the hysterical continuum (Meissner 1988), as well as for patients with various forms of narcissistic character pathology.

Such early narcissistic transference distortions can place the therapeutic alliance in considerable jeopardy. The emergence of a therapeutic alliance requires the capacity both to accept the separate reality of the analyst and to enlist oneself in a meaningful relationship and collaboration with the analyst in the work of effecting therapeutic goals and internal change. In narcissistic transference, however, the patient may place himself in a position of relatively grandiose isolation from the analyst—rejecting and demeaning the analyst's contributions, as though the analyst's interpretations or clarifications were meaningless or even worthless. The patient wards off any initiatives from the analyst as a threat to his rigidly protected, fragile narcissistic core. Such patients may to some degree establish a misalliance, in which they cooperate with external requirements of analysis but withhold themselves commitment to the analytic process and maintain a posture of splendid isolation and contempt, or, in less dramatic forms, a sense of distance or removal from the implications of the analytic process that allows for seemingly effective analytic work, but without any meaningful analytic effect.

Some narcissistic patients, on the other hand, may tend to idealize the analyst. Here the narcissistic misalliance is based on magical expectations and the illusion of attachment to an idealized, all-powerful object. Modell (1975) has described this constellation most succinctly: "What substitutes for therapeutic alliance is a magical belief that to be in the presence of the idealized analyst will effect a change—[the patient] will acquire the idealized characteristics not by means of an active identification but by means of a magical process. As one patient described it, choosing the right analyst is like joining the proper club—one derives a sense of identity by means of a contiguity" (p. 280). The inherent risk with such patients, of course, is that the implicit narcissistic contract allows them to enter the analytic process with a hidden agenda of their own. These patients will comply with expectations of the analytic situation, perform all the externals of the analytic work, even to the point of elaborate production of dreams and associations—in effect, being "good" patients. But their belief is that this compliance will be responded to by the exercise of analytic omnipotence to bring about changes they want.

Setting the Analytic Stage

As Langs (1975a) observed, the therapeutic alliance embraces both conscious and unconscious, explicit and implicit components, which express the respective needs and ego capacities of both patient and therapist as they enter into the therapeutic interaction. In structuring the therapeutic situation, the therapist expresses something about the reality of his own personality, his working style, values, and therapeutic stance. Any wish for physical contact or gratification, especially gratification of the patient's neurotic needs and wishes, is denied. Any efforts or needs on the part of the therapist to try to establish the therapeutic alliance by seductive giving, coaxing, persuading, or seducing of patients are regarded as antitherapeutic and damaging to the patient's autonomy, and set the therapy in the direction of seeking gratification rather than effective therapeutic work (Chessick 1979, 1983a). Structuring the therapeutic situation so that it is not excessively anxiety-provoking for the patient can be accomplished by developing a personal relationship in which the analyst is, and is experienced by the patient as, trustworthy, reliable, responsible, capable, honest, consistent, constant in his own sense of identity and autonomy, and sincerely interested in the patient's well-being. This is not a part to be acted, but requires convergence between his role as therapist and his existence as fellow human being (Stocking 1973).

Setting the ground rules and boundaries of the therapeutic interaction makes an appeal to the rational and adult ego in the patient as it conveys a sense of the therapist's own identity and role within the therapy. In so doing, the therapist effectively serves as a model for identification and a screen onto which the patient projects transference derivatives (Langs 1975b; Meissner 1981).

Excessive rigidity or controlling behavior should be avoided in negotiating and maintaining details of the therapeutic contract so as to provide a model of reasonable flexibility and compromise for patients who have difficulty making such reasonable adaptations (Schulz 1980). The therapist also conveys in a concrete manner aspects of his therapeutic stance, his anonymity, concern for the patient, neutrality, and an attitude of interested understanding and commitment. In addition, he conveys a sense of essential confidentiality. He also communicates, if possible, a sense of mutual engagement with the patient in a process that has the character of an experiment in which both patient and therapist are committed to exploration and understanding of the patient's inner life and experience. The therapist also conveys a sense of his own security, a clear sense of his own boundaries and integrity, his lack of anxiety in the face of the patient's distress and turmoil, and his intention to join in an alliance with the patient's reasonable ego and against the patient's excessive superego restrictions and instinctual turmoil (Boyer 1983).

The structuring approach involves setting ground rules for therapy, the rationale for which was discussed in chapter 9. These include deciding on a fee, determining times and frequency of therapy sessions, their duration, arrangements for billing and payment of fees, including payment for missed appointments (Boyer 1983; Langs 1975a, 1975b). The ground rules also include some stipulation of the respective roles and responsibilities of both patient and therapist. The structuring approach implicitly imposes responsibility on the patient for observing terms of the therapeutic contract and engaging meaningfully and productively in the work of therapy. At all points in the negotiations involved in setting up the therapeutic framework, there is an implicit assumption that the patient is responsible not only for his participation in the therapy but also for some part of the effectiveness of the therapeutic effort and its ultimate outcome.

The role and responsibility of the therapist should also be articulated. Boyer (1983) states that his role in the process is to be present for the interviews, to be on time, and to seek to understand what is going on in the patient and to help him understand that when possible. He also tells the patient that he does not give advice, that he expects at times he will be wrong, and that the patient's responses will indicate when that is so. Chessick (1979, 1983a) has offered a somewhat more detailed description of the therapist's contribution to establishing the therapeutic framework and the therapeutic alliance. His list includes: consistent presence at the agreed-upon sessions; being reliably on time; keeping awake and professionally interested in the patient and nothing else (no distractions, such as telephone calls, etc.); keeping to a firm starting and finishing time for sessions; paying close attention to payment of fees; attempting sincerely and seriously to understand the patient's material and situation, and communicate this understanding by interpretation; to approach the therapy from a stance of objective observation and study and with a sense of physicianly vocation; to provide a room that is quiet, comfortable, properly lighted, and consistent; to avoid moral judgments or any temptation to introduce material from the therapist's own life and attitudes; to avoid temper tantrums or other extreme emotional reactions whether hostile, retaliatory, or exploitative toward the patient; and, finally, to maintain a consistent, clear distinction between fact and fantasy to facilitate the therapist's capacity to avoid countertransference entanglements and traps. As Chessick (1979) states, citing Winnicott (1958), this amounts to the therapist's behaving in the therapeutic interaction as a relatively mature adult, who is realistically and consistently dedicated to the work of therapy.

However, there are issues in the initial transactions between analyst and patient that transcend the formal therapeutic framework. As Jacobs (1991) observes:

> In short, it is the messages sent and received by the patient and analyst as they begin to work together and enter upon the initial period of mutual exploration that become the basis for the establishment of an unspoken contract that goes beyond formal arrangements or technical procedures. Certain rules and limits are established and certain values communicated. Moreover, each party discovers a good deal about the other. Some of what we learn, of course, becomes immediately enmeshed in transference responses. This is true of the analyst as well as the patient and transferences developing even as early as the first session can have the most profound effect on the course and outcome of treatment. . . . Concerned throughout its duration about the proper conduct of the analysis, he [the analyst] nonetheless knows that he must pay special attention to the opening phase because of its enduring impact on both participants. (pp. 12–13)

Structuring Versus Holding

In terms of the "holding" metaphor, the aim of the earliest phase of therapy is to establish the therapeutic relationship in which the therapist becomes such a secure holding object for the patient. As this occurs, the ground is laid for further internalization of adequate holding introjects. Obstacles to this process are several. (1) The holding inevitably fails to mitigate the inner sense of loneliness, and the enraged patient seeks revenge against the inadequate and offending therapist. Not only does his fantasy include destruction of the therapist, but he also fears the therapist's rageful response in reaction to the patient's hostile assault and rejection. (2) The analyst, insofar as his holding is inadequate, becomes the target for hostile projections from the patient's destructive introjects. The relationship is thus seen as mutually hostile and destructive. (3) Insofar as the object is endowed with good qualities of holding and soothing, it can become an object for envy by the needy patient. The treatment focuses on these dynamic impediments and tries to work them through by a combination of clarification, confrontation, and interpretation in a supportive therapeutic context. Often therapists who employ holding tend to use of transitional objects: sending postcards during absences or vacations, providing tokens enabling the patient to keep the object in memory, allowing extra appointments or telephone calls, and so on. The therapist must strike a balance between fostering regression and infantile dependence versus security in the relationship.

In more primitive character disorders (borderline and narcissistic), the therapist may have to clarify, confront, and interpret the patient's transference distortions, particularly when they concern his role as caring object and his distinguishing himself from the patient's projections. Dangerous acting out may also have to be confronted. The patient learns that the therapist is an enduring and reliable object, and that he is indestructible (Winnicott 1969).

The good-enough therapist works in a tenuous area between the patient's feeling empathically understood and feeling deprivation and rage when misunderstood. The therapist's activity becomes a matrix of holding, reflecting his active presence within the therapeutic interaction, often expressed in the form of questions or clarifications or repeated definitions of the work that patient and therapist are undertaking. An important issue in such engagements is the need to regulate the psychological distance between patient and therapist. The therapist aims at maintaining a degree of optimal closeness that avoids fears of either engulfment or abandonment. Like Freud's (1921) porcupines, excessive closeness risks the danger of the object's sharp quills, and excessive distance raises the threat of abandonment and isolation.

Establishment of such a holding or sustaining relationship is no easy matter. Patients may have been burned before and enter any relationship with suspicion. To establish a therapeutic alliance with such patients, the analyst often has to overcome a degree of paranoid distrust or schizoid noninvolvement. Extra appointments and telephone contacts reinforce the therapist's role as a holding and sustaining object. Use of such maneuvers should be explored in terms of their positive contribution to the therapeutic endeavor. There is always the risk of the therapist's masochistic submission to the patient's angry or controlling tactics or the need to counter his sense of helplessness by portraying himself as omnipotent and all-caring. The transference distortions in many such patients are based on projections which destroy the therapeutic alliance. Efforts of the therapist to contain these projections leads to establishment of a transitional relatedness in which the patient feels comforted and protected by an omnipotent maternal presence that wards off threat of separation anxieties.

Despite different emphases, the holding approach and the structuring approach may not be that far apart in terms of clinical practice. It is not unusual for those using a structuring approach to regard establishing and maintaining the therapeutic framework as a way of operationalizing the concept of holding. At the same time, those who espouse the holding or containing approach often address themselves to issues of activity, limit setting, and establishing ground rules as aspects of the therapist's holding function. Nevertheless, the basic assumptions and attitude seem to differ in these approaches. The structuring approach assumes a capacity for at least minimal responsibility and reliability in the patient and places an implicit demand that the patient respond in those terms. The holding approach, in contrast, regards the patient as suffering from a basic defect in these areas, which the holding function is meant to correct.

Each approach runs certain risks. The structuring approach can be used in an excessively demanding, rigid, controlling, or intrusive way. It may place a demand on the patient that exceeds his present capabilities. It may also run the countertransference risks of forcing the patient to adopt a submitting posture in the face of pressures toward structure and responsibility. The therapist runs the risk of becoming an aggressor to the patient's passively compliant and victimized self, can assume a position of power in relation to the patient's impotence, or can infringe on the patient's autonomy. The holding approach, in contrast, assumes that the patient is not capable of responsible or reliable response and creates an oral environment that can in some contexts reinforce unrealistic expectations and idealizations, supporting the patient's passivity and dependence (Appelbaum 1978–79).

The Work of the Opening Phase

To return to our discussion of the opening phase, working through of the patient's initial resistances and anxieties sets the analytic process in motion. The beginning of the analysis places greater priority on establishing the alliance than on anything else. But that process is neither simple nor straightforward. Use of alliance building comments, however empathically attuned they may be, cannot accomplish that task—at least not in all patients. Such statements may only obscure the lack of empathic attunement in the analyst or may put an undue emphasis on an appeal to reason that tends to limit transference-emergence more than facilitating it. More is accomplished by careful attention to the multiple parameters of the alliance as operational principles than by verbal interventions. Empathic attunement is the sine qua non of this process, but empathic expression without the other components of the alliance in place seems vacuous. As Adler (1980) observed, "the judicious use of statements and techniques that ultimately provide models for collaboration, observation, and integration, set the stage for the solidification of the therapeutic alliance in later phases of analysis" (p. 555).

As the initial resistances fade, the patient begins to feel the regressive pulls of the analysis. Thus while diminishing anxiety and resistance facilitate the patient's engagement in free association, the concomitant regressive pulls tend to weaken repressive barriers so that new levels of resistance and anxiety are mobilized. This gradual activation of increasingly primitive levels of resistance and anxiety is a familiar aspect of the analytic process and need not be commented on further at this point.

To focus these issues in terms of our present concern, the primary impact of the work of the opening phase is the activation of latent introjects, which correlates with the degree of regression and the diminution of resistance. The establishment of the therapeutic alliance sets the buffering context within which analytic regression and lessening of resistances can begin to take place. Activation of introjective configurations follows on this process. It may, however, require significant and prolonged phases of regression and modification of resistances before the full dimensions of the introjective economy become apparent. It is this deepening of resistances and related anxieties, however, that marks the progression from the opening phase of the analysis to later stages.

CHAPTER SIXTEEN

Therapeutic Management of Alliance Deviations

For the general run of neurotic patients, the alliance poses no particular technical difficulties, but one can never ignore or take the alliance aspect of analysis for granted. When therapists make such presumptions, alliance difficulties and complications are most likely to come into play. At a minimum, the therapist needs to ascertain whether and to what extent he and the patient are operating within a common ground of assumptions and acceptance of the requirements of the analytic frame. If patient and analyst are operating on the basis of different sets of rules and expectations, difficulties within the alliance would not be surprising. Part of the therapeutic task from the very beginning of the process, then, is to ascertain and negotiate the rules and terms of the analytic work as a mutual task undertaken by both participants in their respective roles.

For some patients, adherence to rules of the game can be a significant difficulty. Narcissistic patients, for example, for whom adherence to any rules and constraints is a matter of resentment and resistance, will continually test the therapeutic alliance, probe its limits, and seek out ways to circumvent its prescriptions, making the framework of the therapeutic drama the focus of therapeutic processing (Doroff 1976). The analyst is forced, in such circumstances, to tend the alliance and do what he can to reconstitute it and get the therapeutic program back on track. Some patients can present particular difficulties in this regard, such that most of the analytic or therapeutic work will be taken up with efforts to deal with and explore alliance difficulties. In these cases, therapeutic alliance interpretation takes precedence over transference interpretation.[1]

Alliance in the Borderline Spectrum

For many borderline patients, difficulties with the alliance can often become the dominant focus of therapeutic concerns and efforts. Although establishing and maintaining the alliance plays a particular role with patients in the borderline spectrum (Meissner 1986b, 1988; Slochower 1992), we should not think that only borderline patients experience such difficulties. Ostensibly "borderline" patients establish and maintain effective therapeutic alliances frequently enough to undermine any one-to-one correspondence between borderline pathology and alliance problems. Some patients are able to maintain a reasonably strong and consistent therapeutic alliance in the face of regressive, perverted, and highly pathological fixations and disturbances that would indicate an essentially borderline level of psychic integration. Yet patients with apparently intact psychic structure who encounter severe difficulties in the alliance sector are not uncommon. One problem is that our notions of what enables one patient to engage meaningfully in the therapeutic alliance and another to encounter significant difficulties are not well developed. Another is that some patients who appear to function at a higher level may turn out, on closer scrutiny, to belong diagnostically in the borderline spectrum, but not necessarily the borderline pathology as described by Kernberg (1968, 1975), Gunderson (1984), and DSM-III, DSM-III-R, and DSM-IV. Such patients may be only episodically borderline, or manifest borderline characteristics only under regressive strain of one kind or another—for example, in an analytic or therapeutic regression (Meissner 1984a, 1988). Other patients seem to establish a meaningful therapeutic alliance, but much to the analyst's dismay turn out to have been concealing certain pathological behaviors, like multiple personality disorders (Kluft 1986, 1991) or eating disorders (Zerbe 1993). In the analytic setting we are not likely to meet the severity of pathology implied in these diagnostic categories, nor are we likely to put them on the analytic couch. We more often encounter patients whose pathology lies in the upper ranges of the borderline spectrum, who for most of their functioning days appear neurotic or even normal, yet under conditions of trauma or stress, or in the course of an analytically induced therapeutic regression, show signs of regressive functioning and borderline features.[2]

Despite the tenuousness of borderline therapeutic alliances, there is a consensus that establishing and maintaining the therapeutic alliance is essential for any effective therapy (Dickes 1967; Gabbard et al. 1988; Meissner 1988). Consensus on how to do that is harder to come by. Kernberg (1968, 1976b) recommends early confrontation and interpretation of negative transferences to clear the way for a possible therapeutic alliance, or transformation into more advanced transferences (Kernberg 1993). Gill and Muslin (1976) also opt for early transference interpretation to intercept impasses or premature terminations. In contrast, Modell (1978) puts the emphasis on therapeutic alliance in its holding variation before transference interpretation. Kohut (1971, 1977) and Adler (1979) prefer the selfobject route, delaying interpretations in the interest of helping the patient develop greater self-cohesion or soothing introjects. The empirical results of Gabbard's group (Gabbard et al. 1988) support the role of transference interpretations in consolidating the therapeutic alliance with borderline patients. My preference (Meissner 1988) is for addressing disruption in therapeutic alliance rather than transference, a path somewhere between the early interpreters and those who put priority on the therapeutic alliance. Focusing on the therapeutic alliance disruption or misalliance is a form of early interpretation, opening the alliance for exploration. Transference—however decisive its influence may be—has to take a back seat for the moment; however, its time will come.

Regressive Crises

A difficult conundrum arises, however, in cases in which the patient's regressive potential can give rise to situations of crisis or self-destructive acting out, suicidal or otherwise. The analyst must determine whether it is advisable and to what extent he should relax the terms of the therapeutic frame and therapeutic alliance in the interest of helping the patient through such a crisis (Dickes 1967; Langs 1976). The analyst must steer a course between potential countertransference traps—between the Scylla of permissiveness and acquiescence and the Charybdis of moralistic restraint. Such acting out may have the hidden purpose of eliciting concerned reactions from the analyst—an invitation for the analyst to match the patient's wish to act out by worrying, forbidding, disapproving, and setting limits (de Blecourt 1993).[3] Some patients lack a functional capacity for a therapeutic alliance and instead form a narcissistic alliance corresponding to their wish for narcissistic gratification (Corwin 1974). A path through the dilemma can sometimes—not always—be found through the therapeutic alliance, engaging the patient in mutual exploration of the implications and consequences of his projected course of action, both for the patient and for the analysis and the patient's relation to the analyst.

Urgent and anxiety-ridden telephone calls, for example, are not unusual (see my discussion of the use of the telephone with reference to the therapeutic frame in chapter 9). Judgment is called for, including some assessment of the extent to which bending the frame has a constructive effect for the patient and some calculation of its implications for the therapeutic alliance. A short-term benefit, let us say in allaying the patient's immediate anxiety, may have a further cost in undermining the therapeutic alliance. The course of action that should be followed allows the patient to endure the crisis of anxiety and infringes on the therapeutic alliance minimally. Optimally, when exceptions bend the parameters of the alliance, these can be explored and understood within an alliance perspective.

Adaptations in the Alliance

For certain patients, any attempt on the part of the analyst to interpret either transference or transference resistances (including resistances to the transference) becomes a traumatic repetition of parental attitudes that inflict painful and humiliating wounds on the patient's narcissism and sense of self. By and large, these tend to be patients within the borderline spectrum (Meissner 1984a, 1988) whose self-structure is fragile and marked by narcissistic and even paranoid features (Jimenez 1993). Boris (1992) observes about such patients, "Such a Self, gorged by the identifications which go to make up first pairing, then grouping, so seriously lacks the relations involved in coupling that it is almost choked. To ask the self to identify with the analyst in what is sometimes called the therapeutic alliance is a disservice. First of all it means the terrible loss of the identifications out of which the Self is constructed (often ingeniously and with concealed pride), and second, it means opening up the inclination to look for, perhaps to lust for, the very differences of which coupling is made" (p. 589). We must walk cautiously here. The therapeutic alliance does invite the patient to step away from his pathology, but not in the fashion envisioned in Boris' statement. The invitation to enter the therapeutic frame does not impose any identifications, but seeks the engagement of ego capacities necessary for therapeutic work. Undoing of familiar and defensively reinforced introjective configurations can take place only over time and as a result of the analytic process, and their replacement by more constructive and adaptive identifications is a goal of therapy, not a point of departure (Meissner 1981). The question Boris raises is whether such developmentally and defensively impaired patients can establish a footing in the therapeutic alliance that allows any degree of therapeutic action.

In such cases, a minimal holding model of therapeutic alliance may prevail, but not without risks and not without evolving eventually into a more developed form of therapeutic alliance. The model of maternal holding presumes a pathological model of maternal deprivation, emphasizing the patient's role as victim and minimizing the place of aggression and conflict in object relationships (Mitchell 1988). If the analyst gratifies the patient on this account, mutually reinforcing fantasies of magical cure may result. In cases of character pathology, inappropriate helplessness and repeated demands for extratherapeutic concessions and exceptions to the therapeutic alliance can be accompanied by rageful attacks on the unresponsive therapist that elicit further negative reactions (Meissner 1988; Slochower 1991). As Slochower (1991) comments: "While the underlying vulnerability is very real, the dramatized and repetitive demands for, e.g., extra sessions, phone conversations, personal information, physical contact, etc., often have complicated emotional effects on the analyst. The analyst may fluctuate between a wish to repair profound early deprivation, a conviction that the analytic line must be held (to 'contain the tantrum'), and anger with these patients for their intrusiveness and unconscious destructiveness" (p. 711).

Under such pressures, even empathic holding can be squelched by the patient's continued angry demands and rejections of any empathic efforts by the analyst. The analyst has little recourse but to stay on course and not be drawn into any possible countertransference traps, between playing the patient's victim or responding to the patient's hostility with some form of hostile counterresponse (Olinick 1964). Slochower (1991, 1992) put it in terms of letting her patient know that she could not destroy her analyst, but that the patient was powerful enough to make a real impact. She argues that adopting a noninterpretive, nonempathic, and nonintrusive stance provided a kind of holding environment, but this understanding would give a different spin to the idea of a holding environment. I would understand the point to be that a firm and mildly aggressive response to the patient's demandingness both avoided certain countertransference traps and maintained the integrity of the therapeutic frame. Yet avoidance of some countertransference traps leaves the analyst vulnerable to others. The patient's demands seek to erode the analytic space and contaminate it inappropriately with reality.

Slochower (1991) distinguishes three variations of the holding environment in response to primitive needs of more disturbed patients, who tend to elicit negative countertransference responses in analysts. One variation is brought on by the regressed and dependent patient who imposes special demands on the analyst and seeks to modify the analytic situation in some fashion. Another variation comes from the narcissistic patient who ignores or represses dependency needs and remains affectively isolated, much like the narcissistic self-sufficiency described by Modell (1976). The analyst may feel impotent, ignored, bored, annoyed, or impatient (Thomson 1993). A third type of patient makes holding impossible by unrelenting attacks and demands which often drive the analyst to use retaliative interpretations or to conclude that the patient is unanalyzable.

Empathic Mirroring

At times, in order to gain or communicate empathy, the therapist uses empathic mirroring (which is not synonymous with empathy) as a deliberate technique. Goodman (1992) refers to empathic mirroring as "the process of reflecting the patient's words or affective tone to communicate an understanding of the patient's subjective experience, often validating that experience in the moment, in order to facilitate the patient's elaboration of his thoughts and feelings" (pp. 635–636). The mirroring may reflect the analyst's empathic experience of the patient, or it may stem from other observational or experiential data. In any case, it can help build empathic continuity with the patient where it is fragile or tenuous. To the extent that it hits the mark, it enables the patient to feel more accepted and understood.

Empathic mirroring also helps to clarify the patient's sense of himself. I have elsewhere (Meissner 1981, 1982, 1986b) argued that detailed exploration of the patient's sense of self is a salient component of the therapeutic process in that it unveils the organization of the patient's pathological introjects. If the therapist attunes himself to this wavelength, the patient conveys much about his experience of himself in the course of the therapy. Empathic mirroring facilitates this process insofar as it conveys an atmosphere of nonjudgmental acceptance and empathic resonance that encourages and supports further self-exploration and self-revelation by the patient. But rather than viewing empathic attunement as therapeutically effective in itself, I prefer to emphasize the entree it provides into clarification of the introjective configurations forming the patient's sense of self and self-images, which is important insofar as these configurations become the target for therapeutic exploration and ultimate change.

Transference Management

Understanding patterns of interaction between transference and therapeutic alliance leads inevitably to the question of transference management. In this section, I shall discuss issues of transference management under four headings: (1) priority of alliance factors over transference factors in dealing with transference distortions, including the use of clarifying or interpretive interventions; (2) the relationship of transference expressions to forming and sustaining therapeutic misalliances; (3) the implications of the interaction of projections and introjections in transference; and (4) forms of misalliance resulting from transference dynamics.

Alliance before Transference

I have discussed the reasons for focusing on the therapeutic alliance and its disruption as a first priority, and dealing with transference manifestations second. Issues pertaining to the alliance must be paid constant attention, and any deviation, distortion, or disruption of the alliance must be dealt with immediately and directly. The attitude and expectancy toward transference factors is somewhat different. In general, I prefer to give ample space and opportunity for transference manifestations to develop and to come into focus. Transference manifestations compel some form of intervention from the therapist only at points where they create significant resistance to the treatment process, or at points at which they become sufficiently disruptive or regressive so as to undermine or disrupt the therapeutic alliance.

The basic rule of thumb is that transference and therapeutic alliance are oppositional and generally inversely proportional, in the sense that the more prominent and influential the transference elements, the less stable and effective is the therapeutic alliance and vice versa. Therapists emphasizing the centrality of transference tend to see any shift toward alliance factors as avoiding or minimizing the significance of transference, but, whatever the oppositional context within which they operate, the therapeutic alliance and transference are also linked in an interactive process. Thus transference can only be clarified, interpreted, and effectively dealt with to the degree that a workable therapeutic alliance is in effect. The meaningful development of the transference may also require some preexisting foundation in the therapeutic alliance.

This issue raises the questions of what factors are necessary for stimulation and development of a full-blown transference or transference neurosis. Patients frequently enter the therapeutic relationship with a significant misalliance riding on underlying transference determinants. Only when the alliance has in some degree been consolidated or stabilized, even in inchoative ways, will the transference elements come into focus. Some form of preliminary alliance, whether a narcissistic alliance or a working or therapeutic alliance, is necessary for the activation and mobilization of more regressive transference elements. In such cases, the patient may need a sense of security, confidence, and trust in the relationship with the therapist in order to express transference elements. Metaphors of holding or containment reflect this dimension of the therapeutic alliance in that they imply a supportive and sustaining environment within which the therapeutic process evolves.[4]

While alliance factors and transference stand in opposition, this line of demarcation is somewhat obscured in the so-called "selfobject" transferences.[5] To the extent that the neurotic or self-related need expressed in the "selfobject" transference is responded to in the alliance by the analytic object, there would seem to be a high risk for development of a transference/countertransference interaction. For example, if the ideal-hungry self finds an object which responds to its need to idealize and serves as an idealized object, the transference on the part of the subject would seem to correspond to a countertransference on the part of the object. This would be analogous to the case of a negative transference, for example, in which the victimized and vulnerable self of the patient would be matched by a sadistic, hostile, or destructive image of the therapist. Although a good therapeutic alliance would not respond in any way to the sense of victimization in this sort of negative transference, it would respond to the basic need expressed in the "selfobject" transferences. While the alliance for an idealizing subject might not immediately satisfy his need to idealize, it would offer a context of understanding, security, and confidence within which his idealizing need would be accepted and empathically understood. If the underlying sense of narcissistic inferiority contributes to the patient's need to idealize, then participation in a meaningful therapeutic alliance would provide some restitutive balm. This view of the therapeutic interaction comes close to the notion of a corrective emotional experience, but it is far from being simply that; rather, it involves processes that are activated within the interpersonal relationship and involve the patterning of projections and introjections underlying the significant internalizations central to the process of cure (Meissner 1981).

Relation to Therapeutic Misalliance

Transferences lie at the root of most therapeutic misalliances (Langs 1976). Whenever the therapist recognizes a misalliance, he has good reason to search for transference components that may contribute to it. As Freud (1912, 1915a) observed, a degree of benign and positive attachment to the therapist may be necessary to allow the patient to feel sufficiently comfortable to proceed with the analytic work. This degree of positive transference, which usually is admissible to consciousness and facilitates the patient's involvement with the therapist, can contribute to establishing a therapeutic alliance. This form of relatively conscious, benign, and constructive transference does not necessarily contribute to a therapeutic misalliance, although we cannot exclude that possibility. Only when transference, usually in a negative form, becomes a resistance to forming the therapeutic relationship should it be a concern for interpretation. Negative transferences, whether in the merely negative or paranoid form, always contribute to formation of a therapeutic misalliance. The therapist may be seen as judgmental, unsympathetic, rigid, sadistic, hostile, powerful, controlling, threatening, abandoning, and so on.[6] Such patients may experience a depressive response that incorporates omnipotent denial and control to fend off fears of the analyst's power (Riviere 1936). Such transferential distortions and their concurrent misalliances lie at the root of many therapeutic impasses. As Kantrowitz (1993a) notes, "When impasses occur, transferences and countertransferences have interfered with the mutual commitment to the task of free association, interpretation, and creation of new meaning in treatment. The relative contribution of these transferences and countertransferences will vary for each patient-analyst pair and in each impasse" (p. 1024). If these aggressive dynamics extend to the psychotic level, the transference becomes paranoid and the alliance disrupted.

Narcissistic transferences are somewhat similar to positive transferences in that they may or may not contribute to the therapeutic misalliance. If the intensity of the narcissistic transference is relatively muted and mild, the degree of distortion introduced into the therapeutic relationship may not significantly distort the potential therapeutic alliance. But even in higher-order narcissistic or neurotic patients, the degree of idealization or mirroring must be carefully assessed for its impact on the therapeutic alliance. At times in such patients the distortion may not be severe, but it may contribute to a subtle narcissistic alliance, preventing evolution toward a more meaningful therapeutic alliance.[7]

Shame can also contribute to a misalliance (Broucek 1991; Jacobson 1993; Morrison 1984, 1989; Wurmser 1981). The patient's wish to keep some aspect of his pathology or other aspect of his life experience concealed from the analyst reflects both a perversion of the alliance and a transference resistance. A patient's concealment of homosexual inclinations, for example, provides a signal of such a misalliance. Behind the misalliance may lie the further possibility of some form of negative transference.

As the narcissistic distortion becomes more severe, however, risk of narcissistic alliance increases, as well as the tendency to form a narcissistically determined therapeutic misalliance. In such cases, risk of a transference/countertransference interaction in response to the patient's narcissistic need is high. The narcissistic need for an illusion of self-sufficiency may create an impasse out of a desire to paralyze the analytic process, immobilize the analyst, and forestall either termination or effective analytic change (Maldonado 1984). As Novick (1980) pointed out, such narcissistically determined misalliances (which he refers to as forms of "negative therapeutic alliance") can express themselves in terms of the over- or undervaluation of the analyst's skill and effectiveness. Overvaluation reflects an omnipotent quest derived from the fantasy of the perfect parent/analyst whose magical technique can ease all pain and conflict. This can create a countertransference seduction for the analyst, whose own narcissistic need to perform therapeutic wonders may make him vulnerable and give rise to a collusive misalliance.

The situation with selfobject transferences is similar in regard to the transference/countertransference risk. To the extent that the selfobject interaction takes place on this level, it always involves some degree of therapeutic misalliance. It is far more preferable to respond to the needs expressed in the selfobject transference in terms of the alliance rather than the transference/countertransference option. By the same token, transitional object transferences and the demand placed on the object to respond in terms of transitional relatedness always involves, to my mind, some degree of therapeutic misalliance. At the bottom of the heap, transference psychosis represents an acute, regressive, and usually long-lasting disruption and breakdown of the therapeutic alliance, but can be taken as reflecting a persistent underlying therapeutic misalliance.

Patterns of Projection and Introjection

As already suggested, such transference distortions may occur with mobilization of preformed transference elements. In the case of the young man described in chapter 15, whose preformed paranoid transference threatened to disrupt the analysis, his anticipations of involvement in the analysis activated preformed transference elements, which placed him in a paranoid position characterized by severe persecutory anxiety, fright, and a corresponding impulse to flee the analysis. To establish the psychoanalytic situation, the analyst had to assume a more active and confronting posture. It was necessary to point out to the patient the nature of his distortions, that they must be coming from other areas of his experience than those involved in the present situation, and that if he let his fears get the better of him, he was in danger of destroying the analysis. In this particular patient, the basic capacity of his ego to observe and assess reality enabled him to respond positively to this strong intervention. Although this did not change the basically paranoid quality of his transference and subsequently elaborated transference neurosis, it broke through the paranoid defense sufficiently to allow more adaptive portions of his ego to engage in the analytic work.

The reverse pattern was described by Kogan (1992) in which the analyst was cast in the role of the weak and impotent father/analyst. The patient, whose history included wounding his father during the father's attempt to save the patient from a suicidal attempt, sought to destroy the therapeutic alliance by breaking off the therapeutic relation and thus destroying the transference object. In addition to his demeaning attacks on the analyst, he joined a religious cult, in which he could subject himself to a powerful leader who imposed painful and humiliating ceremonies on him. Through a spiritual union with this godlike figure, he hoped to acquire the power to ward off the threatening identification with the depressed and deteriorating father. In the midst of these religious obsessions, he decided to quit his job and leave treatment. The analyst, in addition to his feelings of frustration and anger, felt fearful and powerless to prevent this self-destructive acting out and began to doubt his own capabilities as an analyst and the advisability of trying to analyze this patient. Only when the analyst refocused the therapeutic alliance was he able to gain any purchase on this deteriorating situation. He was unable to interrupt the acting out—the patient left the treatment, joined a cult commune, and suffered a psychotic episode—but he was able to reconstitute the relation sufficiently to allow the patient to return for further treatment that ultimately stabilized his fragile ego boundaries and facilitated the emergence of a more secure sense of self.

Forms of Misalliance

A frequent target for emergence of misalliances is the analyst's authority. Freud (1915a) had noted the use of transference love by certain patients as a way of undermining the analyst's authority. Along the same line, Joseph (1993) reported a case in which the patient turned the analysis into a sadomasochistic experience and erotized the transference in order to minimize any differences between Joseph and herself, thus denying any authority or effectiveness to her analyst's efforts.

Among narcissistic patients, a common motivating force behind stalemates or impasses is envy of the analyst's knowledge, skill, and power, especially his position as an acknowledged healer to whom the disadvantaged and distressed patient must turn to for help. Freud (1937) argued that envy-linked complexes like feminine penis envy and masculine fear of homosexual submission were among the most difficult resistances. While Freud's perspective seems to have been limited to the context of envy directed to a male analyst, similar issues can emerge with female analysts, who share the same perils provoked by their power, position, and prestige. The transference resistances are much the same, although cast in somewhat different form as a function of the analyst's gender—e.g., sadomasochistic struggles over power and control in female-female dyads or envious feelings regarding marital status or pregnancy (Lester 1993). The misalliance distortion may take the form of rejection of or excessive compliance with or subjection to the analyst's authoritative position. Males frequently refuse to accept any interpretation or improvement from the father or mother substitute. In females, hopeless and resentful submission to the fate of penis-lack leads to a depressive resolution (Feldman and de Paola 1994). In both cases, the invitation to join the analyst in a meaningful and mutually contributory authority relation is declined in favor of transference resistance, and the therapeutic alliance is undermined. The misalliance for the male paradigm takes the form of rejection of authority, and, for the female paradigm, denial of personal authority.

The task in such situations, whether the authority relation is imbalanced by reason of transference love or some other narcissistic or defensive need on the part of the patient or analyst, is to re-create the analytic space and correct the distortion of the therapeutic alliance (Hernández 1993). Whether the patient rejects or denies the analyst's authority, or whether he follows the path of compliance and subjection, the analyst must be alert to the imbalance in the authority relation and move to address the misalliance directly. In cases where the underlying motivation is narcissistic and/or envious—trying to defeat the analyst and render the analysis meaningless, negating anything experienced as good from the analyst, seeking omnipotent control and devaluation, often with intense paranoid conflicts, suspiciousness, and hatred—establishing or maintaining the therapeutic alliance calls for careful self-monitoring by the analyst to ensure that he is not contributing to the misalliance by his own overly authoritarian or narcissistically determined approach to the patient. This is a primary task in the opening phase of the analysis, directed principally to the narcissistic alliance, but if the issue persists into later stages of the analysis, an optimistic prognosis is correspondingly compromised.

Such disruptions of the alliance are not restricted to the initial phase but may occur in later phases, particularly when the alliance has not been solidly established and there is fairly intense contamination by transference factors. A clinical experience may clarify the place of alliance adjustment in dealing with such disruptive transference distortions. One highly threatened young woman defensively assumed an argumentative and competitive stance through most of her analysis. She particularly resisted any attempts on my part to clarify her resistance, to work through her defensiveness and the obviously concealed layer of intense anxiety, fear, and an overwhelming sense of weakness and vulnerability that motivated her posture within the analysis. Even the most tactful observations or clarifications and the most gentle, relatively innocuous interpretations were taken as personal attacks, meant only to demean and defeat her.

This attitude became increasingly intense and began to threaten not only the work within the analysis, but the patient's continuing in the analytic situation. She finally angrily and bitterly accused me of making her lie on the couch as a humiliating exercise in which she had to submit herself unwillingly to my probings and questionings. It was for her a degrading exposure of those parts of herself about which she felt most ashamed and vulnerable. Her associations clearly related this to a gynecological examination, with her legs spread and strapped helplessly, her most private parts open to the cold, uncaring observation of the analyst/gynecologist.

At this point I asked the patient why she was lying on the couch anyway. The question startled and confused her. It had never occurred to her that lying on the couch was a matter of choice. She had automatically and unquestioningly thought that that was what was expected of her. I suggested that lying on the couch might not be the most useful way for her to go about the analysis, and that she might think about whether she wanted to do something different. When she returned for the next hour, she announced that she had decided to sit in the chair facing me. We did this, and during the ensuing months the patient's extremely argumentative stance disappeared, along with the paranoid distortions. We were able to establish a relatively solid alliance, and many of her defensive attitudes and their underlying unconscious derivatives were exposed, analyzed, and productively worked through. She finally decided to return to the couch—now as a matter of her free and deliberate choice, thereby deepening her involvement and commitment to the analysis.

CHAPTER SEVENTEEN

Interpretation

Interpretation is the primary and basic technical tool in psychoanalytically oriented psychotherapy and psychoanalysis and the essential process in developing insight and gradual resolution of underlying neurotic conflicts. While interpretation is always central to the therapeutic process, in different contexts various aspects of the interpretive process tend to play a differential and at times weightier role. While content remains important, with more primitive patients the mood and manner of interpretation may be even more significant than with healthier neurotic patients. It may be useful, therefore, to consider the nature of psychoanalytic interpretation as well as the therapist's function as interpreter.

Interpretation as Process

Interpretation aims at gaining understanding, and its object is some meaning, set of meanings, or connection of meanings. It is an effort to make sense out of something, or to understand the meaning of a connection or a relationship between events, contexts, behaviors, or whatever. It does not render judgment, but rather aims at translating meaning (Boris 1973). Interpretation, therefore, is not a statement of fact but of meaning, and by its very nature can be no more than tentative, exploratory, and hypothetical (Adler and Myerson 1973b; Kernberg 1979). When the interpretive process is working well, therapist and patient are engaged in the exploration of hypotheses arrived at by a collaborative process, based on the patient's intrapsychic content (Jacobson 1993; Treurniet 1993). Interpretation is not something that the therapist does to the patient; rather, it involves mutual engagement on the part of both therapist and patient. Greenberg (1995) even describes it as a form of negotiation. In a well-working therapeutic process, interpretation is as likely to arise from the patient as from the therapist (Stocking 1973).[1]

Consistency in the therapist's attitude toward the patient and in his interpretive effort seems to be a necessary component of effective interpretation.

The experience of seeking understanding in an empathic relationship with the therapist provides an experience for the patient that is qualitatively different from many experiences in his development, particularly in his relationships with his parents. It creates an ambiance in which gradual introjection of the analyst as an accepting, understanding, and reasonable figure can take place (Boyer 1983). While this experience can be corrective, the authentic corrective flows from the therapeutic alliance rather than in any real relation.[2]

Thus the emphasis often found in discussions of the therapeutic alliance on the analyst's warmth, kindness, and humaneness do not belong properly to the therapeutic alliance but to the real relation. Hanly (1994) has commented on the role of humaneness or "human influence" in the interpretive process. Interpretation is never coldly scientific, unempathic, indifferent, or dehumanizing, as some advocates of the caring attitude seem to suggest. The interpretive process in analysis is consistently empathic; if it is not, it is neither analytic nor interpretive. As Hanly notes: "When interpretations and other interventions are only being read from a theory, rather than being read, with the help of a theory, from the text provided by the patient and his associations, no matter what dosages of human influence the analyst's view of the working alliance may require, the patient will be bereft of this necessary condition for his work. Yet human influence is not of equal importance with interpretation, because its therapeutic efficacy depends upon interpretation. In psychoanalysis it is interpretation that liberates the process of association, seeks out and clears the way to remembering and working through" (p. 465). That is, interpretation emerges from the meaningful matrix of relationship provided by the therapeutic alliance. A more careful discrimination between therapeutic alliance and reality would make it clear that the basis for effective interpretation in the therapeutic alliance is different than any loose connection with "human influence" or "humaneness."

There is room for openness and honesty in making interpretations. The therapist can often usefully acknowledge his uncertainty or doubts, or offer his hypothesis tentatively as only one aspect of the problem, or as a suggestion that the patient may wish to consider, revise, reject, or accept. There is no need to reinforce the patient's sense of inferiority by an implication of the therapist's deeper understanding, sense of infallibility, or superiority. In view of the often uncertain nature of interpretations, it can even be useful for the therapist to be wrong and to acknowledge it (Appel 1974).[3]

Interpretations may also take the form of questions, which offer possible directions of thinking and meanings or can elucidate relationships and connections that facilitate the inquiry (Olinick 1954). Questions nonetheless carry an inherent risk of placing a demand on the patient or of carrying within them an element of confrontation, which may elicit reactions of conformity, resentment, envy, and even rage, and with certain patients are more usefully avoided.

Interpretive Strategy

Caution is called for in making interpretations early in the treatment process, when the therapeutic alliance is poorly or only partially established, as the patient may experience them as critical or accusatory and they may only cause narcissistic injuries or intensify negative transference reactions (Chessick 1982). Similarly, as others have noted (Little 1958; Wallerstein 1967), when patients are functioning in a more regressive mode, transference interpretations have little utility because the interpretation may be overridden by the dynamics of a delusional transference in which the differentiation between fantasy and reality has been eroded and the analyst is experienced as an idealized or diabolized parent. Interpretations have a better chance of being understood and accepted when the therapeutic alliance is intact.

The capacity for the patient to engage in the process of interpretation is in part a function of the level of pathology. At the level of classically neurotic and most narcissistic pathology and at the higher end of the borderline spectrum (Meissner 1988), interpretation becomes the primary therapeutic technique and, by and large, does not differ from ordinary interpretive processes. At lower levels of borderline pathology, however, the effectiveness of interpretations is increasingly compromised. Moreover, the same gradation in severity plays a role in mobilization of countertransference difficulties that may inhibit or interfere with the interpretive process.

Transference Interpretation

Interpretation of transference requires that the therapist maintain a position of technical neutrality and a firm boundary between the patient's transference fantasies and the reality of the therapeutic situation. The therapist must take care that he is not drawn into reactivation of more pathological and primitive object relations reflected in the patient's transference. Therapy with more primitive patients may involve a significant amount of nonverbal communication that plays a vital role in shaping the therapeutic situation. These nonverbal aspects most often reflect the influence of transferences contributing to various misalliances that require exploration and resolution. Negative and disruptive transferences may arise from the beginning of the therapy, especially in more primitively organized patients, and require early interpretation. My preference, based on the role of the therapeutic alliance in establishing the therapeutic situation, is to focus on the alliance aspect of the problem, whether the transference aspects are available for processing or not. When transferences are more modulated, less primitive, and generally positive, they may facilitate establishing the therapeutic situation and lead to gradual development of the therapeutic alliance. These more positive transferences do not demand immediate response but can be tolerated as long as they do not contribute excessively to resistance, but they must be kept on the agenda of issues to be interpreted at an appropriate time. Even when transferences contribute to the therapeutic ambiance, they require interpretation and, one hopes, resolution at some point.

Interpretation and Therapeutic Misalliances

I have argued that early transference distortions can be more effectively conceptualized and dealt with in alliance terms, particularly in the early phases of treatment where the resources and opportunities for transference interpretation as such are relatively nonexistent. Often, dealing with such emergent therapeutic misalliances is less a matter of interpretation than of a combination of confrontation and clarification. The patient's distortions may have their roots in transference determinants and reactions, but at this early phase of treatment the therapist has little knowledge of that material, so it is relatively unavailable for effective interpretation. But the therapist is aware of the patient's behavior and the manner in which he reacts to the therapist's interventions in the here and now. This can be focused on from the very first as distortions of alliance. As Jacobson (1993) notes, "The initial bond formed in the opening phase becomes strengthened through this process of meaningful and helpful interpretation of its distortions, a process we often conceptualize in terms of the strengthening of the therapeutic alliance" (p. 529). In the course of such an exploration, it is not unusual for dynamic, defensive, or even adaptive aspects of the patient's interaction with the therapist to come to light. But the opportunities for any deeper interpretation, genetic or otherwise, are not only scanty, but may in the early phases of therapy prove to be premature and even damaging. Gentle confrontation about the meaning of the patient's behavior and its implications for the therapeutic alliance, in contrast, often helps to engage the patient in the therapeutic process and generate some degree of curiosity about the meaning of his behavior.

Such early clarifications and confrontations and at times low-level interpretations are directed toward establishing the therapeutic alliance (Hanly 1994; Sandler et al. 1973). Success is often a matter of the accuracy, timeliness, and empathy of such interventions. The manner may be more important than the substance. In addition, premature oedipal interpretations may make it more difficult for pre-oedipal transferences to establish themselves. Along the same lines, the Blancks (1974) have emphasized the importance of supporting the patient's ego in the course of making interpretations. They distinguish between ego interpretations, designed to help the patient understand his deficits in order to facilitate further growth, and id interpretations, which deal primarily with unconscious derivatives in order to delineate unconscious wishes and related points of fixation or regression. They emphasize that interpretations must be made in proportion to the capacity of the patient's ego to assimilate and synthesize them. In addition, if the patient requires a more supportive relation that would be interfered with by any kind of interpretation (transference, genetic, or otherwise), the demands of the relationship take precedence. This emphasis is somewhat reminiscent of the emphasis on selfobject transferences and the techniques for dealing with them proposed by the self psychologists.

Affirmative Interpretations

In the face of transference and countertransference difficulties, use of affirmative interpretations based in the alliance has much to recommend it. Interpretations are affirmative when they show empathic understanding of what lies behind the patient's behavior, when the therapist can appreciate the adaptive value of the patient's behavior, and when the therapist can accept the patient's motivation for maintaining his lifestyle in spite of its difficulties. Affirmative interpretations are experienced as empathic, appreciative and respectful. The implicit message in the therapist's affirmative attitude is that the patient is in no danger of encountering trauma similar to any he has experienced in the past and that the prospective relationship with the therapist will be sufficiently safe for him to risk exposure of his unconscious wishes and fantasies (Schaffer 1986).[4]

Interpretations should aim always at being positive and affirmative. This principle has been enunciated by a number of contributors in terms of ego-building (Blanck and Blanck 1974), alliance facilitating (Boyer and Giovacchini 1980; Boyer 1983), or reinforcing self-worth, autonomy, and adaptive value of the patient and his actions (Kris 1990; Schafer 1983; Schaffer 1986). In terms of the therapeutic alliance, interpretations are affirmative to the extent that they support and consolidate the therapeutic alliance. Even when the therapist is drawing attention to negative aspects of the patient's behavior, he will take care to interject a positive and sustaining note. Even when concern for maintaining the patient's sense of self-worth, autonomy, and capacity, is involved, affirmation may not play an immediate role in a given interpretive statement at an isolated point in the therapeutic exchange, but it must not be overlooked. The therapist, if he is wise, will find a way to include an affirmative note in the mix of interpretive elements.

Less affirmative interpretations, on the contrary, may focus on ways in which the patient's behavior is maladaptive, unrealistic, contradictory, or infantile, and may give little regard to the motivating forces underlying the patient's attachment to his self-defeating patterns. These interpretations send the implicit message to the patient that these behaviors and patterns should be stopped as soon as possible and that the therapist is unappreciative, relatively disrespectful, and unempathic.

For many patients, the consequences of exploring and exposing unconscious fantasies and wishes are threatening and dangerous. This affirmative analytic attitude is of the utmost importance in transference interpretations. Analysis of transference manifestations are not affirmative when they portray the patient's transference as distorted or destructive. The therapist's failure to confirm the patient's experience of the relationship is liable to be experienced as rejecting or humiliating, making the therapist a threatening or dangerous object and undermining any attachment or collaboration. If the therapist can approach transference as plausible and even adaptive, with appreciation for underlying motivating forces, the patient's reaction is more likely to regard the interaction with the therapist as safe and to allow further exploration of the transference phenomenon (Schafer 1983).

The issue has more to do with the therapist's attitudes, feelings, and manner of interpretation than the specific content or phraseology. This aspect of the interpretive process only underlines the importance of countertransference factors as they enter into and color the interpretive process. Where interpretations have a negative cast, one can suspect unresolved and unmodulated countertransference factors. Interpretations emerging from a context of valid and accurate empathy are more likely to be affirmative than negative. The patient's introjection of the therapist's interpretive stance is an essential aspect of the process of modifying the patient's pathogenic superego. To the extent that negative elements enter into the interpretive process, they would hardly contribute to this important aspect of the therapeutic dynamics.

Interpretation of the Alliance

Not only is clarification and interpretation of the therapeutic alliance important, but I would further argue the dependence of the interpretive process on the therapeutic alliance. The interpretive process assumes that the therapeutic alliance is effective and reflects the level of the patient's ability to integrate the interpretation and to participate in the process. Any interpretive hypothesis requires validation through continuing collaborative effort of both therapist and patient (Stocking 1973). Thus, an effective therapeutic alliance or at least working alliance is mandatory for useful interpretation and involves development of the patient's curiosity about his own motivations and the reasons and influences that contribute to his attitudes and behaviors.

The interpretive process not only requires some degree of therapeutic alliance but should also reinforce and stabilize it. This may require focusing frequently on existential transactions involved in the therapeutic alliance itself;

this may bring into focus contributing transference processes and lead eventually in the direction of dynamic and genetic interpretations. In analytic work with many narcissistic or more primitive character disorders, the interpretive process may be exquisitely sensitive to alliance factors. When the alliance is identifiably fragile, distorted, or disrupted, interpretations must be used with care as they can easily be distorted by the patient's projective needs. However thoughtfully, carefully, empathically, and gently interpretations may be offered, they may be transformed into pathogenic input. If patients have even some slender footing in a working alliance, it can be reassuring and relieving for them to be able to express and discuss their hostile, competitive, ambivalent, and even murderously destructive impulses toward the therapist. The alliance in a sense serves as a buffer against the toxic influences of these pathological affects. The sense of collaborative consolidation with a strong and resilient object strengthens the patient's capacity to tolerate and deal with these feelings. But patients who lack a sufficiently strong alliance, or in whom the alliance has been disrupted by a regressive crisis, may find it difficult to distinguish between discussing such hostile and destructive feelings and acting upon them. The sense of alliance with the therapist's ego strengths is essential to allow the patient to experience such affects and to deal with them in a more objective, therapeutic, and nontraumatic fashion (Appel 1974).

Likewise, interpretation of important object relations should only be undertaken in the context of a reasonably good working alliance. It may not be useful to try to clarify or confront the patient's convictions about important objects, since disruption of such object connections may be more damaging than helpful. Patients can be brought gradually to a point of understanding more realistic aspects of their relationships, but this can be achieved only in the context of a solid therapeutic alliance. The time may come when it is helpful for the patient to recognize that in some degree his hostility toward a negative object was justified, but this can only be achieved insofar as negative distorting elements in the relationship have been sorted out and understood in dynamic and/or genetic terms (Blanck and Blanck 1974). The purpose of interpretation is to assist the patient in building intrapsychic structure, a process that can be a subtle, prolonged, step-by-step effort with a persistent focus on the therapeutic alliance.

Interpretations that do not contribute to or support the therapeutic alliance are not useful. These would include interpretations that tend to inflict narcissistic injury on the patient, especially early in the treatment process (Chessick 1979). One of the difficulties with more primitive patients is that, if the therapist makes an observation or an interpretation that the patient did not think of first, the patient is confronted with the basic separateness and individuality of the therapist, a realization that shatters his illusion of merger with a good and protective object (Modell 1978). Borderline patients may react to interpretations with shame, envy, rage, and depression. These difficulties at times have led to the conclusion that interpretation should be avoided (Schaffer 1986). Some therapists therefore emphasize the importance of the holding environment and correspondingly deemphasize the work of interpretation in the therapeutic process.

When one is dealing with patients in whom the pathology is more primitive, labile, and vulnerable to regression, interpretation has to be used with great care. The therapist's effort must be constantly directed toward maintaining the fragments of healthy ego-functioning in the patient and supporting the patient's sense of self-worth and autonomy. Any effort on the part of the therapist that smacks of feeding the patient's infantile hunger and symbiotic wishes can only undermine the patient's autonomy and his capacity for contributing to the therapeutic work. Absolving the patient of any degree of responsibility for maintaining the therapeutic work neither reinforces the therapeutic alliance nor provides an adequate framework for meaningful interpretation (Appel 1974). One is always confronted with the difficulty of maintaining an appropriate and useful degree of ego distance in the work of interpretation, neither pressing forward excessively so as to undermine the patient's responsibility and initiative and stimulate wishes for dependence and merger, nor excessively withdrawing or withholding interpretive contributions and running the risk of stirring fears of abandonment, inadequacy, and helplessness (Rangell 1955).

Fantasy and Reality

Clarification of the boundaries between the patient's fantasy life and its derivatives and reality pervades the interpretive process from beginning to end. I would add that interpretation aims at maintaining boundaries between the patient's fantasy distortions and aspects of the therapy that are real and specific to the analytic structure—in particular, the therapeutic alliance. Even at the earliest stages of interpretive work with many patients, the therapist must work toward establishing the rudiments of a working alliance, which may require clarification and at least phenomenological interpretation of the patient's experience in the therapeutic relationship as reflecting misalliance more than alliance.

Achievement of the clarification and differentiation between fantasy and reality at later stages in the therapy is often complex and difficult. It is helpful for the therapist to keep in mind the primary objectives of the therapeutic work, namely, consistently affirming the reality of the treatment situation by interpreting current distortions and helping the patient toward meaningful self-exploration and free-association rather than expending his energies on grappling with and controlling the therapist. This approach aims at reconstituting the therapeutic alliance and getting the therapeutic work back on track. However, in cases where transference-based distortions can be brought into focus and some degree of working alliance is available, drawing the patient's attention to his distortions of the therapeutic reality may not be the most effective tactic.

Transference and Misalliance

Following Freud's suggestion, transferences of relatively mild, benign, and constructive nature, whether simply positive and libidinal or narcissistic, do not call for specific therapeutic response, as long as they are contributory to a meaningful and effective therapeutic alliance. To the degree that they interfere with that progression, they must become objects for therapeutic scrutiny and exploration. All other forms of transference, insofar as they tend to undermine the therapeutic alliance and create therapeutic misalliances, call for therapeutic intervention. In all of these cases, the rule of thumb regarding the priority of alliance over transference as the object of therapeutic effort would hold true—it is the resulting misalliance that must first be identified, explored, and understood. Once this task is at least partially accomplished, or as it is gradually being accomplished, more specific and identifiable transference elements can be brought into play. In negative and narcissistic transferences, the line between transference elements and misalliance can be more cleanly drawn. In the self-object and transitional object transferences, this line is often blurred. In any case, attention to alliance aspects consistently takes precedence and becomes a vehicle for the next step in the process, namely, focusing, exploring, and coming to understand underlying transference dynamics.

The model of transference as developing through progressive interaction of projections and introjections provides a useful framework for conceptualizing and ultimately interpreting the transference dynamics and their implications. In these terms, transference can be understood as a reflection of the patient's self-organization, specifically conceptualized in terms of introjective configurations which form the basis for projective elements. In this sense, displacement transferences express the patient's sense of himself in relationship with specific objects. As the object representation from some previous object relationship is attributed to the therapist, the subject simultaneously adopts a similar role in relation to that displaced object. The nature of the object representation and the position of the subject in relation to it conveys important communications about the individual's own sense of self. In contrast, in the projective transferences, some aspect of the self as integrated within the introjective structure is projected onto the therapist as object. In this case, projection also reflects characteristics of the self-system (Meissner 1986b).

In both cases, a cardinal principle of good therapeutic management is to avoid potential entanglement in a transference/countertransference interaction. In the displacement transference, part of the impulse in the subject is to reenact the previous relationship, but the transference creates no significant pressures within the therapeutic relationship for the therapist to play out that object role. In contrast, in a projective transference, there is an inherent exigency in the projection pressuring the object to fit into the projective requirements, so that, first, the projection is in some degree validated and reinforced and, second, that the corresponding introjective configuration which remains internalized can be confirmed in the ongoing interaction with the projected part.[5] For example, the patient who projects some aspect of his own aggressive introjective configuration onto the therapist and consequently sees the therapist as critical or hostile or threatening, does so in some degree to preserve his internal sense of himself as weak, vulnerable, and victimized. If the projection is not validated and sustained, the mechanism falters and prevents the subject's own inner sense of victimization based on the victim-introject from being effectively sustained.

If possible, the patient can be encouraged to explore dimensions of his transference distortion to bring to light latent transferential components and thereby reveal hidden dimensions of the underlying introjective configuration. For some patients, any sense of the reality of the therapist is achieved only after long periods of engagement and increasing familiarity and only after considerable working through of projective distortions (Olinick 1954). Again, the patient's capacity to accept, realize, and integrate interpretive material that would allow him to gain a firmer footing and orientation in reality is in part a function of the therapeutic alliance, which may be fragile, tenuous, and often minimal. As Modell (1976) points out with reference to the cocoon transference, development of tolerance for separateness leads to the therapeutic action being increasingly organized around the interpretive process. The question is not whether the interpretive process is oriented toward establishing a clearer and more adaptive sense of reality, but in what measure and with what pacing.

The dilemma is similar to that posed by Fairbairn (1958) in distinguishing between the dynamics of a closed system as opposed to an open system. To the extent that the patient's psychic economy is trapped in a closed system, the patient can deal only with the reality of his inner psychic world. To the extent that this system becomes open, input from external reality can be brought into conjunction with the inner dynamics and open the way to more realistic and adaptive solutions. The transference in Fairbairn's terms would be such a closed system and would stand in opposition to the real relationship to an object as a form of open system, or to the therapeutic alliance, also an open system. To the extent that the closed system dynamics are operating, the subject can only relate to the object in transferential terms, so that real or nontransferential qualities of the object hardly enter into determining the patient's reaction to and interaction with that object. The therapeutic problem is how to open the closed system. It may be that open system considerations have to be postponed until the dynamics and patterns of the closed system can be adequately explored, understood, and (it is our hope) resolved, so that the system becomes more open to the outside world.

Alliance as Matrix of Interpretation

While interpretation itself operates on a more or less cognitive level to produce meaningful insight and consequently facilitate therapeutic change and growth within the patient, other factors having to do with alliance provide the context within which interpretation can be productively communicated. Hanly (1994) focuses the relation between therapeutic alliance and interpretation by regarding the alliance as a necessary, but not sufficient, condition for therapeutic change, in contrast to interpretation, which is regarded as merely sufficient. I would argue that analysts cannot feel so sanguine about the effectiveness of any interventions to conclude that they are either necessary or sufficient. Therapeutic alliance may contribute to therapeutic change under certain conditions, but in most cases it falls short of sufficiency. By the same token, therapeutic effects can be experienced as a result of a variety of therapeutic interventions even when the therapeutic alliance is lacking or minimal. Interpretation itself is by the same standards neither necessary nor sufficient: other interventions may prove effective, or change may emerge without any identifiable interpretive contribution. However, interpretation and therapeutic alliance do interact to produce an effect. Interpretations outside the therapeutic alliance are at high risk of having an adverse or no effect, and a therapeutic alliance that does not eventuate in meaningful interpretations leaves room for other factors (e.g., transference cure) to play themselves out. In any case, therapeutic alliance and interpretation do not stand in opposition, even though they can be drawn into patterns of mutual resistance. The oppositional forms of alliance frequently characterized as defensive against unconscious derivatives (especially transference) are in effect forms of therapeutic misalliance.

The critical concern is mobilization of growth potential and facilitation of a more coherent, consolidated, and adaptive sense of self in the patient. Addressing himself to this dimension of analytic experience, Khan (1972b) observed:

> The etiology of the dislocation of self, as Winnicott pointed out, starts always from maladaptive environmental care. We encounter the self of a patient clinically only in *moments* of true regression to dependence and

> holding. Quite often, such moments of self-experience actualize outside the analytic or therapeutic situation and our task then is how to enable the patient to provide ego coverage for them. Interpretation, as such, cannot engender self-experience in the patient, although, once these experiences actualize, interpretations enable the patient's ego to find and elaborate symbolic equations through which these experiences can become a property of the inner psychic reality of the patient—conscious and unconscious . . . .
>
> The two distinct styles of my relating to the patient I can differentiate as: (1) Listening to what the patient verbally communicates, in the patently classical situation as it has evolved, and deciphering its meaning in terms of structural conflicts (ego, id and superego) and through its transferential interpersonal expression in the here-and-now of the analytic situation. (2) Through a psychic, affective, and environmental holding of the person of the patient in the clinical situation, I facilitate certain experiences that I cannot anticipate or program, any more than the patient can. When these actualize, they are surprising, both for the patient and for me, and release quite unexpected new processes in the patient. (pp. 98–99)

Undoubtedly this holding aspect of the analytic interaction, as a limited expression of therapeutic alliance, plays a more prominent role in more primitive forms of personality organization. This "holding" may provide a kind of minimal condition without which the analytic transaction cannot take place. Berry (1975) observed: "In many cases, especially those in which paranoid factors are dominant, and in all cases where one reaches this kernel, the factors of presence, of good will and of listening, play a role which I see as the minimal condition necessary for the acceptance of an interpretation. Without this condition and this preliminary work ('holding'), the interpretation risks being received like milk, like a gift, an attack or a persecution, its contents not being comprehended. Without this 'minimal condition' the interpretation cannot be mutative" (p. 366).

The term "holding" describes the operation of those alliance factors on the part of the analyst that respond to the most primitive and maternally dependent vulnerabilities in the patient. Just as the mother's holding is attenuated, modified, and transformed in relation to developmental changes in the child, so the analyst remains attuned to the evolving vulnerabilities and sensitivities of the patient. In reference to the analyst's later contribution to the progression of the therapeutic alliance, the term "holding" is less appropriate, although it continues to express the reciprocal responsiveness that is optimally maintained throughout development. The holding needed for the infant involves specific qualities quite different from holding provided by a parent for the adolescent, for example.

From the perspective of the present study, these appraisals of analytic "holding" can be extrapolated to all analyses—the holding metaphor is expressive in broader terms of the therapeutic alliance. As I have suggested, the analytic situation, particularly emergence and development of transference, carries an essentially paranoid dynamic that is built into the structure of the transference and can be responded to in meaningful therapeutic terms only by the careful establishing and maintaining of the therapeutic alliance. Particularly important in this regard is the transition from the earliest phases of narcissistic alliance to a position of secondary trust which assures the patient of the analyst's continuing good will and support in the face of the patient's wishes to separate.

Can the analyst respond in such a way as neither to drive the patient back into a state of self-encapsulation, withdrawal, or isolation (equivalent to a paranoid entrenchment), nor to force the patient into a position of false-self compliance or conformity? The muting of elements of conflict and pathogenic ambivalence in the therapeutic alliance opens the way for the exercise of more effective ego resources and thus allows the patient's capacities for adaptive learning and development of insight increasingly to assert themselves.

Interpretive Principles

Some principles for effective transference interpretations, based on an understanding of the reciprocal interconnection and interaction between transference and therapeutic alliance, especially in the form of misalliances, follow.

1. Effective interpretation requires some degree of focusing of transference dynamics on the self-related configurations involved in the transference. In both displacement and projective transferences, the subject is making a statement about his self and his feelings toward himself. This is particularly important in dealing with projective transferences, where the projective element may be readily identifiable in the transference, but where the corresponding introjective dimension, which serves as the source of the projection, remains concealed or repressed. In identifying the projection, therefore, the therapist must remain alert to further data that will allow him to bring into focus that hidden aspect of the patient's self which must be clarified in order for effective interpretation to be made. Thus, if the patient projects an idealizing image onto the therapist, an effective interpretation must await the surfacing of aspects of the patient's own narcissistic superiority in order to connect the projective content and the underlying introjective configuration.

2. An adequate interpretation of transference derivatives must include complementary aspects of the introjective configurations. Thus, patients who project their own aggression must be helped to become aware of their own corresponding role as victim, as well as the reverse, namely, that these same patients carry within themselves as an inherent part of their internalized self-

organization elements of aggressiveness, power and destructiveness. Both the victimized and the aggressive aspects must be acknowledged on a conscious level. By the same token, both the inferior and the superior aspects of the narcissistic configuration must be brought into conscious awareness in order to serve as the basis for adequate interpretation. Since they form in both cases a reciprocally defensive whole within the psychic economy, any attempt to deal interpretively with one side of the configuration without dealing equally with the other side is doomed to failure.

3. Interpretive strategy differs depending on the underlying mechanism by which transference arises. In the case of displacement transferences, interpretation of alliance factors is given precedence over interpretation of the transference dynamics themselves. The transference dynamics are brought into focus by clarification and elucidation of implications of the interaction between patient and therapist in the therapeutic situation. Exploration, clarification, and interpretation of the alliance issues opens the way to a deeper understanding of transference factors.

Direct interpretation of genetic factors contributing to transference is effective not only in clarifying and diminishing effects of the transference, but also in restoring the disrupted or distorted therapeutic alliance. This approach is not possible in early stages of therapy before adequate understanding of the patient's history and developmental experience has been gained. But where such genetic material is either directly expressed in the patient's material or arrived at by way of genetic reconstruction, it can be utilized in this fashion.

4. In contrast to displacement transferences, projective transferences do not successfully yield to genetic interpretation. The same priorities obtain in dealing with alliance factors before transference factors, and dealing with alliance issues as a way of gaining access to underlying transference dynamics. Here, interpretive emphasis must fall specifically on dynamic aspects of transference as they operate in the therapeutic situation. Delineation of projective and introjective components is essential, and focusing of aspects of the immediate misalliance frequently proves meaningful for that effort. This not only clarifies elements involved in the transference itself, but also connects the transference dynamics specifically to the underlying introjective configuration, embracing, as suggested above, the dual aspects of the introjective configuration.

Interpretation of a mirror transference, for example, would follow a series of progressive steps involving (1) clarification and focusing of the alliance distortion and the dimensions and implications of the therapeutic misalliance, (2) addressing dimensions of the underlying introjective configuration, specifically the narcissistic configuration, involving not only the patient's needs connected with the grandiose self for mirroring but also the underlying narcissistically inferior configuration to which the grandiosity is related as a defensive organization. Interpretation of these transference components is not complete, as I have emphasized, until both aspects of the narcissistic configuration have been clarified, explored, and interpreted. The difficulty with this technical approach stems from the fact that for most patients involved in a mirroring form of narcissistic transference, the aspects of worthlessness and shamefulness inherent in the inferior narcissistic configuration are well concealed, often repressed, and not easy of therapeutic access. Nonetheless, interpretation remains inadequate until all of these aspects have been brought into play and adequately encompassed. The genetic aspects, whether directly obtained or reconstructed, can be brought usefully into the interpretive process only when the patient has become aware of the dimensions of his narcissistic disorder and has achieved a degree of wonder and curiosity about the origins, specifically of the respective narcissistic configurations which form such a vital part of his self-organization.

CHAPTER EIGHTEEN

Internalization

A central aspect of the therapeutic process is the role of internalizations during therapeutic involvement (Meissner 1981, 1991; Schafer 1968). Mechanisms and processes of internalization are elicited throughout the analytic process and vary in quality and type, depending on aspects of the analytic relation. Those caught up in the vicissitudes of transference and countertransference tend to reflect the inherent dynamics of conflict, drive, and defense. Those reflective of a well-developed therapeutic alliance tend to be more secondary process, integrative, and constructive, expressing higher-order and more evolved and differentiated integrations of ego-superego functions and adaptive potentialities. The former type of transferentially based internalizations go by the name of introjections (Meissner 1971); the latter form of better integrated, less defensively motivated, and less drive-related internalizations are forms of identification and lead in the direction of a better consolidated and articulated psychic structure and sense of personal identity (Meissner 1972). The aim of the analytic process, therefore, is to maximize conditions for identification and minimize the effects of introjection, especially those introjective formations at the core of the patient's pathology. The ultimate resolution of transference derivatives and consolidation and development of the therapeutic alliance are the basis for this achievement in analysis.

Identification

Identification with the analyst has long been thought essential to the analytic process and the basis for effective interpretation (Sterba 1940). Such identification can be regarded as both a necessary component of and therapeutic derivative of the therapeutic alliance. I would propose, in contradiction to many therapeutic alliance theorists (Greenson 1967; Roland 1967), that the technical basis for constructive and therapeutically useful identifications is not the real relation, but the therapeutic alliance. Constructive identifications can emerge in relation to the analyst's real personality, but I would regard these as accidental to the analytic process; the basis for identification within the process is the therapeutic alliance. Thus I would not rule out identifications with the real person of the analyst, as they may play a role in the analytic outcome, but such internalizations are matters of personal influence—based on inherent qualities of the analyst's personality and not part of the technical specifics of the analytic process.

Internalizations generally can be either constructive and therapeutic or pathological (Lampl-deGroot 1956). Internalizations derived from the transference are forms of introjection that incorporate instinctual derivatives, infantile needs, and defensive organizations in varying degrees (Meissner 1971, 1981), and are cast in aggressive and/or narcissistic terms. Whether the patient internalizes an image of the analyst as hostile, critical, and judgmental, for example, or whether the internalization is based on narcissistic forms of idealization or omnipotence derived from the idealized parental imago (Kohut 1971) or their defensively motivated opposites, the result is a form of introjection that undermines therapeutic alliance. Since identifications are less caught up in defensive vicissitudes than introjections and are on a relatively more autonomous level of integrated ego functioning, they do not so much structure the analytic situation as underlie and qualify the ego's capacity to involve itself constructively in the analytic process (Meissner 1981). At issue is the implementation and facilitation of the patient's capacity for identification. As Rangell (1992) notes: "Change does not come about from interpretations alone. From his experience of the analytic relationship, the therapeutic alliance, the transference neurosis and the analyst's handling of it, and the common ground of a shared reality, the patient is exposed to the challenge and possibility of a new identification. Besides his activities and attitudes toward the patient's neurosis and the sum of his free associations, the analyst's analytic behaviour, such as towards time, money, appointments, and adventitious events, serves itself as a model for identification" (p. 418). This is substantially the role of the therapeutic alliance as developed here.

Identifications give rise to secondary autonomous structures of the ego and superego that enable the patient to relate to the analyst as an analytic and separate object (Meissner 1981). Identification is that aspect of the developmental process by which sufficiently differentiated and integrated ego structures are established, allowing the patient to tolerate the anxiety provoked by the analytic regression and to engage in a meaningful alliance with the analyst in analytic work (Langs 1976).

Identification and the Alliance

Identifications provide the base on which the therapeutic alliance is erected and the matrix from which important identifications will derive in the course of analytic work. The strength inherent in the therapeutic alliance enables the patient to tolerate the regressive reactivation of pathogenic introjects along with the associated painful conflicts and drive derivatives. As Olinick (1976) observed: "By an accretion of small changes and shifts of pattern and attention resulting from the ongoing analytic work, the identifications with the analyst-object can become internalizations of the analyzing function of the analyst. The intersubjective or interpersonal becomes intrapsychic and structurally differentiated. The object attachments to the analyst, arising from transferential, neutralized, as well as more realistic bonds, are gradually transformed into an alliance that, while still subject to regressive changes, moves in the direction of augmented analyzing functions" (p. 6).

Motivations that support and work through the therapeutic alliance play a critical role in the process. While positive transference can add a benign component to this motivational mix, motivation based only on such transference remains fragile and unreliable; when positive transference fuels the analytic process, it can quickly turn sour and become a source of considerable resistance (Novick 1970). Even when the therapeutic alliance seems to be firmly and comfortably established, it can be undermined by the regressive pull of activated transference derivatives, more readily when the patient's pathology lies closer to the primitive end of the spectrum (Meissner 1988).

One objective of the analytic process is gradual enlargement of the patient's capacity for identification, specifically with the analyst, but not exclusively so. This elaboration of the therapeutic alliance stands outside the matrix of introjective and projective interplay underlying transference neurosis. In fact, in some sense therapeutic alliance and transference neurosis stand in opposition. As the transference neurosis begins to intensify and flourish, the therapeutic alliance is placed under considerable stress. An important aspect of the analysis is the continual reinforcement and preservation of a meaningful alliance in the face of regressive vicissitudes.

In thinking about the interweaving roles of therapeutic alliance and transference, we can recall that introjective and identificatory processes occur at all levels of the child's developmental experience. The quality of these processes varies at different levels, but the two processes continue to interact in complex ways. In general, as the child develops, the defensive need to resolve intolerable ambivalences drives patterns of internalization in the direction of introjection rather than identification (Meissner 1974, 1981). But this does not mean that these processes occur in either-or fashion nor that defensively motivated introjections are not concurrently shadowed by meaningful identifications. Identifications may arise not only through reprocessing of introjective contents—identification with the introject—but also more directly in relation to evolving object representations. In some sense, the ego's capacity for internalizing significant early developmental experiences, such as those related to basic trust, involves certain global and rudimentary patterns of identification which are difficult to specify (Meissner 1986b).

The focus of my discussion at this juncture is on the dynamic quality of the identificatory contribution to structuring the analytic situation, anticipating the more dynamic role of identifications in the evolution of therapeutic alliance in the analytic process. However, here I would like to draw attention to the role of identifications in promoting the progressive shifts in alliance during the course of an analysis.

Building the Alliance

The beginning of an analysis poses expectable problems of starting a relationship and putting in motion a process that may be as important as any experience in the patient's life. The patient feels highly vulnerable in the supine position and in the unusual conditions of the analytic situation. Moreover, the patient soon begins to feel the pull of regressive pressures, which only add to the sense of vulnerability. These pressures increase the titer of anxiety, stimulate defensive reactions, and present the problem of finding some basis in the relation with the analyst for a sense of security and confidence. A considerable degree of stress, then, is put on the patient's inherent capacities for trust.

In a situation of vulnerability and dependence, patients may experience stirrings of infantile needs and seek to engage the analyst in nonthreatening terms. Insofar as patients can fall back on identificatory systems that allow a basic sense of trust to enter the relationship, they can begin to tolerate the degree of lowered narcissistic defenses that permits them to entrust themselves to the risks and uncertainties of a precarious relationship such as the analytic one. To the extent that such capacities are imperiled or constrained by pathogenic introjective influences, entering into the analytic relationship becomes all the more difficult. Thus, almost from the first moment of the analysis, important internalization systems are brought into play and influence the direction of analytic work.

The patient's initial problematic dependence normally increases as the analytic work proceeds and as analytic regression takes effect. The analysis moves toward increasing mobilization of infantile residues in the patient's personality, toward activation of the infantile neurosis, and with it reemergence of infantile introjects. This development puts increasing pressure on the therapeutic alliance as the transference neurosis comes into the analytic relation. And although pathogenic introjects come to play a prominent part in the analytic relation, identificatory elements provide the basis for a continuing alliance. If the regressive activation of the introjects overwhelms the identificatory systems, or if a misalliance or transference/countertransference interaction develops, the analytic relation is placed in jeopardy. If the crisis cannot be worked through and resolved, it may be necessary to interrupt or terminate the analysis.

These modifications reflect the dynamics of transference/countertransference interactions involving the interplay of introjections and projections as articulated within the therapeutic alliance. Another parallel aspect of the therapeutic process involves integration of more autonomous and adaptive internalizations, specifically through the therapeutic alliance (Meissner 1981). Identifications take place in parallel with introjective elements. The capacity for constructive identifications increases as transference vicissitudes are gradually worked through. As pathogenic configurations give way to more moderated and realistic forms of self-integration, the path is open for more meaningful and selective identifications, which tend to be based in the alliance.

As transference elements are resolved, more of the therapeutic interaction tends to be based on emergent alliance factors. Without any intentional effort on his part, the therapist serves as a model for identification, in a sense that transcends technique. Positive and constructive identifications that contribute to a more authentic self and more mature identity cannot be fabricated merely by technical interventions. They arise from the matrix of interaction evolving between analyst and analysand and reflect qualities of the analyst's personality and character, which serve as a model with which the patient identifies. The process of identification is facilitated first by the personal qualities and self-integration the analyst brings to the process, and second by his firm yet flexible and empathic adherence to the structure of the therapeutic alliance.

From time to time the patient may find himself wishing to be like the therapist or he may find himself responding to a variety of situations with attitudes, thoughts, or feelings that he links with the therapist. The therapist's task is to neither encourage nor discourage such identifications, but to allow them to follow their natural course unimpeded by countertransference interferences. To the extent that this can be achieved, the patient's identifications become selective, differentiated, autonomous, self-generative, creative, and provide the basis for the potential integration of an authentic sense of self.

In interpreting, clarifying, and working through of introjective components, especially when they come to their full expression in the transference neurosis, significant shifts occur in the therapeutic alliance. These changes reflect alterations in the basic patterns of identification. As the underlying dependencies are resolved, there are increasing signs of the patient's autonomy, in the sense of a growing capacity to carry on the work of the analysis independently of the analyst—signs of a developing observing work ego (Olinick 1976). The patient may feel more comfortable about coming a few minutes late when circumstances reasonably call for it and may more freely and responsibly negotiate

(Goldberg 1987), or even decide, on appropriate occasions, when to miss an appointment. The patient may begin to show initiative in clarifying and interpreting his own analytic productions and in relating their content to various realms of his experience, including his infantile experience. With these shifts, one may observe various imitative adoptions of the analyst's words, attitudes, mannerisms, and even ways of thinking about and processing analytic material.[1] This phase of the analytic experience as can be seen as a trial internalization, based more on introjective dynamics than true identification in which the patient attempts to assimilate aspects of the analyst's analytic role and personality that seem useful and adaptive to the patient (these aspects may even be idealized to some degree), trying them on to see whether and in what way they might fit.

These fragmentary internalizations directly influence the quality of the therapeutic alliance. The character of alliance in the early phase, when the patient is establishing basic trust and increasing dependence, is quite different from that in a later phase, when the patient is establishing and consolidating a sense of autonomous functioning within the analysis. The analyst's approach to the alliance and the ways in which he supports it must shift accordingly. In the earlier phase, the analyst supports the regressive aspects, tolerates the patient's often intense dependency, and tries to facilitate empathic understanding required for the patient to enter into the analytic process. As the regressive phase continues, the analyst maximizes the conditions for regression by tending to be passive and silent and providing the fullest opportunity for pathogenic introjective configurations to express themselves. The analyst's concern in this phase is focused on the alliance, making sure that it is not regressively undermined and that no influences arise (countertransference or otherwise) that would lead to a therapeutic misalliance (Langs 1975a).

As the patient moves into a more autonomous phase, the quality of the alliance also shifts. The analyst becomes more concerned with fostering the patient's nascent attempts at independent functioning and avoiding those subtle defeats and devaluations that can frustrate and even kill the patient's highly vulnerable attempts at self-definition and growth. The analyst must be careful not to convey the attitude that the patient does not really understand his difficulties and that only the wisdom of the analyst can bring illumination and success in the analytic work. The model here is in some respects that of the good parent, who does not defeat or devalue the child because the child is clumsy, awkward, or ineffectual in his attempts to do more complex things, but rather values the child's attempts and encourages his efforts, helping the child to do better than he might otherwise have done.

Thus, the good analyst must learn to moderate and minimize his own interpretative function as analysis progresses in the interest of supporting potential growth and autonomous functioning in the patient. In the course of this process, the patient develops a sense of confidence in his own ability to deal with inner states and feelings and real-life problems. These are all steps in establishing a sense of personal identity, which integrates the various stages of identification that have marked the progression of the alliance.

From Introjection to Identification

Each level of resolution of the infantile derivatives that are bound up in the transference neurosis involves a corresponding revivification and reworking of a developmental level of introjective organization and economy. At each level, then, the introjective organization is to some degree regressively dissolved and the potential for working through correlated developmental issues is reopened. The failure or deviation within significant object relations of the child shifted the balance of internalization processes away from constructive and positive identifications toward defensive, drive-derivative pathogenic introjects. The same internal process is revived in analysis, in terms of the relationship between patient and analyst. In reworking developmental crises with the analytic object, one hopes that the balance in the introjective organization is shifted away from the ambivalence and pathogenic defensiveness inherent in the original introjects toward a more positively toned introjective organization.

The intent of the analytic process is increasingly to mitigate introjective components and to allow for expansion and amplification of identificatory processes. A major concern in assessing analyzability is evaluation of the intensity and scope of the introjective aspects of the patient's psychic organization, as well as an assessment of the patient's identificatory capacity. The importance and complexity of these criteria of analyzability cannot be overestimated (Knapp et al. 1960; Olinick 1976; Sashin et al. 1975; Zetzel 1970; Zetzel and Meissner 1973).

While the Eriksonian epigenetic schema provides a reasonably ready vocabulary with which to address issues embedded in the therapeutic alliance (see chapter 8), these are not the only issues involved. For instance, narcissism and the capacity for nonpathogenic narcissistic investment in the self (self-esteem) may play a major role and bring up as yet unresolved questions. The analytic effort, however, reactivates the introjective resolution and makes it available for reworking in which the therapeutic resolution will shift from an introjective mode toward an identificatory one. During this process the therapeutic alliance undergoes highly specific vicissitudes of its own. These modifications occur independently, but not separately from the working through of the vicissitudes of transference and the transference neurosis. Thus, structural modifications through which the analytic situation and process pass are composed of interlocking components of both therapeutic alliance and transferential derivatives.

At each step of the elaboration of therapeutic alliance, then, critical defensive issues and introjective alignments are reworked to allow for the emergence of positive identificatory processes. These underlying identifications carry with them ego-building and increasingly secondary process and autonomous levels of functioning, which reinforce and differentiate the therapeutic alliance. As the therapeutic alliance develops, it is accompanied by internalization of significant ego capacities and strengths and progress toward a stable, secondarily autonomous structuralization of the patient's internal world and self-organization (Nersessian 1989).

In addressing the elaboration and integration of a cohesive, functional sense of self in the patient, I do not imply that the patient did not have a sense of self before entering analysis. However, aspects of it were conflicted, caught up in defensive struggles, or maladaptive or deficient in certain areas. In the most analyzable patients, the sense of cohesive self is already fundamentally established, and the analytic reworking of certain elements contributes to a reintegration, preserving and building on that underlying cohesion. It is rare in well-conducted analyses for patients to regress to a point of fragmentation of the sense of self, but in cases where developmental arrest or defect has severely affected the level of self-organization, restructuring of the self may take on a more significant role.

Development of the therapeutic alliance, in this frame of reference, cannot be regarded as simply an emergence of specified qualities in the patient's ego, or even as an integration of ego and superego. Rather, it is a matter of a complex organization that reflects the interplay between the structural components of the psychic apparatus, both ego and superego, and the integration of a cohesive and adaptive sense of self. The emergence of this sense of self and identity cannot be divorced from the processing of narcissism.

One of the major instinctual components, deeply embedded in the introjective organization and providing the introjects their special quality in the organization of the patient's pathological sense of self, is the inherent narcissistic investment. In the dissolution of these pathogenic structures, the narcissism bound into them becomes available for developmental reworking, leading to narcissistic transformation.

In the progressive elaboration of the therapeutic alliance, underlying instinctual components undergo various vicissitudes. Aggressive and libidinal components may be sublimated or neutralized, while narcissistic components are more likely to undergo transformation. These transformations—an integral part of the processing of the therapeutic alliance, as well as of formation of a cohesive sense of self—constitute a central instinctual dimension of the shift from an introjective organization to patterns of constructive identification.

The function of narcissism and the organization of these internalization processes are still not fully understood. However, later transformations of narcissism, as correlates of development of the self and a sense of identity, have been described by Kohut (1966) in terms of creativity, ability to be empathic, capacity to contemplate our own impermanence or transience, sense of humor, and wisdom. The resemblance and overlap between these qualities of narcissistic transformation and the emergent qualities of Erikson's adult psychosocial crises—specifically generativity and wisdom—are worthy of note. As already suggested, narcissistic elements of the transference organization frequently remain unresolved at the point of termination of the analytic relationship. In relation to the evolution of therapeutic alliance, however, resolution of these elements and their integration is possible. Subsequent reworking, resolution, and integration of these narcissistic elements allows narcissistic transformations to take place and contributes to the highest level of human capacity (Kohut 1966) and to resolution of further developmental stages in the life cycle (Erikson 1959).

The analysis, in consequence, not only seeks to activate the interpretive resources for delineating and renouncing these introjects and their inherent attachments, but also aims at mobilizing forces that enable the patient to internalize the analytic introject as a replacement for pathogenic residuals. The patient, in turn, must work through the narcissistic perils of loss of love, loss of the needed relationship which has served to sustain self-integrity, or even, at its most pathogenic, loss of self-cohesion. For many classical neurotics, whose pathology involves predominantly structural conflict, this renunciation, followed by turning to the analytic introject, is difficult enough. For more severe personality disorders, in which narcissistic issues pervade the pathology, it is even more difficult, and in some cases impossible.

Projective Mechanisms and Countertransference

A final concern in regard to the progressive shift from introjection to identification has to do with the role of countertransference. My comments here focus on the formation of the analytic introject. In previous discussions of the nature of introjection (Meissner 1974a, 1981), I argued that the child's introjections during development are influenced not only by internal determinants but also by extrinsic factors, including projections from significant figures around the child. The child's family emotional matrix is characterized by interplay of introjections and projections between parents and the child, as well as those stemming from other family members. In pathogenic family situations, the pathologically affected child often acts out elements of such parental projections (Meissner 1964, 1970, 1978a, 1978c).

In analogous fashion, organization of the analytic introject reflects the basic interaction of projections and introjections deriving from both the patient and the analyst (Little 1951; Meissner 1981; Orr 1954). The analyst's projective contribution depends to some degree on his own introjective organization. This countertransference projective interference may impede or distort the progressive organization of the patient's introjects. As Searles (1965) commented:

> To the degree that the patient needs to keep his personality incorporated within what he conceives (largely through projection) to be the personality of the analyst, or to the degree that he needs to utilize the personality of the analyst (again, as the patient perceives that personality, distorted by many projections of his own repressed self-images) as a nucleus for his own functioning self, to that degree the patient's efforts towards individuation are unsuccessful. And insofar as the therapist himself needs to keep the patient's personality incorporated within his own, or to keep his own personality incorporated within that of the patient, he is hampering the patient's efforts to achieve the goal of an independently functioning self. (p. 62)

It is not merely that the analyst's introjective organization can give rise to projections and thus impede analytic work. The patient's pathogenic dynamics may seize on any projective element in the analytic object and even strive to elicit such elements from the analyst. In immersing himself in the therapeutic relationship, the analyst is subjected to extraordinary pressures pulling him into a pattern of responding that will confirm and reinforce the patient's inner pathogenic needs—and thus support the patient's own inner introjective economy.

Here we can say that the patient's projections induce a response in the inner world of the analyst. They evoke a corresponding introjection on the part of the analyst, which in turn may serve as the basis of further projections. This form of introjective induction within the analyst has been described as "counteridentification" (Fliess 1953; Grinberg 1962), and it is this interplay of projections and introjections between analyst and patient that constitutes at least one version of the illusory matrix of transference with its inherent creative potential. This matrix is also the "analytic space" within which, according to some theorists, projective and introjective mechanisms support the empathic communication so essential to effective therapy. As Schafer (1959) has noted:

> a subtle and relatively conflict-free interplay of introjective and projective mechanisms occurs, enhancing the object of contemplation as well as the subject's experience; thus the relationship between the two. Preconscious or conscious experimental fantasies concerning the object and the relationship express this interplay of mechanisms. . . . Empathy involves experiencing in some fashion the feelings of another person. This experience can only be approximate or roughly congruent, since the other self is not directly or

> fully knowable. The shared experience is based to a great extent on remembered, corresponding affective states of one's own. Observing a patient's life at any one point, we tentatively project onto him the feelings we once felt under similar circumstances, and then test this projection by further observation. . . . Affect may therefore be said to play a double role in the comprehension of empathy. There is a re-creation of affect, that is, becoming able to feel approximately as the other person does through revival of past inner experience of a similar nature supplemented by projection and reality testing; also there is translation of one's own reactive affects into stimulus patterns in the other person. . . . This double role of affect is a cardinal aspect of the frequently referred to introjective component of empathic comprehending; it amounts to carrying on a relationship with another person internally, and with a relatively high degree of cathexis. The free availability of affect signals in this process presupposes superego tolerance, associated relaxation of ego defense and control, and hypercathexis of one's own body ego. (pp. 346–348)

The statement has merit with respect to empathic attunement, but the effort to base it on projective devices is questionable. Projection, as I have discussed it in reference to the therapeutic alliance, is counter to real empathy because it involves attribution of one's own self derivatives to the other rather than an affective resonance with something within that other. By the same token, as long as the analyst is able to utilize these currents of introjection and projection in ways that facilitate his openness to the patient, his capability for empathic responsiveness can serve as a major therapeutic tool. But this requires not only that the analyst be sufficiently in touch with these aspects of his experience and but also that his own internal identification to be consolidated and integrated enough to allow this dimension of regressive experience to take place, without bridging over into internal self-modifications or countertransference expressions.

Moeller (1977) has emphasized the role of empathy in elucidating self-representational aspects of the patient's transference. The present volume has aimed at identifying self-representations as determining components of transference reactions. Transference can develop out of the interplay of projection and introjection, related to objective aspects—representations of what the parents, for example, were like—and subjective elements—representations of the patient's own infantile self as determined in early interactions with the parents (Horowitz and Zilberg 1983). Projections in the transference can draw the analyst into the parental role, where the dynamics allow the patient to assume his familiar infantile role. When the analyst responds with projections and introjections of his own, the countertransference is put into play. The transference and the countertransference create a collusive and illusional matrix within which the dynamics of the neurosis are re-created with all the inherent potential for renovation and metamorphosis as well as regression and repetition.

It is with regard to this aspect of the analytic process that the analytic insistence on neutrality becomes most telling. The tendency for such introjective and projective components to play themselves out at an unconscious level emphasizes the difficulties inherent in the analytic process. Furthermore, this aspect of the transference/countertransference interaction makes it apparent that analysts cannot rely on mere technique or analytic behavior to carry them through countertransference vicissitudes. Ultimately, they must rely on awareness of their own introjective configurations and the extent to which these have been effectively analyzed and resolved.

The Analytic Introject

In this sense, then, the critical contribution of the analytic process focuses on facilitating the analytic introject. The renunciation of pathogenic introjects provides the impetus for a more meaningful, less ambivalent, and less conflict-ridden internalization derived from the analytic object relationship. The analyst, in turn, continually makes himself available as an object for internalization. The dynamic aspects of positive transference also contribute to the matrix for internalization. Only when the infantile attachments underlying the pathogenic introjects have been resolved can the inherent potential of the therapeutic relationship begin to assert itself.

The effectiveness of the analytic introject depends in part on inherent qualities of the analytic object and in part on the status of the alliance. The analyst presents himself as calm and trustworthy, both sympathetic and empathic, a nonjudgmental and consistent participant in the analytic process, the collaborative observer of the patient's behavior and productions.

The propensity for introjecting the analytic object is also facilitated by a supportive, positive therapeutic alliance. The gradual resolution of pathogenic impediments and development of the therapeutic alliance are self-reinforcing in that they lay the ground for more meaningful and effective forms of therapeutic internalization. As Boyer and Giovacchini (1967) comment in reference to the analyst's interpretations: "As the analytic imago is introjected and as interpretive activity becomes internalized, the patient's range of secondary process functioning is expanded. The analyst superimposes his secondary process upon the patient's primary process, leading to greater ego structure. In a positive feed-back sequence, this enables the patient to introject more helpful aspects of the analytic relationship, which, in turn, leads to further structuralization and then to greater ability for internalization, etc. This increase in secondary process activity gradually extends to the patient's everyday life and no longer requires analytic reinforcement" (pp. 233–234). The shaping of the analytic introject is increasingly determined by the patient's adaptive ego resources rather than by the defensive pressures which played such a role in organizing the pathogenic introjects. Consequently, the analytic introject tends to be less ambivalent, less inherently conflicted, less subject to drive pressures and derivatives, and finally less susceptible to regressive pulls. The stage is set for the induction of more constructive ego identifications along the lines of "identification with the introject" (Meissner 1972; Sandler 1960).

As the progressive subphase of the analysis advances, the emphasis shifts from transference neurosis to therapeutic alliance. As the component elements of the transference neurosis, derived from the underlying pathogenic introjects, are gradually clarified, worked through, and resolved, the patient's capacity for forming a meaningful analytic introject and the correlated potential for constructive identifications come more to the fore. What I am suggesting here, in somewhat schematic fashion, is that progressive working through of elements of the transference neurosis induces a shift within the analytic relationship in which corresponding elements of the therapeutic alliance are mobilized and placed in significant relief. This opens the way for reworking of alliance issues in a meaningful way. The developmental model is useful in considering this perspective, in that it provides a schema within which these processes can be articulated.

There is a progressive evolution within the therapeutic alliance, correlated with the relative resolution of levels of transference involvement. Thus, the gradual opening and resolution of issues of infantile dependence in transference terms shift the equilibrium in the analytic relationship to an emphasis on issues of basic trust. Similarly, work on issues of control and power may bring into focus dimensions of the patient's emergent autonomy within the analytic relationship. In this sense, the analysis opens the way for further reworking of developmental experiences in terms of the emergence and processing of the analytic introject. The prospects for such reworking, may always be limited, in some degree, and in some forms of character pathology and more primitive forms of personality organization, may be quite limited indeed.

Too little attention has been paid to analysis of the therapeutic alliance as such (Hani 1973). I would suggest that the development of the therapeutic alliance provides the matrix in which more constructive and transmuting identifications (as opposed to introjections) take place. At all stages of analytic work, qualities of the relationship to the analyst play a predominant role and his empathic responsiveness and facilitative stance are critical. The analyst places himself in the difficult position of continuing the work of the analysis and the resolution of transference elements while simultaneously making way for and supporting the emergence of alliance components. It is important that these alliance elements be brought within the perspective of the analytic work so that analytic internalizations do not take place in an implicit or haphazard fashion.

The patient's first attempts to establish some degree of autonomy within the analytic relationship, for example, must be respected in fact as well as in action. They are also appropriate and important objects of analytic reflection. The analysand should have the opportunity not only to experience an emerging autonomy in relation to the analyst, but also to explore the vicissitudes of autonomy in his own life experience. In this way, the analysand's autonomy can be facilitated, consolidated, and made a more specifically reflective, self-conscious, developmental possession. Such scrutiny also provides insight into the patient's own inner needs and propensities, which undermine the sense of autonomy, both past and present.

However, development of insight into these dimensions of the patient's ego functioning and self-organization has a limited value which must be supplemented and sustained in terms of the patient's evolving autonomy within the analytic relationship. This aspect of the patient's experience, rather than simple insight, serves as the matrix for internalization.

Alliance and the Emergence of Identity

The terminal point in development of the therapeutic alliance is the emergence of a cohesive, mature, and adaptive sense of self. Erikson formulates this concept under the rubric of identity, and it can be loosely employed in the present context as well. In an abstract sense, one can say that establishing a stable and adaptive sense of identity is the ultimate step in the analytic process. But in many analyses one may envision the process more in terms of resolution of fundamental aspects of the transference neurosis and the underlying infantile conflicts, as well as unleashing the developmental potential for the subsequent formation of a more effective and stable sense of identity. To the extent that earlier issues implicit in the therapeutic alliance have been mobilized, gradual reworking of the elements of the patient's self occurs, ultimately leading in the direction of consolidation of a sense of identity.

The idea of analytic development of the patient's self through identifications with the analyst has its detractors. Boris (1992), for example, writes: "To ask the Self to identify with the analyst in what is sometimes called the therapeutic alliance is a disservice. First of all it means the terrible loss of the identifications out of which the Self is constructed (often ingeniously and with concealed pride), and second, it means opening up the inclination to look for, mayhaps to lust for, the very differences of which coupling is made" (p. 589). To the contrary, the identifications I have in mind (Meissner 1972, 1981) contribute to the integration of a constructive and adaptive self-structure—no disservice to any patient. The identifications Boris seems to have in mind are more in the line of what I have described as introjections (Meissner 1970, 1971, 1981)—internalizations that are poorly integrated into the self-system and are drive-determined and defensive in function. If analysis were to offer no more than the loss of the patient's pathogenic introjections and the presumptive loss of a sense of self, we would hardly count it as therapeutic. What makes it therapeutic is its capacity to enable the patient to replace pathogenic formations with more adaptive internal configurations than those previously constituting the core of the self.

As Cooper (1992) points out, analysts use more than one model of psychic change in the analytic process. The repair model operates from the perspective of the effects of developmental trauma and directs its efforts to helping the patient understand his maladaptive and self-destructive patterns of behavior and his reluctance to change. The growth model facilitates the latent and impaired developmental potential in the patient by providing a facilitating and secure context within the analysis, usually conceived along the lines of the good parent who can provide what is needed for mobilization of such short-circuited and frustrated capacities in the patient. Most analysts find themselves enacting both models in one or other degree with different patients and even with the same patient. But whatever models are called upon, they represent aspects of the therapeutic alliance.

That consolidation of identifications leading to an achieved sense of identity, however, may take place only over a considerable period of time, even after termination In this light, the analytic process is an open-ended process, continuing to gradually modify and shape the patient's personality, not only within its actual course, but also on into the patient's life. The effective working through of the analytic process sets into motion certain critical mechanisms within which the expanded issues of a stable sense of self and the related narcissistic crises are progressively resolved and integrated.

Inevitably, during this process, the patient and analyst have to face the issue of separation. If the question has not been broached earlier in the analysis around issues of minor interruptions or absences or in the context of the requisite mourning involved in progression from earlier to later phases of the analysis, then it will come to a head in the termination phase. The patient's achievement of and acceptance of his emerging autonomy and identity lead inexorably toward termination and separation from the analyst and the residues of dependence that tie them together. The analytic work, by which the basis for self-organization is shifted from an introjective to an identificatory basis, prepares this ground. Intermingling of presence and absence in the analytic relation sets the stage, as Treurniet (1993) comments: "As an object, we exist only in so far as we have been created by our patients, just as the cuddly toy is created by a child. . . . Patients do not get better by internalising the good image of us that they have created. What we do, in fact, have to offer our patients is our progressive absence" (p. 880). In the context of the therapeutic alliance, the trauma of separation is experienced in a new way as an integrative rather than disintegrative factor.

I shall not detail the subsequent Eriksonian phases which stretch out into the broad range of the life cycle. Intimacy, generativity, and integrity in general reach beyond the specific therapeutic interaction between the patient and the analyst. Nonetheless, these abiding issues permeate the progressive integration and adaptive functioning of the patient beyond analysis. One can hope that the rudiments established by the analytic process will extend themselves into the resolution of future crises, so that the patient can maintain a sense of self-coherence and effective adaptation throughout the life cycle.

CHAPTER NINETEEN

Termination

The question of termination work centering on therapeutic alliance has been little discussed in the literature. Zetzel (1956, 1958) suggested that therapeutic alliance had to be worked through and resolved in the termination phase, but she never made clear how this was to be done, and the suggestion was contaminated by her view of therapeutic alliance as incorporating transference elements. She may well have had the resolution of transference components involved in residual dependence and attachment in mind. In her view, resolution of dependence and issues of separation were essential to facilitate movement toward autonomy, but this also implied acceptance of limitations in the analysis and the analyst (Zetzel 1965, 1966). Similarly, Greenson (1971) felt that the therapeutic alliance receded during the terminal phase of analysis, to be replaced by a resurgence of the real relation. Along the same line, Binstock (1973), who considered transference and therapeutic alliance as reciprocally related, also saw alliance as expanding into a real relationship as a result of successful termination work. We can take for granted the basic analytic view regarding resolution of transferences as part of the termination phase, an aspect of the process that has been thoroughly explored and understood (Blum 1989; Dewald 1982; Firestein 1978, 1982; Gillman 1982; Novick 1982; Panel 1975). The question remains, however, whether it is the residues of the transference neurosis that are, one hopes, worked through in the termination phase, or is it the therapeutic alliance itself that must be resolved? Must the therapeutic alliance be regarded as resistance to the regressive pull of transference? One's view on these questions has a good deal to do with technical management of termination. I shall focus specifically on the therapeutic alliance.

The first consideration is that the therapeutic alliance toward the end of the analytic process is not the same as that at the beginning. If the therapeutic alliance has undergone the development one might wish for during the course of analysis,[1] one would expect to find the patient's level of mature trust, relatively secure autonomy, and emerging and to some degree consolidated identity reasonably well established. For such patients, the analytic process has unleashed developmental potentials that their neurosis may have impeded or thwarted. When analysis has worked well, the work of termination is more readily accomplished and is usually propelled by the developmental dynamic in the patient himself. The evolution of trust and emergence of a mature sense of autonomy, along with attendant qualities of personal authority, responsibility, unencumbered freedom and initiative, together with a secure identity, tend to lessen the patient's need for analytic support and reinforce those elements in himself that draw him inexorably toward greater self-reliance and independence (Kantrowitz et al. 1990a, 1990b, 1990c). The analyst is then viewed more as a helpful and constructive person who has played a vital role but whose importance has faded in the light of the patient's increased capacity to determine his own life course and accept responsibility for his own destiny. Termination is the obvious next step. In this sense, the therapeutic alliance is not resolved in termination, but in itself contributes to or provides the basis for effective termination work and provides the matrix of significant internalizations achieved during the course of the analysis.

But this is an idealized picture. Few analyses, in my experience, ever achieve such a rosy resolution. Not only do unresolved transference residues remain active to the end of the analysis and beyond (Oremland et al. 1975; Norman et al. 1976), but modifications in boundaries and neutrality complicate resolution of the transference neurosis (Langs 1976). Termination work around transference is more often filled with compromise and partial fulfillment of expectations. Even when transferences have been for the most part worked through, elements of the therapeutic alliance (or, more exactly, of residual misalliance) can remain only partially resolved. Termination may become the vital testing ground for the patient's growth in autonomy and responsibility. It is not unusual, with termination looming, for regressive phenomena to assert themselves and for uncertain or poorly consolidated gains in the alliance sector to become undermined. Patients who have had difficulties with trust may begin to experience doubts and find themselves less trusting of analyst and their relation with him. Patients whose autonomy has been fragile may experience a resurgence of feelings of dependency and increasing insecurity about their capacity to face life without analytic support. In the best of cases, these regressive movements are short-lived and can be worked through relatively easily. But patients whose relation to the analyst has become fetishized (Renik 1992), for example, will have difficulties in the termination phase insofar as termination means surrender of the dependent relation to the analyst and is experienced as loss without gain. Despite disclaimers to the contrary, the patient resists and avoids the work of termination. In more severe cases, such misalliances can become a major focus of termination work and require an extensive period of processing before termination can take place. Ferraro (1995) has emphasized the importance of alliance issues in addressing the demand for confrontation of such issues in the terminal phase and the often precarious balance in the outcome of analysis depending on their successful management and resolution.

A critical question that cannot be answered until analyst and analysand are ready to cross this bridge is whether identifiable gains of the analysis remain dependent on continuing analytic contact or whether they have been effectively internalized and structurally integrated as an independent possession of the patient. Some patients give every indication of effective growth and successful enhancement of functioning, only to find themselves beginning to falter shortly after leaving the analysis. The failure to internalize gains of the analysis effectively suggests a lack of adequate integration of the therapeutic alliance and persistence of transference components.

I would regard it as essential from the perspective of the therapeutic alliance that the analyst remain attuned to these issues and bring them into focus for continued exploration and interpretation. As always in dealing with alliance difficulties, the index of suspicion for possible transference derivatives in the mix must be high. Failings or flaggings of the therapeutic alliance are often a key indicator of the persistence and influence of unresolved transference components. These should be identified and addressed, but they may not tell the whole story. For many patients, the unwelcome prospects dictated by development in the therapeutic alliance may pose significant threats. The immanence of termination can give these reluctances a prominence they might otherwise lack. In most patients, the prospect of facing life and the separateness of independent existence, of assuming responsibility for oneself and one's fate, of dealing with the inevitable vicissitudes and disappointments of life on their own, does not come as a welcome eventuality. Patients may try to find ways to delay, avoid, circumvent, or temporize with the prospect of coming to terms with the reality principle more or less definitively. When such is the case, the analyst faces a decision as to how far he should go in temporizing over the inevitable termination and to what extent it is advisable to nudge the patient toward a reluctant termination. For some patients, the push is necessary to enable them to finally stand on their own feet—like the mother bird forcing fledglings from the nest so that they can use their own wings. For other patients, the analyst is better advised to wait for the potential in the patient to find its own path.[2]

Countertransference Difficulties

The termination process can also be complicated by countertransference issues. Working through the termination is not just a matter of what happens in the patient, but it is also a matter of the degree to which the analyst can facilitate appropriate developments in the therapeutic alliance and encourage the patient to work toward termination. Termination in this sense is a product of the collaborative engagement of both analyst and patient. The analyst's countertransference issues may come to play a significant role in how these difficulties are negotiated. Conflicts over dependency and the therapist's role as a helping and sustaining object can provide the basis for a collusive mesh with the patient's own inability to tolerate these aspects. The need to see the patient as needing help can play a role here, buttressed by the therapist's own need to see himself as helping and as important to the patient. It is narcissistically troubling, if not painful, to see one's self as no longer needed or valued as before. Many parents have the same problem in allowing their adolescent children to grow up. If there is a mourning process involved in the patient's giving up the analyst and his dependence on him in the interest of further growth and independence, there is a parallel process in the analyst, who must release the patient and assume a position of diminished value and significance in the patient's experience. Narcissistic issues are inevitably involved and can give rise to countertransference difficulties if not carefully monitored.

This perspective on termination has been well expressed by Schafer (1973):

> It is during termination that all the unspoken promises, expectations, transferences, and resistances on the part of both persons in the therapeutic relationship may come to light. . . . Among the problems that emerge is that of facing the limitations of what therapy can do. These limitations concern the therapist in quite a powerful personal way. Through them he must recognize that his effectiveness as a healer is quite limited, which means that important narcissistic ideas about himself and ideals for himself are forcefully contradicted by experience. The roots of these ideas and ideals lie in infantile fantasies of omnipotence, which no one ever renounces completely. . . . On this account, the terminating patient, who is still saddled with problems—and who quite likely is expressing dissatisfaction with the therapist—is bound to become very much of a disappointment and threat to the therapist. . . . One of the best protections against disruptive countertransference response to the terminating patient is a reasonable and stable sense of one's own goodness. (pp. 140–141)

Such narcissistic countertransference difficulties arise particularly in training analyses. The training analyst may find himself setting excessively high goals for the candidate or, conversely, too readily tolerating the candidate's unresolved conflicts and transferences. The analyst's own professional identity, his sense of himself as keeper of the analytic tradition and protector of training standards, or, in a more personal vein, his sense that the candidate will go forth as a representative of the analyst's own competence and as the bearer of the analyst's ego ideal rather than as his own person, can reflect such countertransference issues. To the extent that the analysis can be conducted within the boundaries of the therapeutic alliance, this affords analyst and candidate the best guide and resource for avoiding or at least being aware of the effects of such countertransference problems.

Countertransference difficulties must be counterposed to the patient's incapacity to accomplish the work of termination. Facing separation from the therapist and the inevitable mourning process associated with it, there is a tendency for regression to prior pathogenic introjective configurations. As these formations are reactivated under separation pressures, the tendency for associated projections and negative transference elements to reemerge is significant, and these dimensions must be reworked in the interest of sustaining a therapeutic alliance that will facilitate the patient's mourning process. However, one frequently finds that the capacity for internalization, which is required to make this process a therapeutically useful one, is impaired, particularly in patients at the lower level of character pathology. A straightforward termination in these cases may not be possible, and the alternative course of attenuating the therapy over time may be necessary (Zetzel 1971). Patients may ultimately be seen on rare occasions at intervals of years, or may even maintain therapeutic contact by occasional telephone calls or letters. The therapeutic contact may never actually be terminated. In these circumstances, the therapeutic alliance remains contaminated with elements of misalliance. The sustaining function of the therapist, rooted in unresolved and unresolvable transference attachments, as an important object in the maintenance of the economy of psychic equilibrium in the patient cannot be underestimated in this context. Langs (1974, 1976) has argued that any modification of definitive termination involves unresolved sectors of misalliance. Similarly, Bird (1972) argued that any attenuation of termination would interfere with resolution of the transference. Even in these circumstances, however, I would maintain that the degree to which effective termination work can be achieved depends on a meaningful therapeutic alliance and that this aspect of the therapeutic relation often must be compromised in the actual working through of termination in whatever form.

In patients in whom aspects of the therapeutic alliance have been relatively compromised, the capacity to separate and internalize may be correspondingly compromised to some degree, but there is nonetheless sufficient capacity to tolerate mourning and to effect a meaningful separation. The separation work, as a matter of principle, should be attempted with as little dilution as possible. The issues require both tolerance of separation and continuing support from the therapist. The work of termination is more problematic, requires more time, may suffer regression more easily, and requires occasional reworking and reinforcement, in contrast to the typical termination work with neurotic patients.

Evolution of the therapeutic alliance and modification of transference derivatives should move the patient toward not only an increased capacity for termination work, but toward greater acceptance of responsibility for the therapeutic outcome and its impact on the patient's sense of self and its reverberations for the patient's future life. This dawning acceptance on the part of the patient sets the stage for meaningful mourning in the sense that, however valued the analyst and the analytic process, the patient has less need for them and can entertain the possibility that surrender of these valued attachments are to his interest and benefit. Whatever the regressive pulls toward continued dependence, the path to further growth and maturity lies in resignation of these infantile needs and greater acceptance of responsibility for oneself and one's destiny. This part of the analytic resolution lies completely in the analysand's hands; it is a piece of termination work that only he can do and to which the analyst can be no more than an observer or facilitator. The facilitation lies in development of the therapeutic alliance that provides the sustaining qualities for the difficult termination work of separation and mourning.

Post-termination Contacts

A separate issue related to the resolution of the therapeutic alliance, especially in patients for whom that resolution has been compromised, is post-termination contacts. Schachter (1992) has proposed that such contacts be planned as part of the termination procedure to assess gains and limitations of the analytic process. The psychological distance afforded by the passage of time and separation can provide a more meaningful perspective on effectiveness of the therapeutic effort, particularly the degree to which analytic gains have been effectively internalized and preserved. Follow-up studies indicate that transferences are more often modulated than successfully resolved (Norman et al. 1976; Oremland et al. 1975; Pfeffer 1959, 1961, 1963; Schlessinger and Robbins 1983). There is no available assessment specifically of therapeutic alliance resolution, but my experience suggests that similar results are likely.

Schachter's (1990) data reveal that indicating to the patient that the analyst will remain available to him for further help is common practice, but initiating such a post-termination meeting is not. Such an arrangement might undermine the patient's autonomy or reactivate unresolved transference needs and even precipitate regressive reactions. There is often a presumption that analysands will be able to deal with any unresolved conflictual or neurotic issues through an expectable mourning process and as a function of effective internalizations realized during the analysis. The fear is that post-termination contacts would interfere with that process. This seems to run counter to personal experience of analysts, who often return to their training analyst for further therapeutic work.

Some of this reluctance seems connected with concerns that the analyst will be seen as too much of a real person and that this would undermine the analytic relation should further therapy be required. The available data, however, suggest not only that such follow-up contacts have no deleterious effects, but that in many instances they can further resolve transference issues or help to maintain therapeutic gains (Schachter 1990).

Schachter (1992) addresses the role of alliance in this context, making the point that a solid therapeutic alliance should provide a basis for sufficient trust and acceptance of the analyst's physicianly interest and concern to permit continued use of the analyst as an important resource in the patient's life when it is helpful. Schachter follows Stone's (1961) view of the therapeutic alliance, about which I have expressed my reservations (see chapter 1). To the extent that the analyst remains a helpful object of dependence and relatively immature trust for the patient, return to the analytic resource may reflect unresolved transference rather than therapeutic alliance. To the extent that termination work consolidated a more mature and constructive therapeutic alliance, the basis is laid for a growth-enhancing relationship beyond termination. In such circumstances, Schachter's recommendations can be warmly endorsed. By the same token, where such optimal resolution of transferences and therapeutic alliance have not been accomplished, the opportunity to return for extended subsequent analytic work may further contribute to exactly such effects. One can never be certain about the extent to which termination work has been fully accomplished—the task is fraught with incomplete effects and many a loose end.

Not to be overlooked in this context is the potential countertransference trap provided by the analyst's reluctance to allow the patient to live his life without need of or help from the analyst. A solid therapeutic alliance will facilitate both the patient's freedom and autonomy and the analyst's tolerance of the narcissistic injury of his faded usefulness. Then again, if the therapeutic alliance is reliable enough, the prospects for further therapeutic effort are good, and no patient should be denied the opportunity to realize such effects. In practice, I frequently indicate to the patient at some point that we have expended great effort and expense to develop a relationship that can serve as a resource for the patient in the future and that it is eminently reasonable for the patient to make use of it when and if he feels the need. Schachter (1992) recommends that such post-termination meetings be explicitly planned, and he offers persuasive reasons for so doing. I prefer to leave the initiative for opening such contact to the patient, which seems more respectful of the patient's autonomy and freedom.

Patients may also entertain frequent fantasies of a personal or social relation with the analyst after termination. Freud (1937) seemed to leave this possibility open when he wrote: "Not every good relation between an analyst and his subject during and after analysis was to be regarded as a transference; there were also friendly relations which were based on reality and which proved to be viable" (p. 222). And Schachter (1992) adds his imprimatur: "There are examples which replicate Freud's observation that patient and analyst may, following termination, develop a genuine friendship that seems healthy rather than neurotic. Indeed, this does not seem a surprising outcome of a strong working alliance, i.e., of the patient's realistic trust in and belief in the analyst's genuine concern for his [or] her wellbeing" (p. 150). These respective opinions both seem to derive from an inadequate respect for the distinction between therapeutic alliance and the real relation. Therapeutic alliance should not be used to justify real involvement with the patient, even after termination. Where friendly relations are allowed to develop, it should be with the mutual recognition that any therapeutic connection has been broken and permanently so.

A special circumstance in which this arrangement becomes more complex and obscure is in the post-termination relationship between training analyst and candidate. All of the strictures of therapeutic analysis apply, but are complicated by the fact that the parties in question become colleagues, participants in joint processes and activities connected with their professional lives and their collaboration in the same professional groups. How post-termination interactions are managed in this context are matters of personal inclination of the involved parties and are best left to their individual judgment and discretion. Even here, however, attainments in the area of the therapeutic alliance in the analysis will facilitate the grounds on which such relationships work themselves out. I have seen instances in this training context where parameters of the therapeutic alliance were eased or not given due attention and respect, in which otherwise productive analytic gains have been eroded and contaminated unnecessarily to the detriment of the training analysis experience of the candidate. Failure to maintain the therapeutic alliance in the termination phase and premature efforts to shift the basis of the analytic relation to a more collegial basis have resulted in unfortunate and at times quite destructive effects. Even in termination of a well-conducted analysis, particularly in the context of a productive training analysis, unrecognized and unresolved transference residues can come alive with unexpected and undesirable consequences when requirements of the therapeutic alliance are not firmly maintained. In my judgment, the eventual status of training analyst–candidate collegiality is best served by persistent efforts to deal with unresolved transference issues before the end of the analysis. The post-termination evolution of these elements is best left to take their course and find common ground comfortable to both analyst and his graduate candidate. The best guarantee and facilitating influence to a comfortable and constructive outcome is the therapeutic alliance.

Optimally, patients, whether candidates or not, leave analysis with a sense of personal competence, a sense of their own individuality and personal value, and a feeling of separateness and freedom from dependence on the analyst which allows them to take responsibility for the course of their own lives. They retain, we might hope, a bond of affection toward the analyst, but one uncontaminated by feelings of dependence. They now have an identity that is truly their own, independent of the analyst. Here again we can draw a parallel between the analyst and the good parent, who not only allows the child to separate and individuate, but who helpfully and constructively facilitates the child's further venture into adult autonomy and identity.

APPENDIX

General Guidelines Related to the Maintenance of Boundaries in the Practice of Psychotherapy by Physicians (Adult Patients)

Introduction

The maintenance of appropriate professional boundaries between doctor and patient is clinically and ethically central to the practice of psychotherapy. Attention to boundary issues helps both to enhance the effectiveness of the therapeutic process and to avoid exploitation of patients. Although each case in which questions about appropriate boundaries arise must be considered in its context, some general guidelines can be articulated in this area.

These guidelines were developed in conjunction with the Massachusetts Psychiatric Society, the Boston Psychoanalytic Institute, and the Massachusetts Medical Society.

Guidelines

The Board of Registration in Medicine is charged by statute with regulating the practice of medicine "in order to promote the public health, safety, and welfare." Within the scope of the Board's authority is the responsibility to define the safe practice of medicine as well as conduct which falls outside such practice. In seeking to provide a better understanding of the expectations it holds for physicians practicing in this state, the Board believes it is useful to issue guidelines which discuss appropriate and inappropriate conduct in areas in which issues of safe practice frequently arise. Guidelines should be distinguished from rules and regulations. These guidelines are intended to identify a framework for the practice of psychotherapy. Generally speaking, when following the guidelines, physicians need provide no further justification for their behavior. Al-

These guidelines were developed by the Massachusetts Board of Registration in Medicine, in conjunction with the Massachusetts Psychiatric Society, the Boston Psychoanalytic Institute, and the Massachusetts Medical Society.

though practice outside the guidelines may be appropriate under some circumstances, such deviations must support therapeutic objectives.

For the purposes of these guidelines, the practice of psychotherapy (in contrast to "counseling" as done routinely in most forms of medical practice) is defined as the intentional use of verbal techniques to explore or alter the patient's emotional life in order to effect symptom reduction or behavior change. Although psychiatry is the medical specialty most often associated with psychotherapy, other physicians may also engage patients in regular sessions described above as psychotherapy. Psychiatrists may offer medical treatments instead of psychotherapy or as an adjunct to psychotherapy. These guidelines apply to all physicians who hold themselves out as practicing psychotherapy or who engage patients in regular sessions as described above.

Since the boundary conditions of psychotherapeutic practice fall into a number of categories, guidelines relating to boundaries must address each of these conditions separately.

Establishing and Maintaining Boundaries in a Psychotherapeutic Relationship

Establishment of boundaries for a psychotherapeutic relationship should begin early in therapy. Although appropriate boundaries may vary with the psychotherapeutic approach employed, the physician, and not the patient, bears the responsibility for defining and maintaining proper personal distance in the relationship. Maintenance of boundaries requires ongoing attention. Boundary crossings should occasion thoughtful review by the physician of whether corrective actions are required.

Appointment Place and Time

In general, physicians practicing psychotherapy should see their patients in the setting, at the hours, and in the allotted periods of time that are appropriate to this mode of treatment. This generally means that treatment should take place during the physician's usual working hours and in an office setting. Home offices are appropriate, provided the usage is separate from the physician's general living quarters.

Some of the exceptions to the usual practice of restricting treatment contacts to office settings include behavioral therapy (e.g., in vivo desensitization); supportive therapy (e.g., meetings in the hospital cafeteria with a severely regressed inpatient); home visits to the homebound or through an organized outreach effort; visits to hospitalized patients; or emergency situations.

Billing Practices

Fees charged to patients for psychotherapy, along with arrangements concerning billing for missed or canceled sessions, telephone contacts, vacations, and so forth, should be negotiated early in the doctor-patient relationship. It should be clear to both parties how insurance coverage will be applied to the fees. Physicians' bills should accurately reflect the services that were rendered. It is not appropriate to collude with patients to render inaccurate bills, even when the goal is to increase third-party coverage available for patients treatment. There is a long and accepted tradition to charge reduced fees or to reduce or forgive outstanding balances when patients are otherwise unable to afford care. Barter arrangements as payment for treatment are problematic and generally should be avoided.

Other Economic Relationships

A physician should never exploit the physician-patient relationship for personal gain. While some economic relationships may be impossible to avoid (patient owns the only auto repair shop within a reasonable distance) or may be sufficiently remote (patient owns stock in a large department store where physician shops), it is essential that the patient not be exploited and that the therapy not be compromised as a result of any economic relationship. Economic relationships that should be avoided include selling objects or services (other than medical services) to the patient; employing or being employed by the patient; and entering into joint ventures with the patient. When considering the purchase of an object or service from a patient, a physician must ensure that such a purchase is never exploitative, confusing, or harmful to the psychotherapy.

Physical Contact

Physical contact with patients is appropriate for the purposes of physical examination and medical treatment, consistent with the psychotherapeutic treatment being provided. Beyond these legitimate medical purposes, physicians practicing psychotherapy generally should limit physical contact with their patients to a handshake at the start or end of a session when this seems called for. When patients are distressed, a comforting pat of reassurance on the hand or shoulder may also be appropriate. Physical contact beyond this may be perceived as flirtatious or sexual and should be avoided. More explicit sexual contact and outright flirtatious behavior is not permitted. Behavioral therapies may legitimately involve other forms of non-intimate physical contact in a public setting.

Self-Disclosure

Self-disclosure, in general, should be kept to a minimum in psychotherapy. There are, however, a few circumstances in which self-disclosure may be appropriate. First, patients have a right to know the physician's training and qualifications when deciding whether to establish a physician / patient relationship. Second, in the treatment of addictions, disclosure of the psychotherapist's own history of substance abuse treatment has become common. Finally, there are infrequent occasions when self-disclosure can have an important therapeutic impact. These situations need to be well thought out, and it must be clear that these disclosures serve the patient, not the therapist. It is never appropriate for physicians practicing psychotherapy to discuss their own current emotional problems or to disclose details of their sexual lives.

Gifts

Many physicians practicing psychotherapy will discourage patients from presenting gifts, preferring to discuss with them the feelings underlying their desire to offer a gift. However, it is not inappropriate for physicians to accept gifts of minimal value from psychotherapy patients. Physicians should not accept gifts of substantial value or of a sexual or intimate nature from psychotherapy patients.

It may be appropriate for patients to express their gratitude for the care they have received by making a voluntary gift or donation to the organizations or facilities for which their physicians work. In such cases, if gifts are of substantial value, it is preferable for patients to discuss their interests in making donations with an independent physician, to make sure that patients are not being exploited.

There may be occasions on which it is appropriate for physicians to present gifts to psychotherapy patients. Gifts of small value may be useful in establishing therapeutic relationships with adolescents and severely regressed adult patients. Physicians may also present gifts to mark important occasions in psychotherapy patients' lives, e.g., the birth of a child. Physicians should never present gifts of substantial value to their psychotherapy patients. Gifts should never be of a sexual or intimate nature.

Nonsexual Social Relations

Certain social relationships with patients may be impossible to avoid, especially in small towns and in certain subcultures (e.g., when the patient runs the only hardware store in town, when the patient has a child in the same school as the physician's child, or when the patient has chosen the physician for psychotherapy because the doctor is known to belong to the same religious or cultural group as the patient). In such situations, the doctors practicing psychotherapy still have some obligations as physicians, even when not acting in the physician role, and should take special care to respect the dignity and privacy of the patient. In such social settings, the fostering of a personal relationship with a psychotherapy patient is inappropriate, whether this be through physical contact, gifts, self-disclosure, or other means.

For example, while the acknowledgment of significant personal milestones or events with a gift of small value is described as appropriate above, even these benign extensions of personal interest may be inappropriate in a social setting, where a vulnerable or confused patient may misinterpret that interest. Similarly, physicians practicing psychotherapy should avoid such potentially intimate encounters as sharing meals, transportation, or attending social gatherings when the therapeutic relationship may suffer or be compromised as a result of the social contact, or where a patient may perceive the physician's conduct to reflect a romantic or sexual interest.

Patients' Families

The psychotherapeutic treatment of a patient also places limits on the behavior that is appropriate with respect to that patient's family members and others intimately involved in the patient's life. Personal relationships with these other individuals in the patient's life should be avoided during the course of treatment. Also, the patient's right to confidentiality is relevant to these family members, with whom physicians practicing psychotherapy may not discuss the patient's condition and treatment without the explicit permission of the patient. Indeed, state law prohibits any disclosure of psychotherapist-patient communications except under specific circumstances.

Among the exceptions to this rule are situations in which disclosure is necessary to protect the safety of the patient or of third parties. Even then, disclosure should be limited to the minimum amount of information needed to achieve the desired end. It is not a breach of a patient's right to confidentiality for a physician-psychotherapist to undertake general psychoeducation with the patient's family on issues of diagnosis and treatment, without disclosing specific information regarding the patients care. Nor does it violate a patient's rights to obtain data for diagnostic or treatment purposes from informants, as long as information about the patient's treatment is not revealed in the process.

Changes in Behavior Regarding Boundaries

Physicians practicing psychotherapy should pay particular attention to changes in the pattern of behavior in any of these areas as treatment continues over time. Although exceptions to any of the principles outlined above occasionally may be indicated, changes in behavior, especially simultaneous changes in more than one area, should be cause for self-examination by the psychotherapist. In such circumstances, consultation from colleagues is highly recommended, as is thorough documentation.

Circumstances in Which Termination Should Be Considered Because Boundaries Cannot Be Maintained

Most boundary crossings are not threatening to the continued existence of the therapeutic relationship, although they require self-examination by the physician and may require discussion with the patient. Certain boundary problems, however, may only be resolved by termination of the psychotherapeutic relationship. These include circumstances in which the physician's subjective reactions to the patient—positive or negative in character—make it difficult to guarantee that boundaries will be maintained. Termination is usually required when the physician has engaged in overtly seductive or sexualized behavior. Patients may be permitted somewhat greater latitude in acting out their feelings, but extreme behaviors, such as significant intrusions into the personal life of the physician, may also necessitate termination. Physicians considering termination of a psychotherapeutic relationship because of problems in maintaining boundaries may find the consultation of a colleague particularly useful.

Patients facing termination fall into three categories. Some patients will not require follow-up care, in which case a reasonable date for termination can be established, without need for referral. A second group of patients would benefit from further treatment and require referral to other appropriate therapists. If diligent efforts fail to identify therapists willing to assume responsibility for their care, a decision must be made as to whether patients' interests are best served by continuing in treatment with their current therapists or by terminating treatment in the absence of definitive follow-up plans. Consultation with experienced psychotherapists is very helpful in such cases. The final group of patients are those in emergent circumstances. They should not be terminated from treatment until another qualified therapist is available and willing to assume responsibility for their care.

Notes

Chapter 1. History and Definition

1. We can trace the alliance concept from Zetzel's (1956) formulation, following Sterba's (1934) view of the therapeutic split in the ego, and further elaboration by Greenson (1965) as the "working alliance."

2. See also Treurniet 1993.

3. See Baker's (1993) discussion of the analyst as "new object."

4. Likewise, engagement in the alliance requires a degree of intelligence and insight into the nature of the analytic process, as well as capacity to enter into the interpretive process, both essential ingredients in analyzability.

5. Ogden (1994) has advanced the concept of the "intersubjective analytic third," which arises in dialectical tension between the interacting subjectivities of analyst and patient. This "third" complement to subjectivity constantly is transformed by understandings developed by analyst and analysand. I find this a genial expression of the essence of the therapeutic alliance. See also Quinodoz' (1994) reservations.

The tension between the classical intrapsychic focus of analysis and the two-person interactive perspective has been nicely formulated by Schwaber (1995): "The psychoanalytic domain is the intrapsychic; *interaction* between the two participants suggests an external purview. We may reason that our interest remains in what occurs within, but that simultaneously we try to elucidate and describe what takes place in the relationship between analyst and patient. In this way however we straddle both spheres—inner and outer—though perhaps retaining some misgivings about the conceptual ramifications of doing so. For it should be clear with whatever model we espouse that *unless we maintain our focus on what is inner, what is intrapsychic, we are pursuing a way of theorising—and of listening—that is inherently not psychoanalytic.* How then can we credibly employ the concept of interaction within our psychoanalytic lexicon? We may do so, I would propose, by adding *and paying heed to* the qualifier—*as it is experienced;* interaction—*from whose point of view?* Experienced—from whose vantage-point? Each of us—analyst, patient, outside observer—may agree about the fact of an occurrence, while we may vary, subtly or widely, about what it means or how it feels" (pp. 557–558).

6. Benjamin's (1994) caricature requires comment. She writes: "The intersubjective position emphasizes the analyst's countertransference identification with the patient as distinct from the classical view that the analyst controls himself and holds fast to the mast of reality in order to carry the patient through the treacherous waters of the transference" (p.

546). The alternatives are not countertransference vs. reality; the therapeutic alliance is a distinct alternative which is inherently intersubjective. Something similar can be said about the Ornsteins' (1994) division of closed-system transferences (the classical model based on displacement or projection) vs. open-system (selfobject) transferences. Classical transferences cannot be confined to a closed system, and they remain as open to intersubjective understanding and influences as selfobject transferences.

7. Spence et al. (1994) have found that the co-occurrence of the personal pronouns *you* and *me* may provide an index of the strength of the therapeutic alliance. They hypothesize that a high proportion of co-occurring pairs reflects a sense of security in entering the analytic space and that a degree of low separation (in time and space during the analytic hour) between *you* and/or *me* and similar indexicals may reflect the degree to which the patient shares the analytic space with the analyst.

8. A review of the Menninger study indicates that failure to establish a meaningful alliance, for whatever reason, contributed significantly to the failure rate (Colson et al. 1982). For an interesting process study demonstrating the central role of therapeutic alliance in psychotherapy see Elliott 1983.

9. Moreover, the alliance concept has applications well beyond individual psychotherapy or analysis. It plays a central role in family therapy (Shapiro et al. 1977), in the therapy of children (Evans 1976; Frankl and Hellman 1962; Geleerd 1962), and in the treatment of adolescents (Schimel 1974; Schowalter 1976; Shapiro et al. 1977); it serves as an important factor of analyzability (Hani 1973); in the vicissitudes of patient compliance or noncompliance in general medicine (Trostle et al. 1983) and in pharmacotherapy (Gutheil 1982; see also Gabbard 1994a, 1994c) ; it is vital in the management of psychiatric emergency room crises (Rosenberg 1994); and it forms an effective component of successful psychotherapy with eating disorders (Bruch 1973, 1978; Crisp et al. 1985; Russell 1970), multiple personalities (Allen 1993; Kluft 1992), and even schizophrenia (Frank and Gunderson 1990; Pao 1983; Robbins 1993; Selzer et al. 1984). Even in prescribing drug treatment—whether in psychiatry or general medicine—the role of therapeutic alliance has been described as the "pharmacotherapeutic alliance" (Gutheil 1982; Adelman 1985; Gabbard 1994a, 1994c).

10. This form of unobjectionable transference is sometimes confused with therapeutic alliance; see Fosshage 1994. It may play an important role in supportive psychotherapy (Wallerstein 1985), but it is preferable to keep it conceptually separate from therapeutic alliance.

11. In a reevaluation of Sterba's views, Friedman (1992) described the ego-split underlying alliance as a form of dissociative state of detachment and self-observation that is activated by transference and serves the purpose of interpretation of transference resistances. Although Sterba planted a seed that matured into later views of alliance, it is a far cry from the alliance concept as developed in this study.

12. The persistence of this paradox might create an insoluble dilemma (Nunberg 1948, 1955). To the extent that irrational motives, e.g., hidden gratifications from engaging in the analysis or seeking to gratify a rivalry with a sibling, might be attributed to the therapeutic alliance (Sandler et al. 1973), they would seemingly reflect emotional or transferential contaminants rather than the alliance itself. Underlying this debate is the unresolved question of whether or not all motivation must be reduced to drive derivatives.

13. Curtis (1970) objected to both terms on the ground that the essence of transference was irrationality and immaturity.

14. See chapter 4 on the role of the analyst's reality in the analytic situation.

15. In terms of the present construction, these qualities belong to the real aspects of the analyst's personality rather than to therapeutic alliance. See chapter 4.

16. The term *working* in this view connotes restriction of the therapeutic relationship to the necessary and sufficient conditions for the patient and therapist to work together, suggesting that the concept of the alliance is limited or constrained to some degree. While this usage is acceptable, the distinction need not be pressed excessively. I shall use the term *working* to express a limited but sufficient alliance and *therapeutic* when the fuller connotations of alliance are in question.

17. Even in Winnicott, the term *holding* assumes various meanings—correct and well-timed interpretation, or a willingness to wait and not interpret, or a protective and comforting emotional attunement to the patient (a sort of environmental provision), or the Kleinian notion of containing (Sandbank 1993).

18. Mayer and Spence (1994) refer to early patterns of mother-infant interaction as a genotype that appears in transformations or phenotypes in the analytic situation, and these are anything but carbon copies.

19. See also Benjamin 1994.

20. At times, the containment metaphor can lead to infantilization of the therapeutic alliance. Bollas (1990), for example, refers to the "sense in infancy that one is inside a container that is alive, psychic. . . . To varying degrees this alliance—*the experience of being inside a process to which one contributes*—will indeed be transferred to the clinical space as the patient reconstructs his experience of being contained . . . by the other." This seems to override the distinction between metaphor and method, and thus, in my view, miscasts the root meaning of the therapeutic alliance.

Chapter 2. Alliance and Transference

1. Langs (1976) regarded these as forms of "genetic transference" insofar as they involved displacements from the past.

2. The authors mention projection of superego derivatives and aspects of self-representations, and I add aspects of the patient's introjective configuration (Meissner 1978, 1981, 1986b, 1988) as contributing to this transferential mechanism. There is controversy about whether the mechanism of such transferences should be regarded as projection or projective identification. Langs (1976) insisted on projective identification, on the ground that an interactional component is called into play. In my view this does not distinguish the process from simple projection, which involves an effort to draw the object into conformity with the projection, whenever another person is the object (Meissner 1980, 1987b).

3. Langs (1976) added another form of transference based on introjection of the analyst—introjective transference or transference identification. This seems to have more to do with the patient's internalization of the analyst than with transference. Another wrinkle comes from Modell (1990) in his distinction of *dependent / containing* from *iconic / projective* transferences. The former reflects a symbolic actualization of developmental conflicts, while the latter recreates specific imagos. The former is also a form of response to the actual therapeutic setting, while the latter rests on projection of internal intentions. The former provides a containing function resembling Modell's articulation of the "holding environment," while the latter comes closer to a form of projective transference. See Killingmo's (1995) discussion and the analysis of the holding environment and its relation the alliance in chapter 1.

4. An effort to reinforce this distinction came from Thompson (1938a, 1938b) who contrasted the irrational quality of transference responses to the analyst with more realistic responses. Another discriminating feature between positive transference and therapeutic alliance was suggested by Schowalter (1976)—therapeutic alliance will help carry the analysis

through periods of negative transference without eliminating or distorting them, but positive transference will not.

5. This dichotomy also undergirds Hanly's (1994) assessment of therapeutic alliance.

6. See also Ticho (1971). Friedman (1969) also introduced the element of hope as a motivating force for analytic work and change—specifically in relation to the therapeutic alliance.

7. See also Knapp's discussion of Swartz's (1969) paper, pp. 319–322.

8. The oppositional aspect of transference and therapeutic alliance is seen dramatically in forms of erotic transference, in which the intensity of transference desires and affects can override and obliterate any semblance of therapeutic alliance. Such patients lose any sense of the unreality or inappropriateness of their feelings, and the demand for real gratification and response from the analyst dominates (Blum 1994b). The demand for reality thus bypasses and subverts not only the ambiguity of transference and the maintenance of the therapeutic frame, but also acceptance of responsible action in the therapeutic alliance.

9. Flournoy (1971) applied this notion to the analyst—his mature transference allowed him to use his reason and understanding in the service of the analysis and contributes to establishing the alliance.

10. Langs (1976) commented on the confusion arising from neglect of the distinction between transference and nontransference and conflating transference and the therapeutic relation. In his view, wishes to understand and develop belong to nontransferential aspects of the therapeutic relation.

11. See also Sandler et al. 1973.

12. See further discussion of this distinction below.

13. The issues here are technical rather than conceptual, which is why Brenner (1979, 1980) objected to the alliance concept. I am using the clinical example only to clarify the distinction and not to address the technical question.

14. The dilemma in dealing with intensely experienced transferences, especially erotic transferences, was underscored by Lachmann (1994). Labeling such transferences as regressive or pathological, or retreating from them by recourse to genetic interpretation or by appeal to therapeutic alliance and the "rules" of analysis, runs the risk of devaluing the patient's experience and increasing the degree of shame and guilt. This form of countertransference enactment is likely to evoke anger and hurt in the patient. Management of such intensive transferences within the therapeutic alliance calls for something quite different.

15. In his delineation of selfobject experiences, Wolf (1993) makes a distinction between object relations and selfobject relation: the former is impersonal, without personal meaning or involvement; the latter involves personal feelings and influences the subject's self-feeling. In addition to the obvious difficulties object relations theorists would have with it, such a formulation, in self psychological terms, has replaced "object" with "selfobject." As Jacobson (1993) notes, extension of the selfobject concept from situations of incomplete boundaries or lack of differentiation—its original meaning—to include all levels of development and object-relatedness jeopardizes conceptual precision. He comments: "The consequences of limiting oneself to a single model, any single model, was presaged by what I believe to be an ancient adage: 'If the only tool you have at your disposal is a hammer, every problem you encounter is likely to resemble a nail' " (p. 542).

16. Novick (1980) described a form of "negative therapeutic alliance" in which patient and analyst colluded to produce a therapeutic failure. This is a form of misalliance in my terminology.

17. I find myself in disagreement with Hanly's (1994) view that the therapeutic alliance can be dependent on a defensive idealizing transference. The alliance may be narcissistic, but

as such it represents a form of misalliance based on transference. A more adequate and authentic therapeutic alliance requires resolution of the transference as determinative.

Chapter 3. Alliance and Countertransference

1. Some analysts, for example, Green (1975), endorse a view of countertransference as embracing all of the analyst's reactions to the patient—not the view I am advocating here.

2. This distinction parallels Wile's (1972) distinction between "therapist-related" (subjective) and "patient-induced" (objective) countertransferences.

3. Efforts to extend the notion of countertransference to include the manner in which self-organization of the analyst interacts with the self-organization of the patient in the sense that each depends on the other for self-regulation (Thomson 1993) lead to a possible form of misalliance. To the extent that the analyst depends on the relation to the patient for self-regulation he suffers from a deficit of autonomy and is vulnerable to transference/countertransference vicissitudes. This does not exclude the range of interpersonal interactions by which each influences and affects the other. Meaningful empathic attunement does not require mutual self-object enmeshment.

4. See the discussion of empathy in chapter 10.

5. Some early usages (Weigert 1954a) mingled countertransference with therapeutic alliance, as a corollary of the patient's positive transference abetting alliance. Greenson (1974), for example, thought a modest degree of positive countertransference contributed to the working alliance.

6. Efforts to cast reactions or interactions of the analyst's real personality with the real personality of the patient as "characterological countertransferences" (Schafer 1993; Schoenewolf 1993) tend to erode the boundary between real and transferential—specifically countertransferential. Treurniet (1993) has even suggested that broadening of countertransference and its overdependence on projective identification may not only distort the meaning of countertransference, but also may serve as a defense against the impact of the real analytic relation. Schafer's comments, for example, on the patriarchal and condescending tone in Freud's (1915a) discussion of transference-love regarding the erotic transferences of female patients, might better view these qualities as belonging to Freud's real personality rather than to any form of countertransference. See my discussion in chapter 4 of the reality of analyst and patient as they enter the psychoanalytic space.

7. Olinick (1993) refers to "structural actualities" of transference which can affect the analyst's capacity to function effectively, yet not be part of countertransference. He includes (1) multiple, obscure, shifting meanings of transference, (2) struggles emerging around transference, (3) affective ambiance of transference, (4) inauthentic or dissembling behavior in which transference is expressed, (5) confusing transference repetitions, and (6) the narcissistic peremptoriness of some transferences. To the extent that they do not lead to countertransference responses they may induce counterreactions of various kinds, which I would regard as aspects of the real interaction between analyst and patient.

8. Transference and countertransference sometimes occur without a transference/countertransference interaction. The view of countertransference as inherently interactive has become increasingly operative in analytic thinking (Gabbard 1994e).

9. These processes have been described by Grinberg (1962) in terms of projective identifications and projective counteridentifications. This basically Kleinian usage is not followed in this discussion for technical and theoretical reasons that are discussed more fully elsewhere (Meissner 1980, 1987b).

10. These distinctions are paralleled by Wile's (1972) distinction between "resonant" (concordant) and "reciprocal" (complementary) countertransference.

11. Concordant countertransferences should be kept distinct from empathy, even when similar mechanisms may be involved. Empathy makes attunement to the affective inner state of another possible, thereby contributing to therapeutic alliance; concordant countertransference leads to collusive identification, thereby serving resistances and contributing to possible misalliance. Reich (1966) distinguished empathy as a form of unconscious receptiveness leading to deeper analytic comprehension, from countertransference, in which trial identifications too close to the analyst's unresolved conflicts can result in distortions of understanding and countertransference acting out. Even an exclusive focus on empathy can become a countertransference-enactment of merger fantasies (Brickman 1993). Rayner (1992) also notes that empathic attunement and projective identification (the presumed mechanism of countertransference) function at different levels of activity, i.e., fantasy activity vs. sensory resonance.

12. Renik (1992) has drawn attention to efforts to treat the analyst as a fetish, cognitively overriding any distinction between fantasy and reality and often leading to breaking off treatment prematurely or drifting into an interminable process. The patient has no wish to terminate and thus interrupt the fetishized relation to the analyst.

13. See McLaughlin (1975) on the countertransference dynamics of the sleepy analyst.

14. A similar pattern of victimization may have been played out in the Dora case (Meissner 1984–85).

Chapter 4. The Analyst as Participant

1. The list of writers recognizing the relevance of the real relation but compounding it with elements of alliance includes Fleming (1946), Thompson (1946), Berman (1949), A. Freud (1954a, 1954b), Stone (1954), Heimann (1956), Rycroft (1956, 1958), Fairbairn (1957, 1958), Little (1957), Nacht (1957, 1964), Reich (1958), Paul (1959), Benassy (1960), Loewald (1960), Tarachow (1962a, 1962b), Olinick (1964), Giovacchini (1965), Rangell (1968), Flournoy 1971), Bird (1972), and Dewald (1976).

2. Keeping transferential factors distinct from reality factors is compounded by their interaction in the patient's analytic experience—a point emphasized by many (Langs 1976; Macalpine 1950). Szasz (1963) even argued that any determination of what was transference depended on the judgment of the analyst, who had no greater claim on that decision than the patient, a view echoed in subsequent claims for the validity of the patient's psychic reality (Kantrowitz 1993; Schwaber 1983b, 1992). Again I would argue that the co-occurrence and interaction of transferential and reality factors do not mean there is no distinction and difference between them. Even Szasz agreed that one purpose of analysis was to help the patient discriminate between them.

3. In Benedek's (1953) case, the woman saw a drawing done by the male therapist and commented positively. The analyst interpreted this in terms of competition with men and specifically her brother, exemplifying such an undermining of alliance. The patient felt misunderstood, misjudged, and aware of the therapist's countertransference, which led to anger, resentment, and an eventual impasse.

4. One line of analytic thinking acknowledges the role of reality, but downplays it to avoid underemphasis on transference. Thus, Abend (1982) wrote, "My own position is that for all practical purposes the reality relationship is always experienced by the analysand (and the analyst, too, of course, though we hope to a lesser degree) as inextricably intertwined with

its unconscious reverberations and meanings. It is to these latter that the analyst's attention should always be directed" (p. 367). *E contra,* I would argue that both reality and its unconscious meanings are proper objects of the analyst's attention. Part of the problem here is Abend's lack of attention to alliance as distinct from reality.

5. Controversy over the meaning of the real is a vital part of psychoanalytic history, beginning with Freud's seduction hypothesis (Bergmann 1993a, 1993b).

6. Frank (1968, 1974a, 1974b) located the basis for hope and therapeutic progress in interactions between real characteristics of patient and therapist; in the view developed here, the basis for hope and progress lies in the alliance rather than reality.

7. There seem to be special difficulties in analyses of children. The child's need to find a relation to the real object may not serve the therapy well, but its transformation into an effective alliance can (see Evans 1976). Tendencies to respond to the child more openly or spontaneously or to adopt a pedagogical role can impinge on the alliance (Shapiro 1984). There are also difficulties arising in the treatment of adolescents with whom the need to interpret reality can become pressing and the parental role looms as a potential countertransference trap (Gesensway 1978).

8. Caper regards this as the analyst's insistence on being real, but failure to distinguish reality from alliance here becomes confusing. The analyst's reality answers to the patient's need to relate to a real object but also erodes the therapeutic structure. Caper (1992) makes the point nicely: "The patient may perversely idealize these collusions as ordinary sociability or friendliness, common human decency, or warmth and empathy. This leads him to feel that when the analyst is actually analyzing (rather than colluding with) this state of mind, he is not a real person, not friendly, warm or empathic. It is therefore quite important to keep in mind, when the patient feels that one is being 'real' and empathic, that one may be unwittingly colluding with the patient's perverse attack on the analyst's, and his own, reality sense" (p. 288).

9. See also Greenson (1965, 1971), Issacharoff (1978), and Greenberg (1995).

10. See also Inderbitzin and Levy (1994) on the attachment of transference to reality.

11. This definition helps to focus the distinction between real relation and alliance. In contrast, Abend's (1982) definition, "The reality relationship between analyst and analysand presumably refers to those features of their contact reflective of their mutual status as adults engaged in a specific activity—psychoanalysis—which has certain agreed upon goals and features of conduct" (p. 367), while less helpful, is equally applicable to the alliance.

12. Some aspects of this interaction have been described in terms of the social system and structure and the respective role behaviors involved in the therapeutic setting (see Newton 1973). In this connection Renik (1993) makes the valid point that "Everything an analyst does in the analytic situation is based upon his or her personal psychology" (p. 4), but this observation should be carried a step further to indicate that the analyst's personal involvement in the transference/countertransference arena is quite different from his involvement in alliance. See the discussion in Almond (1995). This point also touches on issues of therapeutic match, which I would tend to ascribe to the personality and character organization of analyst and analysand—matters pertaining to the real relation. The dimensions of the therapeutic alliance are related but function in a different frame of reference within the analytic process. See Kantrowitz (1992, 1993, 1995) on the therapeutic match and its impact in analysis.

13. See also Weiner (1972). Van der Velde (1985) discussed ways in which the external body image can affect perceptions and transferential determinants of object relations and thus be a nonverbal factor in the development and resolution of transferences in therapy. The

same applies to bodily movements—shifting position, tapping, restlessness, etc. (Jacobs 1973, 1991; McLaughlin 1987).

14. See chapter 10 for further discussion of empathy.

15. Levine (1993) traces the shift in Greenson's usage of *real relationship* from a technical factor facilitating analytic work to a mechanism of cure—even replacing transference. Greenson's mingling of reality and alliance factors gives this criticism substance. In my view, if there is a curative aspect of nontransferential components of the therapeutic relation, it lies in the alliance sector and *not* in reality.

16. Weinstock (1976) offered two cases in which a change in the analyst-patient interaction was reflected in the patient's dream material.

17. Accounts of multiple analyses can be found in Guntrip (1975), Money-Kyrle (1978), Bion (1985), Hurwitz (1986), Little (1990), and Simon (1993).

18. Kantrowitz (1993) views character traits on a continuum between countertransference reactions and habitual, conflict-free patterns of behavior. Thus characterological traits can become conflictual and produce countertransference difficulties, as when an impatient analyst unconsciously ends an hour with a frustrating patient early (countertransference) or expresses this trait in the form of rapid speech (conflict-free). I accept these distinctions, with the understanding that the distinction between countertransference and real aspects of the analyst's character are respected and the varieties of influence of such traits on both transference and therapeutic alliance are kept in mind.

19. Schlesinger (1994a) notes that development of a private language of personal and cryptic meanings between analyst and patient may facilitate the therapeutic alliance, but it may also serve as the basis for subtle collusions that can impede analytic work.

20. This conclusion reflects the burden of the previous discussion of countertransference (see chapter 3).

*Chapter 5. **Reality, Neutrality, and Resistance***

1. Jacobson (1993) notes that some of these developments had been anticipated by Ferenczi.

2. In their discussions of this paper, Natterson and Aronson (in Alger 1966) voice their dissent. The tension between objectivity and engagement is focused by Kovel (1982): "If the therapist is to be objective about me—that is, treat me as I really am—then he cannot treat me as an object. To be objective about another human means recognizing her or his subjectivity with its values as a real agency. But one cannot recognize subjectivity at a distance: it has to be encountered, engaged. And how can we really, truly be *neutral* in such a case? For if I am neutral, then I am disengaged. Neutrality can be read as not caring" (p. 112).

3. Weiner (1972) recommended avoidance of any self-exposure in the face of an inadequate alliance or negative transference. This brings to a focus some of my objections to Renik's (1995a) espousal of self-disclosure, seemingly as a blanket recommendation calculated to counter any authoritarian or idealizing tendencies that might arise in the analytic dialogue. While the ideal of anonymity is never fully realizable, it is stretching it a bit to contend that it is either meaningless or that it is inevitably linked with an authoritarian stance on the part of the analyst. I propose that the alliance perspective would offer a middle ground within which Renik's recommendations would find a compatible home. In that context, the issue of self-disclosure versus relative anonymity can be determined by the terms of the alliance. This alternative would remove the issue from the dichotomous ground of self-disclosure versus authoritarianism. Both self-disclosure and authoritarian attitudes can pro-

vide fertile ground for misalliances. Moreover, Renik seems to argue for a mutuality of disclosure and interpretation that echoes Ferenczi's experiments in mutual analysis, but in a new key. Renik's criticism of Ferenczi—"Ferenczi's much criticized experiment in 'mutual analysis' (in which he and the patient took turns upon the couch saying whatever came to mind) went astray not because Ferenczi's self-disclosure was excessive, but because his self-disclosure was organized in relation to a misguided objective. Ferenczi tried to accomplish the simultaneous analysis of two individuals within a single analytic setting—an over-ambitious effort that was doomed to failure" (p. 487)—might have reverberations, mutatis mutandis, for Renik's own recommendations.

4. Winnicott (1956) held a similar position regarding treatment of more primitive personalities but did not connect it with the alliance concept. See also Khan 1960a, 1960b, 1969.

5. Tauber (1954) strongly recommended telling patients about his thoughts and dreams about them, a position that was criticized by Langs (1976) as excessive and expressive of countertransference. But Langs' unyielding position may lend itself to other countertransference variants.

6. The basic issues do not change with the character of the community, and the therapist must be concerned with preserving a sufficient degree of anonymity that will allow him to continue to work effectively. The particular difficulties for preserving anonymity in a small community are discussed in Beskind et al. (1993).

7. Bollas (1994) suggests that the relative absence of the abstinent or neutral analyst can stimulate erotic desire, increasing the intensity of longing for the object.

8. The conclusion has validity even in the treatment of children (see Chused 1982).

9. Mayer (1994) argues for the congruence of neutrality, compassion, and empathy—all consistent with the therapeutic alliance—with respect to analysis of dying patients. Broadening the concept of neutrality, particularly with reference to constructivist views, is discussed by Schachter (1994). See also Meares' (1983) discussion of technical neutrality and impersonality in relation to empathy exemplified in Keats. My view is that both neutrality and abstinence, in contrast with many other dimensions of the therapeutic alliance, remain part of the participation of the analyst in the process, and not of the patient.

10. Nacht (1963) spoke of "gratifying presence," by which he meant an attitude of attentiveness, availability, understanding, and benevolence.

11. While I find Stone's "affirmative affective tone" consistent with my understanding of the alliance (not as part of the therapeutic alliance but as part of the real relation), I have difficulty taking it as far as Hoffer (1993) seems to in his view that love in the analytic relation is the same as love in ordinary life. The wish to establish equality and mutuality in the analytic relation seems to run up against the inevitable imbalances inherent in the alliance. Hoffer seems to want it both ways: analytic love is "real" but not really equal and mutual (see pp. 349, 350–351). A more moderate note is injected by Gabbard (1994b), "that the real issue for the analyst is not whether transference love is similar to or different from 'real love,' but how the analyst should respond to such powerful wishes" (p. 400). See also the discussion of this issue in Bergmann (1994) and Lachmann (1994). I shall return to this issue in the discussion of the role of authority in analysis in chapter 12.

12. See also Nacht (1957).

13. Built into the analytic relation as an inherent part of its structure are all the vicissitudes of subjectivity—both of the analyst and the patient. This aspect of psychoanalysis has come under heavy criticism by Grünbaum (1984, 1993), in that the inherent subjectivity violates positive criteria of scientific validity. Edelson (1983, 1984, 1986), Hanly (1988), Laor

(1985), Meissner (1990), Spruiell (1987), Wallace (1989), and Wallerstein (1986, 1988) have in turn critiqued Grünbaum on precisely this ground. The problem is indigenous to the practice of medicine generally—the influence of the "Rashomon metaphor" in medical practice has been stressed by Eisenberg (1983), that is, even eyewitness accounts are filtered through the subjectivity of the observer.

14. In more primitive character structures, the push for reality can become so intense that the alternatives become fusion or annihilation (Frosch 1983; Scialli 1982).

15. Stone (1961) suggested that Freud's ideas on abstinence were prompted by his own difficulties in managing erotic feelings. See also Schachter (1994).

16. Stein (1986) argues that the explanatory model of the physician-treater is determined not merely by professional ideals and theoretical commitments, but also by situational and subjective influences.

17. Data on the relevance of these considerations for analytic practice and the perspectives on truth and reality, including attitudes toward the desirability or practicality of neutrality, have been provided by Hamilton (1993). These issues may have played their part in the controversy between Freud and Ferenczi (Kirshner 1993).

18. The controversy took place under stressful circumstances that involved interlocking and troublesome transferences, including the fact that both men were seriously ill and dying (Blum 1994a). See Eickhoff (1993), Hoffer (1991), Falzeder and Haynal (1989), and especially Brabant et al. (1994). Freud's rather explicit yet deferential letter to Ferenczi is reproduced in Jones (1957).

19. Other differences extended more deeply into the subsoil of their respective views of reality, analytic truth, and the nature of interpersonal reality. See Kirshner's (1993) discussion of these issues.

20. Bollas (1989) addresses this issue, arguing that the analysand inevitably uses elements of the analyst's personality to express his true self, analogous to the mother's facilitation of the emergence of the child's self. This emphasizes generative rather than deconstructive aspects of the analysis, and the analyst's central role involves his availability as an object for such expression. Similarly, Stone's (1961) case for gratifying the patient's adult needs has its place, but in my view that is in the alliance and not through reality.

Chapter 6. Personal Factors

1. I am distinguishing here between the analytic process and the analytic situation. The situation refers to the setting in which analysis takes place, with its characteristic organization and structure. The process involves factors involved in doing the analysis and its procedures—free association, transference, regression, alliance, countertransference, and so on. For the distinction see Moore and Fine (1990).

2. The focus here is on material reality as opposed to psychic reality. There are discussible questions as to what kind of reality holds primary place in the analytic situation and process (Schwaber 1983b; Modell 1990, 1991).

3. Tallmer's (1989) questionnaire study of death attitudes among analysts included data on a patient group consisting of candidates in analytic training who had experienced death of a training analyst. The reactions varied according to whether the death was sudden or anticipated, the stage of the transference, whether the patient had suffered early losses, and the sort of defenses involved. Early signs of physical and behavioral change in the analyst were often observed even before the candidates were told about the illness. The greater the degree of neutrality and anonymity preserved by the analyst, the larger the scope for fantasies

and fears. Particular issues affecting the patients' responses were how and from whom they learned of the analyst's actual or impending death, the question of referral, and the form of participation in death rituals (e.g., funeral, memorial service). See Kaplan's (1993) case material and discussion of these issues.

4. Tallmer (1989) collected interesting confirmatory data on this question. Responses to a questionnaire on death attitudes distributed to a large group of older analysts included 32 who had discussed the question of their own death with patients, 11 who had dealt with it in a limited and superficial way, and 51 who had not discussed it at all. Replies of this latter group suggest the degree to which discomfort with the subject may have motivated their avoidance. Common defenses were intellectualization, projection, and denial.

5. Cohen (1983) raises an interesting question regarding whether the therapist should communicate information about the patient to a colleague for purposes of referral and whether this constitutes a violation of confidentiality. Such an arrangement may be one option for a given patient, but nothing should be done without approval of the patient. A discussion of whether referral is advisable, whether this is the patient's wish, to whom, and under what circumstances is entirely consistent with the demands of the alliance. Confidentiality, then, would not be at issue. Similar arrangements might be made in any circumstance in which therapy might be transferred to another therapist—e.g., moving, retirement, military service, and so on.

6. Keeping the focus here on terminal illness, the literature is somewhat more generous than that dealing with death of the analyst or therapist. Many analysts and therapists have shared their experience in the treatment of dying patients. The literature includes Coolidge (1969), Dahlberg (1980), Eissler (1955), Gifford (1969), Hildebrand (1992), Norton (1963), Saul (1959), Schwartz and Karasu (1977), and Segal (1958).

7. For issues specific to treatment of children who have suffered loss of a parent or loved one, see Barnes (1964), Birtchnell et al. (1973), Furman (1964), Lebovici (1974), Miller (1971), Nagera (1970), and Plank and Plank (1978). I shall not discuss these problems, but the principles relevant to the alliance are equally applicable.

8. On the question of interruptions and absences in therapy, see Nadelson (1993). For a sensitive treatment of loss in the life of the therapist, see Givelber and Simon (1981).

9. Chronic disabilities also create special problems, e.g., deafness (Farber 1953). For more extended discussion of chronic disabilities and their implications, see Asch and Rousso (1985).

10. The differential between absences of the analyst and those of the patient with regard to payment for missed sessions will be taken up in chapter 9.

11. See reviews in Schwartz (1987), Lasky (1990a), and Grunebaum (1993). Also see Blum's (1994a) comments on the Freud-Ferenczi controversy in this respect.

12. See also Grunebaum (1993).

13. See also Lasky (1990a). For a divergent opinion see Rosner (1986).

14. The issues and dynamics are similar even when the illness is brief and leaves no observable sequelae. See van Dam (1987).

15. This point was underlined by Eissler (1975) as well. See also the excellent discussion of these issues in Durban et al. (1993) and Grunebaum (1993).

16. Freud finally had to refer the Wolf Man to Ruth Mack Brunswick, but there is some question as to whether the Wolf Man's hypochondriacal preoccupations with his nose and mouth may have been influenced by Freud's oral cancer (Durban et al. 1993).

17. See Grotjahn's (1952) account of continuing to analyze despite acute renal colic.

18. See also the review by Kaplan (1993).

Chapter 7. Gender-Related and Accidental Factors

1. Issues related to transgressions of sexual boundaries in the therapeutic setting will be discussed as violations of the therapeutic frame (chapter 9) and as ethical violations (chapter 14). My focus here is on the intersection of reality and transference and their impact on the alliance.

2. Renik (1990) reported a case of homosexual transference in a female patient toward a male analyst. The gender of the analyst also plays a determining role in treatment of children (Tyson 1980). The function of differing gender roles in the therapy of female patients is explored in Kaplan (1985).

3. Canestri (1993) suggests that transference love can manifest itself in same sex dyads, whether male or female, without necessarily involving homosexual implications. By the same token, social stereotypes can influence other aspects of the analytic relation. Kaplan (1979) suggested that male and female therapists differed in their approaches to both authority and empathy, females being strong on empathy and weak on authority, males the opposite. The dichotomy has to be weak at best and has to yield to the capacity for better trained, more experienced, or more gifted therapists to transcend such stereotypes.

4. This configuration is assumed in Freud's (1915a) paper on transference love (Person 1993).

5. Difficulties arising when the therapist is going through a divorce (Johansen 1993) or when both therapist and patient are involved in divorces (Trench 1993)—both gender-related and reality-based vicissitudes—can affect the therapist's countertransference and undermine the alliance.

6. Useful accounts of analytic processes in which pregnancy became an issue are provided by Appelbaum (1988), Blitzer and Murray (1964), Deben-Mager (1993), Etchegoyen (1993), Fox (1958), Friedman (1993), Goldberger (1991), Hannett (1949), Lax (1969), Lester and Notman (1988), Mariotti (1993), Pines (1988, 1990), Rose (1961), and Silver and Campbell (1988). Uyehara et al. (1995) provide a useful survey of common issues experienced especially in candidates with first control cases—a first pregnancy may often coincide with a first control.

7. Charles (1993) challenges this common view on the grounds that empirical studies to support this conclusion are lacking. My argument and clinical experience support the position of Gutheil et al.

8. Currently draconian and legally inexcusable circumstances are exemplified in the treatment of psychiatrist Margaret Bean-Bayog. Her career and professional life were destroyed on the basis of unsubstantiated accusations foisted by the patient's family, the Massachusetts Board of Registration in Medicine, the media, and legal exploitation. Her fault, if any can be found, was in bending the boundaries of the therapeutic frame and in undertaking heroic measures to deal with her patient's psychosis and suicidality. The message to all practitioners is clear—if you try to heal the pain of another beyond certain limits, you will be punished for it. The fallout is that mental health professionals will shy away from treating patients who might need it most—suicidal patients and other severely disturbed patients. See the discussion of the Bean-Bayog case by Maltsberger (1993) and the more developed account in Chafetz and Chafetz (1994).

9. Additional studies of the variations on this theme can be found in Dias and Chebari (1987), Meers (1970), and Panel (1968). Also, references cited above regarding interracial analyses may also involve cultural variants.

10. See also Kogan (1993), who addresses problems of conducting analysis with off-

spring of Holocaust survivors under siege and the threat of missile and gas attacks from Iraq during the Gulf War. She writes: "During the Gulf War, the psychoanalytic setting became a sealed room, which could change at any moment from a consultation room into a shelter against a chemical attack. When a missile was about to fall during a session, both patient and analyst put on the gas masks that Israelis carried with them everywhere. At such times, patients shared life-threatening moments with their analysts—which certainly had a deep effect upon the analysis" (p. 803).

11. The structure of psychoanalytic training facilities may also erode confidentiality in the transmission, use, and processing of candidate information. See Dulchin and Segal (1982a, 1982b).

12. The countertransference implications and reverberations of extended vacations are discussed in de Urtubey (1995).

13. See the further discussion of these issues in chapter 12.

14. Technical and countertransferential difficulties involved in accepting gifts in analysis are discussed by Talan (1989).

Chapter 9. The Therapeutic Framework

1. Quinodoz (1992) argues that the frame serves a containing function, reflecting "the whole complex of conditions needed to generate the particular psychical and affective relationship between analyst and patient whereby a process can become established" (p. 627). See my comments on the alliance and the containing function in chapter 1. See also Milner (1952), Rycroft (1958), and Winnicott (1954).

2. Many of the issues of maintaining boundaries and being able to flexibly adapt boundaries when it makes clinical sense are embedded in the discussion regarding the use of the couch in psychoanalysis. A series of useful perspectives on this question can be found in an issue of *Psychoanalytic Inquiry* (Moraitis 1995).

3. Freud exceeded the therapeutic boundaries and violated the frame more than once —the Rat Man and Wolf Man are only leading examples—and some instances ended disastrously. Mahony (1993) cites the Frick case, among others.

4. Some of the deeper implications and meaning of time and its management in therapy are discussed by Ingram (1979).

5. With such patients, when I have exhausted all resources for confrontation, clarification, interpretation, and limit-setting within the therapeutic context, I set a parameter excluding all unscheduled therapy hours. I then determine with the patient what immediate resources are available in the face of severe anxiety or regressive turmoil. If there is an emergency, it is better for the patient to go to an acute facility, such as a hospital emergency room. Then the therapy can later explore what was involved in the emergency.

6. The physical presence of patient with therapist provides a multiplicity of channels of communication, with particular emphasis on affective communication, that one is deprived of over the phone. See Brenneis (1994b).

I am unsympathetic with the view of Dickes (1967), who rationalized open telephone contacts as increasing the reality of the analyst in the therapeutic relation, thereby strengthening the alliance. Again, the failure to distinguish reality and alliance causes confusion in such thinking. From my perspective, increasing the analyst's reality by eroding boundaries of the therapeutic frame acts counter to the therapeutic alliance, tending more toward misalliance than alliance.

7. A new wrinkle is a 900-number called the "Solutions Line" that has been instituted

as a form of brief therapy. I regard this as a variant of the call-in function of emergency help centers—perhaps useful in terms of crisis intervention but having little long-term therapeutic impact.

8. Again as a matter of personal preference, I do not give patients my private telephone number, and on rare occasions when patients have been able to gain access to it, I make it clear that that is not a channel over which I am willing to communicate with the patient and immediately terminate the conversation. The only number I give patients is my office phone, where access is limited and easily controlled.

9. The lack of fee in the Wolf Man case may have complicated the transference and contributed to a therapeutic misalliance (Langs 1976; Meissner 1977, 1979c).

10. Balsam and Balsam (1974) have contributed a useful discussion of this matter. Eissler (1974) noted that excessive sacrifice on the part of either analyst or patient may introduce masochistic gratification. See also Rothstein's (1995) useful account of beginning analysis with a low fee.

11. My own approach is to bill regularly on a monthly basis and to expect payment of the current bill within the month. If a balance appears on the bill I may inquire about it or not, depending on the degree of reliability and responsibility of the patient. For some patients, nonpayment may reflect hidden deviations from the alliance or other motives related to transferential or resistance factors. Areas of difficulty include nonpayment (Gedo 1963; Hilles 1971; Reider 1977), insurance (Gabbard et al. 1991; Halpert 1972a, 1972b, 1985; Jimenez 1993; Pasternack 1977), or other forms of third-party payment (Eissler 1974; Langs 1976; Rivinus 1977).

12. I have discussed details of charging for missed appointments in chapter 6.

13. See the case of Karen in Meissner (1978). Another account of difficulties created by reducing the fee can be found in Jimenez' (1993) report of this complication in the treatment of a narcissistic and paranoid borderline man. Special considerations come into play in clinics charging no fees or low fees (Lorand and Console 1958; Meyerson and Epstein 1976) and in the treatment of wealthy patients (Eissler 1974). See also Alexander (1954). Langs (1976) argued that any modification of a basic fee will result in transference gratification, increased resistance, and possible misalliance. This can happen, in my view, when the reduced fee is not contained by the alliance.

14. See my reflections on Renik's (1995a) recommendations regarding self-disclosure in the notes to chapter 5.

15. For a divergent opinion regarding the touching taboo, see McLaughlin (1995). While his bid for a measure of flexibility is appealing and in many ways sensible, I would want to balance it with a word of caution regarding the potential countertransference risks and especially for the erosion of alliance factors.

16. Sexual contact between therapist and patient is generally regarded as an ethical violation, but I am treating it here specifically as a boundary violation. Transgression of sexual boundaries wreaks havoc with present and often future therapies and often reflects some pathology in the therapist (Apfel and Simon 1985a, 1985b; Gabbard 1994b; Notman 1993; Pope 1994).

17. I was struck by Levenson's (1992) summary statement: "The cardinal mistake in psychoanalysis is to assume that the patient is sick, distorting, developmentally impaired. The reification of the patient *qua* patient has the effect of protecting the therapist against his or her anxiety, fosters a subtle disdain for the patient, and reinforces the assumption that the patient needs the therapist to explain the patient's life, or to rectify failures in relationships in the patient's earlier life" (p. 569). Taken at face value, the statement from the side of the

therapist describes a severe countertransference distortion, and, from the side of the patient, a neurotic self-image and a reflection of infantile needs and wishes. But it is still true that the patient seeks therapy precisely because he is sick, distorting, and developmentally impaired, that the assignment of the patient to the patient role and an effort to define the patient's problem in some theoretical context is what therapists do and why patients pay them to do it. This seems perfectly compatible with the therapeutic alliance. The further implication that such an approach fosters disdain of the patient and self-inflation on the part of the therapist strays over the line into countertransference.

Chapter 10. Empathy and Alliance

1. The analytic instrument is delicately balanced between a subjective, empathic, introspective stance and a more objective, observational perspective (Jacobson 1993; Treurniet 1980). The integration of these and other sources of information provides the basis for the analytic process (Meissner 1989, 1991; Spencer and Balter 1990). The pre-analytic emergence of the concept of empathy, particularly in the work of Theodor Lipps and his development of *Einfühlung,* and the extensive influence of these ideas on Freud, are traced effectively by Pigman (1995). Pigman notes that empathy came to play an essential role not only in the interaction between analyst and analysand, but also in development of psychoanalytic aesthetics. See also Kris' (1952) observations in this regard.

2. Cavell (1993) makes the point, "First, 'empathy' cannot be a matter of my getting somehow outside my own mind and into yours, but rests rather in discovering and widening the common base we share, exercising my imagination in regard to the beliefs and desires you may have in respect to which your behavior seems more or less reasonable to you" (p. 34). Spence (1993) concurs that "our view of what the other is thinking or feeling is always coloured by our theory of mind" (p. 736). See also Levine (1994) on the same issue. The problem of "other minds" addressed here continues to bedevil philosophical reflection (Pigman 1995).

3. Beres and Arlow (1974) note the more mature functions that contribute to empathic capacity, including developed ego functions and a sufficiency of meaningful human experience as well. See also Levy (1985) and Buie (1981).

4. This consideration also has weight in the self psychology perspective. Schwaber (1979) noted that attuning oneself to the intrapsychic reality of another should not prejudice integrity of one's own self-experience and requires maintenance of one's own autonomy.

5. Greenson (1960) distinguished empathy, a preconscious and temporary experience, from identification, which is essentially unconscious and more permanent. I shall return to the question of the relation between alliance and forms of internalization in chapter 18.

6. Shapiro (1974) acknowledged the difficulty with the notion of "trial identification" and tried to salvage it—unsuccessfully, to my reading. See also Basch's (1983) discussion.

7. See also Tansey and Burke (1985, 1989).

8. Blum (1982) observes not only that good parenting depends on a good deal more than empathy, but that a mother who is only empathic with her frightened and crying child is not of much use if she too is frightened and crying. An analyst who only identifies empathically with his depressed patient does the patient little good by becoming depressed. The direction taken by Lacan (1977, 1981), according to which the experience we have of ourselves and each other is radically alienated by the unconscious, runs counter to the Kohutian perspective (Hamburg 1991).

9. Shapiro (1974) suggests ways in which empathy can be used defensively as a mask

for projection. This question and the relevant distinctions are discussed more fully in chapter 3 on the relation between alliance and countertransference.

10. Some clarifications may be useful at this point. Empathy involves an affective attunement to the other that reads the other in the appropriate register; whereas transference is experienced as transference and not as real. Experiencing it as real is a form of countertransference. Real aspects of the other can similarly be experienced as real; to take them for transference is a form of countertransference. Neither the psychic reality of the analyst (countertransference) nor the psychic reality of the patient (transference) is determinative or normative; to take either as reflecting the real is also countertransference. It is as much a countertransference vicissitude for the analyst to claim his view of reality as representative as to claim that his empathic attunement is in itself a valid index of the patient's subjective state (Brickman 1993). On these terms, then, to take Freud's unobjectionable positive transference as equivalent to therapeutic alliance would be a form of countertransference.

11. Effective use of empathy can be compounded by misconceptions and misuses of it in the therapeutic process. Greenson (1960) spoke of the "pathology of empathy," in the form of either inhibition or excess, the latter signaled by failure to shift back to an observant stance after participation in the patient's feeling. Book (1988) discusses semantic confusions (with sympathy, kindness, approval, or unquestioning acceptance of the patient's experience—a danger in the overemphasis on the patient's psychic reality as determinative), conceptual difficulties (failure to distinguish empathic attunement and empathic responses, mirroring or otherwise communicating empathic understanding), countertransference difficulties (using empathy for purposes of defense or gratification), and technical misuses (overlooking layering in the patient's affective experience or levels of self-other differentiation).

12. Commenting on his patient's need for an affirming and reassuring response from him, Feldman (1993b) wrote: "While it is undoubtedly true that my patient sought the comfort and gratification of an analyst responding in a benign, unquestioning and appreciative way to what he had brought, I was not convinced that he either expected me simply to accept what he had brought without thinking, or that if I had done so it would have provided any more than a temporary and uneasy reassurance. I believe he would consciously or unconsciously have recognised that my enactment of the phantasy of the benign, affectionate mother would have been partly based on my own anxieties and needs—for example on my need to split off and deny any connection between his rejecting mother and myself, and my wish to feel valued and loved by my patient" (p. 283).

13. The patient may simply lack the capacity or willingness to engage empathically with the analyst. Gehrie (1993) cites a case in which therapeutic impasse was due neither to failure of optimal empathy nor to a countertransference problem of the analyst, but to "a reflection of a fundamental inability of this patient to distinguish between past and present, and to process intentionality" (p. 1086).

14. Some analysts make a point of dealing explicitly with technical errors to avoid undermining the therapeutic alliance (Greenson 1967; Langs 1976).

15. Goldberg (1987a) notes that the analyst can find himself apologizing on the basis of his sense of failure to live up to an impossible standard of empathic understanding—another countertransference trap.

16. The technical aspects of stopping disturbances of the alliance are addressed in chapter 16.

17. Jackson's (1992) fine paper connects the work of Schröder, Deutsch, and Ferenczi with Rogers's client-centered therapy and Kohut's self psychology.

18. F. J. Levine (1993) notes the conceptual drift in Kohut's usage of empathy, from an

observational method to its later efferent or communicative meaning. H. B. Levine (1983) adds the clarifying note that "empathy" is a form of understanding as opposed to something the therapist does: "To say something that a therapist or parent did was or was not 'empathic' is a bit of short hand. Actions, other than the act of comprehending, may follow from an empathic understanding and so gain the qualifying adjective, 'empathic,' but these actions are not to be confused with that particular form of understanding itself, which we call 'empathy' " (p. 165). Basch (1983) also noted that common usage tends to interpret selfish or manipulative affective attunement—the confidence man or demagogue, for example—as "unempathic," and altruistic or helpful intentions toward another as "empathic," even though the same affective communicative process is at work.

19. In addition, some evidence suggests that the distinction between empathic attunement and empathic communication is clinically valid. Differences in the evaluation of therapist empathy in brief dynamic therapy by patients, therapists, and supervisors reflect differential focus on empathic understanding by therapists and supervisors, and a focus on empathic communication by patients. See Free et al. (1985) and Frayn (1993) on the role of empathic statements.

Another important consideration pertains to the distinction between empathic listening and the encompassing conditions within which it becomes possible. The difference is clearly illustrated in Schwaber's (1995) contribution to the linkage between empathic listening and interpretation. The preoccupation for her falls on the listening process and its vicissitudes, especially its revelations of transference, countertransference, and transference/countertransference interactions. She pays little attention to the antecedent conditions within which not only her listening, but also the patient's meaningful self-expression, his capacity to remain affectively connected, and his ability to attune himself to her input and to accept her interpretive interventions, are realized. These matters all pertaining to the therapeutic alliance which provide the therapeutic structure and context within the listening process takes place.

20. This view of empathy is found also in Basch (1983), Chessick (1985, 1989), Fleming (1972), Kanzer (1981), Levy (1985), Spencer and Balter (1990), Stone (1981), and Strupp (1973).

21. Chessick (1989) accepts the validity of Schwaber's listening stance but argues that it is but one of a number of listening perspectives required for a more comprehensive listening process. Makari and Shapiro (1993) question whether the myth of an empathically attuned observer of another's subjectivity deserves any less skepticism than the myth of a purely objective external observer.

Arlow (1995) comments on the contemporary emphasis on listening from the perspective of countertransference enactments—what he calls "stilted listening." Commenting on Schwaber's (1992) reported exchange between herself and her patient, in which careful attention to countertransference elements was central, Arlow observes: "Recent contributions by Schwaber (1992), Renik (1993), Jacobs (1986), and others focus on the special attention that must be paid to so-called countertransference enactments. The analyst is advised to direct his or her attention and interest during the session and afterwards toward his/her own reactions, to try to understand the genesis of his/her untoward responses, and to clarify these issues with the patient. The danger here is that it may shift the attention away from the flow of the patient's associations in response to the analyst's interventions onto issues concerning the analyst's theoretical orientation or transient, personal anxieties. Under such circumstances, listening may become confused, overly theoretical, and intellectual in orientation" (pp. 226–227). He then adds, "The focus, however, must remain fixed on the stream of the patient's associations, on the context and the contiguity of the elements in his productions" (p. 229). Listening from the vantage point of the analyst's subjectivity can be recommended to the extent that it facilitates the process, but one should not lose sight of the fact that it is the patient we are trying to understand so that the subjective orientation must complement and not replace objective components of our experience of the patient.

See also Roy Schafer's (1995) effort to focus the tension between objectivity and subjectivity in the thinking of Heinz Hartmann and analysis more generally.

22. Pine (1992) focuses some of the limits of empathy's curative effect on developmental failures.

23. Spence (1982) delineated a series of frameworks or interpretive axioms for psychoanalytic listening, only one of which was empathy. The linguistic and narrative aspects of listening are further discussed by Makari and Shapiro (1993). Jacobs (1973, 1991) has even pointed to the role of bodily kinesic movements as vehicles for empathic understanding.

24. The debate over the role of empirical and theoretical or conceptual factors in psychoanalysis is alive and well—see the exchange of letters between Schwaber and Hamilton (1993). Paniagua (1995) argues to the differential effects of clinical theories specifically on clinical activity. See Meissner (1989, 1991); Stein (1991). Raphling (1995) recognizes the inevitability of the analyst's personal influence on the analysand as an essential component of the analytic process. Every interpretation carries its burden of advocacy and elicits a transference response from the patient, and that recognizing and dealing with these influences is preferable to attempting to minimize or mute them. See my discussion of the role of personal values in the analytic process in chapter 14.

The antithetic view—the opposite pole of the tension between theoretically neutral and theoretically informed empathic listening—is posed by Schwaber (1995). She properly cautions against allowing one's theoretical perspective to intrude on and interfere with analytic listening. Certain points in her argument, however, deserve qualification. The assumption that analysts uniformly take their own experience as more truthful than the patient's can be challenged. The potential for countertransference distortion should not override the capacity for balanced assessment of the experience of both parties as required for empathic listening within the therapeutic alliance context. In addition, the assumption that explaining is equivalently explaining *away* deserves challenge. Her example of the misuse of theory as overriding the patient's experience draws us to the conclusion not that the analysis is incorrect, but that it was misused. Her inference that theory is an interference rather than an aid to empathic understanding is misleading.

25. Modell (1976) views empathy and understanding as aspects of the holding environment, an alliance variant (see chapter 1).

Chapter 11. Personal Qualities in the Alliance

1. Stone (1961) cast his discussion of trust in transference terms, but the distinction of basic versus secondary trust follows a similar progression. He related basic trust to the primary transference as a reflection of primary maternal symbiotic union. Secondary trust would thus be related to the mother of separation.

2. I shall discuss this model further in regard to the issue of authority in the alliance in chapter 12.

3. That Lacan was Loewenstein's analysand lends a curious historical note to this discussion, suggesting that many of the unresolved transference issues between them revolved around issues of autonomy.

4. Modell seems to equate autonomy with agency or mastery in the self—a view with ample philosophical support. To take one such definition: "Autonomy involves the process of assessing facts and their likely consequences in terms of one's stable values and beliefs and undertaking voluntary decisions or actions on this basis" (McCullough 1984). Autonomy so defined is both conscious and rational, and thus consistent with a view of agency as conscious and as an ego function. I would regard the agency of the self as more far-reaching and complex (see Meissner 1993).

5. The main protagonist for the cause of unequivocal autonomy of mental patients has been Szasz (1963, 1974a, 1974b). His rather extreme libertarian views have been contested on several fronts, in particular that to regard mental patients as fully autonomous may not serve their interests (Laor 1982).

Chapter 12. Personal Factors: Authority, Freedom, Responsibility

1. Ferenczi's efforts to undercut the authoritative structure of the analytic relation led to some unfortunate consequences, but he and Rank (1924) were writing in a context in which authoritarian views prevailed, in which it was assumed that the analyst knew best. They, in turn, adopted an authoritarian stance in the interest of shortening treatment (Friedman 1994). As Benjamin (1994) notes: "The attitude of adoration or submission is, of course, an important constituent of the respect for authority figures. The problem of submission to or compliance with authority was central to Freud's efforts to take psychoanalysis out of the sphere of manipulation, hypnosis, or persuasion and make it a rational science that appealed to the patient's own powers. Yet the subtext of Freud's central writings on the transference can be seen as the conflict between the conceptions of psychoanalysis as submission to the physician's rational authority and as a project of liberation. Certainly Freud believed that the analytic situation evoked the erotic transference, as does any physician-patient relationship, because of the physician's charismatic authority, and that this evocation was dangerous indeed" (p. 539).

2. The paradigmatic experiments demonstrating the propensity for subjects to submit to authority figures unquestioningly were those of Milgram (1965).

3. The analyst's authority is not rooted in transference only, as Freud (1916–17) seems to have inferred. See Kanzer (1981), citing Freud: "For the analyst is then called upon to persuade the patient's weak ego 'to transfer to us the authority of his superego' so that we can serve him precisely 'in various functions, as an authority and a substitute for his parents, as a teacher and educator' (Freud 1940, p. 181)" (p. 76). This view of authority, in addition to reflecting Freud's paternalistic bias (Schafer 1993), is congruent with Strachey's (1934) classic formulation of the therapeutic action of psychoanalysis (see Meissner 1991). But such authority lies outside the alliance.

4. Caution is required in interpreting formulations like "Transference desire . . . creates the other as authority" (Gargiulo 1989, p. 154). See also Benjamin (1994) for the opposite canard: "the control, order, and boundaries set by the authority figure actually excite and evoke the wish for erotic submission" (p. 540). Whether one regards transference as evoking authority or vice versa, the proposition contains a truth, but not the whole truth. If desire gives rise to authority as transference, or if transference gives rise to submission, the authority relation involves a good deal more than can be accounted for by transference. In fact, even expert authority can be called into question. Horwitz (1994) notes with regard to consultation: "The idealized scenario of patients who present themselves for examination, receive the therapist's recommendation gratefully and unquestioningly, and follow it obe-

diently and compliantly occurred rarely, if ever, in the past and occurs even less often today. . . . In recent years, the veneer of the infallibility of the expert has worn thin, and patients have correctly been educated not only to be an active part of the process, but also to ask questions about it" (pp. 113–114). See also Friedman (1994).

5. I emphasize the authoritarian-authoritative distinction, in terms of which the analyst should always be, and at his best is, authoritative. But if he is authoritative in his own realm, so too is the patient in his, mutatis mutandis. The analyst should never assume an authoritarian position; to do so sets up a therapeutic misalliance and may express a transference/countertransference interaction. In this respect, Renik's (1995a) assault on anonymity as contributing to the analyst's authority may lead to throwing the baby out with the bath. As he puts it: "I believe Hoffman's (1994) candid admission goes to the heart of the matter: 'The magical aspect of the analyst's authority is enhanced by his or her . . . anonymity. There is a kind of mystique about the analysis that I doubt we want to dispel completely' (p. 198). We may not want to dispel it, but I think we should!" (p. 481). His argument that the analyst can never be effectively anonymous and that the myth of complete analytic anonymity can well be dispelled is essentially correct, but it requires to be complemented by the equally valid idea that the analyst can never fully divest himself of the mantle of authority. His engagement in the analytic process should strive to be authoritative and not authoritarian. Hoffman's "magical aspect of the analyst's authority" is that aspect of authority based on transference; he does not address the aspect of authority based in the alliance—nor does Renik. The transferential aspect of authority cannot be dispensed with, but it can be explored, interpreted, and in some degree resolved. The alliance aspect is one of the factors contributing to the analytic structure, should not be dispensed with, and is open to scrutiny and exploration at any point in the analysis. It is not to be done away with, but has to be brought into meaningful and constructive integration with the patient's emergent authority.

6. Benjamin seems to view the process exclusively in transference terms, but more is involved in this potential identification. We hope for authentic identifications, derived from the therapeutic alliance, rather than introjections from transference. See my further discussion of the role of internalization in chapter 18.

7. An excess of authoritarian certitude and reliance on theory or knowledge can set the therapist up as a target for the patient's wish to beat him at his own game (Levine 1972).

8. I agree with Kernberg's (1993) comment that avoidance of this authoritative role in the interest of empathy, avoidance of authoritarian excess or any imposition on the patient may risk falling into sadomasochistic transference/countertransference deviations quite as much as an excessive dose of such authority.

9. In many adolescent patients, any submission to establishment (authority) figures, including the therapist, may be regarded as an intolerable compromise because establishment types are automatically regarded as suppressive and hostile to freedom (Zuger 1972). The alliance can be a crucial and troublesome aspect of therapy with such patients.

10. On the tension between freedom and determinism in psychoanalysis, see Holt (1965), Meissner (1984b), Wallace (1985), and Wallwork (1991).

11. Ferrell et al. (1984) describe "volitional disability" in relation to noncompliance—a form of resistance—in phobic, compulsive, and addicted patients. The disability is a failure of such patients to take responsibility for their behavior and to adopt effective action. To the extent that it might imply an innate inability to take responsibility, I would challenge it. If adopting this latter view might help to avoid one form of countertransference—avoidance of judgment or anger at the patient—it is equally likely to lead to another.

12. This is one aspect of Schafer's (1976) action language that has merit. Emphasis on the action aspect of all behaviors, whether seemingly passive or not, including feelings, reinforces patient responsibility. The patient's use of language to disown responsibility—"I didn't have any choice," or, "My feelings were too overwhelming," for example—can be confronted and clarified. Another ploy is the use of *need* for *wish* or *want*. Need often involves a disavowal of responsibility, whereas want or wish places the responsibility where it belongs (Halleck 1982, 1988).

Chapter 13. Ethical Dimensions: Confidentiality

1. See also Person (1993), Hernández (1993), and Canestri (1993).
2. See Pellegrino's (1979) excellent discussion of the role of ethical perspectives, not only in medicine but in all the healing professions. Consistent with the view of alliance in this study, Pellegrino emphasized the ethical function and responsible participation of the patient in the therapeutic process. Levine (1972) focused on "creative alliance" as one of the major expressions of ethical perspective in human affairs—specifically with respect to the therapeutic alliance.
3. A useful set of guidelines formulated by the Massachusetts Board of Registration in Medicine in collaboration with other professional therapeutic groups is reproduced in the appendix.
4. In the present discussion, confidentiality will include both confidentiality and privacy in Szasz's terms.
5. Even in hospital inpatient units, where sharing of information about the patient is essential to staff functioning, information conveyed by the therapist should be tailored according to the therapeutic need of the staff and the right to privacy of the patient (Schwartz 1984). The demands of confidentiality can never be abrogated.

Another context where issues of confidentiality arise is in the training of psychoanalytic candidates. The candidate undertakes a required training analysis in which strict confidentiality is mandatory. But for purposes of evaluating the candidate's progression, often information is sought from the training analyst. Various institutes resolve this problem in different ways, one of which is that the training analyst provides no information regarding the candidate's analysis other than when it began and when it was completed. Some of these issues have been discussed in Dulchin and Segal (1982a). See Dulchin and Segal (1982b) for further discussion of the related issue of utilization of confidences from outside third parties. See also the discussion in chapter 7.

6. In Lipton's (1991) brief survey, most analysts did not ask permission, and most tried to report only on terminated cases.
7. As Agich (1985) notes, preservation of confidentiality, even in the general medical context, is governed by the responsibility for preserving the patient's autonomy. This is also a delicate issue in treating adolescents. Schimel (1974) emphasized the importance of candor in developing trust with adolescent patients: "Being candid requires a consideration of the total situation, an expressed awareness of what is true and what is dubious, a dispassionate impartiality, an often hard-won freedom from (or a suspension of) bias and prejudice, as well as a disposition to be favorable or lenient. Trust is candor's counterpart" (p. 251).
8. However, the therapist's own private jottings, musings, and notes to himself are not the patient's property or the property of anyone else except the therapist. The patient should not be given access to them in any form, nor should anyone else.

Chapter 14. Ethical Dimensions: Values

1. See the discussion of freedom in chapter 12.

2. Self-understanding places a high value on truthfulness, openness, and integrity in the analytic transaction (Vanderpool and Weiss 1984). The data on patient deceptiveness and noncompliance indicate that patients are not always truthful or cooperative, from motives of shame, embarrassment, guilt, denial, independence, or a variety of issues of secondary gain. Whatever the motive, deception of self or analyst undermines the therapeutic alliance.

Chapter 15. Establishing the Therapeutic Alliance

1. The narcissistic alliance, as developed here, overlaps the concept of selfobject transferences in significant ways. The narcissistic alliance responds to selfobject needs when and to the extent that they may be operative in a given patient. For many healthier, narcissistically better consolidated patients, these needs remain background features of the analysis. These patients tend to present fewer problems in developing a therapeutic alliance.

Chapter 16. Therapeutic Management of Alliance Deviations

1. See Hani 1973.

2. An unusual series of such unsuccessful cases can be found in Panel 1993a.

3. Winnicott (1956) noted that resistance always indicates some mistake by the analyst that remains until it is uncovered and dealt with. The "always" may be a bit strong.

4. The supportive aspect of the therapeutic alliance differs from supportive interventions—persuasion, advice, encouragement, manipulation—that undermine the therapeutic alliance and suggest underlying misalliances (Greenacre 1959).

5. In an interesting sidelight, the descriptions provided by Stolorow and his collaborators (Stolorow et al. 1987; Stolorow 1993) and other self psychology theorists (Wolf 1993) for repairing ruptures in selfobject transference ties are comparable to techniques for restoring therapeutic alliance disruptions. Wolf lists three factors: (1) an explanation that makes sense to the patient, (2) a positive affective experience in relation to the analyst's empathic stance, and (3) the patient's sense of having an effective role in modifying the analyst's posture. In their view the selfobject tie is restored, whereas my perspective focuses on therapeutic alliance. The question that perplexes me is whether the selfobject needs underlying selfobject transferences are the same as the restored selfobject transferences which undergird the progression to more effective analytic treatment. They seem to me to be different—the latter being synonymous with the therapeutic alliance, the former, not. Selfobject theorists apparently do not recognize any difference.

6. This sort of reaction seems to have occurred in Freud's experience with the Rat Man (Freud 1909; Kanzer 1952).

7. Langs (1975a, 1975b, 1976) pointed to the potential for "misalliance cures."

Chapter 17. Interpretation

1. I would offer a word in passing on the relation of this view of interpretation with the form of hermeneutic deconstruction—or, as Laplanche (1992) calls it, "creative hermeneutic"—emerging in psychoanalytic circles. The issue is alive in viewpoints espoused by Spence (1982) on narrative truth and Schafer (1981) on narrative action in psychoanalysis. The

hermeneutic emphasis on construction of meaning, whether conceived of as an aspect of the analyst's creative interpretive effort or as an aspect of the analytic dialogue (Leavy 1980), undermines neutrality and substitutes a fictive construction for understanding of the relation between the patient's psychic reality and a verifiable external (actual or historical) reality insofar as it can be determined. Criticism of this hermeneutic function and discussion of some of its philosophical underpinnings can be found in Ahumada (1994), particularly disengagement of language from its moorings in real reference, whether psychic or factual. In the interactive view of interpretation I am suggesting, creative and deconstructive elements are respected but are articulated within a not merely consensual but also realistic context. Similar risks can be entertained in the overemphasis on psychic reality to the neglect of material reality and corresponding validation. The issue comes home to roost in the problem of false memories. See the discussions in Brenneis (1994a) and Person and Klar (1994).

2. This distinction separates therapeutic alliance from an alexandrian "corrective emotional experience." Engagement in the therapeutic alliance is inherently corrective, whereas "corrective emotional experience" is a function of the real relation and remains open to therapeutic misalliance.

3. Ornstein's (Ornstein and Ornstein 1994) patient Mr. K, in his mistrustful search for "red words," found that his analyst responded with a frank and open discussion, including the analyst's uncertainty. The threat of impasse was derailed by the analyst's empathic stance. The authors comment: "We hope that the brief segments of this lengthy analysis have demonstrated that interpretations which convey acceptance and understanding as well as periodic explanations (from the patient's perspective), do indeed deepen the analytic dialogue. They do so because 'feeling understood' is a self-consolidating experience, the precondition for lessening defensive operations (Ornstein and Ornstein 1985)" (p. 993). The technique so described is perfectly congruent with the therapeutic alliance.

4. Kris (1990, 1994) noted, in relation to his view of functional neutrality, that such affirmative interpretations have particular merit in the face of the patient's tendency to self-criticism.

5. This combination of projection by the subject, introjection by the object, and pressures on the object to enact the projective role are often addressed as "projective identification,"a term that I find inaccurate and confusing. See Meissner 1980, 1987b.

Chapter 18. Internalization

1. The imitative dimension is not in itself a form of internalization, but a precursor of internalization (Meissner 1974b).

Chapter 19. Termination

1. See the discussion of the developmental aspects of the therapeutic alliance as reflecting developmental experience (chapter 8) and in the course of the analysis (chapters 11 and 12).

2. Freud's (1918) experiment with the Wolf Man of setting an arbitrary termination limit was not at all successful (Meissner 1977, 1979c) and was later seen by Freud (1937) himself as a form of blackmail: "We may be sure that, while part of the material will become accessible under the pressure of the threat, another part will be kept back and thus become buried, as it were, and lost to our therapeutic efforts" (p. 218).

References

Aarons, Z. A. 1975. The analyst's relocation: Its effect on the transference—parameter or catalyst. *International Journal of Psychoanalysis,* 56:303–320.

Abend, S. M. 1979. Unconscious fantasy and theories of cure. *Journal of the American Psychoanalytic Association,* 27:579–596.

——. 1982. Serious illness in the analyst: Countertransference considerations. *Journal of the American Psychoanalytic Association,* 30:365–375.

——. 1986. Countertransference, empathy, and the analytic ideal: The impact of life stresses on analytic capability. *Psychoanalytic Quarterly,* 5m563–575.

Abend, S. M., Porder, M. S., and Willick, M. S. 1983. *Borderline Patients: Psychoanalytic Perspectives.* New York: International Universities Press.

Adelman, S. A. 1985. Pills as transitional objects: A dynamic understanding of the use of medication in psychotherapy. *Psychiatry,* 48:246–253.

Adler, G. 1970. Valuing and devaluing in the psychotherapeutic process. *Archives of General Psychiatry,* 22:454–461.

——. 1979. The myth of the alliance with borderline patients. *American Journal of Psychiatry,* 136:642–645.

——. 1980. Transference, real relationship and alliance. *International Journal of Psychoanalysis,* 61:547–558.

——. 1985. *Borderline Psychopathology and Its Treatment.* New York: Aronson.

——. 1989. Transitional phenomena, projective identification, and the essential ambiguity of the psychoanalytic situation. *Psychoanalytic Quarterly,* 58:81–104.

Adler, G., and Myerson, P. G. 1973. Introduction. In Adler, G., and Myerson, P. G. (eds.), *Confrontation in Psychotherapy.* New York: Science House, 9–19.

Adler, J. S., and Gutheil, T. G. 1977. Fees in beginning private practice. In Gutheil, T. G. (ed.), Money as a clinical issue in psychiatry. *Psychiatric Annals,* 7:35–46.

Agger, E. M. 1993. The analyst's ego. *Psychoanalytic Inquiry,* 13:403–424.

Agich, G. J. 1985. Roles and responsibilities: Theoretical issues in the definition of consultation liaison psychiatry. *Journal of Medicine and Philosophy,* 10:105–126.

Ahumada, J. L. 1994. Interpretation and creationism. *International Journal of Psychoanalysis,* 75:695–707.

Alexander, F. 1954. Some quantitative aspects of psychoanalytic technique. *Journal of the American Psychoanalytic Association,* 2:685–701.

Alexander, L. B., Barber, J. P., Luborsky, L., Crits-Christoph, P., and Auerbach, A. 1993. On what bases do patients choose their therapists? *Journal of Psychotherapy Practice and Research,* 2:135–146.

Alger, I. 1966. The clinical handling of the analyst's responses. *Psychoanalytic Forum,* 1:289–302.

Allen, A. 1971. The fee as a therapeutic tool. *Psychoanalytic Quarterly,* 40:132–140.

Allen, J. G. 1993. Dissociative processes: Theoretical underpinnings of a working model for clinician and patient. *Bulletin of the Menninger Clinic,* 57:287–308.

Allen, J. G., Newsom, G. E., Gabbard, G. O., and Coyne, L. 1984. Scales to assess the therapeutic alliance from a psychoanalytic perspective. *Bulletin of the Menninger Clinic,* 48:383–400.

Allen, S. 1956. Reflections on the wish of the analyst to break or change the basic rule. *Bulletin of the Menninger Clinic,* 20:192–200.

American Psychiatric Association. 1973. The principles of medical ethics with annotations especially applicable to psychiatry. *American Journal of Psychiatry* 130:1057–1064.

——. 1987. Guidelines on confidentiality. *American Journal of Psychiatry,* 144: 1522–1525.

Apfel, R. J., and Simon, B. 1985a. Patient-therapist sexual contact. I. Psychodynamic perspectives on the causes and results. *Psychotherapy and Psychosomatics,* 43:57–62.

——. 1985b. Patient-therapist sexual contact. II. Problems of subsequent psychotherapy. *Psychotherapy and Psychosomatics,* 43:63–68.

Appel, G. 1974. An approach to the treatment of schizoid phenomena. *Psychoanalytic Review,* 61:99–113.

Appelbaum, A., and Diamond, D. 1993. Prologue. *Psychoanalytic Inquiry,* 13:145–152.

Appelbaum, A. H. 1988. Psychoanalysis during pregnancy: The effect of sibling constellation. *Psychoanalytic Inquiry,* 8:177–195.

Appelbaum, S. A. 1978–79. How strictly confidential? *International Journal of Psychoanalytic Psychotherapy,* 7:220–224.

——. 1992. Evils in the private practice of psychotherapy. *Bulletin of the Menninger Clinic,* 56:141–149.

Arlow, J. A. 1979. The role of empathy in the psychoanalytic process: Panel presentation. *Bulletin of the Association for Psychoanalytic Medicine,* 18:64–69.

——. 1995. Stilted listening: Psychoanalysis as discourse. *Psychoanalytic Quarterly,* 64:215–233.

Arlow, J. A., and Brenner, C. 1966. The psychoanalytic situation. In Litman, R. E. (ed.), *Psychoanalysis in the Americas.* New York: International Universities Press, 23–43, 133–138.

Asch, A., and Rousso, H. 1985. Therapists with disabilities: Theoretical and clinical issues. *Psychiatry,* 48:1–12.

Bacal, H. A. 1985. Optimal responsiveness and the therapeutic process. In *Progress in Self Psychology,* vol. 1, ed. A. Goldberg. New York: Guilford Press, 202–227.

Bacal, H. A., and Newman, K. 1990. *Theories of Object Relations: Bridges to Self Psychology*. New York: Columbia University Press.

Bader, M. J. 1993. The analyst's use of humor. *Psychoanalytic Quarterly,* 62:23–51.

——. 1994. The tendency to neglect therapeutic aims in psychoanalysis. *Psychoanalytic Quarterly,* 63:246–270.

Baker, R. 1993. The patient's discovery of the psychoanalyst as a new object. *International Journal of Psychoanalysis,* 74:1223–1233.

Balint, M. 1965. *Primary Love and Psycho-Analytic Technique*. New York: Liveright.

——. 1968. *The Basic Fault: Therapeutic Aspects of Regression*. London: Tavistock.

Balsam, R. M., and Balsam, A. 1974. *Becoming a Psychotherapist: A Clinical Primer*. Boston: Little, Brown.

Baranger, M. 1993. The mind of the analyst: From listening to interpretation. *International Journal of Psychoanalysis,* 74:15–24.

Barnes, M. J. 1964. Reactions to the death of a mother. *Psychoanalytic Study of the Child,* 19:334–357.

Barthes, R. 1982. *A Barthes Reader*, ed. S. Sontag. New York: Hill and Wang.

Basch, M. F. 1983. Empathic understanding: A review of the concept and some theoretical considerations. *Journal of the American Psychoanalytic Association,* 31:101–126.

——. 1984. Selfobjects and selfobject transference: Theoretical implications. In Stepansky, P., and Goldberg, A. (eds.), *Kohut's Legacy.* Hillsdale, N.J.: Analytic Press, 21–41.

——. 1986. How does analysis cure? An appreciation. *Psychoanalytic Inquiry,* 6: 403–428.

——. 1988. *Understanding Psychotherapy: The Science Behind the Art*. New York: Basic Books.

Bassen, C. R. 1988. The impact of the analyst's pregnancy on the course of analysis. *Psychoanalytic Inquiry,* 8:280–298.

Baudry, F. 1991. The relevance of the analyst's character and attitudes to his work. *Journal of the American Psychoanalytic Association,* 39:917–938.

Benassy, M. 1960. Fantasy and reality in transference. *International Journal of Psychoanalysis,* 41:396–400.

Benedek, T. 1953. Dynamics of the countertransference. *Bulletin of the Menninger Clinic,* 17:201–208.

Benjamin, J. 1994. What angel would hear me? The erotics of transference. *Psychoanalytic Inquiry,* 14:535–557.

Beres, D. 1968. The role of empathy in psychotherapy and psychoanalysis. *Journal of the Hillside Hospital,* 17:362–369.

——. 1971. Ego autonomy and ego pathology. *Psychoanalytic Study of the Child,* 26:3–24.

Beres, D., and Arlow, J. A. 1974. Fantasy and identification in empathy. *Psychoanalytic Quarterly,* 43:26–50.

Berezin, M. A. 1957. Note-taking during the psychoanalytic session. *Bulletin of the Philadelphia Association for Psychoanalysis,* 7:96–101.

Berg, M. D. 1977. The externalizing transference. *International Journal of Psychoanalysis,* 58:235–244.

Berger, D. M. 1984. On the way to empathic understanding. *American Journal of Psychotherapy,* 37:111–120.

Bergmann, M. S. 1993a. Reality and psychic reality in Ernst Kris's last papers: An attempt to update his findings. *Psychoanalytic Inquiry,* 13:372–383.

——. 1993b. Reflections on the history of psychoanalysis. *Journal of the American Psychoanalytic Association,* 41:929–955.

——. 1994. The challenge of erotized transference to psychoanalytic technique. *Psychoanalytic Inquiry,* 14:499–518.

Berman, L. 1949. Counter-transferences and attitudes of the analyst in the therapeutic process. *Psychiatry,* 12:159–166.

Bernal y del Rio, V. 1984. The "real" similarities and differences in the psychoanalytic dyad. *Journal of the American Academy of Psychoanalysis,* 12:31–41.

Berry, N. 1975. From fantasy to reality in the transference: A reply to the discussion by Pedro Luzes. *International Journal of Psychoanalysis,* 56:365–366.

Beskind, H., Bartels, S. J., and Brooks, M. 1993. Practical and theoretical dilemmas of dynamic psychotherapy in a small community. In Gold, J. H., and Nemiah, J. C. (eds.), *Beyond Transference: When the Therapist's Real Life Intrudes.* Washington, D.C.: American Psychiatric Press, 1–19.

Betz, B. J. 1970. Attitudinal interactions in psychotherapy. *American Journal of Psychotherapy,* 24:477–484.

Bibring, E. 1937. Therapeutic results of psycho-analysis. *International Journal of Psychoanalysis,* 18:170–189.

Bibring, G. L. 1936. A contribution to the subject of transference resistance. *International Journal of Psychoanalysis,* 17:181–189.

——. 1958. Discussion of Zetzel 1958. Meeting of the American Psychoanalytic Association, New York.

——. 1959. Some considerations of the psychological processes in pregnancy. *Psychoanalytic Study of the Child,* 14:113–121.

Bibring, G. L., Dwyer, T. F., Huntington, D. S., and Valenstein, A. F. 1961. A study of the psychological processes in pregnancy and of the earliest mother-child relationship. *Psychoanalytic Study of the Child,* 16:9–72.

Binstock, W. A. 1973. The therapeutic relationship. *Journal of the American Psychoanalytic Association,* 21:543–557.

Bion, W. R. 1962. *Learning from Experience.* In *Seven Servants: Four Works by Wilfred R. Bion.* New York: Aronson, 1977.

——. 1963. *Elements of Psychoanalysis.* In *Seven Servants: Four Works by Wilfred R. Bion.* New York: Aronson, 1977.

——. 1965. *Transformations.* In *Seven Servants: Four Works by Wilfred R. Bion.* New York: Aronson, 1977.

——. 1970. *Attention and Interpretation.* In *Seven Servants: Four Works by Wilfred R. Bion.* New York: Aronson, 1977.

——. 1985. *All My Sins Remembered: Another Part of a Life*. Abingdon, England: Fleetwood Press.

Bird, B. 1957. A specific peculiarity of acting out. *Journal of the American Psychoanalytic Association*, 5:630–647.

——. 1972. Notes on transference: Universal phenomenon and the hardest part of analysis. *Journal of the American Psychoanalytic Association*, 20:267–301.

Birtchnell, J., Wilson, I. C., Bratfos, O., et al. 1973. *Effects of Early Parent Death*. New York: MSS.

Blanck, G., and Blanck, R. 1974. *Ego Psychology: Theory and Practice*. New York: Columbia University Press.

Bleger, J. 1967. Psychoanalysis of the psychoanalytic frame. *International Journal of Psychoanalysis*, 48:513–519.

Blitzer, J. R., and Murray, J. M. 1964. On the transformation of early narcissism during pregnancy. *International Journal of Psychoanalysis*, 45:89–97.

Blum, H. P. 1971a. On the conception and development of the transference neurosis. *Journal of the American Psychoanalytic Association*, 19:41–53.

——. 1971b. Transference and structure. In Kanzer, Mark (ed.), *The Unconscious Today*. New York: International Universities Press, 117–195.

——. 1973. The concept of erotized transference. *Journal of the American Psychoanalytic Association*, 21:61–76.

——. 1981. Some current and recurrent problems of psychoanalytic technique. *Journal of the American Psychoanalytic Association*, 29:47–68.

——. 1982. Theories of the self and psychoanalytic concepts: Discussion. *Journal of the American Psychoanalytic Association*, 30:959–937.

——. 1989. The concept of termination and the evolution of psychoanalytic thought. *Journal of the American Psychoanalytic Association*, 37:275–295.

——. 1994a. The confusion of tongues and psychic trauma. *International Journal of Psychoanalysis*, 75:871–882.

——. 1994b. Discussion on the erotic transference: Contemporary perspectives. *Psychoanalytic Inquiry*, 14:622–635.

Bollas, C. 1987. *The Shadow of the Object*. London: Free Association.

——. 1989. *Forces of Destiny*. London: Free Association Books.

——. 1990. Origins of the therapeutic alliance. Weekend conference, British Psycho-Analytical Society, "Treatment Alliances: Therapeutic and Anti-Therapeutic." London, October 1990.

——. 1994. Aspects of the erotic transference. *Psychoanalytic Inquiry*, 14:572–590.

Book, H. E. 1988. Empathy: misconceptions and misuses in psychotherapy. *American Journal of Psychiatry*, 145:420–424.

Bordin, E. S. 1979. The generalizability of the psychoanalytic concept of the working alliance. *Psychotherapy: Theory, Research, and Practice*. 16:252–260.

Boris, H. N. 1973. Confrontation in the analysis of transference resistance. In Adler, G., and Myerson, P. G. (eds.), *Confrontation in Psychotherapy*. New York: Science House, 181–206.

——. 1992. The equalizing eye: Unconscious envy: III. *Contemporary Psychoanalysis*, 28:572–593.

Bornstein, M., and Silver, D. 1981. Prologue. *Psychoanalytic Inquiry,* 1:323–327.

Bouvet, M. 1958. Technical variation and the concept of distance. *International Journal of Psychoanalysis,* 39:211–221.

Boyer, L. B. 1978. Countertransference experiences with severely regressed patients. *Contemporary Psychoanalysis,* 14:48–72.

——. 1983. *The Regressed Patient.* New York: Aronson.

Boyer, L. B., and Giovacchini, P. L. 1967. *Psychoanalytic Treatment of Schizophrenic and Characterological Disorders.* New York: Aronson.

——. 1980. *Psychoanalytic Treatment of Schizophrenic, Borderline and Characterological Disorders.* 2nd ed. New York: Aronson.

Brabant, E., Falzeder, E., and Giampieri-Deutsch, P. (eds.). 1994. *The Correspondence of Sigmund Freud and Sandor Ferenczi. Vol. I, 1908–1914.* Cambridge: Harvard University Press.

Bradlow, P. A., and Coen, S. J. 1975. The analyst undisguised in the initial dream in psychoanalysis. *International Journal of Psychoanalysis,* 56:415–426.

Breggin, P. R. 1971. Psychotherapy as applied ethics. *Psychiatry,* 34:59–74.

Brenneis, C. B. 1994a. Belief and suggestion in the recovery of memories of childhood sexual abuse. *Journal of the American Psychoanalytic Association,* 42:1027–1053.

——. 1994b. Observations on psychoanalytic listening. *Psychoanalytic Quarterly,* 63:29–53.

Brenner, C. 1979. Working alliance, therapeutic alliance, and transference. *Journal of the American Psychoanalytic Association,* 27 (Suppl.): 137–157.

——. 1980. Working alliance, therapeutic alliance and transference. In Blum, H. P. (ed.), *Psychoanalytic Explorations of Technique: Discourse on the Theory of Therapy.* New York: International Universities Press, 137–157.

Breuer, J., and Freud, S. 1893–95. Studies on hysteria. *Standard Edition,* 2.

Brice, C. W. 1984. Pathological modes of human relating and therapeutic mutuality: A dialogue between Buber's existential relational theory and object-relations theory. *Psychiatry,* 47:109–123.

Brickman, H. R. 1993. "Between the devil and the deep blue sea": The dyad and the triad in psychoanalytic thought. *International Journal of Psychoanalysis,* 74:905–915.

Brodsky, B. 1959. Liebestod fantasies in a patient faced with a fatal illness. *International Journal of Psychoanalysis,* 40:13–16.

Broucek, F. J. 1991. *Shame and the Self.* New York: Guilford Press.

Bruch, H. 1973. *Eating Disorders: Obesity, Anorexia Nervosa, and the Person Within.* New York: Basic Books.

——. 1978. *The Golden Cage: The Enigma of Anorexia Nervosa.* Cambridge: Harvard University Press.

Brunswick, R. M. 1928. A supplement to Freud's "History of an infantile neurosis." *International Journal of Psychoanalysis,* 9:439–476.

Buber, M. 1958. *I and Thou.* 2nd ed. New York: Scribner's.

Buie, D. H. 1981. Empathy: Its nature and limitations. *Journal of the American Psychoanalytic Association,* 29:281–307.

Burke, W. F., and Tansey, M. J. 1985. Projective identification and countertransference turmoil: Disruptions in the empathic process. *Contemporary Psychoanalysis*, 21:372–402.

Busch, F. 1994. Some ambiguities in the method of free association and their implications for technique. *Journal of the American Psychoanalytic Association*, 42:363–384.

Canestri, J. 1993. A cry of fire: Some considerations on transference love. In Person, E. S., Hagelin, A., and Fonagy, P. (eds.), *On Freud's "Observations on Transference-love."* New Haven: Yale University Press, 146–164.

Caper, R. 1992. Does psychoanalysis heal? A contribution to the theory of psychoanalytic technique. *International Journal of Psychoanalysis*, 73:283–292.

Casement, P. J. 1982. Some pressures on the analyst for physical contact during the reliving of an early trauma. *International Review of Psychoanalysis*, 9:279–286.

Cavell, M. 1988a. Interpretation, psychoanalysis, and the philosophy of mind. *Journal of the American Psychoanalytic Association*, 36:859–879.

——. 1988b. Solipsism and community: Two concepts of mind in psychoanalysis. *Psychoanalysis and Contemporary Thought*, 11:587–613.

——. 1991. The subject of mind. *International Journal of Psychoanalysis*, 72:141–154.

——. 1993. *The Psychoanalytic Mind: From Freud to Philosophy*. Cambridge: Harvard University Press.

Cesio, F. 1993. The oedipal tragedy in the psychoanalytic process: Transference love. In Person, E. S., Hagelin, A., and Fonagy, P. (eds.), *On Freud's "Observations on Transference-love."* New Haven: Yale University Press, 130–145.

Chafetz, G. S., and Chafetz, M. E. 1994. *Obsession: The Bizarre Relationship Between a Prominent Harvard Psychiatrist and Her Suicidal Patient*. New York: Crown.

Charles, S. C. 1993. The doctor-patient relationship and medical malpractice litigation. *Bulletin of the Menninger Clinic*, 57:195–207.

Charles, S. C., Warnecke, R. B., and Wilbert, J. R., et al. 1987. Sued and nonsued physicians. *Psychosomatics*, 28:462–468.

Charles, S. C., Wilbert, J. R., and Franke, K. J. 1985. Sued and nonsued physicians' self-reported reactions to malpractice litigation. *American Journal of Psychiatry*, 142:437–440.

Charles, S. C., Wilbert, J. R., and Kennedy, E. C. 1984. Physicians' self-reports of reactions to malpractice litigation. *American Journal of Psychiatry*, 141:563–565.

Chessick, R. D. 1977. Effects of the therapist's philosophical premises on psychotherapeutic process. *American Journal of Psychotherapy*, 31:252–264.

——. 1978. Countertransference crises with borderline patients. *Current Concepts in Psychiatry* (Jan.-Feb.), 20–24.

——. 1979. A practical approach to the psychotherapy of the borderline patient. *American Journal of Psychotherapy*, 33:531–546.

——. 1982. Intensive psychotherapy of a borderline patient. *Archives of General Psychiatry*, 39:413–419.

——. 1983. Problems in the intensive psychotherapy of the borderline patient. *Dynamic Psychotherapy*, 1:20–32.

——. 1985. Psychoanalytic listening II. *American Journal of Psychotherapy*, 39:30–48.

——. 1989. *The Technique and Practice of Listening in Intensive Psychotherapy*. Northvale, N.J.: Aronson.

Chodoff, P. 1972. The effect of third-party payment on the practice of psychotherapy. *American Journal of Psychiatry*, 129:540–545.

Christie, G. L. 1994. Some psychoanalytic aspects of humour. *International Journal of Psychoanalysis*, 75:479–489.

Chrzanowski, G. 1979. Participant observation and the working alliance. *Journal of the American Academy of Psychoanalysis*, 7:259–269.

Chused, J. F. 1982. The role of analytic neutrality in the use of the child analyst as a new object. *Journal of the American Psychoanalytic Association*, 30:3–28.

——. 1991. The evocative power of enactments. *Journal of the American Psychoanalytic Association*, 39:615–639.

——. 1992. The patient's perception of the analyst: The hidden transference. *Psychoanalytic Quarterly*, 61:161–184.

Chused, J. F. and Raphling, D. L. 1992. The analyst's mistakes. *Journal of the American Psychoanalytic Association*, 40:89–116.

Clark, R. W. 1995. The pope's confessor: A metaphor relating to illness in the analyst. *Journal of the American Psychoanalytic Association*, 43:137–149.

Clifton, A. R. 1974. Regression in the search for a self. *International Journal of Psychoanalytic Psychotherapy*, 3:273–292.

Cohen, J. 1983. Psychotherapists preparing for death: Denial and action. *American Journal of Psychotherapy*, 37:222–226.

Colson, D., Lewis, L., and Horwitz, L. 1982. Negative effects in psychotherapy and psychoanalysis. In Mays, D., and Franks, C. (eds.), *Above All Do Not Harm: Negative Outcome in Psychotherapy*. New York: Aronson.

Coltart, N. 1991. The analysis of an elderly patient. *International Journal of Psychoanalysis*, 72:209–219.

Coolidge, J. C. 1969. Unexpected death in a patient who wished to die. *Journal of the American Psychoanalytic Association*, 17:413–420.

Cooper, A. M. 1986. Some limitations on therapeutic effectiveness: The "burnout syndrome" in psychoanalysis. *Psychoanalytic Quarterly*, 55:576–598.

——. 1992. Psychic change: Development in the theory of psychoanalytic techniques. *International Journal of Psychoanalysis*, 73:245–250.

Corwin, H. A. 1974. The narcissistic alliance and progressive transference neurosis in serious regressive states. *International Journal of Psychoanalytic Psychotherapy*, 3:299–316.

Couch, A. S. 1995. Anna Freud's adult psychoanalytic technique: A defense of classical analysis. *International Journal of Psychoanalysis*, 76:153–171.

Crisp, A. H., Norton, K. R. S., Jurczak, S., Bowyer, C., and Duncan, S. 1985. A treatment approach to anorexia nervosa—Twenty-five years on. *Journal of Psychiatric Research*, 19:393–404.

Curtis, H. C. 1970. Toward a metapsychology of transference. *Bulletin of the Philadelphia Association for Psychoanalysis*, 22:152–159.

——. 1979. The concept of therapeutic alliance: Implications for the "widening scope." *Journal of the American Psychoanalytic Association*, 27 (Suppl.): 159–192.

Dahlberg, C. C. 1980. Perspectives on death, dying, and illness while working with patients. *Journal of the American Academy of Psychoanalysis*, 8:369–380.

Davidson, L. 1980a. Ethnic roots, transcultural methodology and psychoanalysis. *Journal of the American Academy of Psychoanalysis*, 8:273–278.

——. 1980b. *Patients Whom Therapists Find Hard to Treat: A Cross-cultural Perspective*. Forest Hills, N.Y.: Bleuler Psychotherapy Center.

Deben-Mager, D. 1993. Acting out and transference themes induced by successive pregnancies of the analyst. *International Journal of Psychoanalysis*, 74:129–139.

De Blécourt, A. 1993. Transference, countertransference and acting out in psychoanalysis. *International Journal of Psychoanalysis*, 74:757–774.

De Jonghe, F., Rijnierse, P., and Janssen, R. 1991. Aspects of the analytic relationship. *International Journal of Psychoanalysis*, 72:693–707.

——. 1992. The role of support in psychoanalysis. *Journal of the American Psychoanalytic Association*, 40:475–499.

De Urtubey, L. 1995. Countertransference effects of absence. *International Journal of Psychoanalysis*, 76:683–694.

Devereux, G. 1953. Cultural factors in psychoanalytic therapy. *Journal of the American Psychoanalytic Association*, 1:629–655.

Dewald, P. A. 1976. Transference regression and real experience in the psychoanalytic process. *Psychoanalytic Quarterly*, 45:215–230.

——. 1982. Serious illness in the analyst: Transference, countertransference, and reality responses. *Journal of the American Psychoanalytic Association*, 30:347–363.

Diamond, D. 1993. The paternal transference: A bridge to the erotic oedipal transference. *Psychoanalytic Inquiry*, 13:206–225.

Dias, C. G., and Chebari, W. D. 1987. Psychoanalysis and the role of black life and culture in Brazil. *International Review of Psychoanalysis*, 14:185–202.

Dickes, R. 1967. Severe regressive disruptions of the therapeutic alliance. *Journal of the American Psychoanalytic Association*, 15:508– 533.

——. 1975. Technical considerations of the therapeutic and working alliances. *International Journal of Psychoanalytic Psychotherapy*, 14:1–24.

Doroff, D. R. 1976. Developing and maintaining the therapeutic alliance with the narcissistic personality. *Journal of the American Academy of Psychoanalysis*, 4: 137–160.

Dubey, J. 1974. Confidentiality as a requirement of the therapist: Technical necessities for absolute privilege in psychotherapy. *American Journal of Psychiatry*, 131:1093–1096.

Dulchin, J., and Segal, A. J. 1982a. The ambiguity of confidentiality in a psychoanalytic institute. *Psychiatry*, 45:13–25.

——. 1982b. Third-party confidences: The uses of information in a psychoanalytic institute. *Psychiatry*, 45:27–37.

Durban, J., Lazar, R., and Ofer, G. 1993. The cracked container, the containing crack: Chronic illness—its effect on the therapist and the therapeutic process. *International Journal of Psychoanalysis*, 74:705–713.

Edelson, M. 1983. Is testing psychoanalytic hypotheses in the psychoanalytic situation really possible? *Psychoanalytic Study of the Child,* 38:61–109.

——. 1984. *Hypothesis and Evidence in Psychoanalysis*. Chicago: University of Chicago Press.

——. 1986. Causal explanation in science and in psychoanalysis. *Psychoanalytic Study of the Child,* 41:89–127.

Eickhoff, F.-W. 1993. A re-reading of Freud's "Observations on transference love." In Person, E. S., Hagelin, A., and Fonagy, P. (eds.), *On Freud's "Observations on Transference-love."* New Haven: Yale University Press, 33–56.

Eisenberg, L. 1983. The subjective in medicine. *Perspectives in Biology and Medicine,* 27:48–61.

Eissler, K. R. 1955. *The Psychiatrist and the Dying Patient*. New York: International Universities Press.

——. 1974. On some theoretical and technical problems regarding the payment of fees for psychoanalytic treatment. *International Review of Psychoanalysis,* 1:73–101.

——. 1975. On possible effects of aging on the practice of psychoanalysis: An essay. *Journal of the Philadelphia Association for Psychoanalysis,* 2:138–152.

Elliott, R. 1983. "That in your hands": A comprehensive process analysis of a significant event in psychotherapy. *Psychiatry,* 46:113– 129.

Epstein, R. S., and Simon, R. I. 1990. The exploitation index: An early warning indicator of boundary violations in psychotherapy. *Bulletin of the Menninger Clinic,* 54:450–465.

Epstein, R. S., Simon, R. I., and Kay, G. G. 1992. Assessing boundary violations in psychotherapy: Survey results with the exploitation index. *Bulletin of the Menninger Clinic,* 56:150–166.

Erikson, E. H. 1959. *Identity and the Life Cycle*. Psychological Issues, Monograph 1. New York: International Universities Press.

——. 1963. *Childhood and Society*. 2nd ed. New York: Norton.

——. 1964. *Insight and Responsibility*. New York: Norton.

——. 1968. *Identity: Youth and Crisis*. New York: Norton.

Ervin, S. J., Jr. 1975. The right of the psychiatric patient to the confidentiality of his revelations. Address to the Conference on the Confidentiality of Health Records. *Psychiatric Spectator,* 9:2–3.

Esman, A. H. 1989. Psychoanalysis and general psychiatry: Obsessive compulsive disorder as paradigm. *Journal of the American Psychoanalytic Association,* 37:319–336.

Etchegoyen, A. 1993. The analyst's pregnancy and its consequences on her work. *International Journal of Psychoanalysis,* 74:141–149.

Evans, R. 1976. Development of the treatment alliance in the analysis of an adolescent boy. *Psychoanalytic Study of the Child,* 31:193–224.

Faigon, D., and Siquier, M. I. 1992. From authoritative discourse to psychoanalytic discourse: A psychoanalytic view of ethics. *Psychoanalytic Inquiry,* 12:594–611.

Fairbairn, W. R. D. 1936. The effect of the king's death upon patients under analysis. *International Journal of Psychoanalysis,* 17:278–284.

——. 1957. Freud, the psycho-analytic method and mental health. *British Journal of Medical Psychology,* 30:53–62.

——. 1958. On the nature and aims of psycho-analytic treatment. *International Journal of Psychoanalysis,* 39:374–385.

Falzeder, E., and Haynal, A. 1989. "Heilung durch Liebe?" Ein aussergewöhnlicher Dialog in der Geschichte der Psychanalyse. *Jahrbuch der Psychanalyse,* 24:109–127.

Farber, D. J. 1953. Written communication in psychotherapy. *Psychiatry,* 16:365–374.

Feinsilver, D. B. 1983. Reality, transitional relatedness, and containment in the borderline. *Contemporary Psychoanalysis,* 19:537– 569.

Feldman, E., and de Paola, H. 1994. An investigation into the psychoanalytic concept of envy. *International Journal of Psychoanalysis,* 75:217–234.

Feldman, M. 1993a. Aspects of reality and the focus of interpretation. *Psychoanalytic Inquiry,* 13:274–295.

——. 1993b. The dynamics of reassurance. *International Journal of Psychoanalysis,* 74:275–285.

Fenichel, O. 1941. *Problems of Psychoanalytic Technique.* New York: Psychoanalytic Quarterly.

——. 1945. Neurotic acting out. *Psychoanalytic Review,* 32:197–206.

Fenster, S., Phillips, S., and Rapaport, E. 1986. *The Therapist's Pregnancy.* Hillsdale, N.J.: Analytic Press.

Ferenczi, S. 1919. On the technique of psychoanalysis. In *Further Contributions to the Technique of Psychoanalysis.* London: Hogarth, 1950, 177–188.

——. 1932. *The Clinical Diary of Sandor Ferenczi.* Ed. J. Dupont. Cambridge: Harvard University Press, 1988.

——. 1949. Ten letters to Freud. *International Journal of Psychoanalysis,* 30:243–250.

Ferenczi, S., and Rank, O. 1924. *The Development of Psychoanalysis.* New York: Dover, 1956.

Ferraro, F. 1995. Trauma and termination. *International Journal of Psychoanalysis,* 76:51–65.

Ferrell, R. B., and Price, T. R. P. 1993. Effects of malpractice suits on physicians. In Gold, J. H., and Nemiah, J. C. (eds.), *Beyond Transference: When the Therapist's Real Life Intrudes.* Washington, D.C.: American Psychiatric Press, 141–158.

Ferrell, R. B., Price, T. R. P., Gert, B., and Bergen, B. J. 1984. Volitional disability and physician attitudes toward noncompliance. *Journal of Medicine and Philosophy,* 9:333–351.

Fields, M. 1985. Parameters and the analytic process: A contribution to the theory of the "mature transference." *Journal of the American Academy of Psychoanalysis,* 13:15–33.

Finell, J. S 1985. Narcissistic problems in analysis. *International Journal of Psychoanalysis,* 66:433–445.

Firestein, S. K. 1978. *Termination in Psychoanalysis.* New York: International Universities Press.

——. 1982. Termination of psychoanalysis: Theoretical, clinical and pedagogic considerations. *Psychoanalytic Inquiry,* 2:473–497.

Fischer, N. 1971. An interracial analysis: Transference and countertransference significance. *Journal of the American Psychoanalytic Association,* 19:736–745.

Fleming, J. 1946. Observations on the defenses against a transference neurosis. *Psychiatry,* 9:365–374.

——. 1972. Early object deprivation and transference phenomena: The working alliance. *Psychoanalytic Quarterly,* 41:23–49.

——. 1975. Some observations on object constancy in the psychoanalysis of adults. *Journal of the American Psychoanalytic Association,* 23:743–760.

Fliess, R. 1942. The metapsychology of the analyst. *Psychoanalytic Quarterly,* 11: 211–227.

——. 1953. Countertransference and counteridentification. *Journal of the American Psychoanalytic Association,* 1:268–284.

Flournoy, O. 1971. The psychoanalyst and the psychoanalytic process. *International Journal of Psychoanalysis,* 52:127–135.

Fogel, G. I. 1993. A transitional phase in our understanding of the psychoanalytic process: A new look at Ferenczi and Rank. *Journal of the American Psychoanalytic Association,* 41:585–602.

Fosshage, J. L. 1994. Toward reconceptualising transference: Theoretical and clinical considerations. *International Journal of Psychoanalysis,* 75:265–280.

Fox, H. M. 1958. Narcissistic defenses during pregnancy. *Psychoanalytic Quarterly,* 27:340–358.

Fox, R. P. 1984. The principle of abstinence reconsidered. *International Review of Psychoanalysis,* 11:227–236.

Frank, A. F. and Gunderson, J. G. 1990. The role of the therapeutic alliance in the treatment of schizophrenia. *Archives of General Psychiatry,* 47:228–236.

Frank, J. 1968. The role of hope in psychotherapy. *International Journal of Psychiatry,* 5:383–412.

——. 1974a. Psychotherapy: The restoration of morale. *American Journal of Psychiatry,* 131:271–274.

——. 1974b. Therapeutic components of psychotherapy. *Journal of Nervous and Mental Diseases,* 159:325–342.

Frankl, L., and Hellman, I. 1962. Symposium on child analysis: II. The ego's participation in the therapeutic alliance. *International Journal of Psychoanalysis,* 43:333–337.

Franklin, G. 1990. The multiple meanings of neutrality. *Journal of the American Psychoanalytic Association,* 38:195–220.

Frayn, D. H. 1987. An analyst's regressive reverie: A response to the analysand's illness. *International Journal of Psychoanalysis,* 68:271– 277.

——. 1993. Contemporary considerations influencing psychoanalytic interventions. *Canadian Journal of Psychoanalysis,* 1:7–25.

Free, N. K., Green, B. L., Grace, M. C., Chernus, L. A., and Whitman, R. M. 1985. Empathy and outcome in brief focal dynamic therapy. *American Journal of Psychiatry,* 142:917–921.

Freud, A. 1936. *The Ego and the Mechanisms of Defense*. Revised edition. New York: International Universities Press, 1966.
——. 1954a. Problems of technique in adult analysis. *Bulletin of the Philadelphia Association for Psychoanalysis*, 4:44–70.
——. 1954b. The widening scope of indications for psychoanalysis: Discussion. *Journal of the American Psychoanalytic Association*, 2:607–620.
——. 1962. The theory of the parent-infant relationship: Contribution to the discussion. *The Writings of Anna Freud*, Vol. V: *Research at the Hampstead Child-Therapy Clinic and Other Papers 1956– 1965*. New York: International Universities Press, 1969, 187–193.
——. 1965. *Normality and Pathology in Childhood: Assessments of Development*. In *The Writings of Anna Freud*, vol. VI. New York: International Universities Press.
Freud, S. 1905a. Fragment of an analysis of a case of hysteria. *Standard Edition*, 7:1–122.
——. 1905b. Jokes and their relation to the unconscious. *Standard Edition*, 8.
——. 1905c. On psychotherapy. *Standard Edition*, 7:255–268.
——. 1905d. Three essays on the theory of sexuality. *Standard Edition*, 7:123–245.
——. 1909. Notes upon a case of obsessional neurosis. *Standard Edition*, 10:151–320.
——. 1910. Leonardo da Vinci and a memory of his childhood. *Standard Edition*, 11:57–137.
——. 1912a. The dynamics of transference. *Standard Edition*, 12:97– 108.
——. 1912b. Recommendations to physicians practicing psychoanalysis. *Standard Edition*, 12:109–120.
——. 1912–13. Totem and taboo. *Standard Edition*, 13:vii–162.
——. 1913. On beginning the treatment. *Standard Edition*, 12:121– 144.
——. 1914. Remembering, repeating and working through. *Standard Edition*, 12: 145–156.
——. 1915a. Observations on transference-love. *Standard Edition*, 12:157–171.
——. 1915b. The unconscious. *Standard Edition*, 14:159–215.
——. 1916–17. Introductory lectures on psychoanalysis. *Standard Edition*, 16.
——. 1917. Mourning and melancholia. *Standard Edition*, 14:237–260.
——. 1918. From the history of an infantile neurosis. *Standard Edition*, 17:1–123.
——. 1921. Group psychology and the analysis of the ego. *Standard Edition*, 18:65–143.
——. 1923a. The ego and the id. *Stand Edition*, 19:1–66.
——. 1923b. Two encyclopedia articles. *Standard Edition*, 18:233– 259.
——. 1925a. Negation. *Standard Edition*, 19:233–239.
——. 1925b. Some additional notes on dream interpretation as a whole. *Standard Edition*, 19:123–138.
——. 1933. New introductory lectures on psychoanalysis. *Standard Edition*, 22:1–182.
——. 1937. Analysis terminable and interminable. *Standard Edition*, 23:209–253.
——. 1940. An outline of psychoanalysis. *Standard Edition*, 23:139– 207.
Friedman, H. J. 1975. Psychotherapy of borderline patients: The influence of theory on technique. *American Journal of Psychiatry*, 132:1048–1052.

Friedman, L. 1969. The therapeutic alliance. *International Journal of Psychoanalysis,* 50:139–153.

——. 1986. Kohut's testament. *Psychoanalytic Inquiry,* 6:321–347.

——. 1988. *The Anatomy of Psychotherapy.* Hillsdale, N.J.: Analytic Press.

——. 1992. How and why do patients become more objective? Sterba compared with Strachey. *Psychoanalytic Quarterly,* 61:1–17.

——. 1994. Classics revisited: Introduction. *Journal of the American Psychoanalytic Association,* 42:847–9.

Friedman, M. E. 1993. When the analyst becomes pregnant—twice. *Psychoanalytic Inquiry,* 13:226–239.

Frieswyk, S. H., Allen, J., Colson, D., Coyne, L., Gabbard, G., Horwitz. L., and Newsom, G. 1986. The therapeutic alliance: Its place as a process and outcome variable in psychotherapy research. *Journal of Consulting and Clinical Psychology,* 54:32–38.

Fromm-Reichmann, F. 1950. *Principles of Intensive Psychotherapy.* Chicago: University of Chicago Press.

Frosch, J. 1983. *The Psychotic Process.* New York: International Universities Press.

Furer, M. 1967. Some developmental aspects of the superego. *International Journal of Psychoanalysis,* 48:277–280.

Furlong, A. 1992. Some technical and theoretical considerations regarding the missed session. *International Journal of Psychoanalysis,* 73:701–718.

Furman, R. A. 1964. Death of six-year-old's mother during his analysis. *Psychoanalytic Study of the Child,* 19:377–397.

Gabbard, G. O. 1994a. *Dynamic Psychiatry in Clinical Practice: The DSM-IV Edition.* Washington, D.C.: American Psychiatric Press.

——. 1994b. Love and lust in erotic transference. *Journal of the American Psychoanalytic Association,* 42:385–403.

——. 1994c. Mind and brain in psychiatric treatment. *Bulletin of the Menninger Clinic,* 58:427–446.

——. 1994d. Psychotherapists who transgress sexual boundaries with patients. *Bulletin of the Menninger Clinic,* 58:124–135.

——. 1994e. Sexual excitement and countertransference love in the analyst. *Journal of the American Psychoanalytic Association,* 42:1083– 1106.

——. 1995. Countertransference: The emerging common ground. *International Journal of Psychoanalysis,* 76:475–485.

——., Horwitz, L., Frieswyk, S., Allen, J. G., Colson, D. B., Newsom, G., and Coyne, L. 1988. The effect of therapist interventions on the therapeutic alliance with borderline patients. *Journal of the American Psychoanalytic Association,* 36: 697–727.

Gabbard, G. O., Takahashi, T., Davidson, J., Bauman-Bork, M., and Ensroth, K. 1991. A psychodynamic perspective on the clinical impact of insurance review. *American Journal of Psychiatry,* 148:318–323.

Gampel, Y. 1992. Psychoanalysis, ethics, and actuality. *Psychoanalytic Inquiry,* 12: 526–550.

Ganzarain, R. 1991. Extra-analytic contacts: Fantasy and reality. *International Journal of Psychoanalysis,* 72:131–140.
Gardiner, M. (ed.). 1971. *The Wolf-Man by the Wolf-Man.* New York: Basic Books.
Gardner, M. R. 1991. The art of psychoanalysis: On oscillation and other matters. *Journal of the American Psychoanalytic Association,* 39:851–870.
Gargiulo, G. J. 1989. Authority, the self, and psychoanalytic experience. *Psychoanalytic Review,* 76:149–161.
Gay, P. 1988. *Freud: A Life for Our Times.* New York: Norton.
Gedo, J. E. 1963. A note on nonpayment of psychiatric fees. *International Journal of Psychoanalysis,* 44:368–371.
——. 1977. Notes on the psychoanalytic management of archaic transferences. *Journal of the American Psychoanalytic Association,* 25:787–803.
——. 1979. *Beyond Interpretation.* New York: International Universities Press.
——. 1988. *The Mind in Disorder.* Hillsdale, N.J.: Analytic Press.
Gehrie, M. J. 1993. Psychoanalytic technique and the development of the capacity to reflect. *Journal of the American Psychoanalytic Association,* 41:1083–1111.
Geleerd, E. R. 1962. Symposium on child analysis: Contributions to discussion. *International Journal of Psychoanalysis,* 43:338–341.
Gesensway, D. B. 1978. Adolescent resistances in the psychoanalysis of adults. *Journal of the Philadelphia Association for Psychoanalysis,* 5:17–28.
Gifford, S. 1969. Some psychoanalytic theories about death: A selective historical review. *Annual of the New York Academy of Sciences,* 164:638–668.
Gill, M. M. 1979. The analysis of the transference. *Journal of the American Psychoanalytic Association,* 27:263–288.
——. 1982. *Analysis of Transference. Vol I: Theory and Technique.* Madison, Conn.: International Universities Press.
——. 1993. One-person and two-person perspectives: Freud's "Observations on transference love." In Person, E. S., Hagelin, A., and Fonagy, P. (eds.), *On Freud's "Observations on Transference-love."* New Haven: Yale University Press, 114–129.
Gill, M. M., and Muslin, H. L. 1976. Early interpretation of transference. *Journal of the American Psychoanalytic Association,* 24:779–794.
Gill, M. M., Simon, J., Fink, G., Endicott, N. A., and Paul, I. H. 1968. Studies in audio-recorded psychoanalysis. I. General considerations. *Journal of the American Psychoanalytic Association,* 16:230–244.
Gillman, R. D. 1982. The termination phase in psychoanalytic practice: A survey of forty-eight completed cases. *Psychoanalytic Inquiry,* 2:463–472.
Giovacchini, P. L. 1965. Transference, incorporation and synthesis. *International Journal of Psychoanalysis,* 46:287–296.
——. 1972. Technical difficulties in treating some characterological disorders: Countertransference problems. *International Journal of Psychoanalytic Psychotherapy,* 1:112–128.
——. 1973. Character disorders: Form and structure. *International Journal of Psychoanalysis,* 54:153–161.

Gitelson, M. 1952. The emotional position of the analyst in the psycho-analytic situation. *International Journal of Psychoanalysis,* 33:1–10.

——. 1962. The curative factors in psychoanalysis. *International Journal of Psychoanalysis,* 43:194–206.

Gold, J. H., and Nemiah, J. C. (eds.). 1993. *Beyond Transference: When the Therapist's Real Life Intrudes.* Washington, D.C.: American Psychiatric Press.

Goldberg, A., ed. 1978. *The Psychology of the Self: A Casebook.* New York: International Universities Press.

——. 1987a. The place of apology in psychoanalysis and psychotherapy. *International Review of Psychoanalysis,* 14:409–417.

——. 1987b. Psychoanalysis and negotiation. *Psychoanalytic Quarterly,* 56:109–129.

——. 1988. *A Fresh Look at Psychoanalysis: A View from Self Psychology.* Hillsdale, N.J.: Analytic Press.

Goldberg, E. L., Myers, W. A., and Zeifman, I. 1974. Some observations on three interracial analyses. *International Journal of Psychoanalysis,* 55:495–500.

Goldberg, P. 1989. Actively seeking the holding environment: Conscious and unconscious elements in the building of a therapeutic framework. *Contemporary Psychoanalysis,* 25:448–476.

Goldberg, S. H. 1991. Patients' theories of pathogenesis. *Psychoanalytic Quarterly,* 60:245–275.

——. 1994. The evolution of patients' theories of pathogenesis. *Psychoanalytic Quarterly,* 63:54–83.

Goldberger, M. 1991. Pregnancy during analysis—help or hindrance? *Psychoanalytic Quarterly,* 60:207–226.

Goldberger, M., and Evans, D. 1985. On transference manifestations in male patients with female analysts. *International Journal of Psychoanalysis,* 66:295–309.

Goldberger, M., and Holmes, D. E. 1993. Transferences in male patients with female analysts: An update. *Psychoanalytic Inquiry,* 13:173–191.

Good, M. I. 1994. The reconstruction of early childhood trauma: Fantasy, reality, and verification. *Journal of the American Psychoanalytic Association,* 42:79–101.

Goodman, A. 1992. Empathy and inquiry: Integrating empathic mirroring in an interpersonal framework. *Contemporary Psychoanalysis,* 28:631–646.

Goz, R. 1973. Women patients and women therapists: Some issues that come up in psychotherapy. *International Journal of Psychoanalytic Psychotherapy,* 2:298–319.

——. 1975. On knowing the therapist "as a person." *International Journal of Psychoanalytic Psychotherapy,* 4:437–458.

Gray, P. 1982. Developmental lag in the evolution of technique for psychoanalysis of neurotic conflict. *Journal of the American Psychoanalytic Association,* 30:621–656.

——. 1987. On the technique of analysis of the superego: An introduction. *Psychoanalytic Quarterly,* 56:130–154.

——. 1990. The nature of therapeutic action in psychoanalysis. *Journal of the American Psychoanalytic Association,* 38:1083–1097.

——. 1991. On transferred permissive or approving superego fantasies: The analysis of the ego's superego activities. *Psychoanalytic Quarterly,* 60:1–33.

Green, A. 1975. The analyst, symbolization and absence in the analytic setting (on changes in analytic practice and analytic experience). *International Journal of Psychoanalysis*, 56:1–22.

Greenacre, P. 1954. The role of transference. *Journal of the American Psychoanalytic Association*, 2:671–684.

——. 1956. Problems of overidealization of the analyst and of analysis. *Psychoanalytic Study of the Child*, 21:193–212.

——. 1958. Discussion of Zetzel 1958.. Meeting of the American Psychoanalytic Association, New York.

——. 1959. Certain technical problems in the transference relationship. *Journal of the American Psychoanalytic Association*, 7:484–502.

——. 1968. The psychoanalytic process, transference, and acting out. *International Journal of Psychoanalysis*, 49:211–218.

Greenberg, J. 1995. Psychoanalytic technique and the interactive matrix. *Psychoanalytic Quarterly*, 64:1–22.

Greenson, R. R. 1960. Empathy and its vicissitudes. *International Journal of Psychoanalysis*, 41:418–424.

——. 1965. The working alliance and the transference neurosis. *Psychoanalytic Quarterly*, 343:155–181. Reprinted in *Explorations in Psychoanalysis*. New York: International Universities Press, 1978.

——. 1967. *The Technique and Practice of Psychoanalysis*. New York: International Universities Press.

——. 1971. The "real" relationship between the patient and the psychoanalyst. In Kanzer, M. (ed.), *The Unconscious Today*. New York: International Universities Press, 213–232.

——. 1972. Beyond transference and interpretation. *International Journal of Psychoanalysis*, 53:213–217.

——. 1974. Loving, hating, and indifference towards the patient. *International Review of Psychoanalysis*, 1:259–266.

——. 1978. *Explorations in Psychoanalysis*. New York: International Universities Press.

Greenson, R. R., and Wexler, M. 1969. The non-transference relationship in the psychoanalytic situation. *International Journal of Psychoanalysis*, 50:27–39.

Griffith, M. S. 1977. The influences of race on the psychotherapeutic relationship. *Psychiatry*, 40:27–40.

Grinberg, L. 1962. On a specific aspect of countertransference due to the patient's projective identification. *International Journal of Psychoanalysis*, 43:436–440.

Grinberg, L., and Grinberg, R. 1974. Identity and psychoanalysis. *International Review of Psychoanalysis*, 1:499–508.

Grossman, L. 1993. The perverse attitude toward reality. *Psychoanalytic Quarterly*, 62:422–436.

Grotjahn, M. 1952. A psychoanalyst passes a small stone with big troubles. In Pinnar, M., and Miller, B. (eds.), *When Doctors Are Patients*. New York: Norton.

Grubrich-Simitis, I. 1986. Six letters of Sigmund Freud and Sandor Ferenczi on the interrelationship of psychoanalytic theory and technique. *International Review of Psychoanalysis,* 13:259–277.

Grünbaum, A. 1984. *The Foundations of Psychoanalysis: A Philosophical Critique.* Berkeley: University of California Press.

——. 1993. *Validation in the Clinical Theory of Psychoanalysis: A Study in the Philosophy of Psychoanalysis.* Madison, Conn.: International Universities Press.

Grunebaum, H. 1993. The vulnerable therapist: On being ill or injured. In Gold, J. H., and Nemiah, J. C. (eds.), *Beyond Transference: When the Therapist's Real Life Intrudes.* Washington, D.C.: American Psychiatric Press, 21–50.

Grunes, J. M. 1981. Reminiscences, regression, and empathy—A psychotherapeutic approach to the impaired elderly. In Greenspan, S. I., and Pollock, G. H. (eds.), *The Course of Life: Psychoanalytic Contributions Toward Understanding Personality Development. III. Adulthood and the Aging Process.* Adelphi, Md.: Mental Health Study Center, NIMH, 545–548.

Gunderson, J. G. 1984. *Borderline Personality Disorganization.* Washington, D.C.: American Psychiatric Press.

Guntrip, H. 1975. My experience of analysis with Fairbairn and Winnicott. *International Review of Psychoanalysis,* 2:145–156.

Gutheil, T. G. 1977. Introduction. In Gutheil, T. G. (ed.), Money as a clinical issue in psychiatry. *Psychiatric Annals,* 7:6–7.

——. 1982. The psychology of psychopharmacology. *Bulletin of the Menninger Clinic,* 41:321–330.

——. 1989. Borderline personality disorder, boundary violations, and patient-therapist sex: Medicolegal pitfalls. *American Journal of Psychiatry,* 146:597–602.

Gutheil, T. G., Bursztajn, H. J., Brodsky, A., and Alexander, V. (eds.). 1991. *Decision Making in Psychiatry and the Law.* Baltimore: Williams and Wilkins.

Gutheil, T. G., and Gabbard, G. O. 1993. The concept of boundaries in clinical practice: Theoretical and risk-management dimensions. *American Journal of Psychiatry,* 150:188–196.

Gutheil, T. G., and Havens, L. L. 1979. The therapeutic alliance: Contemporary meanings and confusions. *International Review of Psychoanalysis,* 6:467–481.

Guttman, H. A. 1984. Sexual issues in the transference and countertransference between female therapist and male patient. *Journal of the American Academy of Psychoanalysis,* 12:187–197.

Haak, N. 1957. Comments on the analytical situation. *International Journal of Psychoanalysis,* 38:183–195.

Hägglund, T.-B. 1981. The final stage of the dying process. *International Journal of Psychoanalysis,* 62:45–49.

Halleck, S. L. 1982. The concept of responsibility in psychotherapy. *American Journal of Psychotherapy,* 36:292–303.

——. 1988. Which patients are responsible for their illnesses? *American Journal of Psychotherapy,* 42:338–353.

Halpert, E. 1972a. The effect of insurance on psychoanalytic treatment. *Journal of the American Psychoanalytic Association,* 20:122–133.

——. 1972b. A meaning of insurance in psychotherapy. *International Journal of Psychoanalytic Psychotherapy,* 1:62–68.

——. 1985. Insurance. *Journal of the American Psychoanalytic Association,* 33:937–949.

——. 1989. Cardiac preoccupations. *Psychoanalytic Quarterly,* 58:210–226.

Hamburg, P. 1991. Interpretation and empathy: Reading Lacan with Kohut. *International Journal of Psychoanalysis,* 72:347–361.

Hamilton, V. 1993. Truth and reality in psychoanalytic discourse. *International Journal of Psychoanalysis,* 74:63–79.

Hani, A. G. 1973. The rediscovery of the therapeutic alliance. *International Journal of Psychoanalytic Psychotherapy,* 2:449–477.

Hanly, C. M. T. 1988. Review of *The Foundations of Psychoanalysis: A Philosophical Critique,* by Adolf Grünbaum. *Journal of the American Psychoanalytic Association,* 36:521–528.

——. 1990. The concept of truth in psychoanalysis. *International Journal of Psychoanalysis,* 71:375–383.

——. 1994. Reflections on the place of the therapeutic alliance in psychoanalysis. *International Journal of Psychoanalysis,* 75:457–467.

Hannett, F. 1949. Transference reactions to an event in the life of the analyst. *Psychoanalytic Review,* 36:69–81.

Hann-Kende, F. 1933. On the role of transference and countertransference in psychoanalysis. In Devereux, G. (ed.), *Psychoanalysis and the Occult.* New York: International Universities Press, 1953, 158–167.

Harris, I. D. 1960. Unconscious factors common to parents and analysts. *International Journal of Psychoanalysis,* 41:123–129.

Hartley, D. E., and Strupp, H. H. 1983. The therapeutic alliance: its relationship to outcome in brief psychotherapy. In Masling, J. (ed.), *Empirical Studies of Psychoanalytical Theories,* vol. 1. Hillsdale, N.J.: Analytic Press, 7–11.

Hartmann, E. 1966. The psychophysiology of free will: an example of vertical research. In Loewenstein, R. M., Newman, L. M., Schur, M., and Solnit, A. J. (eds.), *Psychoanalysis—A General Psychology.* New York: International Universities Press, 521–536.

Hartmann, H. 1939. *Ego Psychology and the Problem of Adaptation.* New York: International Universities Press, 1958.

——. 1944. Psychoanalysis and sociology. In *Essays on Ego Psychology.* New York: International Universities Press, 1964, 19–36.

——. 1950. Comments on the psychoanalytic theory of the ego. In *Essays on Ego Psychology.* New York: International Universities Press, 1964, 113–141.

——. 1960.. *Psychoanalysis and Moral Values.* New York: International University Press.

Hausner, R. 1985–86. Medication and transitional phenomena. *International Journal of Psychoanalytic Psychotherapy,* 11:375–398.

Havens, L. 1978. Explorations in the uses of language in psychotherapy: Simple empathic statements. *Psychiatry,* 41:336–345.

——. 1979. Explorations in the uses of language in psychotherapy: Complex empathic statements. *Psychiatry,* 42:40–48.

Haynal, A., and Falzeder, E. 1993. Slaying the dragons of the past or cooking the hare in the present: a historical view on affects in the psychoanalytic encounter. *Psychoanalytic Inquiry,* 13:357–371.

Heimann, P. 1956. Dynamics of transference interpretations. *International Journal of Psychoanalysis,* 37:303–310.

——. 1970. In Panel: Discussion of "The non-transference relationship in the psychoanalytic situation." *International Journal of Psychoanalysis,* 51:143–150.

Hernández, M. 1993. Footnote to a footnote to "Observations on transference love." In Person, E. S., Hagelin, A., and Fonagy, P. (eds.), *On Freud's "Observations on Transference-love."* New Haven: Yale University Press, 96–101.

Hildebrand, H. P. 1992. A patient dying with AIDS. *International Review of Psychoanalysis,* 19:457–469.

Hilles, L. 1971. The clinical management of the nonpaying patient. *Bulletin of the Menninger Clinic,* 35:98–112.

Hinkle, B. J. 1977. Living with the demands of confidentiality. *Journal of Legal Medicine,* 5:9–13.

Hoffer, A. 1985. Toward a definition of psychoanalytic neutrality. *Journal of the American Psychoanalytic Association,* 33:771–795.

——. 1990. Review of *The Clinical Diary of Sandor Ferenczi. International Journal of Psychoanalysis,* 71:723–727.

——. 1991. The Freud-Ferenczi controversy—A living legacy. *International Review of Psychoanalysis,* 18:465–472.

——. 1993. Is love in the analytic relationship "real"? *Psychoanalytic Inquiry,* 13: 343–356.

Hoffman, I. Z. 1994. Dialectical thinking and therapeutic action in the psychoanalytic process. *Psychoanalytic Quarterly,* 63:187–218.

Holt, R. R. 1965. Ego autonomy re-evaluated. *International Journal of Psychoanalysis,* 46:151–167.

Horowitz, M. J., and Zilberg, N. 1983. Regressive alterations of the self concept. *American Journal of Psychiatry,* 140:284–289.

Horwitz, L. 1994. The transition process in converting to psychoanalysis. *Bulletin of the Menninger Clinic,* 58:108–123.

Hunter, K. M. 1991. *Doctors' Stories: The Narrative Structure of Medical Knowledge.* Princeton: Princeton University Press.

Hurwitz, M. R. 1986. The analyst, his theory, and the psychoanalytic process. *Psychoanalytic Study of the Child,* 41:439–466.

Inderbitzin, L. B., and Levy, S. T. 1994. On grist for the mill: External reality as defense. *Journal of the American Psychoanalytic Association,* 42:763–788.

Ingram, D. H. 1979. Time and timekeeping in psychoanalysis and psychotherapy. *American Journal of Psychoanalysis,* 39:319–328.

Issacharoff, A. 1978. Beyond countertransference: The "new truth" in the psychoanalytic process. *Contemporary Psychoanalysis,* 14:291–310.

Jackson, S. W. 1992. The listening healer in the history of psychological healing. *American Journal of Psychiatry*, 149:1623–1632.

Jacobs, T. J. 1973. Posture, gesture, the movement in the analyst: Cues to interpretation and countertransference. *Journal of the American Psychoanalytic Association*, 21:77–92.

——. 1986. On countertransference enactments. *Journal of the American Psychoanalytic Association*, 34:289–307.

——. 1991. *The Use of the Self: Countertransference and Communication in the Analytic Situation*. Madison, Conn.: International Universities Press.

Jacobson, J. G. 1993. Developmental observation, multiple models of the mind, and the therapeutic relationship in psychoanalysis. *Psychoanalytic Quarterly*, 62:523–552.

Jimenez, J. P. 1993. A fundamental dilemma of psychoanalytic technique: Reflections on the analysis of a perverse paranoid patient. *International Journal of Psychoanalysis*, 74:487–504.

Johansen, K. H. 1993. Countertransference and divorce of the therapist. In Gold, J. H., and Nemiah, J. C. (eds.), *Beyond Transference: When the Therapist's Real Life Intrudes*. Washington, D.C.: American Psychiatric Press, 87–108.

Jones, E. 1957. *The Life and Work of Sigmund Freud. Vol. 3. The Last Phase 1919–1939*. New York Basic Books.

Jones, E. E. 1993. How will psychoanalysis study itself? *Journal of the American Psychoanalytic Association*, 41 (Suppl.): 91–108.

Joseph, B. 1985. Transference: The total situation. *International Journal of Psychoanalysis*, 66:447–454.

——. 1993. On transference love: Some current observations. In Person, E. S., Hagelin, A., and Fonagy, P. (eds.), *On Freud's "Observations on Transference-love*." New Haven: Yale University Press, 102–113.

Kaiser, H. 1955. The problem of responsibility in psychotherapy. *Psychiatry*, 18: 205–211.

Kanter, S. S., and Kanter, J. A. 1977. Therapeutic setting and management of fees. In Gutheil, T. G. (ed.), Money as a clinical issue in psychiatry. *Psychiatric Annals*, 7:23–34.

Kantor, S. J. 1989. Transference and the beta adrenergic receptor: A case presentation. *Psychiatry*, 52:107–115.

——. 1993. Analyzing a rapid cycler: Can the transference keep up? In Schachter, M. (ed.), *Psychotherapy and Medication: A Dynamic Integration*. Northvale, N.J.: Aronson, 291–311.

Kantrowitz, J. L. 1992. The analyst's style and its impact on the analytic process: overcoming a patient-analyst stalemate. *Journal of the American Psychoanalytic Association*, 40:169–194.

——. 1993a. Impasses in psychoanalysis: Overcoming resistance in situations of stalemate. *Journal of the American Psychoanalytic Association*, 41:1021–1050.

——. 1993b. The uniqueness of the patient-analyst pair: Approaches for elucidating the analyst's role. *International Journal of Psychoanalysis*, 74:893–904.

——. 1995. The beneficial aspects of the patient-analyst match. *International Journal of Psychoanalysis,* 76:299–313.

Kantrowitz, J. L., Katz, A. L., Greenman, D. A., Morris, H., Paolitto, F., Sashin, J., and Solomon, L. 1989. The patient-analyst match and the outcome of psychoanalysis: A pilot study. *Journal of the American Psychoanalytic Association,* 37: 893–919.

Kantrowitz, J. L., Katz, A. L., and Paolitto, F. (1990a) Followup of psychoanalysis five to ten years after termination: I. Stability of change. *Journal of the American Psychoanalytic Association,* 38:471–496.

——. (1990b) Followup of psychoanalysis five to ten years after termination: II. Development of the self-analytic function. *Journal of the American Psychoanalytic Association,* 38:637–654.

Kantrowitz, J. L., Katz, A. L., and Paolitto, F. (1990c) Followup of psychoanalysis five to ten years after termination: III. The relation between the resolution of the transference and the patient-analyst match. *Journal of the American Psychoanalytic Association,* 38:655–678.

Kanzer, M. 1952. The transference neurosis of the Rat Man. *Psychoanalytic Quarterly,* 21:181–189.

——. 1972. Superego aspects of free association and the fundamental rule. *Journal of the American Psychoanalytic Association,* 20:246–266.

——. 1975. The therapeutic and working alliances: an assessment. *International Journal of Psychoanalytic Psychotherapy,* 4:48–68.

——. 1980. Freud's "human influence" on the Rat Man. In Kanzer, M., and Glenn, J. (eds.), *Freud and His Patients.* New York: Aronson, 232–240.

——. 1981. Freud's "analytic pact": The standard therapeutic alliance. *Journal of the American Psychoanalytic Association,* 29:69–87.

Kaplan, A. G. 1979. Toward an analysis of sex-role related issues in the therapeutic relationship. *Psychiatry,* 42:112–120.

——. 1985. Female or male therapists for women patients: New formulations. *Psychiatry,* 48:111–121.

Kaplan, A. H. 1993. The aging and dying psychotherapist: death and illness in the life of the aging psychotherapist. In Gold, J. H., and Nemiah, J. C. (eds.), *Beyond Transference: When the Therapist's Real Life Intrudes.* Washington, D.C.: American Psychiatric Press, 51–70.

Kelman, H. 1987. On resonant cognition. *International Review of Psychoanalysis,* 14:111–123.

Kennedy, J. A. 1952. Problems posed in the analysis of Negro patients. *Psychiatry,* 15:313–327.

Kernberg, O. F. 1968. The treatment of patients with borderline personality organization. *International Journal of Psychoanalysis,* 49:600–619.

——. 1969. A contribution to the ego-psychological critique of the Kleinian school. *International Journal of Psychoanalysis,* 50:317–334.

——. 1970. Factors in the psychoanalytic treatment of narcissistic personalities. *Journal of the American Psychoanalytic Association,* 18:51–85.

——. 1974. Further contributions to the treatment of narcissistic personalities. *International Journal of Psychoanalysis*, 55:215–239.

——. 1975. *Borderline Conditions and Pathological Narcissism*. New York: Aronson.

——. 1976a. *Object-Relations Theory and Clinical Psychoanalysis*. New York: Aronson.

——. 1976b. Technical considerations in the treatment of borderline personality organization. *Journal of the American Psychoanalytic Association*, 24:795–829.

——. 1979. Psychoanalytic psychotherapy with borderline adolescents. *Adolescent Psychiatry*, 7:294–321.

——. 1984. *Severe Personality Disorders: Psychotherapeutic Strategies*. New Haven: Yale University Press.

——. 1993. Convergences and divergences in contemporary psychoanalytic technique. *International Journal of Psychoanalysis*, 74:659–673.

Khan, M. M. R. 1960a. Clinical aspects of the schizoid personality: Affects and technique. *International Journal of Psychoanalysis*, 41:430–437.

——. 1960b. Regression and integration in the analytic setting. *International Journal of Psychoanalysis*, 41:130–146.

——. 1969. Vicissitudes of being, knowing, and experiencing in the therapeutic situation. *British Journal of Medical Psychology*, 42:383–393.

——. 1972a. Dread of surrender to resourceless dependence in the analytic situation. *International Journal of Psychoanalysis*, 53:225–230.

——. 1972b. The finding and becoming of self. *International Journal of Psychoanalytic Psychotherapy*, 1:97–111.

Killingmo, B. 1995. Affirmation in psychoanalysis. *International Journal of Psychoanalysis*, 76:503–518.

King, P. 1974. Notes on the psychoanalysis of older patients—Reappraisal of the potentialities for change during the second half of life. *Journal of Analytic Psychology*, 19:22–37.

——. 1980. The life cycle as indicated by the nature of the transference in the psychoanalysis of the middle-aged and elderly. *International Journal of Psychoanalysis*, 61:153–160.

Kirman, W. J. 1980. Countertransference in facilitating intimacy and communication. *Modern Psychoanalysis*, 5:131–145.

Kirshner, L. A. 1993. Concepts of reality and psychic reality in psychoanalysis as illustrated by the disagreement between Freud and Ferenczi. *International Journal of Psychoanalysis*, 74:219–230.

Klauber, J. 1968. The psychoanalyst as a person. *British Journal of Medical Psychology*, 41:315–322.

Klein, H. S. 1974. Transference and defense in manic states. *International Journal of Psychoanalysis*, 55:261–268.

Kleinman, A. 1978. Clinical relevance of anthropological and cross-cultural research: concepts and strategies. *American Journal of Psychiatry*, 135:427–431.

Kluft, R. P. 1986. High-functioning multiple personality patients: Three cases. *Journal of Nervous and Mental Disease*, 174:722–726.

——. 1991. Multiple personality disorder. In Tasman, A., and Goldfinger, S. M. (eds.), *American Psychiatric Press Review of Psychiatry,* vol. 10. Washington, D.C.: American Psychiatric Press.

——. 1991. Hospital treatment of multiple personality disorder: An overview. *Psychiatric Clinics of North America,* 14:695–719.

——. 1992. Discussion: A specialist's perspective on multiple personality disorder. *Psychoanalytic Inquiry,* 12:139–171.

Knapp, P. H., Levin, S., McCarter, R. H., Werner, H. and Zetzel, E. R. 1960. Suitability for psychoanalysis: A review of one hundred supervised analytic cases. *Psychoanalytic Quarterly,* 29:459–477.

Knight, R. P. 1946. Determinism, "freedom" and psychotherapy. In Knight, R. P. (ed.), *Psychoanalytic Psychiatry and Psychology*. New York: International Universities Press, 365–381.

Kogan, I. 1992. From acting out to words and meaning. *International Journal of Psychoanalysis,* 73:455–465.

——. 1993. Curative factors in the psychoanalyses of holocaust survivors' offspring before and during the Gulf war. *International Journal of Psychoanalysis,* 74:803–814.

Kohut, H. 1959. Introspection, empathy, and psychoanalysis: An examination of the relationship between mode of observation and theory. *Journal of the American Psychoanalytic Association,* 7:459–483.

——. 1965. Autonomy and integration. *Journal of the American Psychoanalytic Association,* 13:851–856.

——. 1966. Forms and transformations of narcissism. *Journal of the American Psychoanalytic Association,* 14:243–272.

——. 1971. *The Analysis of the Self.* New York: International Universities Press.

——. 1977. *The Restoration of the Self.* New York: International Universities Press.

——. 1980. Summarizing reflections. In Goldberg, A. (ed.), *Advances in Self Psychology*. New York: International Universities Press, 473–554.

——. 1984. *How Does Analysis Cure?* Chicago: University of Chicago Press.

Kriechman, A. M. 1984. Illness in the therapist: The eye patch. *Psychiatry,* 47:378–386.

Kris, A. O. 1990. Helping patients by analyzing self-criticism. *Journal of the American Psychoanalytic Association,* 38:605–636.

——. 1994. Freud's treatment of a narcissistic patient. *International Journal of Psychoanalysis,* 75:649–664.

Kris, E. 1956. The personal myth: A problem in psychoanalytic technique. In *Selected Papers of Ernst Kris*. New Haven: Yale University Press, 1975, 272–300.

——. 1952. *Psychoanalytic Explorations in Art*. New York: Schocken Books, 1964.

Krohn, A. 1974. Borderline "empathy" and differentiation of object representations: A contribution to the psychology of object relations. *International Journal of Psychoanalytic Psychotherapy,* 34:142–165.

Kron, R. E. 1971. Psychoanalytic complications of a narcissistic transference. *Journal of the American Psychoanalytic Association,* 19:636–653.

Kubie, L. S. 1971. The destructive potential of humor in psychotherapy. *American Journal of Psychiatry,* 127:861–866.

Kubler-Ross, E. 1969. *On Death and Dying.* New York: Macmillan.

Kulish, N. M. 1984. The effect of the sex of the analyst on the transference. *Bulletin of the Menninger Clinic,* 48:95–110.

——. 1986. Gender and transference: The screen of the phallic mother. *International Review of Psychoanalysis,* 13:393–404.

Kulish, N., and Mayman, M. 1993. Gender-linked determinants of transference and countertransference in psychoanalytic psychotherapy. *Psychoanalytic Inquiry,* 13:286–305.

Kultgen, J. 1985. Veatch's new foundation for medical ethics. *Journal of Medicine and Philosophy,* 10:369–386.

Lacan, J. 1977. *Ecrits: A Selection.* New York: Norton.

——. 1988. *The Seminar of Jacques Lacan. Book II; The Ego in Freud's Theory and in the Technique of Psychoanalysis 1954–1955.* New York: Norton.

Lachmann, F. M. 1994. How can I eroticise thee? Let me count the ways. *Psychoanalytic Inquiry,* 14:604–621.

Lacocque, P.-E., and Loeb, A. J. 1988. Death anxiety: A hidden factor in countertransference hate. *Journal of Religion and Health,* 27:95–108.

Lambley, P., and Cooper, P. 1975. Psychotherapy and race: Interracial therapy under apartheid. *American Journal of Psychotherapy,* 29:179–184.

Lampl-de Groot, J. 1956. The role of identification in psycho-analytic procedure. *International Journal of Psychoanalysis,* 37:456–459.

Langer, S. 1942. *Philosophy in a New Key.* Cambridge: Harvard University Press.

Langs, R. 1973a. The patient's view of the therapist: Reality or fantasy? *International Journal of Psychoanalytic Psychotherapy,* 2:411–431.

——. 1973b. *The Technique of Psychoanalytic Psychotherapy.* 2 vols. New York: Aronson.

——. 1975a. Therapeutic misalliances. *International Journal of Psychoanalytic Psychotherapy,* 4:77–105.

——. 1975b. The therapeutic relationship and deviations in technique. *International Journal of Psychoanalytic Psychotherapy,* 4:106–141.

——. 1976. *The Therapeutic Interaction.* 2 vols. New York: Aronson.

——. 1978–79. Responses to creativity in psychoanalysts. *International Journal of Psychoanalytic Psychotherapy,* 7:189–207.

——. 1982. *Psychotherapy: A Basic Text.* New York: Aronson.

——. 1992. *Science, Systems, and Psychoanalysis.* New York: Karnac Books.

Laor, N. 1982. Old Whig psychiatry: The Szaszian variant. *International Journal of Psychiatry and Related Sciences,* 19:215–225.

——. 1985. Psychoanalysis as science: The inductivist's resistance revisited. *Journal of the American Psychoanalytic Association,* 33:149–166.

Laplanche, J. 1992. Interpretation between determinism and hermeneutics: A restatement of the problem. *International Journal of Psychoanalysis,* 73:429–445.

Laplanche, J., and Pontalis, J.-B. 1973. *The Language of Psychoanalysis*. New York: Norton.

Lasky, R. 1989. Some determinants of the male analyst's capacity to identify with female patients. *International Journal of Psychoanalysis*, 70:405–418.

——. 1990a. Catastrophic illness in the analyst and the analyst's emotional reaction to it. *International Journal of Psychoanalysis*, 71:455–473.

——. 1990b. Keeping the analysis intact when the analyst has suffered a catastrophic illness: Clinical considerations. In Schwartz, H. J., and Schlessing-Silver, A. (eds.), *Illness in the Analyst: Implications for the Treatment Relationship*. Madison, Conn.: International Universities Press.

——. 1992. Some superego conflicts in the analyst who has suffered a catastrophic illness. *International Journal of Psychoanalysis*, 73:127–136.

Lax, R. F. 1969. Some considerations about transference and countertransference manifestations evoked by the analyst's pregnancy. *International Journal of Psychoanalysis*, 50:363–372.

Lear, J. 1993. An interpretation of transference. *International Journal of Psychoanalysis*, 74:739–755.

Leavy, S. A. 1980. *The Psychoanalytic Dialogue*. New Haven: Yale University Press.

——. 1993. Self and sign in free association. *Psychoanalytic Quarterly*, 62:400–421.

Lebovici, S. 1974. Observations on children who have witnessed the violent death of one of their parents: A contribution to the study of traumatization. *International Review of Psychoanalysis*, 1:117–123.

Lederer, W. 1971. Some moral dilemmas encountered in psychotherapy. *Psychiatry*, 34:75–85.

Lester, E. P. 1985. The female analyst and the erotized transference. *International Journal of Psychoanalysis*, 66:283–293.

——. (1985–6) On erotized transference and resistance. *International Journal of Psychoanalytic Psychotherapy*, 11:21–25.

——. 1990. Gender and identity issues in the analytic process. *International Journal of Psychoanalysis*, 71:435–444.

——. 1993. Boundaries and gender: Their interplay in the analytic situation. *Psychoanalytic Inquiry*, 13:153–172.

Lester, E. P., Jodoin, R.-M., and Robertson, B. M. 1989. Countertransference dreams reconsidered: A survey. *International Review of Psychoanalysis*, 16:305–314.

Lester, E. P., and Notman, M. T. 1988. Pregnancy and object relations: Clinical considerations. *Psychoanalytic Inquiry*, 8:196–221.

Levenson, E. 1979. Language and healing. *Journal of the American Academy of Psychoanalysis*, 7:271–282.

——. 1992. Mistakes, errors, and oversights. *Contemporary Psychoanalysis*, 28:555–571.

Levenson, R. 1984. Intimacy, autonomy and gender: Developmental differences and their reflection in adult relationships. *Journal of the American Academy of Psychoanalysis*, 12:529–544.

Levin, D. C. 1969. The self: A contribution to its place in theory and technique. *International Journal of Psychoanalysis,* 50:41–51.

Levine, F. J. 1993. Unconscious fantasy and theories of technique. *Psychoanalytic Inquiry,* 13:326–342.

Levine, H. B. 1983. Some implications of self psychology. *Contemporary Psychoanalysis,* 19:153–171.

——. 1994. The analyst's participation in the analytic process. *International Journal of Psychoanalysis,* 75:665–676.

Levine, M. 1972. *Psychiatry and Ethics.* New York: George Braziller.

Levy, S. T. 1985. Empathy and psychoanalytic technique. *Journal of the American Psychoanalytic Association,* 33:353–378.

Levy, S. T., and Inderbitzin, L. B. 1992. Neutrality, interpretation, and therapeutic intent. *Journal of the American Psychoanalytic Association,* 40:989–1011.

Lewy, E. 1961. Responsibility, free will, and ego psychology. *International Journal of Psychoanalysis,* 42:260–270.

Lichtenberg, J. D. 1983a. An application of the self psychological viewpoint to psychoanalytic technique. In Lichtenberg, J. D., and Kaplan, S. (eds.), *Reflections on Self Psychology,* Hillsdale, N.J.: Analytic Press, 163–185.

——. 1983b. A clinical illustration of construction and reconstruction in the analysis of an adult. *Psychoanalytic Inquiry,* 3:279–294.

Lichtenberg, J. D., Bornstein, M., and Silver, D. (eds.). 1984. *Empathy.* 2 vols. Hillsdale, N.J.: Analytic Press.

Lipson, B. 1974. Confidentiality in life insurance underwriting. Working paper for the Conference on the Confidentiality of Health Records. November 7–9, 1974. Mimeographed.

Lipton, E. L. 1991. The analyst's use of clinical data, and other issues of confidentiality. *Journal of the American Psychoanalytic Association,* 39:967–985.

Lipton, S. D. 1977. The advantages of Freud's technique as shown in his analysis of the Rat Man. *International Journal of Psychoanalysis,* 58:255–273.

——. 1979. An addendum to "The advantages of Freud's technique as shown in his analysis of the Rat Man." *International Journal of Psychoanalysis,* 60:215–216.

Little, M. 1951. Counter-transference and patient's response to it. *International Journal of Psychoanalysis,* 32:32–40.

——. 1957. "R"—the analyst's total response to his patient's needs. *International Journal of Psychoanalysis,* 38:240–254.

——. 1958. On delusional transference (transference psychosis). *International Journal of Psychoanalysis,* 39:134–138.

——. 1966. Transference and borderline states. *International Journal of Psychoanalysis,* 47:476–485.

——. 1990. *Psychotic Anxieties and Containment: A Personal Record of an Analysis with Winnicott.* Northvale, N.J.: Aronson.

Little, R. B. 1967. Transference, countertransference and survival reactions following an analyst's heart attack. *Psychoanalytic Forum,* 2:107–126.

Loewald, H. 1960. On the therapeutic action of psychoanalysis. *International Journal of Psychoanalysis*, 41:16–33.

——. 1975. Psychoanalysis as an art and the fantasy character of the psychoanalytic situation. *Journal of the American Psychoanalytic Association*, 23:277–299.

——. 1986. Transference-countertransference. *Journal of the American Psychoanalytic Association*, 34:275–287.

Loewenstein, R. M. 1954. Some remarks on defences, autonomous ego and psychoanalytic technique. *International Journal of Psychoanalysis*, 35:188–193.

——. 1969. Developments in the theory of transference in the last fifty years. *International Journal of Psychoanalysis*, 50:583–588.

——. 1972. Ego autonomy and psychoanalytic technique. *Psychoanalytic Quarterly*, 41:1–22.

London, N. J. 1985. An appraisal of self psychology. *International Journal of Psychoanalysis*, 66:95–107.

Lorand, S., and Console, W. A. 1958. Therapeutic results in psychoanalytic treatment without fee. *International Journal of Psychoanalysis*, 39:59–64.

Lord, R., Ritvo, S., and Solnit, A. J. 1978. Patients' reactions to the death of the psychoanalyst. *International Journal of Psychoanalysis*, 59:189–197.

Luborsky, L. L. 1984. *Principles of Psychoanalytic Psychotherapy*. New York: Basic Books.

Luborsky, L., and Crits-Christoph, P. 1990. *Understanding Transference: The Core Conflictual Relationship Theme Method*. New York: Basic Books.

Luborsky, L., Mintz, J., Auerbach, A., Christoph, P., Bachrach, H., Todd, T., Johnson, M., Cohen, M., and O'Brien, C. P. 1980. Predicting the outcome of psychotherapy—Findings of the Penn psychotherapy project. *Archives of General Psychiatry*, 37:471–481.

Macalpine, I. 1950. The development of the transference. *Psychoanalytic Quarterly*, 19:501–539.

Mahler, M. S., Pine, F., and Bergman, A. 1975. *The Psychological Birth of the Human Infant*. New York: Basic Books.

Mahony, P. J. 1993. Freud's cases: Are they valuable today? *International Journal of Psychoanalysis*, 74:1027–35.

Makari, G., and Shapiro, T. 1993. On psychoanalytic listening: Language and unconscious communication. *Journal of the American Psychoanalytic Association*, 41:991–1020.

Maldonado, J. L. 1984. Analyst involvement in the psychoanalytical impasse. *International Journal of Psychoanalysis*, 65:263–271.

Maltsberger, J. T. 1993. A career plundered. Presidential Address to the American Association of Suicidology. San Francisco, April 15, 1993.

Maltsberger, J. T., and Buie, D. H. 1974. Countertransference hate in the treatment of suicidal patients. *Archives of General Psychiatry*, 30:625–633.

Margulies, A. 1984. Toward empathy: The uses of wonder. *American Journal of Psychiatry*, 141:1025–1033.

Mariner, A. S. 1967. The problem of therapeutic privacy. *Psychiatry*, 30:60–72.

Mariotti, P. 1993. The analyst's pregnancy: The patient, the analyst, and the space of the unknown. *International Journal of Psychoanalysis*, 74:151–164.

Markson, E. R. 1993. Depression and moral masochism. *International Journal of Psychoanalysis*, 74:931–940.

Marziali, E., Marmar, C., and Krupnick, J. 1981. Therapeutic alliance scales: Development and relationship to psychotherapy outcome. *American Journal of Psychiatry*, 138:361–364.

Massachusetts Board of Registration in Medicine. 1994. *General Guidelines Related to the Maintenance of Boundaries in the Practice of Psychotherapy by Physicians (Adult Patients)*. Boston: Board of Registration in Medicine.

Mayer, E. L. 1994. Some implications for psychoanalytic technique drawn from analysis of a dying patient. *Psychoanalytic Quarterly*, 63:1–19.

Mayer, L. C., and Spence, D. P. 1994. Understanding therapeutic action in the analytic situation: A second look at the developmental metaphor. *Journal of the American Psychoanalytic Association*, 42:789–817.

McCormick, S.J., R. A. 1978. Some neglected aspects of moral responsibility for health. *Perspectives in Biology and Medicine*, 22:31–43.

McCullough, L. B. 1984. Patients with reduced agency: Conceptual, empirical, and ethical considerations. *Journal of Medicine and Philosophy*, 9:329–331.

McDargh, J. 1992. Concluding clinical postscript: On developing a psychological perspective. In *Surveying Sacred Landscapes: A Clinical Case Approach to Religious Experience in Psychotherapy*. New York: Columbia University Press, 172–193.

McDougall, J. 1978. Primitive communication and the use of countertransference. *Contemporary Psychoanalysis*, 14:173–209.

McGlashan, T. H. 1983. The "we-self" in borderline patients: Manifestations of the symbiotic self-object in psychotherapy. *Psychiatry*, 46:351–361.

McLaughlin, J. T. 1975. The sleepy analyst: Some observations on states of consciousness in the analyst at work. *Journal of the American Psychoanalytic Association*, 23:363–382.

——. 1987. The play of transference: Some reflections on enactment in the psychoanalytic situation. *Journal of the American Psychoanalytic Association*, 35:557–582.

——. 1993. Work with patients: The impetus for self-analysis. *Psychoanalytic Inquiry*, 13:365–389.

——. 1995. Touching limits in the analytic dyad. *Psychoanalytic Quarterly*, 64:433–465.

Meares, R. 1983. Keats and the "impersonal" therapist: A note on empathy and the therapeutic screen. *Psychiatry*, 46:73–82.

Meers, D. R. 1970. Contributions of a ghetto culture to symptom formation: Psychoanalytic studies of ego anomalies in childhood. *Psychoanalytic Study of the Child*, 25:209–230.

Mehlman, R. D. 1976. Transference mobilization, transference resolution, and the narcissistic alliance. Presented to the Boston Psychoanalytic Society, February 25, 1976.

Meissner, S.J., W. W. 1964. Thinking about the family—Psychiatric aspects. *Family Process*, 3:1–40.
——. 1970. Notes on identification. I. Origins in Freud. *Psychoanalytic Quarterly*, 39:563–589.
——. 1971. Notes on identification. II. Clarification of related concepts. *Psychoanalytic Quarterly*, 40:277–302.
——. 1972. Notes on identification. III. The concept of identification. *Psychoanalytic Quarterly*, 41:224–260.
——. 1973. Notes on the psychology of hope. *Journal of Religion and Health*, 12:7–29, 120–139.
——. 1974a. Correlative aspects of introjective and projective mechanisms. *American Journal of Psychiatry*, 131:176–180.
——. 1974b. The role of imitative social learning in identificatory processes. *Journal of the American Psychoanalytic Association*, 22:512–536.
——. 1977. The Wolf Man and the paranoid process. *Annual of Psychoanalysis*, 5:23–74.
——. 1978a. The conceptualization of marriage and family dynamics from a psychoanalytic perspective. In: Paolino, T. J., and McCrady, B. S. (eds.), *Marriage and Marital Therapy: Psychoanalytic Behavioral and Systems Theory Perspectives*. New York: Brunner/Mazel, 25–88.
——. 1978b. Notes on some conceptual aspects of the borderline personality. *International Review of Psychoanalysis*, 5:297–311.
——. 1978c. *The Paranoid Process*. New York: Aronson.
——. 1979a. Internalization and object relations. *Journal of the American Psychoanalytic Association*, 27:345–360.
——. 1979b. Threats to confidentiality. *Psychiatric Annals*, 9:54–71.
——. 1979c. The Wolf Man and the paranoid process. *Psychoanalytic Review*, 66: 155–171.
——. 1980. A note on projective identification. *Journal of the American Psychoanalytic Association*, 28:43–67.
——. 1981. *Internalization in Psychoanalysis*. Psychological Issues, Monograph 50. New York: International Universities Press.
——. 1982. Psychotherapy of the paranoid patient. In Giovacchini, P. L., and Boyer, L. B. (eds.), *Technical Factors in the Treatment of the Severely Disturbed Patient*. New York: Aronson, 349–384.
——. 1983. Values in the psychoanalytic situation. *Psychoanalytic Inquiry*, 3:577–598.
——. 1984a. *The Borderline Spectrum: Differential Diagnosis and Developmental Issues*. New York: Aronson.
——. 1984b. *Psychoanalysis and Religious Experience*. New Haven: Yale University Press.
——. 1984–85. Studies on hysteria: Dora. *International Journal of Psychoanalytic Psychotherapy*, 10:567–598.
——. 1986a. Can psychoanalysis find its self? *Journal of the American Psychoanalytic Association*, 34:379–400.

——. 1986b. The earliest internalizations. In Lax, R. F., Bach, S., and Burland, J. A. (eds.), *Self and Object Constancy: Clinical and Theoretical Perspectives*. New York: Guilford Press, 29–72.

——. 1986c. *Psychotherapy and the Paranoid Process*. Northvale, N.J.: Aronson. Paperback edition 1994..

——. 1987a. *Life and Faith: Psychological Perspectives on Religious Experience*. Washington, D.C.: Georgetown University Press.

——. 1987b. Projection and projective identification. In J. Sandler (ed.), *Projection, Identification, Projective Identification*. Madison, Conn.: International Universities Press, 27–49.

——. 1988. *Treatment of Patients in the Borderline Spectrum*. Northvale, N.J.: Aronson.

——. 1989. A note on psychoanalytic facts. *Psychoanalytic Inquiry*, 9:193–219.

——. 1990. Foundations of psychoanalysis reconsidered. *Journal of the American Psychoanalytic Association*, 38:523–557.

——. 1991. *What Is Effective in Psychoanalytic Therapy: The Move from Interpretation to Relation*. Northvale, N.J.: Aronson.

——. 1992. The concept of the therapeutic alliance. *Journal of the American Psychoanalytic Association*, 40:1059–1087.

——. 1993. The self-as-agent in psychoanalysis. *Psychoanalysis and Contemporary Thought*, 16:459–495.

Menaker, E. 1942. The masochistic factor in the psychoanalytic situation. *Psychoanalytic Quarterly*, 9:171–186.

Mendell, D. 1993. Supervising female therapists: A comparison of dynamics while treating male and female patients. *Psychoanalytic Inquiry*, 13:270–285.

Menninger, W. W. 1989. The impact of litigation and court decisions on clinical practice. *Bulletin of the Menninger Clinic*, 53:203–214.

Meyerson, A. T., and Epstein, G. 1976. The psychoanalytic treatment center as a transference object. *Psychoanalytic Quarterly*, 45:274–387.

Milgram, S. 1965. Some conditions of obedience and disobedience to authority. *Human Relations*, 18:57–76.

Miller, J. B. M. 1971. Children's reactions to the death of a parent: A review of the psychoanalytic literature. *Journal of the American Psychoanalytic Association*, 19:697–719.

Milner, M. 1952. Aspects of symbolism in comprehension of the not-self. *International Journal of Psychoanalysis*, 33:181–195.

Mitchell, S. A. 1986. The wings of Icarus: Illusion and the problem of narcissism. *Contemporary Psychoanalysis*, 22:107–132.

Mitchell, S. 1988. *Relational Concepts in Psychoanalysis*. Cambridge: Harvard University Press.

Mitrani, J. L. 1993. Deficiency and envy: Some factors impacting the analytic mind from listening to interpretation. *International Journal of Psychoanalysis*, 74:689–704.

Modell, A. H. 1968. *Object Love and Reality*. New York: International Universities Press.

——. 1975. A narcissistic defense against affects and the illusion of self sufficiency. *International Journal of Psychoanalysis*, 56:275–282.

——. 1976. "The holding environment" and the therapeutic action of psychoanalysis. *Journal of the American Psychoanalytic Association*, 24:285–307.

——. 1978. The conceptualization of the therapeutic action of psychoanalysis: The action of the holding environment. *Bulletin of the Menninger Clinic*, 42:493–504.

——. 1986. The missing elements in Kohut's cure. *Psychoanalytic Inquiry*, 6:367–385.

——. 1988a. The centrality of the psychoanalytic setting and the changing aims of treatment: A perspective from a theory of object relations. *Psychoanalytic Quarterly*, 52:577–596.

——. 1988b. Changing psychic structure through treatment: Preconditions for the resolution of the transference. *Journal of the American Psychoanalytic Association*, 36 (Suppl.): 225–239.

——. 1988c. On the protection and safety of the therapeutic setting. In Rothstein, A. (ed.), *The Therapeutic Action of Psychoanalytic Psychotherapy*. Madison, Conn.: International Universities Press.

——. 1989. The psychoanalytic setting as a container of multiple levels of reality: A perspective on the theory of psychoanalytic treatment. *Psychoanalytic Inquiry*, 9:67–87.

——. 1990. *Other Times, Other Realities: Toward a Theory of Psychoanalytic Treatment*. Cambridge: Harvard University Press.

——. 1991. A confusion of tongues or whose reality is it? *Psychoanalytic Quarterly*, 60:227–244.

——. 1993. *The Private Self*. Cambridge: Harvard University Press.

Moeller, M. L. 1977. Self and object in countertransference. *International Journal of Psychoanalysis*, 58:365–374.

Money-Kyrle, R. E. 1956. Normal countertransference and some of its deviations. *International Journal of Psychoanalysis*, 37:360–366.

——. 1978. *The Collected Papers of Roger Money-Kyrle*. Ed. D. Meltzer and E. O'Shaughnessy. Strath Tay, Perthshire: Clunie Press.

Moore, B. E., and Fine, B. D. (eds.). 1990. *Psychoanalytic Terms and Concepts*. New Haven: Yale University Press.

Moraitis, G. 1993. The analyst's quest for self-awareness. *Psychoanalytic Inquiry*, 13:333–347.

Moraitis, G. (ed.). 1995. The relevance of the couch in contemporary psychoanalysis. *Psychoanalytic Inquiry*, 15.

Morris, H. 1993. Narrative representation, narrative enactment, and the psychoanalytic construction of history. *International Journal of Psychoanalysis*, 74:33–54.

Morrison, A. P. 1984. Working with shame in psychoanalytic treatment. *Journal of the American Psychoanalytic Association*, 32:479–505.

——. 1989. *Shame: The Underside of Narcissism*. Hillsdale, N.J.: Analytic Press.

Moses, I. 1988. The misuse of empathy in psychoanalysis. *Contemporary Psychoanalysis*, 24:577–594.

Nacht, S. 1957. Technical remarks on the handling of the transference neurosis. *International Journal of Psychoanalysis,* 38:196–203.

——. 1958. Variations in technique. *International Journal of Psychoanalysis,* 39:235–237.

——. 1962. The curative factors in psychoanalysis, II. *International Journal of Psychoanalysis,* 43:206–211.

——. 1963. The non-verbal relationship in psychoanalytic treatment. *International Journal of Psychoanalysis,* 44:328–333.

——. 1964. Silence as an integrative factor. *International Journal of Psychoanalysis,* 45:299–303.

Nacht, S., and Viderman, S. 1960. The pre-object universe in the transference situation. *International Journal of Psychoanalysis,* 41:385–388.

Nadelson, C. C. 1993. The therapist's absences. In Gold, J. H., and Nemiah, J. C. (eds.), *Beyond Transference: When the Therapist's Real Life Intrudes.* Washington, D.C.: American Psychiatric Press, 71–85.

Nadelson, T. 1976. Victim, victimizer: Interaction in the psychotherapy of borderline patients. *International Journal of Psychoanalytic Psychotherapy,* 5:115–129.

Nagera, H. 1970. Children's reactions to the death of important objects: A developmental approach. *Psychoanalytic Study of the Child,* 25:360–400.

Nersessian, E. 1989. Changing psychic structure through treatment. *Journal of the American Psychoanalytic Association,* 37:173–186.

——. 1995. Some reflections on curiosity and psychoanalytic technique. *Psychoanalytic Quarterly,* 64:113–135.

Newton, P. M. 1973. Social structure and process in psychotherapy: A sociopsychological analysis of transference, resistance and change. *International Journal of Psychiatry,* 11:480–526.

Noll, J. O., and Hanlon, M. J. 1976. Patient privacy and confidentiality at mental health centers. *American Journal of Psychiatry,* 133:1286–1289.

Norman, H. F., Blacker, K. H., Oremland, J. D., and Barrett, W. G. 1976. The fate of the transference neurosis after termination of a satisfactory analysis. *Journal of the American Psychoanalytic Association,* 24:471–498.

Norton, J. 1963. Treatment of a dying patient. *Psychoanalytic Study of the Child,* 18:541–560.

Notman, M. T. 1993. Countertransference reactions to a patient's sexual encounter with a previous therapist. In Gold, J. H., and Nemiah, J. C. (eds.), *Beyond Transference: When the Therapist's Real Life Intrudes.* Washington, D.C.: American Psychiatric Press, 159–172.

Notman, M. T., and Lester, E. 1988. Pregnancy: Theoretical considerations. *Psychoanalytic Inquiry,* 8:139–159.

Novick, J. 1970. Vicissitudes of the "working alliance" in the analysis of a latency girl. *Psychoanalytic Study of the Child,* 25:231–256.

——. 1980. Negative therapeutic motivation and negative therapeutic alliance. *Psychoanalytic Study of the Child,* 35:299–320.

——. 1982. Termination: Themes and issues. *Psychoanalytic Inquiry,* 2:329–365.

Novick, K. K., and Novick, J. 1994. Postoedipal transformations: Latency, adolescence, and pathogenesis. *Journal of the American Psychoanalytic Association,* 42: 143–169.

Nunberg, H. 1948. *Practice and Theory of Psychoanalysis,* vol. I. New York: International Universities Press.

——. 1955. *Principles of Psychoanalysis.* New York: International Universities Press.

Ogden, T. H. 1979. On projective identification. *International Journal of Psychoanalysis,* 60:357–373.

——. 1994. The concept of interpretive action. *Psychoanalytic Quarterly,* 63:219–245.

Olden, C. 1953. On adult empathy with children. *Psychoanalytic Study of the Child,* 8:111–126.

Olinick, S. L. 1954. Some considerations of the use of questioning as a psychoanalytic technique. *Journal of the American Psychoanalytic Association,* 2:57–66.

——. 1959. The analytic paradox. *Psychiatry,* 22:333–339.

——. 1964. The negative therapeutic reaction. *International Journal of Psychoanalysis,* 45:540–548.

——. 1969. On empathy and regression in service of the other. *British Journal of Medical Psychology,* 42:41–49.

——. 1975. On empathic perception and the problems of reporting psychoanalytic processes. *International Journal of Psychoanalysis,* 56:147–154.

——. 1976. Parallel analyzing functions in work ego and observing ego: The treatment alliance. *Journal of the Philadelphia Association for Psychoanalysis,* 3:3–21.

——. 1993. Structural actualities of the transference and their effects on the analyst's functions. *Psychoanalytic Inquiry,* 13:310–325.

Olinick, S. L., Poland, W. S., Grigg, K. A., and Granatir, W. L. 1973. The psychoanalytic work ego: Process and interpretation. *International Journal of Psychoanalysis,* 54:143–151.

Oremland, J. D., Blacker, K. H., and Norman, H. F. 1975. Incompleteness in "successful" psychoanalyses: A follow-up study. *Journal of the American Psychoanalytic Association,* 23:819–844.

Oremland, J. D., and Windholz, E. 1971. Some specific transference, countertransference and supervisory problems in the analysis of a narcissistic personality. *International Journal of Psychoanalysis,* 52:267–275.

Ornstein, A. 1974. The dread to repeat and the new beginning. *Annual of Psychoanalysis,* 2:231–248.

Ornstein, P. H., and Ornstein, A. 1985. Clinical understanding and explaining: The empathic vantage point. In Goldberg, A. (ed.), *Progress in Self Psychology, vol. I.* New York: Guilford Press, 43–61.

——. 1994. On the conceptualisation of clinical facts in psychoanalysis. *International Journal of Psychoanalysis,* 75:977–994.

Orr, D. W. 1954. Transference and countertransference: A historical survey. *Journal of the American Psychoanalytic Association,* 2:621–670.

Ost, D. E. 1984. The "right" not to know. *Journal of Medicine and Philosophy,* 9:301–312.

Ostow, M. 1962. *Drugs in Psychoanalysis and Psychotherapy*. New York: Basic Books.

Ottenheimer, L. 1972.. Some considerations on moral values and psychoanalysis. In Post, S. C. (ed.), *Moral Values and the Superego Concept in Psychoanalysis.* New York: International Universities Press, 240–243.

——. 1979. Some psychodynamics in the choice of an analyst. *Journal of the American Academy of Psychoanalysis,* 7:339–344.

Panel. 1958. Technical aspects of transference. Reported by D. Leach. *Journal of the American Psychoanalytic Association,* 6:560–566.

——. 1968. Aspects of culture in psychoanalytic theory and practice. Reported by S. W. Jackson. *Journal of the American Psychoanalytic Association,* 16:651–670.

——. 1972. Levels of confidentiality in the psychoanalytic situation. Reported by A. S. Watson. *Journal of the American Psychoanalytic Association,* 20:156–176.

——. 1974. The analyst's emotional life during work. Reported by R. Aaron. *Journal of the American Psychoanalytic Association,* 22:160–169.

——. 1975. Termination: Problems and techniques. Reported by W. S. Robbins. *Journal of the American Psychoanalytic Association,* 23:166–176.

——. 1992. Freudian and Kleinian theory: A dialogue of comparative perspectives. Reported by H. B. Levine. *Journal of the American Psychoanalytic Association,* 40:801–826.

——. 1993a. Learning from our unsuccessful cases. Reported by E. J. Nuetzel. *Journal of the American Psychoanalytic Association,* 41:743–754.

——. 1993b. The life cycle of the analyst: Pregnancy, illness, and disability. Reported by H. J. Schwartz. *Journal of the American Psychoanalytic Association,* 41:191–207.

Paniagua, C. 1995. Common ground, uncommon methods. *International Journal of Psychoanalysis,* 76:357–371.

Pao, P.-N. 1983. Therapeutic empathy and the treatment of schizophrenics. *Psychoanalytic Inquiry,* 3:145–167.

Pasternack, S. A. 1977. The psychotherapy fee: An issue in residency training. *Diseases of the Nervous System,* 38:913–916.

Pattison, E. M. 1967. The experience of dying. *American Journal of Psychotherapy,* 21:32–43.

Paul, L. 1959. A note on the private aspect and professional aspect of the psychoanalyst. *Bulletin of the Philadelphia Psychoanalytic Association,* 9:96–101.

Paul, N. L. 1967. The use of empathy in the resolution of grief. *Perspectives in Biology and Medicine,* 11:153–170.

Pellegrino, E. D. 1979. Toward a reconstruction of medical morality: The primacy of the act of profession and the fact of illness. *Journal of Medicine and Philosophy,* 4:32–56.

Person, E. S. 1983. Women in therapy: Therapist gender as a variable. *International Review of Psychoanalysis,* 16:193–204.

——. 1988. *Dreams of Love and Fateful Encounters.* New York: Norton.

——. 1993. Introduction. In Person, E. S., Hagelin, A., and Fonagy, P. (eds.), *On Freud's "Observations on Transference-love."* New Haven: Yale University Press, 1–14.

Person, E. S., and Klar, H. 1994. Establishing trauma: The difficulty distinguishing between memories and fantasies. *Journal of the American Psychoanalytic Association,* 42:1055–1081.

Peterfreund, E. 1975. How does the analyst listen? On models and strategies in the psychoanalytic process. *Psychoanalysis and Contemporary Science,* 4:59–101.

Peters, M. 1991. Analytic neutrality and the "person" as psychoanalyst. *Psychoanalysis and Psychotherapy,* 9:114–127.

Pfeffer, A. Z. 1959. A procedure for evaluating the results of psychoanalysis: A preliminary report. *Journal of the American Psychoanalytic Association,* 7:418–444.

——. 1961. Follow-up study of a satisfactory analysis. *Journal of the American Psychoanalytic Association,* 9:698–718.

——. 1963. The meaning of the analyst after analysis—A contribution to the theory of therapeutic results. *Journal of the American Psychoanalytic Association,* 11:229–244.

Pickering, G. 1978. Medicine on the brink: The dilemma of a learned profession. *Perspectives in Biology and Medicine,* 21:551–560.

Pigman, G. W. 1995. Freud and the history of empathy. *International Journal of Psychoanalysis,* 76:237–256.

Pine, F. 1992. From technique to a theory of psychic change. *International Journal of Psychoanalysis,* 73:251–254.

——. 1993. A contribution to the analysis of the psychoanalytic process. *Psychoanalytic Quarterly,* 62:185–205.

Pines, D. 1988. Adolescent pregnancy and motherhood: A psychoanalytic perspective. *Psychoanalytic Inquiry,* 8:234–251.

——. 1990. Pregnancy, miscarriage and abortion: A psychoanalytic perspective. *International Journal of Psychoanalysis,* 71:301–307.

Plank, E. N., and Plank, R. 1978. Children and death: As seen through art and autobiographies. *Psychoanalytic Study of the Child,* 33:593–620.

Poland, W. S. 1971. The place of humor in psychotherapy. *American Journal of Psychiatry,* 128:635–637.

——. 1974. On empathy in analytic practice. *Journal of the Philadelphia Association for Psychoanalysis,* 1:284–297.

——. 1975. Tact as a psychoanalytic function. *International Journal of Psychoanalysis,* 56:155–162.

——. 1978. On the analyst's responsibility: An editorial. *Journal of the Philadelphia Association for Psychoanalysis,* 4:187–196.

——. 1984. On the analyst's neutrality. *Journal of the American Psychoanalytic Association,* 32:283–299.

——. 1990. The gift of laughter: On the development of a sense of humor in clinical analysis. *Psychoanalytic Quarterly,* 59:197–225.

——. 1992. From analytic surface to analytic space. *Journal of the American Psychoanalytic Association*, 40:381–404.

Pope, K. S. 1994. *Sexual Involvement With Therapists: Assessment, Subsequent Therapy, Forensics*. Washington, D.C.: American Psychological Association Press.

Post, S. 1980. Origins, elements, and functions of therapeutic empathy. *International Journal of Psychoanalysis*, 61:277–293.

Post, S. C. (ed.). 1972. *Moral Values and the Superego Concept in Psychoanalysis*. New York: International Universities Press.

Puget, J. 1992. Belonging and ethics. *Psychoanalytic Inquiry*, 12:551–569.

Quinodoz, D. 1992. The psychoanalytic setting as the instrument of the container function. *International Journal of Psychoanalysis*, 73:627–635.

Quinodoz, J.-M. 1994. Clinical facts or psychoanalytic clinical facts? *International Journal of Psychoanalysis*, 75:963–976.

Racker, H. 1953. A contribution to the problem of countertransference. *International Journal of Psychoanalysis*, 43:313–324.

——. 1957. The meaning and uses of countertransference. *Psychoanalytic Quarterly*, 26:303–357.

——. 1958. Psychoanalytic technique and the analyst's unconscious masochism. *Psychoanalytic Quarterly*, 27:555–562.

——. 1968. *Transference and Countertransference*. London: Hogarth.

Ramzy, I. 1961. The range and spirit of psychoanalytic technique. *International Journal of Psychoanalysis*, 42:497–505.

——. 1972. The place of values in psychoanalytic theory, practice and training. In Post, S. C. (ed.), *Moral Values and the Superego Concept in Psychoanalysis*. New York: International Universities Press, 205–225.

Rangell, L. 1955. The borderline case (Panel report). *Journal of the American Psychoanalytic Association*, 3:285–298.

——. 1968. The psychoanalytic process. *International Journal of Psychoanalysis*, 49:19–26.

——. 1969. The intrapsychic process and its analysis: A recent line of thought and its current implications. *International Journal of Psychoanalysis*, 50:65–77.

——. 1981. From insight to change. *Journal of the American Psychoanalytic Association*, 29:119–141.

——. 1985. The object in psychoanalytic theory. *Journal of the American Psychoanalytic Association*, 33:301–334.

——. 1992. The psychoanalytic theory of change. *International Journal of Psychoanalysis*, 73:415–428.

Rapaport, D. 1957. The theory of ego autonomy: A generalization. In Gill, M. M. (ed.), *The Collected Papers of David Rapaport*. New York: Basic Books, 1967, 722–744.

Raphling, D. L. 1994. A patient who was not sexually abused. *Journal of the American Psychoanalytical Association*, 42:65–78.

——. 1995. Interpretation and expectation: The anxiety of influence. *Journal of the American Psychoanalytical Association*, 43:95–111.

Raphling, D. L., and Chused, J. F. 1988. Transference across gender lines. *Journal of the American Psychoanalytic Association,* 36:77–104.

Rappaport, E. A. 1956. The management of an erotized transference. *Psychoanalytic Quarterly,* 25:515–529.

——. 1959. The first dream in an erotized transference. *International Journal of Psychoanalysis,* 40:240–245.

Rayner, E. 1992. Matching, attunement and the psychoanalytic dialogue. *International Journal of Psychoanalysis,* 73:39–54.

Redlich, F., and Mollica, R. 1976. Overview: Ethical issues in contemporary psychiatry. *American Journal of Psychiatry,* 133:125–136.

Reed, G. S. 1993. On the value of explicit reconstruction. *Psychoanalytic Quarterly,* 62:52–73.

Reich, A. 1958. A special variation of technique. *International Journal of Psychoanalysis,* 39:230–234.

——. 1960. Further remarks on countertransference. *International Journal of Psychoanalysis,* 41:389–395.

——. 1966. Empathy and countertransference. In *Psychoanalytic Contributions.* New York: International Universities Press, 1973, 344–360.

Reider, A. E. 1977. Therapeutic process and an unpaid bill. In Gutheil, T. G. (ed.), Money as a clinical issue in psychiatry. *Psychiatric Annals,* 7:8–22.

Reik, T. 1948. *Listening with the Third Ear: The Inner Experience of a Psychoanalyst.* New York: Farrar, Straus, and Giroux, 1983.

Renik, O. 1990. Analysis of a woman's homosexual strivings by a male analyst. *Psychoanalytic Quarterly,* 59:41–53.

——. 1992. Use of the analyst as a fetish. *Psychoanalytic Quarterly,* 61:542–563.

——. 1993. Analytic interaction: Conceptualizing technique in light of the analyst's irreducible subjectivity. *Psychoanalytic Quarterly,* 62:553–571.

——. 1995a. The ideal of the anonymous analyst and the problem of self-disclosure. *Psychoanalytic Quarterly,* 64:466–495.

——. 1995b. The role of an analyst's expectations in clinical technique: Reflections on the concept of resistance. *Journal of the American Psychoanalytic Association,* 43:83–94.

Rhodes, L. A. 1984. "This will clear your mind": The use of metaphors for medication in psychiatric settings. *Culture, Medicine and Psychiatry,* 8:49–70.

Rieff, P. 1959. *Freud: The Mind of the Moralist.* New York: Viking Press.

Rioch, J. M. 1943. The transference phenomenon in psychoanalytic therapy. *Psychiatry,* 6:147–156.

Riviere, J. 1936. A contribution to the analysis of the negative therapeutic reaction. *International Journal of Psychoanalysis,* 17:304–320.

Rivinus, T. M. 1977. The abuse of social security income. In Gutheil, T. G. (ed.), Money as a clinical issue in psychiatry. *Psychiatric Annals,* 7:69–73.

Roazen, P. 1972. The impact of psychoanalysis on values. In Post, S. C. (ed.), *Moral Values and the Superego Concept in Psychoanalysis.* New York: International Universities Press, 197–204.

Robbins, M. 1988. Use of audiotape recording in impasses with severely disturbed patients. *Journal of the American Psychoanalytic Association,* 36:61–75.

——. 1993. *Experiences of Schizophrenia: An Integration of the Personal, Scientific, and Therapeutic.* New York: Guilford Press.

Robertson, B. M., and Yack, M.-E. 1993. A candidate dreams of her patient: A report and some observations on the supervisory process. *International Journal of Psychoanalysis,* 74:993–1003.

Rochlin, G. 1965. *Griefs and Discontents: The Forces of Change.* Boston: Little, Brown.

Roland, A. 1967. The reality of the psychoanalytic relationship and situation in the handling of transference-resistance. *International Journal of Psychoanalysis,* 48: 504–510.

Roose, S. P. 1990. The use of medication in combination with psychoanalytic psychotherapy or psychoanalysis. In Michels, R. (ed.), *Psychiatry,* vol. 1. Philadelphia: Lippincott, 1–8.

Roose, S. P., and Stern, R. H. 1995. Medication use in training cases: A survey. *Journal of the American Psychoanalytic Association,* 43:163–170.

Rose. G. J. 1961. Pregenital aspects of pregnancy fantasies. *International Journal of Psychoanalysis,* 42:544–549.

Rosenbaum, M. 1965. Dreams in which the analyst appears undisguised—A clinical and statistical study. *International Journal of Psychoanalysis,* 46:429–437.

Rosenberg, R. C. 1994. The therapeutic alliance and the psychiatric emergence room crisis as opportunity. *Psychiatric Annals,* 24:610–614.

Rosner, S. 1986. The seriously ill or dying analyst and the limits of neutrality. *Psychoanalytic Psychology,* 3:357–371.

Roth, N. 1978. Fear of death in the aging. *American Journal of Psychotherapy,* 32:552–560.

Rothstein, A. 1980. Toward a critique of the psychology of the self. *Psychoanalytic Quarterly,* 49:425–455.

——. 1986. The seduction of money: A brief note on an expression of transference love. *Psychoanalytic Quarterly,* 55:296–300.

——. 1995. Psychoanalytic technique and the creation of analysands: On beginning analysis with patients who are reluctant to pay the analyst's fee. *Psychoanalytic Quarterly,* 64:306–325.

Roughton, R. E. 1993. Useful aspects of acting out: Repetition, enactment, and actualization. *Journal of the American Psychoanalytic Association,* 41:443–472.

Russell, G. F. M. 1970. Anorexia nervosa: Its identity as an illness and its treatment. In Price, J. H. (ed.), *Modern Trends in Psychological Medicine.* New York: Appleton-Century Crofts, 131–164.

Rycroft, C. 1956. The nature and function of the analyst's communication to the patient. *International Journal of Psychoanalysis,* 37:469–472.

——. 1958. An enquiry into the function of words in the psychoanalytic situation. *International Journal of Psychoanalysis,* 39:408–415.

Sandbank, T. 1993. Psychoanalysis and maternal work—some parallels. *International Journal of Psychoanalysis*, 74:715–727.

Sandler, A. 1978. Problems in the psychoanalysis of an aging narcissistic patient. *Journal of Geriatric Psychiatry*, 11:5–36.

Sandler, J. 1960. The background of safety. *International Journal of Psychoanalysis*, 41:352–356.

——. 1976. Countertransference and role-responsiveness. *International Review of Psychoanalysis*, 3:32–37.

Sandler, J., Dare, C., and Holder, A. 1973. *The Patient and the Analyst: The Basis of the Psychoanalytic Process*. New York: International Universities Press.

Sandler, J., Holder, A., Kawenoka, M., Kennedy, H., and Neurath, L. 1969. Notes on some theoretical and clinical aspects of transference. *International Journal of Psychoanalysis*, 50:633–645.

Sarwer-Foner, G. J. 1960. *The Dynamics of Psychiatric Drug Therapy*. Springfield, Ill.: C. C. Thomas.

Sashin, J. I., Eldred, S. H., and van Amerongen, S. T. 1975. A search for predictive factors in institute supervised cases: A retrospective study of 183 cases from 1959–1966 at the Boston Psychoanalytic Society and Institute. *International Journal of Psychoanalysis*, 56:343–359.

Saul, L. J. 1959. Reactions of a man to natural death. *Psychoanalytic Quarterly*, 28:383–386.

Schachter, J. 1990. Post-termination patient-analyst contact: I. Analysts' attitudes and experience; II. Impact on patients. *International Journal of Psychoanalysis*, 71:475–486.

——. 1992. Concepts of termination and post-termination patient-analyst contact. *International Journal of Psychoanalysis*, 73:137–154.

——. 1994. Abstinence and neutrality: Development and diverse views. *International Journal of Psychoanalysis*, 75:709–720.

——. 1995. The analyst under stress: Issues of technique. *Journal of the American Psychoanalytic Association*, 43:11–14.

Schachter, J., and Butts, H. F. 1968. Transference and countertransference in interracial analyses. *Journal of the American Psychoanalytic Association*, 16:792–808.

Schafer, R. 1959. Generative empathy in the treatment situation. *Psychoanalytic Quarterly*, 28:342–373.

——. 1970. The psychoanalytic vision of reality. *International Journal of Psychoanalysis*, 51:279–297.

——. 1973. The termination of brief psychoanalytic psychotherapy. *International Journal of Psychoanalytic Psychotherapy*, 2:135–148.

——. 1976. *A New Language for Psychoanalysis*. New Haven: Yale University Press.

——. 1981. *Narrative Actions in Psychoanalysis*. Worcester, Mass.: Clark University Press.

——. 1983. *The Analytic Attitude*. New York: Basic Books.

——. 1993. Five readings of Freud's "Observations on transference love." In Person, E. S., Hagelin, A., and Fonagy, P. (eds.), *On Freud's "Observations on Transference-love."* New Haven: Yale University Press, 75–95.

——. 1995. In the wake of Heinz Hartmann. *International Journal of Psychoanalysis,* 76:223–235.

Schaffer, N. D. 1986. The borderline patient and affirmative interpretation. *Bulletin of the Menninger Clinic,* 50:148–162.

Schevin, F. F. 1963. Countertransference and identity phenomena manifested in a case of "phallus girl" identity. *Journal of the American Psychoanalytic Association,* 11:331–344.

Schimel, J. L. 1974. Two alliances in the treatment of adolescents: Toward a working alliance with parents and a therapeutic alliance with the adolescent. *Journal of the American Academy of Psychoanalysis,* 2:243–253.

Schlesinger, H. J. 1981. The process of empathic response. *Psychoanalytic Inquiry,* 1:393–416.

——. 1994a. How the analyst listens: The prestages of interpretation. *International Journal of Psychoanalysis,* 75:31–37.

——. 1994b. The role of the intellect in the process of defense. *Bulletin of the Menninger Clinic,* 58:15–36.

Schlessinger, N., and Robbins, F. P. 1983. *A Developmental View of the Psychoanalytic Process: Follow-up Studies and Their Consequences.* Madison, Conn.: International Universities Press.

Schoenewolf, G. 1993. *Counterresistance: The Therapist's Interference with the Therapeutic Process.* Northvale, N.J.: Aronson.

Schowalter, J. E. 1976. Therapeutic alliance and the role of speech in child analysis. *Psychoanalytic Study of the Child,* 31:415–436.

Schulz, C. G. 1980. All-or-none phenomena in the therapy of severe disorders. In Strauss, J. S., et al. (eds.), *The Psychotherapy of Schizophrenia.* New York: Plenum, 181–190.

Schur, M. 1972. *Freud: Living and Dying.* New York: International Universities Press.

Schwaber, E. A. 1979. On the "self" within the matrix of analytic theory—some clinical reflections and reconsiderations. *International Journal of Psychoanalysis,* 60:467–479.

——. 1981a. Empathy: a mode of analytic listening. *Psychoanalytic Inquiry,* 1:357–392.

——. 1981b. Narcissism, self psychology and the listening perspective. *Annual of Psychoanalysis,* 9:115–131.

——. 1983a. A particular perspective on analytic listening. *Psychoanalytic Study of the Child,* 38:519–546.

——. 1983b. Psychoanalytic listening and psychic reality. *International Review of Psychoanalysis,* 10:379–392.

——. 1986. Reconstruction and perceptual experience: further thoughts on psychoanalytic listening. *Journal of the American Psychoanalytic Association,* 34:911–932.

——. 1992. Countertransference: the analyst's retreat from the patient's vantage point. *International Journal of Psychoanalysis,* 73:349–361.

——. 1995. Towards a definition of the term and concept of interaction. *International Journal of Psychoanalysis,* 76:557–564.

Schwaber, E. A., and Hamilton, V. 1993. Letters to the editor: Truth and reality in psychoanalytic discourse. *International Journal of Psychoanalysis,* 74:1065–8.

Schwartz, A. M., and Karasu, T. B. 1977. Psychotherapy with the dying patient. *American Journal of Psychotherapy,* 31:19–35.

Schwartz, H. J. 1987. Illness in the doctor: Implications for the psychoanalytic process. *Journal of the American Psychoanalytic Association,* 35:657–692.

Schwartz, H. J., and Schlessinger-Silver, A.-L. 1990. *Illness in the Analyst: Implications for the Treatment Relationship.* Madison, Conn.: International Universities Press.

Schwartz, R. S. 1984. Confidentiality and secret-keeping on an inpatient unit. *Psychiatry,* 47:279–284.

Schwarz, I. G. 1974. Forced termination of analysis revisited. *International Review of Psychoanalysis,* 1:283–290.

Scialli, J. V. K. 1982. Multiple identity processes and the development of the observing ego. *Journal of the American Academy of Psychoanalysis,* 10:387–405.

Searles, H. F. 1965. *Collected Papers on Schizophrenia and Related Subjects.* New York: International Universities Press.

——. 1978. Psychoanalytic therapy with the borderline adult: Some principles concerning technique. In Masterson, J. F. (ed.), *New Perspectives on Psychotherapy of the Borderline Adult.* New York: Brunner/Mazel,

——. 1978–79. Concerning transference and countertransference. *International Journal of Psychoanalytic Psychotherapy,* 7:165–188.

——. 1984. Transference responses in borderline patients. *Psychiatry,* 47:37–49.

——. 1985. Separation and loss in psychoanalytic therapy with borderline patients: Further remarks. *American Journal of Psychoanalysis,* 45:9–27.

Segal, H. 1958. Fear of death: Notes on the analysis of an old man. *International Journal of Psychoanalysis,* 39:178–181.

——. 1964. *Introduction to the Work of Melanie Klein.* New York: Basic Books.

——. 1989. Psychoanalysis and freedom of thought. In Sandler, J. (ed.), *Dimensions of Psychoanalysis.* London: Karnac Books, 51–64.

Selzer, M. A., Carsky, M., Gilbert, B., Weiss, W., Klein, M., and Wagner, S. 1984. The shared field: A precursor stage in the development of a psychotherapeutic alliance with the hospitalized chronic schizophrenic patient. *Psychiatry,* 47:324–332.

Shainess, N. 1979. Analyzability and capacity for change in middle life. *Journal of the American Academy of Psychoanalysis,* 7:385–403.

Shapiro, D. 1989. *Psychotherapy of Neurotic Character.* New York: Basic Books.

Shapiro, E. R., Shapiro, R. L., Zinner, J., and Berkowitz, D. A. 1977. The borderline ego and the working alliance: Indications for family and individual treatment in adolescence. *International Journal of Psychoanalysis,* 58:77–87.

Shapiro, T. 1974. The development and distortions of empathy. *Psychoanalytic Quarterly*, 43:4–25.

——. 1981. Empathy: A critical reevaluation. *Psychoanalytic Inquiry*, 1:423–448.

——. 1984. On neutrality. *Journal of the American Psychoanalytic Association*, 32: 269–282.

Silber, A. 1969. A patient's gift: Its meaning and function. *International Journal of Psychoanalysis*, 50:335–341.

Silver, A.-L. 1982. Resuming the work with a life-threatening illness. *Contemporary Psychoanalysis*, 18:314–326.

Silver, D., and Campbell, B. K. 1988. Failure of psychological gestation. *Psychoanalytic Inquiry*, 8:222–233.

Simon, B. 1992. "Incest—See under Oedipus complex": The history of an error in psychoanalysis. *Journal of the American Psychoanalytic Association*, 40:955–988.

——. 1993. In search of psychoanalytic technique: Perspectives from on the couch and from behind the couch. *Journal of the American Psychoanalytic Association*, 41:1051–82.

Simon, J., Fink, G., Gill, M. M., Endicott, N. A., and Paul, I. H. 1970. Studies in audio-recorded psychoanalysis. II. The effect of recording upon the analyst. *Journal of the American Psychoanalytic Association*, 18:86–101.

Skolnikoff, A. Z. 1993. The analyst's experience in the psychoanalytic situation: A continuum between objective and subjective reality. *Psychoanalytic Inquiry*, 13: 296–309.

Slavin, M. O., and Kriegman, D. 1992. *The Adaptive Design of the Human Psyche*. New York: Guilford Press.

Slochower, J. 1991. Variations in the analytic holding environment. *International Journal of Psychoanalysis*, 72:709–718.

Slochower, J. 1992. A hateful borderline patient and the holding environment. *Contemporary Psychoanalysis*, 28:72–88.

Slovenko, R. 1976. On confidentiality. *Contemporary Psychoanalysis*, 12:109–139.

Smith, H. F. 1993. Engagements in the analytic work. *Psychoanalytic Inquiry*, 13: 425–454.

Smith, J. H. 1991. *Arguing with Lacan: Ego Psychology and Language*. New Haven: Yale University Press.

Sonnenberg, S. M. 1995. Analytic listening and the analyst's self-analysis. *International Journal of Psychoanalysis*, 76:335–342.

Spence, D. P. 1982. *Narrative Truth and Historical Truth*. New York: Norton.

——. 1993. Beneath the analytic surface: The analysand's theory of mind. *International Journal of Psychoanalysis*, 74:729–738.

Spence, D. P., Mayes, L. C., and Dahl, H. 1994. Monitoring the analytic surface. *Journal of the American Psychoanalytical Association*, 42:43–64.

Spencer, J. H., and Balter, L. 1990. Psychoanalytic observation. *Journal of the American Psychoanalytic Association*, 38:393–421.

Spiegel, J. P. 1976. Cultural aspects of transference and countertransference revisited. *Journal of the American Academy of Psychoanalysis*, 4:447–467.

Spitz, R. E. 1965. *The First Year of Life*. New York: International Universities Press.

Spotnitz, H. 1969. *Modern Psychoanalysis of the Schizophrenic Patient*. New York: Grune and Stratton.

Spruiell, V. 1983. The rules and frames of the psychoanalytic situation. *Psychoanalytic Quarterly*, 52:1–33.

——. 1984. The analyst at work. *International Journal of Psychoanalysis*, 6:13–30.

——. 1987. The foundations of psychoanalysis: An essay on a philosophical book by Adolf Grünbaum. *International Review of Psychoanalysis*, 14:169–183.

Stein, H. F. 1986. "Sick people" and "trolls": A contribution to the understanding of the dynamics of physician explanatory models. *Culture, Medicine and Psychiatry*, 10:221–229.

Stein, M. 1981. The unobjectionable part of the transference. *Journal of the American Psychoanalytic Association*, 29:869–892.

——. 1988. Writing about psychoanalysis. II. Analysts who write, patients who read. *Journal of the American Psychoanalytic Association*, 36:393–408.

Stein, S. 1991. The influence of theory on the psychoanalyst's countertransference. *International Journal of Psychoanalysis*, 72:325–334.

Sterba, R. 1934. The fate of the ego in psychoanalytic therapy. *International Journal of Psychoanalysis*, 15:117–126.

——. 1940. The dynamics of the dissolution of the transference resistance. *Psychoanalytic Quarterly*, 9:363–379.

——. 1941. The relaxation of the analyst. *Psychiatry*, 4:339–342.

Stern, D. B. 1988. Not misusing empathy. *Contemporary Psychoanalysis*, 24:598–611.

Stern, D. N. 1985. *The Interpersonal World of the Infant: A View from Psychoanalysis and Developmental Psychology*. New York: Basic Books.

Stern, M. M. 1970. Therapeutic playback, self objectification and the analytic process. *Journal of the American Psychoanalytic Association*, 18:562–598.

Stern, S. 1992. The opposing currents technique: For eating disorders and other false-self problems. *Contemporary Psychoanalysis*, 28:594–615.

Stewart, W. A. 1963. An inquiry into the concept of working through. *Journal of the American Psychoanalytic Association*, 11:474–499.

Stocking, M. 1973. Confrontation in psychotherapy: Considerations arising from the psychoanalytic treatment of a child. In Adler, G., and Myerson, P. G. (eds.), *Confrontation in Psychotherapy*. New York: Science House, 319–345.

Stolorow, R. 1983. Self psychology: A structural psychology. In Lichtenberg, J. D., and Kaplan, S. (eds.), *Reflections on Self Psychology*. Hillsdale, N.J.: Analytic Press, 287–296.

——. 1986. Critical reflections on the theory of self psychology: An inside view. *Psychoanalytic Inquiry*, 6:387–402.

——. 1993. An intersubjective view of the therapeutic process. *Bulletin of the Menninger Clinic*, 57:450–457.

Stolorow, R., Atwood, G. E., and Lachmann, F. M. 1981. Transference and countertransference in the analysis of developmental arrests. *Bulletin of the Menninger Clinic*, 45:20–28.

Stolorow, R., Brandschaft, B., and Atwood, G. E. 1983. Intersubjectivity in psychoanalytic treatment: With special reference to archaic states. *Bulletin of the Menninger Clinic*, 47:117–128.

——. 1987. *Psychoanalytic Treatment: An Intersubjective Approach*. Hillsdale, N.J.: Analytic Press.

Stolorow, R., and Lachmann, F. 1980. *Psychoanalysis of Developmental Arrests: Theory and Treatment*. New York: International Universities Press.

——. 1984. Transference: The future of an illusion. *Annual of Psychoanalysis*, 12/13:19–37.

Stone, L. 1954. The widening scope of indications for psychoanalysis. *Journal of the American Psychoanalytic Association*, 2:567–594.

——. 1961. *The Psychoanalytic Situation*. New York: International Universities Press.

——. 1967. The psychoanalytic situation and the transference: Postscript to an earlier communication. *Journal of the American Psychoanalytic Association*, 15:3–58.

——. 1981. Notes on the noninterpretive elements in the psychoanalytic situation and process. *Journal of the American Psychoanalytic Association*, 29:89–118.

Stoudemire, A. 1983. The onset and adaptation to cancer: Psychodynamics of an ill physician. *Psychiatry*, 46:377–386.

Strachey, J. 1934. The nature of the therapeutic action of psychoanalysis. *International Journal of Psychoanalysis*, 50 1969.: 275–292.

Strenger, C. 1989. The classic and the romantic vision in psychoanalysis. *International Journal of Psychoanalysis*, 70:593–610.

Strupp, H. 1960. *Psychotherapists in Action*. New York: Grune and Stratton.

——. 1973. Toward a reformulation of the psychotherapeutic influence. *International Journal of Psychiatry*, 11:263–354.

Sullivan, H. S. 1953. *The Interpersonal Theory of Psychiatry*. New York: Norton.

——. 1956. *Clinical Studies in Psychiatry*. In *The Collected Works of Harry Stack Sullivan, M.D.* Vol. II. New York: Norton.

Sutherland, J. 1993. The autonomous self. *Bulletin of the Menninger Clinic*, 57:3–32.

Swartz, J. 1969. The erotized transference and other transference problems. *Psychoanalytic Forum*, 3:307–333.

Szasz, T. 1962. The problem of privacy in training analysis: Selections from a questionnaire study of psychoanalytic practices and opinions. *Psychiatry*, 25: 195–207.

——. 1963. *Law, Liberty and Psychiatry: An Inquiry into the Social Use of Mental Health Practices*. New York: Macmillan.

——. 1974a. *The Ethics of Psychoanalysis: The Theory and Method of Autonomous Psychotherapy*. New York: Basic Books.

——. 1974b. *The Myth of Mental Illness: Foundation of a Theory of Personal Conduct*. New York: Harper and Row.

Talan, K. H. 1989. Gifts in psychoanalysis: Theoretical and technical issues. *Psychoanalytic Study of the Child,* 44:149–163.

Tallmer, M. 1989. The death of an analyst. *Psychoanalytic Review,* 76:529–542.

Tansey, M. H., and Burke, W. F. 1985. Projective identification and the empathic process: Interactional communications. *Contemporary Psychoanalysis,* 21:42–69.

——. 1989. *Understanding Countertransference: From Projective Identification to Empathy*. Hillsdale, N.J.: Analytic Press.

Tarachow, S. 1962a. Interpretation and reality in psychotherapy. *International Journal of Psychoanalysis,* 43:377–387.

——. 1962b. The problem of reality and the therapeutic task. *Journal of the Hillside Hospital,* 11:21–28.

Tarnower, W. 1966. Extra-analytic contacts between the psychoanalyst and the patient. *Psychoanalytic Quarterly,* 35:399–413.

Tasman, A. 1982. Loss of self-cohesion in terminal illness. *Journal of the American Academy of Psychoanalysis,* 10:515–526.

Tauber, E. S. 1954. Exploring the therapeutic use of countertransference data. *Psychiatry,* 17:331–336.

Terman, D. 1989. Therapeutic change: Perspective of self psychology. *Psychoanalytic Inquiry,* 9:88–100.

Thomä, H., and Kächele, H. 1987. *Psychoanalytic Practice. Vol. 1: Principles*. Berlin: Springer Verlag.

Thompson, C. 1938a. Development of awareness of transference in a markedly detached personality. *International Journal of Psychoanalysis,* 19:229–309.

——. 1938b. Notes on the psychoanalytic significance of the choice of analyst. *Psychiatry,* 1:205–216.

——. 1946. Transference as a therapeutic instrument. *Psychiatry,* 9:273–278.

Thomson, P. G. 1993. The influence of the analyst's narcissistic vulnerability on his work. *Psychoanalytic Inquiry,* 13:348–364.

Ticho, E. A. 1971. Recent developments in psychoanalysis and psychotherapy. *Bulletin of the Menninger Clinic,* 35:447–460.

——. 1972. The effect of the analyst's personality on psychoanalytic treatment. *Psychoanalytic Forum,* 4:135–172.

Torras de Beà, E. 1992. Towards a "good enough" training analysis. *International Review of Psychoanalysis,* 19:159–167.

Trad, P. V. 1992. The future as prologue for the past. *Contemporary Psychoanalysis,* 28:647–672.

Trench, J. M. 1993. When both therapist and patient are divorcing: The role of supervision. In Gold, J. H., and Nemiah, J. C. (eds.), *Beyond Transference: When the Therapist's Real Life Intrudes*. Washington, D.C.: American Psychiatric Press, 109–123.

Treurniet, N. 1980. On the relation between the concepts of self and ego in Kohut's psychology of the self. *International Journal of Psychoanalysis,* 61:325–333.

——. 1983. Psychoanalysis and self psychology: A metapsychological essay with a clinical illustration. *Journal of the American Psychoanalytic Association,* 31:59–100.

——. 1993. What is psychoanalysis now? *International Journal of Psychoanalysis*, 74:873–891.

Trostle, J. A., Hauser, W. A., and Susser, I. S. 1983. The logic of noncompliance: Management of epilepsy from the patient's point of view. *Culture, Medicine and Psychiatry*, 7:35–56.

Tyson, P. 1980. The gender of the analyst: In relation to transference and countertransference manifestations in prelatency children. *Psychoanalytic Study of the Child*, 35:321–338.

Uchill, A. B. 1978. Deviation from confidentiality and the therapeutic holding environment. *International Journal of Psychoanalytic Psychotherapy*, 7:208–219.

Uyehara, L. A., Austrian, S., Upton, L. G., Warner, R. H., and Williamson, R. A. 1995. Telling about the analyst's pregnancy. *Journal of the American Psychoanalytical Association*, 43:113–135.

Van Dam, H. 1987. Countertransference during an analyst's brief illness. *Journal of the American Psychoanalytic Association*, 35:647–655.

Van Niel, M. S. 1993. Pregnancy: The obvious and evocative real event in a therapist's life. In Gold, J. H., and Nemiah, J. C. (eds.), *Beyond Transference: When the Therapist's Real Life Intrudes*. Washington, D.C.: American Psychiatric Press, 125–140.

Vanderpool, H. Y., and Weiss, G. B. 1984. Patient truthfulness: A test of models of the therapist-patient relationship. *Journal of Medicine and Philosophy*, 9:353–372.

Van der Velde, C. D. 1985. Body images of one's self and of others: Developmental and clinical significance. *American Journal of Psychiatry*, 142:527–537.

Veatch, R. M. 1981. *A Theory of Medical Ethics*. New York: Basic Books.

Viederman, M. 1976. The influence of the person of the analyst on structural change: A case report. *Psychoanalytic Quarterly*, 45:231–249.

——. 1991. The real person of the analyst and his role in the process of psychoanalytic cure. *Journal of the American Psychoanalytic Association*, 39:451–489.

Voth, H. M. 1972a. Love affair between doctor and patient. *American Journal of Psychotherapy*, 26:394–400.

——. 1972b. Responsibility in the practice of psychoanalysis and psychotherapy. *American Journal of Psychotherapy*, 26:69–83.

Waelder, R. 1936. The problem of freedom in psychoanalysis and the problem of reality-testing. *International Journal of Psychoanalysis*, 17:89–108.

Wallace, E. R. 1985. *Historiography and Causation in Psychoanalysis*. Hillsdale, N.J.: Analytic Press.

——. 1989. Pitfalls of a one-sided image of science: Adolf Grünbaum's *Foundations of Psychoanalysis*. *Journal of the American Psychoanalytic Association*, 37:493–529.

Wallerstein, R. S. 1967. Reconstruction and mastery in the transference psychosis. *Journal of the American Psychoanalytic Association*, 15:551–583.

——. 1985. *Forty-two Lives in Treatment: A Study of Psychoanalysis and Psychotherapy*. New York: Guilford Press.

——. 1986. Psychoanalysis as a science: A response to the new challenges. *Psychoanalytic Quarterly*, 55:414–451.

——. 1988. Psychoanalysis, psychoanalytic science, and psychoanalytic research—1986. *Journal of the American Psychoanalytic Association,* 36:3–30.

——. 1993. On transference love: Revisiting Freud. In Person, E. S., Hagelin, A., and Fonagy, P. (eds.), *On Freud's "Observations on Transference-love."* New Haven: Yale University Press, 57–74.

Wallwork, E. 1991. *Psychoanalysis and Ethics.* New Haven: Yale University Press.

Warner, R. 1976–77. The relationship between language and disease concepts. *International Journal of Psychiatry in Medicine,* 7:57–68.

Webb, R. E., Bushnell, D. F., and Widseth, J. C. 1993. Tiresias and the breast: Thinking of Lacan, interpretation, and caring. *International Journal of Psychoanalysis,* 74:597–612.

Weigert, E. 1954a. Countertransference and self-analysis of the psychoanalyst. *International Journal of Psychoanalysis,* 35:242–246.

——. 1954b. The importance of flexibility in psychoanalytic technique. *Journal of the American Psychoanalytic Association,* 2:702–710.

Weiner, M. F. 1972. Self-exposure by the therapist as a therapeutic technique. *American Journal of Psychotherapy,* 26:42–51.

Weinstock, C. 1976. Dreams stimulated by the analyst-patient relationship. *Journal of the American Academy of Psychoanalysis,* 4:161–170.

Weir, R. 1980. Truthtelling in medicine. *Perspectives in Biology and Medicine,* 24:95–112.

Weisman, A. D. 1965. *The Existential Core of Psychoanalysis.* Boston: Little, Brown.

Weiss, S. S. 1972. Some thoughts and clinical vignettes on translocation of an analytic practice. *International Journal of Psychoanalysis,* 53:505–514.

Westin, A. F. (ed.). 1977. *Computers, Health Records, and Citizen Rights.* Washington, D.C.: National Bureau of Standards. Quoted by Herrington, B. S. *Psychiatric News,* 12 (11):8.

Wile, D. B. 1972. Negative countertransference and therapist discouragement. *International Journal of Psychoanalytic Psychotherapy,* 1(3): 36–67.

——. 1977. Ideological conflicts between clients and psychotherapists. *American Journal of Psychotherapy,* 31:437–449.

Winnicott, D. W. 1949. Hate in the countertransference. *International Journal of Psychoanalysis,* 30:69–75.

——. 1953. Transitional objects and transitional phenomena. In *Playing and Reality.* New York: Basic Books, 1971, 1–25.

——. 1954. Metapsychological and clinical aspects of regression within the psychoanalytical set-up. In *Collected Papers by D. W. Winnicott.* London: Tavistock, 278–294.

——. 1956. On transference. *International Journal of Psychoanalysis,* 37:386–388.

——. 1958. *Collected Papers.* New York: Basic Books.

——. 1960a. Ego distortion in terms of true and false self. In *The Maturational Processes and the Facilitating Environment.* New York: International Universities Press, 1965, 140–152.

——. 1960b. The theory of the parent-infant relationship. *International Journal of Psychoanalysis,* 41:585–595.

——. 1962. The aims of psychoanalytical treatment. In *The Maturational Processes and the Facilitating Environment.* New York: International Universities Press, 1965, 166–170.

——. 1963. Psychiatric disorders in terms of infantile maturational processes. In *The Maturational Processes and the Facilitating Environment.* New York: International Universities Press 1965. 230–241.

——. 1965. *The Maturational Processes and the Facilitating Environment.* New York: International Universities Press.

——. 1971. *Playing and Reality.* New York: Basic Books.

Wittkower, E. D., and Robertson, B. M. 1977. Sex differences in psychoanalytic treatment. *American Journal of Psychotherapy,* 31:66–75.

Wohlberg, G. W. 1975. A black patient with a white therapist. *International Journal of Psychoanalytic Psychotherapy,* 4:540–562.

Wolf, E. 1988. *Treating the Self: Elements of Clinical Self Psychology.* New York: Guilford Press.

——. 1993. Disruptions of the therapeutic relationship in psychoanalysis: A view from self psychology. *International Journal of Psychoanalysis,* 74:675–687.

Wurmser, L. 1978. *The Hidden Dimension.* New York: Aronson.

——. 1981. *The Mask of Shame.* Baltimore: Johns Hopkins University Press.

Wylie, H. W., and Wylie, M. L. 1987. An effect of pharmacotherapy on the psychoanalytic process: Case report of a modified analysis. *American Journal of Psychiatry,* 144:489–492.

Zaphiropoulos, M. L. 1982. Transcultural parameters in the transference and countertransference. *Journal of the American Academy of Psychoanalysis,* 10:571–582.

Zavitzianos, G. 1974. Transference, therapeutic alliance and the principle of multiple function of the ego (factors of analyzability). *Journal of the Philadelphia Association for Psychoanalysis,* 1:298–313.

Zerbe, K. J. 1993. Selves that starve and suffocate: The continuum of eating disorders and dissociative phenomena. *Bulletin of the Menninger Clinic,* 57:319–327.

——. 1995. Integrating feminist and psychodynamic principles in the treatment of an eating disorder patient: Implications for using countertransference responses. *Bulletin of the Menninger Clinic,* 59:160–176.

Zetzel, E. R. 1956. The concept of transference. In *The Capacity for Emotional Growth.* New York: International Universities Press, 1970, 168–181.

——. 1958. Therapeutic alliance and the psychoanalysis of hysteria. In Zetzel, *The Capacity for Emotional Growth.* New York: International Universities Press, 1970, 182–196.

——. 1965. The theory of therapy in relation to a developmental model of the psychic apparatus. *International Journal of Psychoanalysis,* 46:39–52.

——. 1966. The analytic situation. In *Psychoanalysis in the Americas,* ed. by R. E. Litman. New York: International Universities Press, 86–106.

——. 1970. *The Capacity for Emotional Growth*. New York: International Universities Press.

——. 1971. A developmental approach to the borderline patient. *American Journal of Psychiatry*, 127:867–871.

Zetzel, E. R., and Meissner, S.J., W. W. 1973. *Basic Concepts in Psychoanalytic Psychiatry*. New York: Basic Books.

Zilboorg, G. 1943. Fear of death. *Psychoanalytic Quarterly*, 12:465–475.

——. 1956. Psychoanalytic borderlines. *American Journal of Psychiatry*, 112:709–710.

Zinberg, N. 1967. Psychoanalytic training and psychoanalytic values. *International Journal of Psychoanalysis*, 48:88–96.

Zuger, B. 1972. Understanding human freedom: A necessary ingredient in treating adolescents. *American Journal of Psychotherapy*, 26:263–267.

Index

abandonment, 94, 95, 96, 101, 233
abstinence, 8–9, 10, 13, 14, 23, 71; need for, 74–78, 88; principle of, 85, 91
access to records, 201
accidental factors, 152
acting out, 8, 48, 50, 55, 56; harmful, 76, 218, 242, 247; paranoid, 103; on telephone, 148; fee issues in, 149
active technique, 85
"actualization," 87
actual reality, 64–65
adaptations in alliance, 248–49
adolescents, 17
advice, 91, 240
affection, displays of, 85
affective attunement, 159, 164, 167, 169
affective communication, 19
affective resonance, 158
"affirmative affective tone," 311*n*11
affirmative interpretation, 261–62
aggression, 20, 110, 279
aggressive projections, 47, 48
aggressor-introject, 47, 48
aging, 103–04
alter ego, 35
ambiguity, 27, 64
ambivalence, 130, 231, 232, 274, 278
anal period, 130, 131, 132, 134
analysand. *See* patient
"Analysis Terminable and Interminable" (Freud), 9
analyst: attitudes of, 5–6; personality of, 7, 63, 67, 75, 77; role of, 12, 145–46, 240–41; errors of, 14, 15, 28, 71, 75, 163–64; authority of, 23–24; as participant, 62–65; as model, 75, 239–40; death of, 93–95; illness of, 99–102; aging, 103–04; empathy and, 159–61; need for gratification, 192; responsibilities of, 196, 197, 198, 217–18. *See also* countertransference; real relationship
analytic atmosphere, 8
analytic interaction, 231
analytic introject, 280–81, 283–85
analytic listening, 41, 50–51, 80, 119, 168, 170, 319*n*21. *See also* empathic listening
analytic narrative, 79–80
analytic object, 283
analytic pact, 9, 10, 142, 200. *See also* therapeutic framework
analytic process, 3, 10, 23; elements in, 4, 5, 282–83; motivations in, 28–29; quest for meaning in, 74–75; opening phase, 237–38; objectives of, 274, 275, 278; end of, 288–90; defined, 312*n*1
analytic regression, 229, 230, 235, 237; trust and, 178, 179
analytic situation, 24, 143, 234, 235, 236; reality factors in, 92–93; gender issues in, 107–10; pregnancy, 110–14; accidental factors in, 114–24; paranoid dynamic in, 269; defined, 312*n*1
analytic space, 21, 281
analytic split, 165
analytic work, 195, 286
analyzing ego, 13
anal zone, 131
anger, 95
annihilation, 20–21, 95
anonymity, 18, 74, 76, 77, 141, 159, 188
anxiety, 47, 141, 237, 244; tolerance for, 147–48
appearance: neutrality of, 75
appointments, 146; guidelines for, 298. *See also* missed appointments
archaic response, 35

asymmetrical relation, 188, 191
attachment, 9
authenticity, 210, 213–14
authoritarian attitude, 23, 81, 85, 114
authoritarianism, 6, 73, 153, 188, 191
authority: in alliance, 188, 190–93; new notion of, 189–90
autonomous ego, 10
autonomous functioning, 72, 194
autonomy, 25, 38, 128, 132; of analyst, 6, 46, 113; roots of, 131–33; role of, 180–85
avoidance, 71, 113, 162

barter, 299
basic trust, 131, 176, 177, 229, 277; undermining, 230; capacity for, 231, 232, 234
Bean-Bayog, Margaret, 314*n*8
behavioral therapy, 298
billing practices, 299
blaming devices, 84
borderline patients, 21, 37, 38, 231, 242; collaboration with, 33; gender issues and, 109; boundaries for, 143–44; empathy with, 161, 165; alliance and, 245–47; interpretation and, 259, 264
borderline rage, 144
boundaries, 73, 81, 92, 155; in reality, 90, 91; illness issue, 99, 100; gender issue, 109; in framework, 143–45; fee issue, 150; need for, 259; termination and, 289–90; guidelines for, 297–98, 302
breach of alliance, 98

castration anxiety, 102, 108, 184
casual conversation, 203
character, 72–73
"characterological countertransference," 307*n*6
character pathology, 248
character transference, 23
child analysis, 14, 17, 309*n*7
childhood affects, 7, 30
childhood traumata, 84, 85–86
closing phase, 15. *See also* termination
"cocoon" transference, 19, 34
cohesive self. *See* self-cohesion
collaboration, 8, 10, 21, 190, 291
collusion, 66, 84, 95, 121, 291; gender issues and, 108, 109, 112
collusive avoidance, 96
communications model, 189
complementary identification, 43–44
compliance, 6, 49, 50, 124, 184, 255
compulsion to cure, 103
conceptual empathy, 158
concordant countertransference, 308*n*11
concordant identification, 43–44
confidentiality, 143, 201, 301; threats to, 202–07
conflict, 6, 19, 36, 272
confrontation, 40–41, 56, 260
consistency, 141, 257–58
containment, 20–21, 251, 305*n*20
containment-separateness subphase, 45
contamination. *See* transferential contaminants
contract. *See* therapeutic contract
corrective emotional experience, 8, 37, 88, 100, 252, 258, 325*n*2
couch, 144, 235
counteraggression, 55
"counteridentification," 281
counterprojective response, 43
counterreaction, 39
countertransference, 3, 4, 23, 32; defined, 39–41; model, 42–44; phases in, 44–46; misalliance and, 46–50; therapeutic response to, 50–57; authority and, 192; freedom and, 195; values and, 220–21; interference, 276, 281; at termination, 290–93
countertransference enactment, 40, 51–52
countertransference hate, 48
countertransference trap, 57, 100, 204, 294; sources of, 247, 249
covenant, 142
cultural issues, 93, 108, 109, 116–17, 197
curiosity, 15, 28, 76, 120, 262

death, 93–97, 103–04, 313*n*3
decision making, 143, 151–52, 180
defense systems, 230, 232
defensive issues, 181, 272, 273, 278, 279, 286
denial, 94, 99, 100, 112, 113, 162, 255
dependency issues, 26, 31, 36, 67; trust and, 175–76, 177; willing dependence, 179; autonomy and, 182; tolerance for, 238; interpretive process and, 262
depression, 95, 96, 198, 252, 255
deprivation, 9, 14, 25
destructive impulses, 263
detachment, 77
devaluation, 49, 50, 55
developmental aspect, 128, 169, 280, 284, 285; facets of, 129–35; epigenetic progression in, 136–39; empathy and, 155
developmental crises, 111, 274, 278
deviations in alliance, 76; types of, 245–49; empathic mirroring in, 249–50; transference

management in, 250–54; misalliance and, 254–56
diatrophic attitude, 14, 19, 32
"diatrophic function," 11
displacement, 22, 23, 67, 164
displacement transference, 270
distance, 73, 90, 102, 242
distortion, 12, 14; cognitive, 6; causes of, 31, 37–38; in alliance, 33, 44, 46–47, 49; collusive, 51; transferential, 117, 233, 242, 260; countertransference, 157. *See also* narcissistic alliance
divorce, 314*n*5
dominance, 191
dreams, 109
drive elements, 10, 133, 272, 284
drugs. *See* medication

eating disorders, 246
economic relationships, 299
egalitarian attitude, 6, 114, 153, 180
ego, 7, 9, 10, 132, 273, 279; adaptive ego, 11, 286
ego autonomy, 133
ego-derivative, 24
ego-functioning, 132, 285
ego-ideal, 103
ego-interests, 24
ego interpretation, 260
ego psychology, 8, 63, 181
ego-split, 7, 10, 11, 304*n*11
emergencies, 298
"emotional coldness" of analyst, 8
emotional discharge, 20
emotional reactivity, 53–55
empathic acceptance, 35, 85, 96
empathic attunement, 18, 243, 250, 282, 319*n*19; role of, 156–57, 158, 160, 162, 165, 169
empathic communication, 281–82, 319*n*19
empathic connection subphase, 45–46
empathic experience, 157–58
empathic failure, 164, 173
empathic holding, 19, 249
empathic listening, 166–68, 170, 319*n*19
empathic mirroring, 161, 167, 169, 249–50
empathic resonance, 155, 158, 160, 163, 165, 250
empathic response, 32
empathic understanding, 40, 95, 162, 164
empathy, 6, 9, 77, 228; of analyst, 34, 35, 159–61; defined, 154–55; identification and, 156–57; role of, 158–59, 168–69, 171–72, 282; limits of, 161–62, 169–71; vs. transference, 164–66
empowerment, 191
entitlement, 50, 81, 101, 143, 144
envy, 41, 255
epigenetic schema, 130, 136–38, 174, 179, 278
erotic stimulation, 131
erotized transference, 50, 81, 106, 109, 191, 255, 306*n*8
ethical issues, 7, 200–01. *See also* confidentiality; values
evaluation, 212, 213
exclusive subjectivity, 41
expectations, 6–7, 23, 28, 43, 81, 170
experience, 16
expert authority, 191
externalization, 22
extra-analytic contact, 122–23
extra sessions, 146–47

false self, 17, 18, 133–34
false-self compliance, 269
families, 301
fantasies, 9, 23, 24, 262; unconscious, 16, 32; in analytic process, 29, 65–66; of superiority, 49; cure fantasy, 248; at termination, 294–95
fantasy and reality, 76, 78; boundaries between, 21, 81, 165; interpretation and, 264–65
father transference, 31
fees. *See* financial issues
Ferenczi, S., 84–87, 88
fetish, 80, 289
financial arrangements, 93, 101, 143, 200, 206; reduced fees, 81, 106; importance of, 148–50
fixation, 91, 261
fragmentation of self, 279
framework. *See* therapeutic framework
free association, 195, 236, 244
freedom, 180, 194–95, 214
Freud, S.: on good relationship, 7; on alliance, 8–10; on transference, 22, 23–24; debate with Ferenczi, 84–87, 88
frustration, 47, 49, 50
frustration-gratification, 89
"functional neutrality," 75
fundamental rule, 9

gender issues, 107–10, 184, 191
genetic fallacy, 175
genetic interpretation, 270, 271
gifts, 120–21, 150, 300
good-enough therapist, 18, 242
grandiosity, 41, 57, 143, 228, 270–71

gratification, 9, 13, 28, 66, 190; transference gratification, 11, 164; withholding, 74; appropriate, 75–76; boundaries in, 89, 90; sexual, 109; denial of, 239
Greenson, R. R., 13, 15
grief, 95
ground rules, 9, 12, 18, 182; importance of, 62, 239, 240
growth model, 267, 286
guilt, 101, 104, 112, 134

Hartmann, H., 210–11
health values, 212, 213
helplessness, 47, 248
holding approach, 241–43, 248, 249, 251, 268, 269
holding environment, 34, 244; concept of, 17–21, 232–34
holding introjects, 241
home visits, 298
homosexual issues, 213, 255
honesty, 201
hopefulness, 11, 49, 130, 179
hospitalization, 115, 201, 217–18, 298
humaneness, 9, 13, 258
humor, 69, 78
hyperautonomous domination, 131
hyperindependence, 181, 182, 183, 184

id, 7, 9
id-derivative, 24
idealization, 42, 191, 253; of analyst, 31, 56, 118
idealized object, 36–37, 228
idealized selfobject, 228
idealizing interaction, 49
identification, 7, 12; with analyst, 10, 13, 14, 193; empathy and, 156, 161, 173; values and, 221; conditions for, 231, 232; kinds of, 272–74; role in alliance, 275–77; introjection to, 278–80; countertransference and, 280–83
identification-signal affect subphase, 45
identity: loss of, 95; emergence of, 285–87
id interpretation, 260–61
"idiolects," 83
illness, 97–102
illusions, 21, 41; illusory expectations, 228
illusory matrix, 281–82
imagination, 158
immortality: illusion of, 94
impasse. *See* therapeutic impasse
impotence: feelings of, 47
incestuous negative transference enactment, 50
independence, 181, 182, 184, 277
independent objectivity, 42
individuality, 8, 77
individuation, 26, 32
industry, 135–36, 137, 138, 186–87
ineffectiveness: feelings of, 47
infantile conflict, 4, 50, 95, 132, 284, 285
infantile expectations, 10, 52–53
infantile needs, 9, 273, 275
infantile sexuality, 135
infantile traumata, 50, 84, 85
infantile trust, 174, 175, 176
infantile wishes, 24, 32
inferiority: sense of, 186, 258
informed consent, 115, 124, 143, 180
initiative, 134–35, 137, 185–86
insight, 10, 16, 91, 167, 187, 267
instinctual derivatives, 10, 273, 279
insurance companies, 93
insurance forms, 205–08
interactional perspective, 154
interlocking projections, 40
internalization, 42, 193, 283, 292; by therapist, 43–44; role of, 56–57; empathy and, 156, 161, 173; sources of, 186, 187, 231; of values, 221
internal processing phase, 45–46
interpersonal experience, 7
interpretation, 6, 14, 183; withholding, 47; interaction and, 52–53; empathy and, 172–73; of transference, 233, 259–60; nature of, 257–59; misalliance and, 260–61, 265–67; affirmative, 261–62; of alliance, 262–64, 267–69; principles of, 269–71
interpretive process, 257–59, 262
interpretive strategy, 259, 270
interruption of analysis, 20, 118–19, 236
"intersubjective analytic third," 303*n*5
intersubjective psychic space, 62
intersubjectivity, 6, 43
intrapsychic structure, 257, 263
intrasubjective psychic space, 62
introductory phase, 15
introjection, 37, 40; process of, 42, 43, 278–80; conditions for, 231, 232; patterns of, 252, 253–54; analytic introject, 283–85
introjective configuration, 43, 44, 55, 98, 244, 250; sources of, 265, 266; interpretation and, 269–70
introjective transference, 305*n*3
intrusion, 76
intuition, 9, 162, 228
involvement vs. noninvolvement, 62

irrationality, 16
irrational willingness, 227
isolation, 19, 94, 104
isolation-involvement, 89

judgment, 212–13

Kant, I., 180

language, 83, 155
latency, 132, 134, 135–36
latent introjects, 244
legal issues. *See* medicolegal issues
libidinal issues, 10, 24, 25, 31, 214, 279
libidinally based transference, 22
life insurance, 205
limitations: of analyst, 69; on freedom, 194
limit-setting, 56, 217
listening. *See* analytic listening
litigation, 109
logistics of therapy, 5
loneliness, 95, 96, 104
loss, 95, 96
love, 13, 65. *See also* transference love

magical expectations, 10, 21, 28, 52, 227, 228, 238–39
malpractice, 109, 115–16
managerial authority, 191
masochistic countertransference, 164
masochistic patients, 71
masochistic submission, 48, 131, 242
masochistic transference, 106
mastery, 26, 75
maternal deprivation, 20, 32
maternal model, 19
maternal selfobject empathy, 171
maternal transference, 11, 109
"matrix transference," 26–27
maturational multidimensionality, 136
mature transference, 11, 26
medical model, 77, 189, 197–98
medication, 93, 123–24
medicolegal issues, 144–45, 197, 201, 208
memory, 79
mental set subphase, 44–45
merger, 26
metacommunication, 80, 158
metaphor, 83
Mill, J. S., 180
mirroring, 35, 37, 43, 76, 77, 253. *See also* empathic mirroring
mirror transference, 270–71
misalliance. *See* therapeutic misalliance
mismatch, 81–84
missed appointments, 102, 143, 148–49, 183, 299
money, 114–15
moral standards, 200
mother-child interaction, 12–13, 27, 84, 155, 229; importance of, 29, 128, 129, 136, 229
motivation for analytic work, 10, 11, 13, 16, 19, 274; sources of, 24–25; alliance motivation, 28–30
"Mourning and Melancholia" (Freud), 96
mourning process, 94, 96, 97; at termination, 291, 292, 293
moving office, 119–20
multiple personality disorder, 246
mutative interpretation, 16, 19, 86, 173
mutative support, 16
mutual analysis, 84, 86
mutual empathic attunement, 172–73
mutual interaction, 5–7, 77, 155, 187, 188, 257; empathy and, 161–62, 171

narcissism, 21, 33, 132, 259; function of, 279–80
narcissistic alliance, 38, 269; capacity for, 227–29; distortions in, 229–32, 238; and therapeutic alliance, 234
narcissistic assault, 41
narcissistic character disorder, 18, 231, 238
narcissistic countertransference, 291–92
narcissistic defensive alliance, 177
narcissistic distortion, 38, 253
narcissistic equilibrium, 228
narcissistic gratification, 247
narcissistic inferiority, 37, 42, 57
narcissistic injury, 177, 234, 294
narcissistic investment, 278, 279
narcissistic invulnerability, 94, 100
narcissistic misalliance, 234
narcissistic rage, 19
narcissistic transference, 22, 35, 41, 48; positive transference and, 37–38; elements of, 236, 237; misalliance and, 252–53; interpretation and, 270, 271
narcissistic vulnerability, 47, 49, 107, 177
narrative incommensurability, 78–80
needs, 34, 36
negative therapeutic alliance, 253
negative transference, 27, 29, 36, 37, 165, 236; elements of, 31, 55–56, 251–52, 259; interpretation of, 246
negotiation, 6, 257

neutrality, 13, 18, 23, 25, 69, 71; of analyst, 8, 9, 113; deviations from, 13; selfobject and, 35; necessity of, 74–78, 259, 283; termination and, 289–90
neutralization, 75
noncountertransference, 41
nonneutrality, 211
nontherapeutic space, 143
nontransference, 27
nonverbal communication, 158, 259

object cathexis, 66
object-constancy, 128
"objective countertransference," 40
objectivity, 6, 211–12
object loss, 235
object need, 32, 33
object relationship, 157, 235, 263; role of, 12, 20, 60; capacity for, 16, 24
object representation, 157
"observant ego," 10
observation, 155, 167–68
obsessional patient, 132–33
obsessive-compulsive syndrome, 133
oedipal interpretation, 260
oedipal phase, 26, 132, 155
ontogenetic evolution, 128
ontogeny, 130, 183
open communication, 201
opening phase, 15, 237–38, 243–44; tasks of, 255–56
oscillating dimensions, 36
outcome of therapy, 7, 16, 196, 201; factors in, 82, 166, 290, 293
overidentification, 41
overzealousness, 9

paranoid features, 33
parental model, 11, 19
participant observation, 6
paternalism, 188, 191, 198
paternal transference, 109
pathogenic introject, 43, 131, 250, 274, 275, 276, 277
pathogenic superego, 262
pathogenesis, 78
patient: as collaborator, 4, 8; interaction with analyst, 5–7; individuality of, 8, 77; as victim, 20; good-enough patient, 57; death of, 95–96; elderly, 104; role of, 145–46; empathy in, 162–64. *See also* identification; transference *and other aspects of alliance*
personality disorder, 197
personal myth, 79
phallic eroticism, 134
phallic period, 130
philosophical issues, 83
physical contact, 151, 239; guidelines for, 299–300
play age, 134
playfulness, 185
political issues, 116–17
positive transference, 37, 274, 283; elements of, 10, 16, 31, 236; unobjectionable, 16, 22, 24, 26, 29, 31
post-oedipal phase, 132, 155
post-termination contact, 293–96
power issues, 75, 77, 189, 191
preformed transference, 30
pregenital experience, 13
pregnancy, 93, 110–14
premature closure, 131, 162, 169, 178, 246
pre-oedipal material, 109
pre-oedipal transference, 4, 260
prephallic material, 109
pressure of interaction subphase, 45
preverbal affective attunement, 155
"primary love" relations, 34
primary objects, 27, 28
primary relationship, 4, 66, 175
"primary transference," 4
primitive character disorder, 90, 263–64
"primitive communications," 46
primitive transference, 26
"primordial transference," 11
privacy, 141, 201, 207
projection, 20, 22, 37, 164, 236; countertransference and, 42, 43; destructive, 242; patterns of, 252, 253–54; projective transference, 265, 266, 269, 270; mechanisms of, 280–83
"projective identification," 40
protector: analyst as, 23
pseudo-autonomous functions, 181
psychic reality, 64–65
Psychoanalysis and Moral Values (Hartmann), 210
psychoanalytic empathy, 77
psychoanalytic process, 75, 141
"psychoanalytic work ego," 5
psychopathology, 213
puberty, 135

questions, 258

racial issues, 104–06
rage, 20, 109, 144

rapport, 8, 11
rapprochement stage, 134
"rational alliance," 5
rationality, 16, 180; conscious, 7
"rational transference," 11
Rat Man, 150, 235
reality, 10, 21, 23, 61, 79; consensual, 6; in analytic process, 65–66; patient demands for, 88–91. *See also* fantasy and reality
reality-based issues, 92–93
reality testing, 7, 12, 155
real relationship, 3, 4, 5, 17, 40, 41; vs. alliance, 25–26, 31, 65, 67; transference and, 63–65; personality in, 68–72; character in, 72–73; as resistance, 78–81; mismatch and, 81–84; differing views on, 84–87; role in analytic process, 87–88; termination and, 288, 295
reason, 10
reasonable ego, 13
reasonable willingness, 227
reception phase, 44–45
reciprocal partnership, 6
recording analytic session, 121–22
records, 204–05
referrals, 200
regression, 12, 17, 33, 244, 261; at termination, 289
regression, malignant, 53
regressive crises, 247
regressive impulses, 8
regressive phase, 277
regressive pressures, 275, 284
regressive transference, 251
rejection of authority, 255
relaxation technique, 85
religious perspective, 83
remembering, 33, 86
repair model, 286
repetitive dimension, 36
"representational conjunction," 44
"representational disjunction," 44
rescue fantasies, 109, 144
rescue theory, 83
resistance to treatment, 7, 24, 47, 237, 244; transference and, 10, 26–28; real relation and, 78–81; empathy and, 164–66
resolution, 36
resonant empathy. *See* empathic resonance
respect for patient, 8
responsibility, 137, 143, 185, 195–99
restitutive aggression, 47
rigidity, 76, 89, 90
roles, 145–46
sadistic gratification, 97
sadomasochistic conflict, 48, 98, 255
scheduling appointments, 102, 143
schizoid patients, 19, 43
scholarly communication, 203–04
secondary trust, 130–31, 269; development of, 176–77, 178, 179
self, 7, 36, 42, 131
self-analysis, 46, 53
self-awareness, 41
self-cohesion, 35, 95, 278, 280
self-destructive impulse, 197
self-detachment, 77
self-disclosure, 151; guidelines for, 300
self-esteem, 48, 100, 131, 278
self-experience, 18
self-experiential empathy, 158, 163
self-exposure, 75
self-fulfillment, 190
selfhood, 214
self-image, 48
self-injury, 76
self-integration, 131, 276
self-integrity, 280
self-justification, 84
self-knowledge, 41, 210, 213
self-monitoring, 50, 51, 53, 220
self-object differentiation, 155
selfobject experience, 306*n*15
selfobject needs, 234
selfobject transference, 11, 22, 66, 265; role of, 34–37, 49–50, 251, 253
self-organization, 33, 180, 214, 279, 285, 307*n*3
self-other experience, 109, 157
self-regulation, 307*n*3
self-representation, 44, 282
self-revelation, 75, 102, 159; problem of, 76, 77; death and, 94, 95
self-structure, 285–86
self-sufficiency, 19
self-system, 25, 265
self-trust: of analyst, 176
self-understanding, 212, 213, 215
sense of self, 184, 267, 279, 285, 286
separation, 26, 32, 95, 101; issues of, 235, 286, 287; separation work, 292
separation-individuation, 183
sexual curiosity, 134
sexual relations, 50
sexual stereotypes, 107, 108
shame, 51, 253
signal affect, 45
social learning, 133

social relations, 300–301
social violence, 117
specific/nonspecific factors, 7
split. *See* ego-split
spontaneity, 185, 186
stability, 141
stalemate, 33, 48, 71, 82
Sterba, R., 10–11
"stilted listening," 319*n*21
stimulus nutriment, 133
"structural actualities" of transference, 307*n*7
structural theory, 10
structuring approach, 240, 241–43
Studies on Hysteria (Breuer and Freud), 8
subjection, 255
"subjective countertransference," 40
subjective experience, 155, 156
subjectivity, 311*n*3
submission, 6, 191
suicide, 115, 116, 217, 218
superego, 7, 9, 24; aging and, 103; values and, 213, 214; integration with ego, 279
superego externalization, 23
superego structures, 132, 273
supportive therapy, 298
symbiotic dyad, 43
symbiotic reunion, 26
sympathy, 8, 155

Tarasoff case, 218
teaching conferences, 202
technical neutrality, 77
telephone contact, 147–48, 202–03, 247, 292, 299
terminal phase, 15, 286
termination, 120, 288–90; countertransference and, 290–93; post-termination contact, 293–96; guidelines, 302
therapeutic alliance, 3, 4–7; defined, 7–8; individual views on, 8–13; concerns regarding, 14–17; holding environment in, 17–21, 232–34; conditions for, 226–27; impediments to, 234–39; analytic stage for, 239–41; opening phase, 243–44; analysis of, 284–85
therapeutic contract, 5, 142–43
therapeutic framework, 47, 142, 182; fee issues, 114–15; defined, 140–41; deviations in, 152–53; responsibility in, 195–96, 201. *See also individual components*
therapeutic impasse, 21, 71, 82, 84, 246, 252
therapeutic interaction, 46
"therapeutic interest," 15
therapeutic management, 53
therapeutic misalliance, 3, 23, 31, 41, 53, 276; causes of, 36, 75, 80, 159, 181, 238–39; transference and, 37–38, 252–53, 265–67; countertransference and, 46–50; forms of, 83–84, 118, 121, 254–56; personal factors in, 95, 96; expressions of, 148, 185; destructive, 199; interpretation and, 260–61; at termination, 289–90, 292
therapeutic omnipotence, 47
therapeutic regression, 24, 245, 246
therapeutic relationship, 4–5
therapeutic space, 143
therapeutic split, 11, 12
therapeutic zeal, 8
time of analytic hour, 93
training analysis, 323*n*5
training analyst, 293, 295
training situation, 117–18
transference, 3, 4, 5; individual views on, 8–13; vs. alliance, 22–24, 25–28; motivation and, 24–25, 28–30; alliance interplay and, 30–34; and therapeutic misalliance, 37–38; real relation and, 63–65
transference/countertransference interaction, 22, 23, 36, 38, 182; factors in, 39, 40, 251, 253; analysis of, 42, 43–44; as interactive process, 44–46; aggressive aspects of, 47–48; narcissistic aspects of, 49–50; erotic aspects of, 50; avoiding, 266; sources of, 276, 283
transference desire, 87
transference fantasies, 101, 104
transference identification, 305*n*3
transference illusion, 80
transference interpretation, 33, 34, 245, 262
transference love, 23–24, 81, 254, 314*n*3
transference neurosis, 12, 13, 14, 19, 29; elements of, 22, 251, 275, 284, 285; emergence of, 179, 238; conditions for, 229, 230, 274
transference psychosis, 22, 38, 236, 253
transference resistance, 10, 67
transference resolution, 82
transferential contaminants, 26, 27, 30, 153, 236
transferential trap, 91
transitional object, 21
transitional object transference, 38, 253, 265
transitional transference, 22
transsubjective psychic space, 62–63
trauma, 84, 85–86
trial identification, 46, 156–57
trial internalization, 277

trust, 12, 24, 26, 128, 228; capacity for, 71–72; roots of, 130–31, 174–75; role in alliance, 177–80. *See also* basic trust; secondary trust
trustworthiness: of analyst, 6
truth: quest for, 215
truthfulness, 8, 23, 200
twinship, 35

unconscious: uncovering of, 75, 76
unconscious communication, 157–58
unconscious countertransference, 46
unconscious derivatives, 267
unconscious transference, 29
unobjectionable positive transference, 16, 22, 24, 26, 29, 31

vacations, 143
validation, 169
value judgments, 211
value neutrality, 209
values, 77, 209; role of, 210–15; technical and personal, 215–20, 221
victim-introject, 42, 48, 56, 266
victimization, 36, 56, 98, 110, 251, 266
violence, 116, 201
"volitional disability," 322*n*11

will, 7, 132
willingness, 24, 185, 227, 234
wishes, 23, 34, 56, 261, 262
Wolf Man, 150, 204, 234
work ego, 196
working alliance, 13, 16, 66, 262, 263
working model subphase, 45

Zetzel, E. R., 11–13